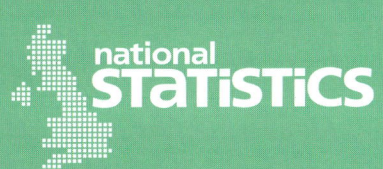

Winter 2006
No 32

Health Statistics Quarterly

In this issue

palgrave
macmillan

About the Office for National Statistics

The Office for National Statistics (ONS) is the Government Agency responsible for compiling, analysing and disseminating many of the United Kingdom's economic, social and demographic statistics, including the retail prices index, trade figures and labour market data, as well as the periodic census of the population and health statistics. It is also the agency that administers the statutory registration of births, marriages and deaths in England and Wales. The Director of ONS is also the National Statistician and the Registrar General for England and Wales.

A National Statistics publication

National Statistics are produced to high professional standards set out in the National Statistics Code of Practice. They undergo regular quality assurance reviews to ensure that they meet customer needs. They are produced free from any political influence.

About Health Statistics Quarterly and Population Trends

Health Statistics Quarterly and Population Trends are journals of the Office for National Statistics. Each is published four times a year in February, May, August and November and March, June, September and December, respectively. In addition to bringing together articles on a wide range of population and health topics, *Health Statistics Quarterly and Population Trends* contain regular series of tables on a wide range of subjects for which ONS is responsible, including the most recently available statistics.

Subscription

Annual subscription, including postage, is £100; single issues are £27.50.

Online

Health Statistics Quarterly and Population Trends can be viewed or downloaded as Adobe Acrobat PDF files from the National Statistics website www.statistics.gov.uk/products/p6725.asp *(Health Statistics Quarterly)* or *www.statistics.gov.uk/products/p6303.asp (Population Trends).*

Contributions

Articles: 5,000 words max.

Dates for submissions

Title \ Issue	Spring	Summer	Autumn	Winter
Health Statistics Quarterly	by 11 Sept	by 11 Dec	by 22 Mar	by 21 June
Population Trends	by 23 Oct	by 2 Feb	by 4 May	by 26 July

Please send to:

Clare Parrish, executive secretary
Health Statistics Quarterly
Office for National Statistics
Zone D2/22
1 Drummond Gate
London SW1V 2QQ
Tel: 020 7533 5125
E-mail: clare.parrish@ons.gsi.gov.uk

Contact points at ONS

People with enquiries about the statistics published regularly in *Health Statistics Quarterly and Population Trends* can contact the following enquiry points.

Topic enquiries

Abortions: 020 7972 5537 (Department of Health)
    E-mail: abortion.statistics@dh.gsi.gov.uk
Births: 01329 813758
    E-mail: vsob@ons.gsi.gov.uk
Conceptions: 01329 813758
    E-mail: vsob@ons.gsi.gov.uk
Expectation of life: 020 7533 5222
    E-mail: lifetables@ons.gsi.gov.uk
Marriages and divorces: 01329 813758
    E-mail: vsob@ons.gsi.gov.uk
Migration: 01329 813872/813255
Mortality: 01329 813758
    E-mail: vsob@ons.gsi.gov.uk
Population estimates: 01329 813318
    E-mail: pop.info@ons.gsi.gov.uk
Population projections:
    National – 020 7533 5222
    E-mail: natpopproj@ons.gsi.gov.uk
    Subnational – 01329 813474/813865

General enquiries

National Statistics Customer Contact Centre
Room 1015 Government Buildings
Cardiff Road
Newport NP10 8XG
Tel: 0845 601 3034
E-mail: info@statistics.gsi.gov.uk
Website: www.statistics.gov.uk

ISBN 0-230-00317-6

ISSN 1465-1645

in brief

Alcohol-related deaths – latest figures for 2005

Latest figures on alcohol-related death rates in the UK in 2005 were released on 7 November. These showed that rates in the UK increased from 6.9 per 100,000 population in 1991 to 12.9 in 2005. The number of alcohol-related deaths more than doubled from 4,144 in 1991 to 8,386 in 2005. These figures are based on a harmonised definition of alcohol-related deaths that has been agreed across the UK. The definition was described in In Brief in *Health Statistics Quarterly* 31 where alcohol-related death rates in the UK from 1991–2004 were reported.

Since publication, errors have been found in some of the figures quoted in that edition. These have now been corrected and released with new data for 2005 on the National Statistics website: www.statistics.gov.uk/cci/nugget.asp?id=1091

The latest figures for 2005 show that in the UK in 2005 the male death rate, at 17.9 deaths per 100,000 population, was more than twice the rate for females (8.3 deaths per 100,000) and males accounted for two-thirds of the total number of deaths.

For men the death rates in all age groups increased between 1991 and 2005. The biggest increase was for men aged 35–54. Rates in this age group more than doubled during this period from 13.4 to 29.9 deaths per 100,000. However the highest rates in each year were for men aged 55–74. In 2005 the rate in this age group was 43.4 per 100,000.

The death rates by age group for females were consistently lower than rates for males, however the trends showed a broadly similar pattern by age. The death rate for women aged 35–54 nearly doubled between 1991 and 2005, from 7.2 to 14.2 per 100,000 population, a larger increase than the rate for women in any other age group. The highest rates in each year were for the age group 55–74 however. In 2005 there were 19.2 alcohol-related deaths per 100,000 population for women in this age group.

Recent Publications

Contraception and sexual health, 2005/06 (October, available at www.statistics.gov. uk/statbase/ product.asp?vlnk=6988).

Focus on Ethnicity and Religion (Palgrave Macmillan, £50, October, ISBN 1-4039-9328-9).

Focus on Gender (October, available at www.statistics.gov.uk/statbase/ product. asp?vlnk=109238).

Population Trends 125 (Palgrave Macmillan, £27.50, September, ISBN 0-230-00320-6).

To order any of the above publications from Palgrave Macmillan please contact www. palgrave.com/ons

All publications are also available free of charge at www.statistics.gov.uk

Health indicators

England and Wales

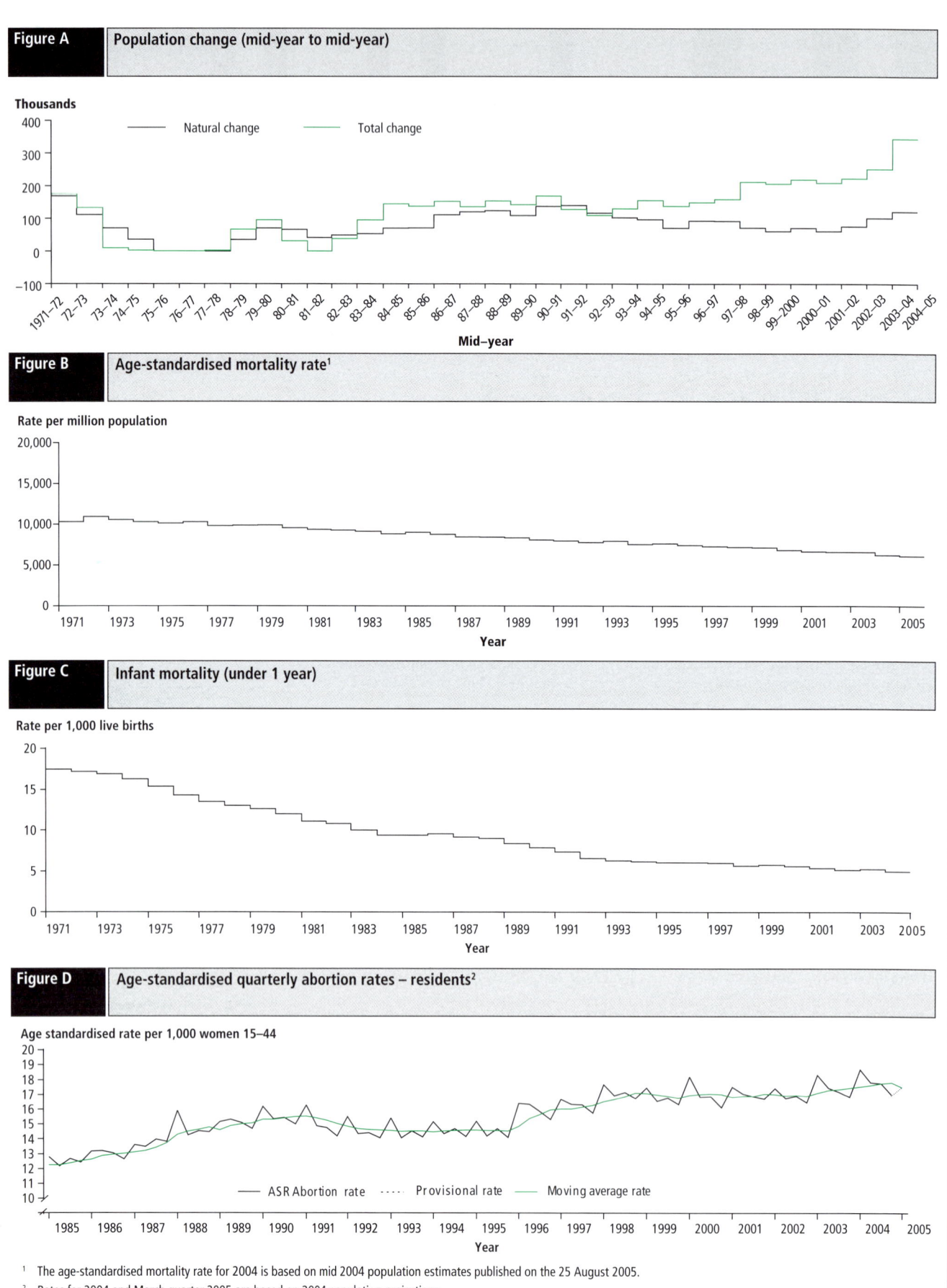

| Figure A | Population change (mid-year to mid-year) |

Thousands

Legend: Natural change — Total change

Mid–year

| Figure B | Age-standardised mortality rate[1] |

Rate per million population

Year

| Figure C | Infant mortality (under 1 year) |

Rate per 1,000 live births

Year

| Figure D | Age-standardised quarterly abortion rates – residents[2] |

Age standardised rate per 1,000 women 15–44

Legend: ASR Abortion rate ···· Provisional rate — Moving average rate

Year

[1] The age-standardised mortality rate for 2004 is based on mid 2004 population estimates published on the 25 August 2005.

[2] Rates for 2004 and March quarter 2005 are based on 2004 population projections.

Health Statistics Quarterly 32

ISBN 0-230-00317-6

CORRECTION

Table 1 Life expectancy at birth[1] (years) and relative position (rank order[2]) of local authorities in England and Wales, 2003–2005 and 1993–1995

Page 106

The data for male life expectancy at birth in Wales for 1993–1995 should read: 73.42

The difference in male life expectancy in Wales between 2003–2005 and 1993–1995 (years) should read 2.73

The pdf on the ONS website www.statistics.gov.ul/statbase/product. asp?vlnk=6725 shows the correct information.

Office for National Statistics

November 2006

Basingstoke: Palgrave Macmillan

Trends in injury and poisoning mortality using the ICE on injury statistics matrix, England and Wales, 1979–2004

Clare Griffiths, Oliver Wright and
Cleo Rooney
Office for National Statistics

Introduction

Although deaths from injury and poisoning account for less than 5 per cent of all deaths in England and Wales[1] it is important to examine them in more detail for several reasons. Deaths from injury and poisoning account for over half of deaths at ages 15–34. In men in this age group, the five most common causes of death are all categories of injury or poisoning, as are five of the top ten in women.[2] Thus deaths from injury and poisoning have a large impact in terms of premature deaths and potential years of life lost. Many of the events that lead to injuries are thought to be largely preventable through public policies, and so resulting deaths should be largely avoidable; for example, motor vehicle accidents can be prevented through promotion of behaviour change, legislation and enforcement, and design of roads, vehicles and safety devices.

There is a need for consistent and comparable information on injury mortality over time, to highlight increasing hazards, and monitor the effects of interventions. This is particularly difficult when new revisions of the International Classification of Diseases (ICD), used to code cause of death, are introduced. The standard ICD classification has two dimensions for classifying the underlying cause for deaths from injury and poisoning – the mechanism of death, for example poisoning or drowning, and the intent, for example unintentional, suicide, homicide. In the ICD, intent takes precedence over mechanism, so deaths are first grouped according to whether they were unintentional (accidental in the ICD), suicide, homicide etc and then within these categories they are classified according to mechanism.

This article shows trends in injury and poisoning mortality in England and Wales using a matrix of mechanism (e.g. fall, fire) by intent (e.g. accident, suicide) developed by the International Collaborative Effort (ICE) on injury statistics. Overall injury and poisoning mortality rates have declined for both males and females. Declines were greatest during the 1980s and early 1990s, with rates falling only slightly since. Rates were generally higher for males and were highest in the elderly. Transport death rates declined substantially. Death rates from falls declined to the mid 1990s but then increased. There were increases in death rates from drug abuse/dependence in both sexes and in homicide rates among males.

In many standard tabulations it is common to separate out accidents by mechanism but present the other intents as a whole. This reflects, in part, the larger numbers of deaths that are accidental compared to other intents and in part the different groups that have been interested in preventing particular subsets of injury deaths, such as motor vehicle accidents, accidents in the home, the workplace or in children. There are good reasons for doing this, when thinking about some methods of prevention, but it can underemphasise the overall importance of unintentional injuries. It is also useful to be able to look easily at comparisons of mechanisms across all intents. For example, the headline indicator of drug-misuse mortality in England and Wales includes all deaths due to poisoning with one or more controlled drug, whatever the intent or coroner's verdict.[3] This is not easy with the standard ICD shortlists. The mechanism of death is important when looking at preventing injury deaths by modification of products/environment, for example gun control legislation, or improvements in car safety. Categorising deaths by intent is important when looking at interventions that aim to prevent deaths across all mechanisms of death for the same intent, for example provision of mental health services and antidepressant prescribing to prevent suicides.

The ICE matrix

Why analyse data using the ICE matrix

The International Collaborative Effort (ICE) on injury statistics matrix classifies injury and poisoning deaths according to both mechanism and intent, using standard groups of ICD codes.[4,5,6,7] This was done in an effort to standardise how comparisons across mechanisms and intents are carried out, as there are a number of potential ways of doing this. Intent may be established and reported in very different ways in different countries, and this may distort international comparisons. An example is the apparently very low rate of accidental drownings in England and Wales, compared to other ICE participant countries.[8] This is largely an artefact due to a much larger proportion of our drowning deaths being coded as suicide and particularly as 'undetermined intent'. The latter reflects coroners' 'open' verdicts where there is no evidence of intent. In many countries such deaths are simply assumed to be accidental. Use of the matrix facilitates comparison of deaths between countries independent of these potential complications. A study carried out in the 1990s using the matrix showed that France had mortality rates from injury and poisoning twice those in England and Wales and rates for poisoning and falls were nearly twice as high in Denmark as in the comparison countries.[9]

ONS has used the ICE matrix to look at injury and poisoning mortality in England and Wales in two annual reports.[10,11] Presentation of data using the ICE matrix allows easy access to information on both mechanism and intent.

Modifications of the matrix in our analysis

We modified the matrix from the international version in the following ways:

- **Grouped deaths with an underlying cause of Y33.9 with deaths from homicide (unspecified mechanism)**. This code is used for the underlying cause for deaths in England and Wales which have been registered before legal proceedings have been completed and the inquest has therefore been adjourned. These deaths are known as accelerated registrations. It has been possible to register these deaths in this way since 1978 and these deaths were identified in ICD-9 using code E988.8.[1] A large proportion of these deaths are subsequently found to be homicides, so to exclude them from the homicide grouping would underestimate deaths from homicide. These deaths accounted for 52 per cent of homicides in 2004.

- **Included deaths from 'Mental and behavioural disorders due to psychoactive substance use' (F10–F19) with poisoning**. In England and Wales, over 90 per cent of these deaths are in fact acute poisonings where the coroner has given a verdict of drug misuse or addiction, instead of one of accident, suicide or an open verdict.[12] To leave out these deaths would underestimate mortality from poisoning; including them increases the number of deaths in this mechanism by 1,260 (54 per cent) (Table 1). These deaths are referred to as deaths from drug abuse/dependence in the article.

- **Included deaths coded to E887 (fracture, cause unspecified) in ICD-9 and the nearest equivalent to this in ICD-10 (deaths with an underlying cause of X59- unspecified accident, with a secondary cause of S72 – fracture of femur (Box One)) with deaths from falls.** Previous analysis showed that these codes in ICD-10 give a good approximation to the E887 code in ICD-9. Many deaths from falls simply state the resulting fracture on the death certificate and to leave these deaths out of the falls category would underestimate deaths from falls.[13] Including them increases the number of deaths included in this mechanism by 2,042 deaths (67 per cent) (Table 1).

- **Added deaths from osteoporosis (M80–M81) to the falls mechanism.** This is because it is possible, in both ICD-9 in England and Wales and in ICD-10 in most countries, for deaths from fractures following falls to be coded as due to osteoporosis.[13] In 2004, over 80 per cent of deaths from osteoporosis were stated to have involved a pathological fracture.[1] In order not to further underestimate falls we therefore included osteoporosis deaths in our analysis – increasing the number of deaths included in this mechanism by 1,478 (48 per cent) (Table 1). These deaths do not have an intent recorded, as they are not within the injury and poisoning chapter of the ICD, but they are most likely to be unintentional deaths. We have kept them separate in the results presented to show their contribution to overall numbers.

Box one

Secondary cause of death

Deaths where the underlying cause is an external cause are also assigned at least one nature of injury code (from Chapter XIX, S00–T98). Thus, it is possible to have more than one nature of injury code for a single death. For example, a car occupant injured in a transport accident (V40–V49) may have suffered a fracture to the skull (S02) and femur (S72), as well as injuries of the spleen (S36). However, it is necessary to select which one of the nature of injury codes is to be identified as the one causing death. This one cause code is referred to by ONS as the secondary cause. To do this, WHO provides selection guidelines or 'rules' to ensure that the most useful information is derived from the death certificate and that it is done uniformly.[14]

The codes from ICD-10 and ICD-9 used in this analysis for each intent and mechanism category are shown in Appendix A.

Data and Methods

Mortality data

Mortality data were extracted from the deaths databases held by ONS. Most deaths from injury and poisoning are certified by a coroner – 84 per cent in 2004. The exception to this is deaths from falls and fractures, usually in the elderly, which are often certified by doctors, after consultation with the coroner, if there is no public interest that requires an

Table 1	Injury and poisoning deaths by mechanism and intent, 2004

England and Wales

Numbers

Persons	Intent							
Mechanism	Unintentional	Suicide	Undetermined probable homicide	Homicide and intervention/	Legal abuse/ dependence	Drug	Osteoporosis	TOTAL
a) Y33.9 included with homicide, with F10–F19 and M80–M81 added								
Cut/pierce	13	110	18	141				282
Drowning	169	87	148	5				409
Fall and fracture	2,915	99	55	0			1,478	4,547
Fire/flame, hot object/substance	283	39	31	14				367
Firearm	2	81	14	18				115
Machinery	10							10
Transport	2,728	6		1				2,735
Natural/environmental	139							139
Overexertion	0							0
Poisoning	927	888	514	9		1,260		3,598
Struck by, against	49		1	7				57
Suffocation	480	1,748	309	28				2,565
Other specified	123	145	60	5	1			334
Unspecified	2,897	103	140	530				3,670
Total	**10,735**	**3,306**	**1,290**	**758**	**1**	**1,260**	**1,478**	**18,828**
b) Additional adjustment made: X59 with S72 secondary cause removed from unspecified and added to fall								
Cut/pierce	13	110	18	141				282
Drowning	169	87	148	5				409
Fall and fracture	4,957	99	55	0			1,478	6,589
Fire/flame, hot object/substance	283	39	31	14				367
Firearm	2	81	14	18				115
Machinery	10							10
Transport	2,728	6		1				2,735
Natural/environmental	139							139
Overexertion	0							0
Poisoning	927	888	514	9		1,260		3,598
Struck by, against	49		1	7				57
Suffocation	480	1,748	309	28				2,565
Other specified	123	145	60	5	1			334
Unspecified	855	103	140	530				1,628
Total	**10,735**	**3,306**	**1,290**	**758**	**1**	**1,260**	**1,478**	**18,828**

inquest. Data for 1981 have been excluded from analysis by mechanism of death because of the registrars' strike of that year, which reduced the amount of detail supplied to ONS for deaths from injury and poisoning.

Annual mortality statistics for the years up to and including 1992 were published by the year in which the death was registered. Each year, the file of deaths used for analysis therefore contained details of some deaths that had occurred in previous years but had not been registered in the year of death. It omitted deaths that had occurred during the calendar year but had not been registered before the end of the year. The two categories were assumed to balance out each year. A large proportion of deaths in these groups were from injury and poisoning, because of the time taken to hold an inquest and subsequently register the death. Mortality statistics for 1993 onwards have been tabulated by the year in which the deaths occurred, not when they were registered. The annual file is closed in September following the year end, so deaths registered after this date are never included in the annual files used for routine outputs and analysis.

1979 was chosen as the start year for analysis because this was the first year that ICD-9 coding was used in England and Wales. ICD-10 was introduced in 2001.

ONS usually combines deaths from suicide and injury/poisoning of undetermined intent to give an overall estimate of suicides in England and Wales.[15] In this analysis, however, we have presented them separately

to show any differences in the distribution of mechanisms within the two intents.

Mortality rates and populations

To take into account differences in age/sex distributions over time, we calculated directly age-standardised mortality rates for males and females separately for each cell of the matrix, using the European Standard Population.[16] Revised mid-year population estimates based on the 2001 Census were used to calculate the rates for 1982 to 2002. For 1992 to 2002, these were final revised populations published in Autumn 2004. For 1982 to 1991, these were final revised populations published in Spring 2003. Populations prior to 1982 were not revised following the 2001 Census.[17]

Results

Trends and patterns in overall injury and poisoning mortality

Overall injury and poisoning mortality rates have declined since 1979 for both males and females from 528 per million population for males and 305 per million for females in 1979 to 398 per million and 178 per million respectively in 2004 (Figure 1). For both sexes, declines were greatest during the 1980s and early 1990s; rates for males declined almost 20 per cent between 1979 and 1993, and for females the decline

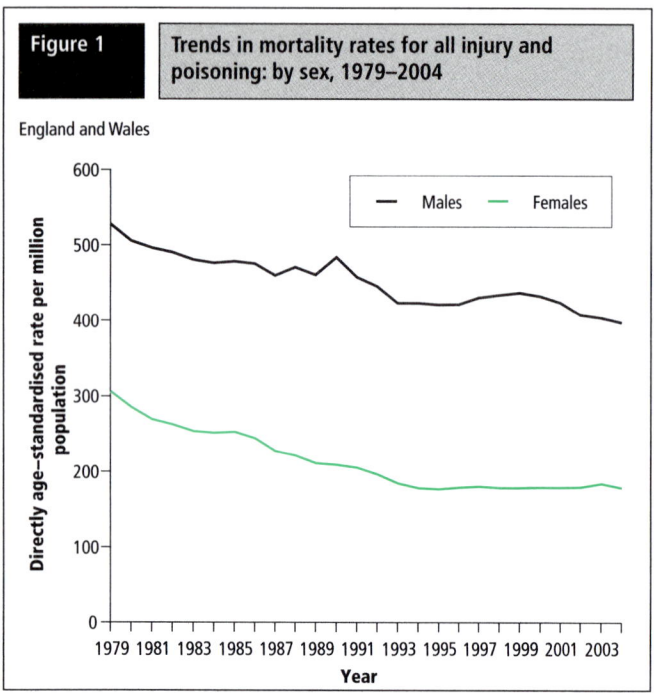

Figure 1 Trends in mortality rates for all injury and poisoning: by sex, 1979–2004

England and Wales

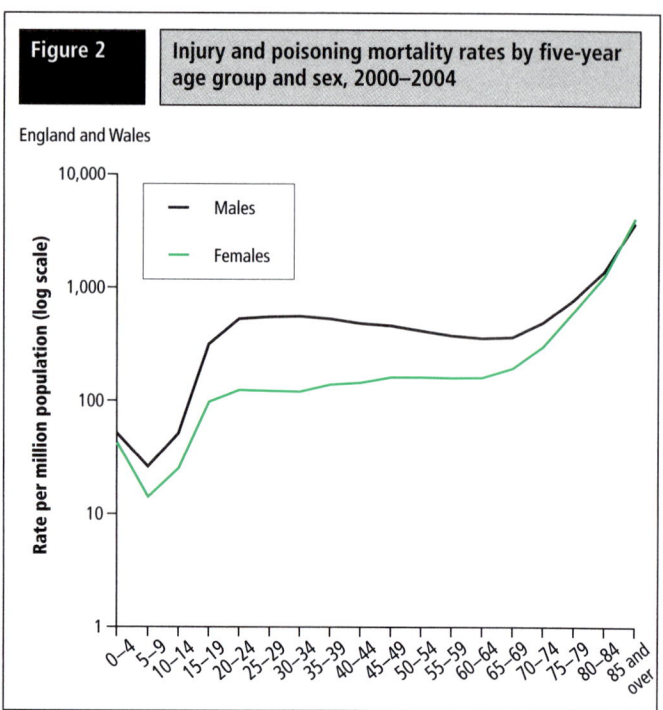

Figure 2 Injury and poisoning mortality rates by five-year age group and sex, 2000–2004

England and Wales

was almost 40 per cent. In contrast, between 1993 and 2004, rates for males declined 6 per cent, after increasing during the mid to late 1990s, and for females rates declined only 3 per cent between 1993 and 2004.

Injury and poisoning mortality rates also vary substantially by age and sex. The highest rates are in the oldest age group, and this is the only age group where rates are higher for females than for males (Figure 2). This is likely to be at least partly due to the fact that in the 85 and over age group, women are generally older than men and thus have higher mortality. Rates are substantially higher for males than females between ages 15 and 64, with this gap starting to narrow for ages 65–69 and older. At ages up to 15, rates are also more similar between males and females, but are still higher among males, even in the 0–4 age group. For both sexes rates decrease between the 0–4 and 5–9 age group then begin to

increase to ages 20–24. In men, rates decline from ages 20–24 to 65–69 and then start to increase to the oldest age group. For women, the pattern is different, with rates slowly increasing from ages 20–24 to 65–69, and then increasing more rapidly to the oldest age groups (Figure 2).

Looking at trends by broad age group, rates in the 75 and over age group for both males and females were far higher than in any other age group throughout the period 1979–2004. Rates in this age group declined to the mid 1990s before beginning to rise again. In females, rates under 15 and at ages 35–74 declined over the period. However, mortality in the 15–34 age group changed very little. For males, the under 15s also had the lowest rates and they declined throughout the period. Rates in the age groups 15–34, 35–54 and 55–74 were more variable – in the early part of the period rates were higher in the 55–74 age group, but these declined

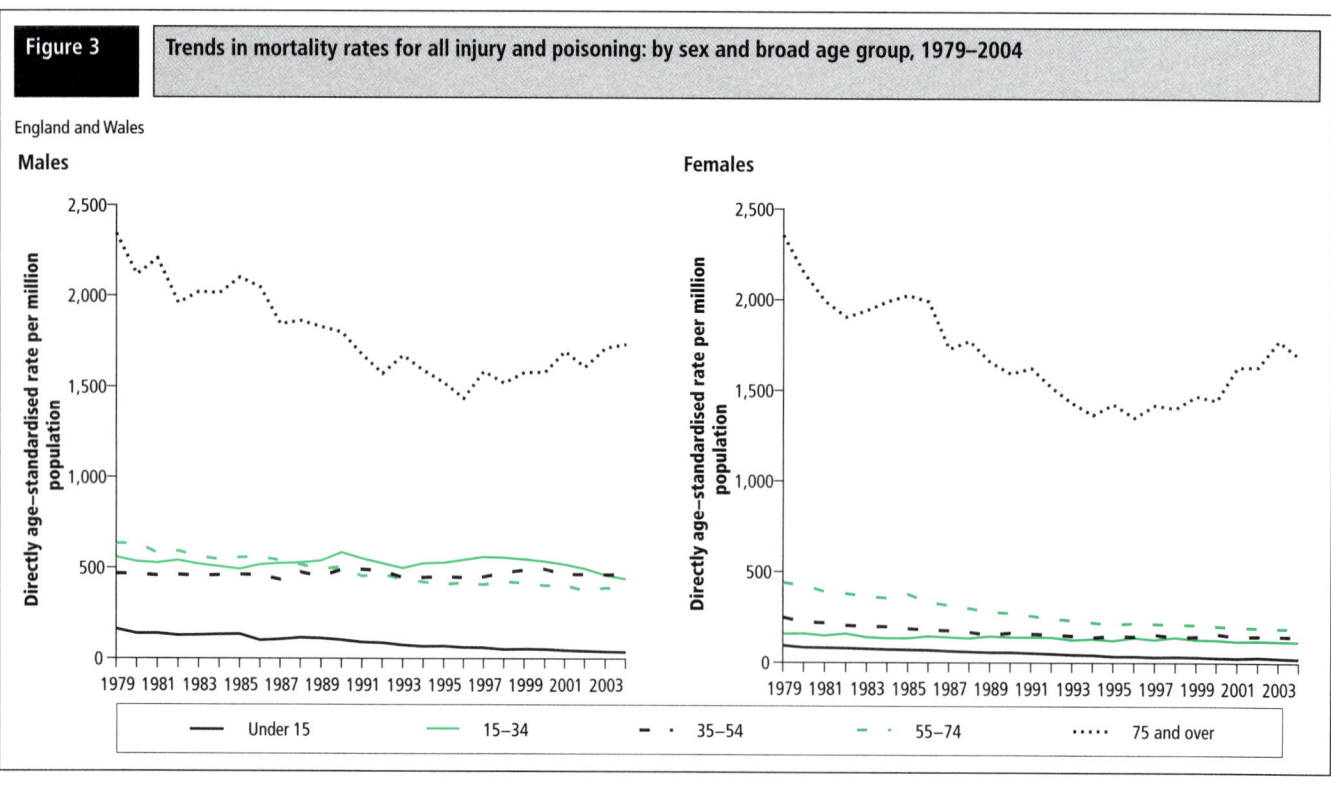

Figure 3 Trends in mortality rates for all injury and poisoning: by sex and broad age group, 1979–2004

England and Wales

Males

Females

Under 15 — 15–34 — · 35–54 — — 55–74 ····· 75 and over

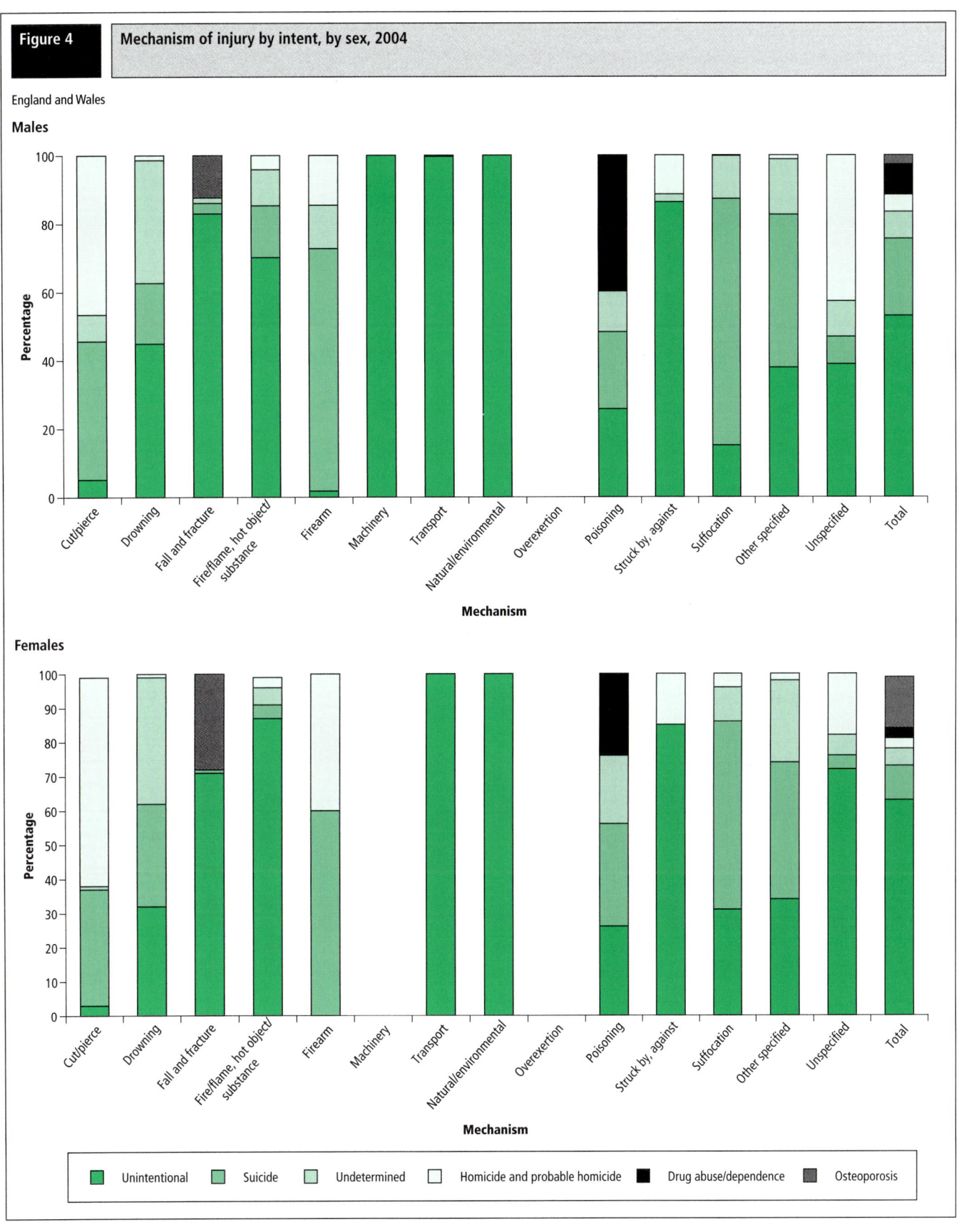

Figure 4 Mechanism of injury by intent, by sex, 2004

England and Wales

Males

Females

substantially, so that by 2004, men in this age group had lower rates than men in the other two age groups. Rates in the 35–54 age group did not decline over the period, so they went from being the lowest of the three middle age groups to being the highest. The 15–34 age group had the highest rates of the three from the early 1990s until 2002, but in 2003 and 2004 their rate was below that of the 35–54 age group (Figure 3).

Patterns of mortality by intent, within mechanism

In 2004, the majority of falls and fractures were unintentional (83 per cent for males and 71 per cent for females) (Figure 4). If we assume that deaths from osteoporosis were also unintentional, these proportions increase to 95 and 99 per cent. The majority of deaths from cutting/piercing injuries were homicides (47 per cent for males and 61 per cent for females) and the majority of deaths from suffocation, which includes hanging and asphyxiation by plastic bags, were suicides (72 per cent for males and 55 per cent for females). Poisoning, by contrast, was split across four main intents – drug abuse/dependence (40 per cent for males and 24 per cent for females), unintentional (26 per cent for both males and females), suicide (22 per cent and 30 per cent) and undetermined intent (12 per cent and 20 per cent).

Almost all deaths due to transport incidents were unintentional. This is partly due to ICD coding rules – even deaths with a verdict of 'death by dangerous driving' or an open verdict are coded as unintentional. This is largely because measures aimed at improving road safety, including enforcement of legislation on speeds, seat belts, drink driving etc, as well as design of roads and vehicles are aimed at preventing all motor vehicle deaths.

Since 1979 an increased proportion of poisonings have been recorded as due to drug abuse/dependence (11 per cent for males and 6 per cent for females in 1979 compared with 40 and 24 per cent in 2004) (data not shown). Other mechanisms had a more similar distribution of intents in 1979 compared with 2004.

Patterns of mortality by mechanism, within intent

In 2004 the most common mechanisms for unintentional injuries among males were transport and falls (35 and 34 per cent respectively). In 1979, a much higher percentage of unintentional deaths were due to transport (53 per cent) (Table 2). For females, the majority of unintentional deaths in both 1979 and 2004 were due to falls/fractures (48 per cent in 1979 and 62 per cent in 2004), followed by transport (27 per cent and 13 per cent). In 2004, for suicides, suffocation was the most common mechanism for males (57 per cent), compared with poisoning in 1979 (44 per cent). There was a similar percentage allocated to both suffocation (40 per cent) and poisoning (41 per cent) for females. In 1979, 59 per cent of female suicides were due to poisoning.

As might be expected, deaths from undetermined intent were more mixed in terms of the mechanisms involved. In 1979 for both sexes, the two most common mechanisms were poisoning (37 per cent for males and 56 per cent for females) and drowning (28 per cent for males and 26 per cent for females). By 2004, a reduced proportion were drownings (12 per cent for males and 11 per cent for females) and an increased proportion due to suffocation (28 per cent for males and 15 per cent for females compared with 7 per cent and 1 per cent respectively in 1979).

For deaths from homicide the picture is less clear. This is because a large proportion are 'probable homicides', registered when the inquest is adjourned. A large proportion of homicides therefore have an unspecified mechanism (74 per cent for males and 60 per cent for females in 2004 compared with 39 per cent and 38 per cent in 1979). The coroner cannot give detailed cause information before completion of legal proceedings. For homicides with a stated mechanism, the most common was cutting/piercing injuries for males in both 1979 and 2004 and for females in 2004. For females in 1979 suffocation was the most common mechanism.

However, because of the increase in homicides with no information on mechanism, these changes are hard to interpret.

Trends in injury and poisoning mortality by intent

For males, the most common intent group for injury and poisoning deaths was unintentional across the period 1979 to 2004, with a substantial decline from 353 per million in 1979 to 205 per million in 2004 (Figure 5). Suicide rates fell across the period but only slightly from 109 per

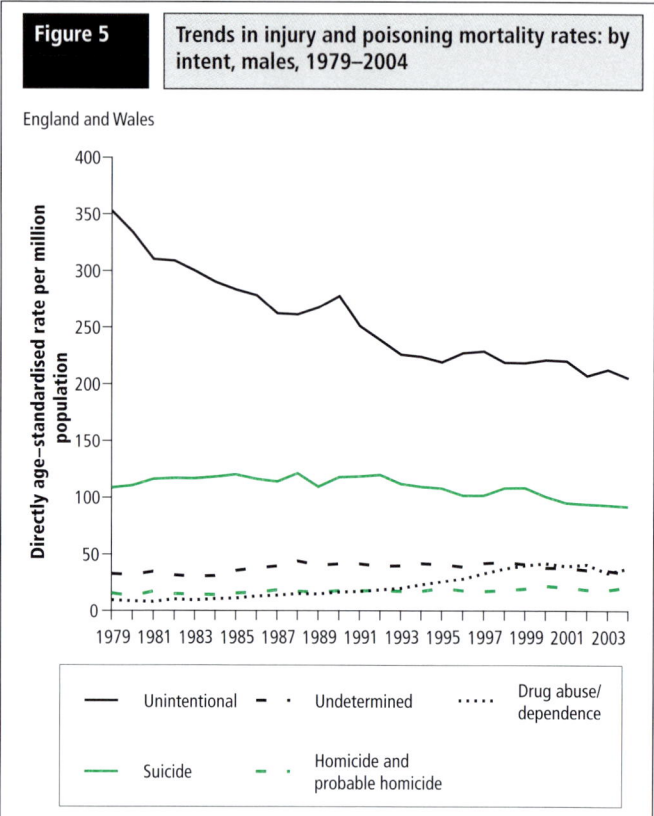

Figure 5 — Trends in injury and poisoning mortality rates: by intent, males, 1979–2004

England and Wales

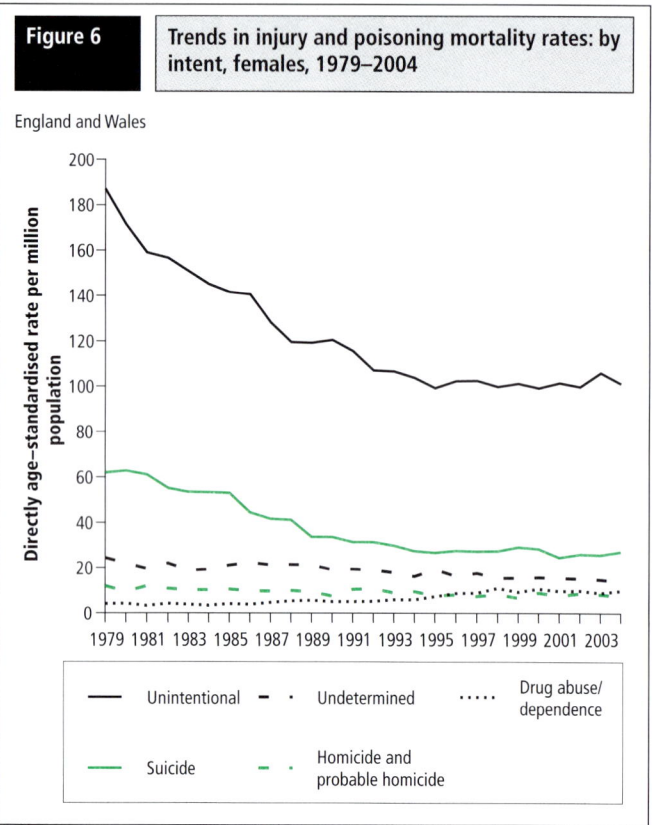

Figure 6 — Trends in injury and poisoning mortality rates: by intent, females, 1979–2004

England and Wales

| Table 2 | Percentage of deaths by mechanism within intent groups: by sex, 2004 and 1979 |

England and Wales

Percentages

Mechanism	Intent						Total
	Unintentional	Suicide	Undetermined	Homicide and probable homicide	Drug abuse/ dependence	Osteoporosis	
2004							
Males							
Cut/pierce	0	3	2	18	0	0	2
Drowning	2	2	12	1	0	0	3
Fall and fracture	34	3	4	0	0	100	21
Fire/flame, hot object/substance	3	1	3	2	0	0	2
Firearm	0	3	2	3	0	0	1
Machinery	0	0	0	0	0	0	0
Transport	35	0	0	0	0	0	19
Natural/environmental	1	0	0	0	0	0	1
Overexertion	0	0	0	0	0	0	0
Poisoning	11	22	34	1	100	0	23
Struck by, against	1	0	0	1	0	0	0
Suffocation	5	57	28	1	0	0	18
Other specified	2	4	5	1	0	0	2
Unspecified	6	3	11	74	0	0	9
Total	100	100	100	100	100	100	100
Females							
Cut/pierce	0	3	0	20	0	0	1
Drowning	1	4	11	0	0	0	2
Fall and fracture	62	3	4	0	0	100	55
Fire/flame, hot object/substance	3	1	2	2	0	0	2
Firearm	0	0	0	1	0	0	0
Machinery	0	0	0	0	0	0	0
Transport	13	0	0	0	0	0	8
Natural/environmental	1	0	0	0	0	0	1
Overexertion	0	0	0	0	0	0	0
Poisoning	6	41	53	2	100	0	14
Struck by, against	0	0	0	1	0	0	0
Suffocation	4	40	15	12	0	0	8
Other specified	1	4	5	1	0	0	1
Unspecified	10	3	10	60	0	0	9
Total	100	100	100	100	100	100	100
1979							
Males							
Cut/pierce	0	4	1	32	0	0	2
Drowning	4	6	28	1	0	0	6
Fall and fracture	19	5	9	0	0	100	16
Fire/flame, hot object/substance	4	2	4	1	0	0	4
Firearm	0	7	3	6	0	0	2
Machinery	2	0	0	0	0	0	1
Transport	53	0	0	0	0	0	35
Natural/environmental	3	0	0	0	0	0	2
Overexertion	0	0	0	0	0	0	0
Poisoning	5	44	37	2	100	0	16
Struck by, against	1	0	0	9	0	0	1
Suffocation	5	28	7	6	0	0	10
Other specified	2	5	4	5	0	0	3
Unspecified	1	0	8	39	0	0	2
Total	100	100	100	100	100	100	100
Females							
Cut/pierce	0	2	0	21	0	0	1
Drowning	1	10	26	2	0	0	4
Fall and fracture	48	5	6	0	0	100	40
Fire/flame, hot object/substance	7	2	2	2	0	0	5
Firearm	0	1	1	5	0	0	0
Machinery	0	0	0	0	0	0	0
Transport	27	0	0	0	0	0	18
Natural/environmental	4	0	1	0	0	0	3
Overexertion	0	0	0	0	0	0	0
Poisoning	6	59	56	1	100	0	18
Struck by, against	0	0	0	3	0	0	0
Suffocation	5	17	1	24	0	0	7
Other specified	1	3	1	3	0	0	1
Unspecified	1	0	5	38	0	0	2
Total	100	100	100	100	100	100	100

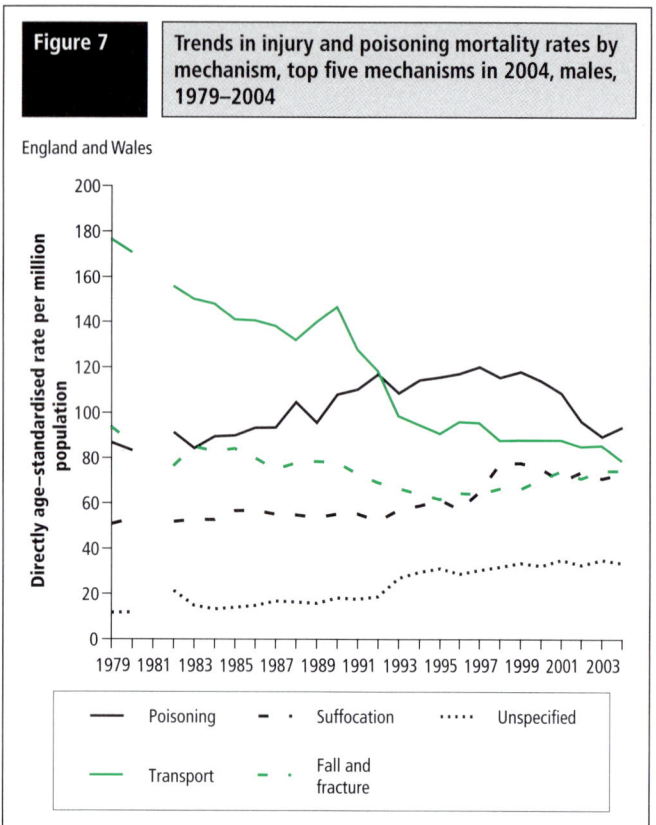

Figure 7 Trends in injury and poisoning mortality rates by mechanism, top five mechanisms in 2004, males, 1979–2004

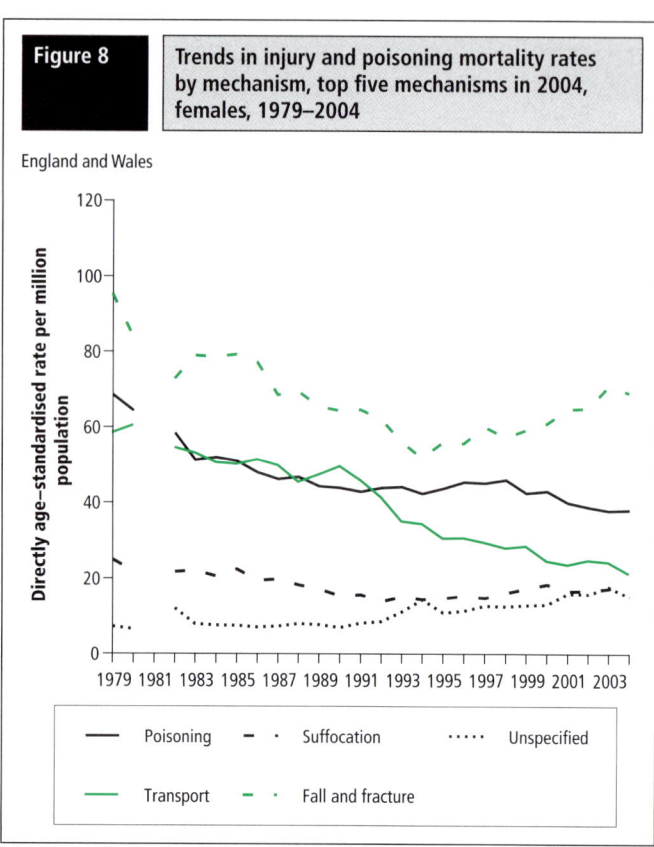

Figure 8 Trends in injury and poisoning mortality rates by mechanism, top five mechanisms in 2004, females, 1979–2004

million in 1979 to 92 per million in 2004. Death from undetermined intent rose during the early and mid 1980s, with a peak rate of 44 per million in 1988. For the next 11 years, rates remained fairly stable before decreasing consistently from 1998 to stand at 33 per million in 2004 – the same rate as in 1979. ONS normally combines suicide and undetermined intent when presenting overall suicide trends for England and Wales. Over the period there was an increase in drug abuse/dependence death rates, from 9 per million in 1979 to 37 per million in 2004, though the peak was 42 per million in 2000. Homicide rates increased from 16 per million in 1979 to 21 per million in 2004, with a peak of 22 per million in 2000.

Among females, the most common intent was also unintentional, with a substantial decrease between 1979 (187 deaths per million population) and 1995, when the lowest rate in the period of 99 per million was recorded (Figure 6). Since 1995 rates have remained stable at around 100 per million. Suicide was the second most common intent, and suicide rates among females declined from 62 per million in 1979 to 27 per million in 1995. Since then rates have been fairly stable. Deaths with undetermined intent declined from 24 per million in 1979 to 14 per million in 2004. Deaths from homicide also declined, from 12 per million in 1979 to 8 per million in 2004. Deaths from drug abuse/dependence increased from 4 per million in 1979, varying between 9 per million and 11 per million during 1996 to 2004.

Trends in injury and poisoning mortality by mechanism

The five most common mechanisms in 2004 for both males and females were poisoning, transport, suffocation, falls and fractures and unspecified. Figures 7 and 8 show trends for these mechanisms from 1979 to 2004. For males, there was a large decrease in transport death rates, from 176 per million in 1979 to 79 per million in 2004 (Figure 7). Since 1993, poisoning has been the most common mechanism for males, with rates increasing from 87 per million in 1979 to a peak of 120 per million in 1997. Rates then declined to 2003. Deaths from falls and fractures declined from 94 per million in 1979 to a low of 62 per million in 1995. Since then rates have increased to stand at 74 per million in 2004. Rates for suffocation and for unspecified mechanisms both increased over the period.

For females, the most common mechanism throughout the period was falls and fractures. Death rates for these followed a similar pattern to that seen for males, declining from 95 per million in 1979 to a low of 52 per million in 1994, increasing since then, to stand at 69 per million in 2004 (Figure 8). There was a decline in deaths from poisoning, though rates did increase slightly during the 1990s before decreasing again. Rates for transport incidents also declined during the period, from 58 per million in 1979 to 21 per million in 2004. The pattern for suffocation was different to that for males, with rates declining to the early 1990s and then increasing, to stand at 19 per million in 2004. Deaths with unspecified mechanism increased throughout the period.

Figures 9 and 10 present trends in death rates for the less common mechanisms. For males, rates for drowning, fire/flame and firearm all declined (Figure 9). Rates for cutting/piercing injuries have been more variable, but have increased in recent years. Rates for deaths involving machinery decreased to almost zero by 2004. For females, rates for fire/flame and drowning decreased from around 16 per million in 1979 to around 4 per million in 2004 (Figure 10). Rates for natural/environmental factors and cutting/piercing injuries also declined overall during the period, but rates for cutting/piercing injuries have been stable in recent years.

As discussed above, the distribution of intents for deaths from poisoning shows an interesting pattern over the period. For males, the overall rate for mortality from poisoning has increased from 87 per million in 1979 to a peak of 120 per million in 1997, declining to 2003, as described above. Within this there has been a shift in the distribution of the intent of the deceased, which may tell us something about changes in the types of these deaths. From 1979, throughout the 1980s, suicide was consistently the most common intent, but from the early 1990s this pattern started to change, with unintentional deaths and deaths from drug abuse/dependence becoming increasingly more important (Figure 11). By 2004, both of these intents had higher rates than suicide. For females, the overall trend is one of decline, particularly in suicides. Deaths from drug abuse/dependence have increased over the period.

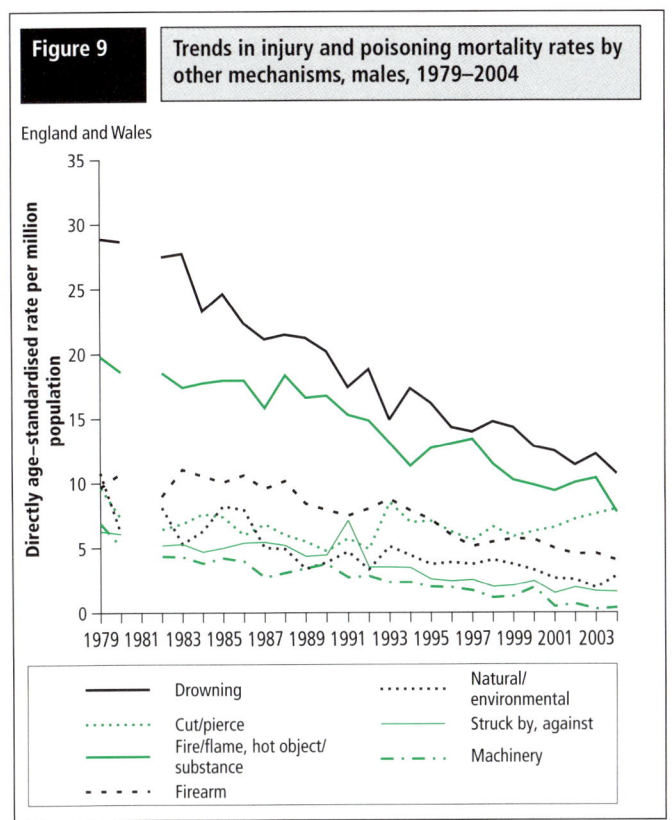

Figure 9 | **Trends in injury and poisoning mortality rates by other mechanisms, males, 1979–2004**

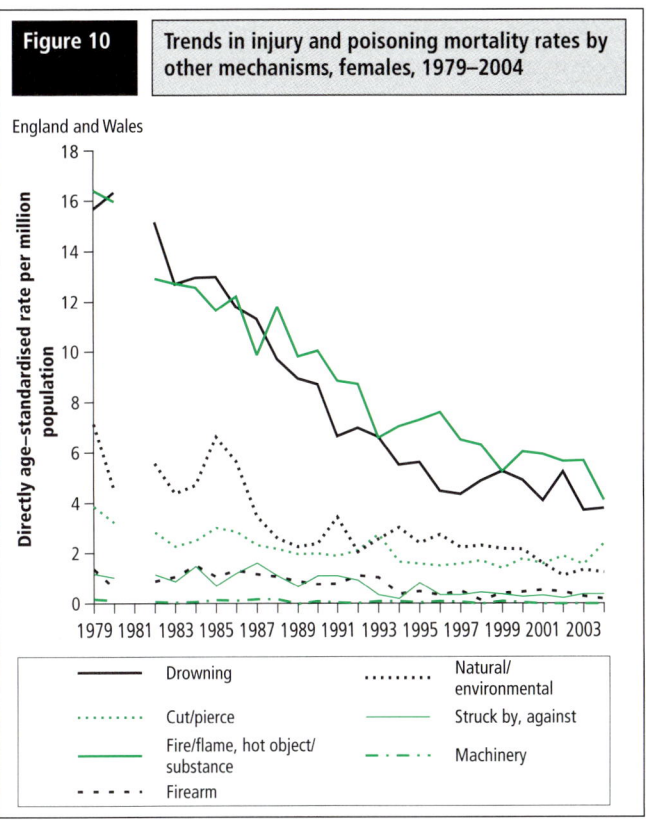

Figure 10 | **Trends in injury and poisoning mortality rates by other mechanisms, females, 1979–2004**

Patterns of injury and poisoning mortality for the top four mechanisms by age

Mortality varies by five-year age group according to the mechanism of death. For falls, in both males and females there is a strong relationship with age, with rates increasing dramatically from ages 5–9, with the lowest rates, to age 85 plus, where rates for falls are substantially higher than for the other main mechanisms of death (Figure 12). The other mechanisms show more similar patterns to each other by age, particularly in males. In males, for poisoning and suffocation, rates are lowest in the

5–9 age group. For transport, rates are lowest in the 0–4 age group. Rates rise steeply to a peak in young adulthood. The age group of the peak varies by mechanism – for transport it is in men aged 20–24, whereas for poisoning and suffocation it is in men aged 30–34. For each of these, rates then start to decline, before rising again in the older age groups.

For females, rates for transport, poisoning and suffocation are lowest in the 5–9 age group. Rates then rise with age, but there is only a clear peak in young adults for transport, where the peak is in 15 to 19-year-olds. Rates for transport then decrease, levelling off between ages 30 and 59

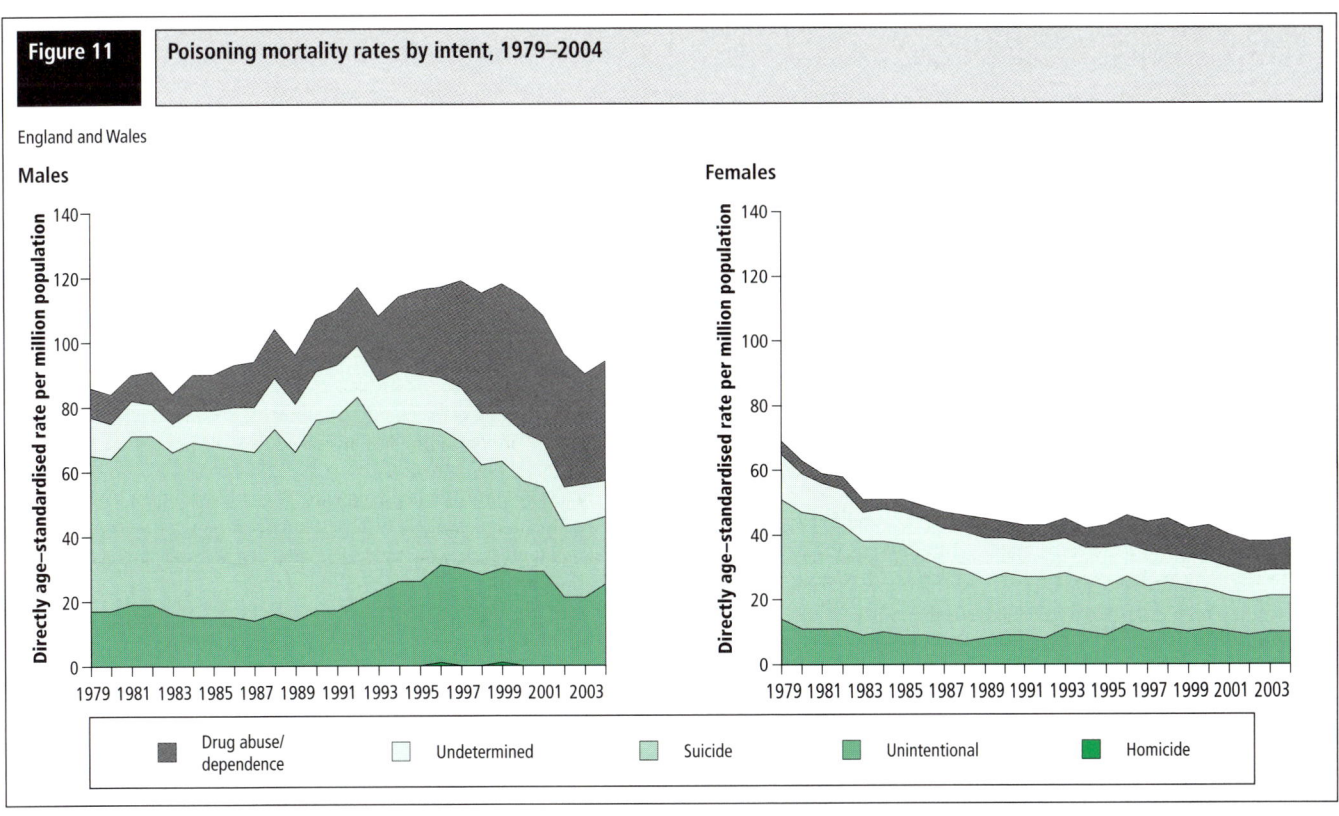

Figure 11 | **Poisoning mortality rates by intent, 1979–2004**

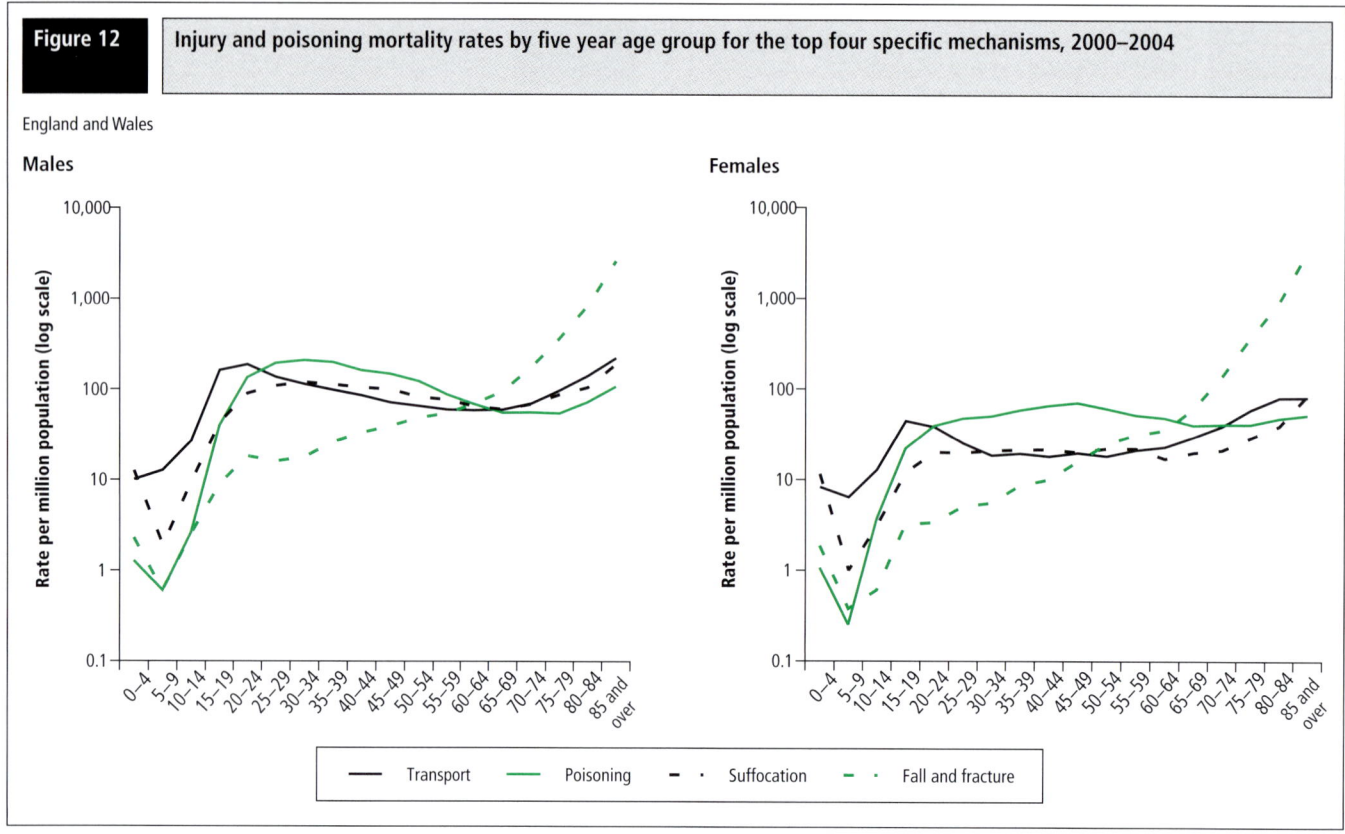

Figure 12 | Injury and poisoning mortality rates by five year age group for the top four specific mechanisms, 2000–2004

England and Wales

Males

Females

Transport — Poisoning — · Suffocation — · · Fall and fracture

before starting to rise again from age 60–64. For suffocation, rates are stable between ages 20–24 and 65–69, where they again start to rise. For poisoning, rates peak in the 45–49 age group.

Discussion

Overall injury and poisoning mortality rates have declined since 1979 for both males and females; for both sexes the reductions in rates were greatest during the 1980s and early 1990s, with rates decreasing only slightly since then. Overall rates were significantly higher for males than for females and were highest in the elderly, throughout the period 1979 to 2004, and have increased since the 1990s in this age group.

Transport incidents have seen a large decline. Various national and local Government campaigns and regulations have targeted road safety. Compulsory seatbelt wearing for front-seat passengers was introduced in 1982 and for adult back-seat passengers in 1991. Soon after the law came into effect there was 90 per cent wearing by car drivers and front-seat passengers. The introduction of the breathalyser test came in 1967,[18] predating the period examined in our article.

Deaths from falls and fractures declined to the mid 1990s but then increased in more recent years. Some of this may be related to aging of the population, though this should be minimised through age standardising the rates. There has been a large shift away from holding inquests in deaths from falls in the elderly to allowing doctors to certify the death after consulting the coroner. It is possible, though it is difficult to find evidence to check, that this could have led to an increased willingness amongst doctors to certify deaths as due to falls and fractures. However, research is needed to establish whether this is a real increase in risk of dying from falls, and what the reasons for such a rise could be.

Deaths from fires have decreased substantially in both sexes. This is despite an increase over the same time period in total fires and domestic fires in the UK.[19] Deaths from drowning have also declined over the same period, although the reasons for this decline are unclear.

Homicide rates have increased among males, particularly young adults, but have decreased in women and not changed much in infants and children. This pattern is similar to the trends in suicide rates. ONS mortality data do not provide any information about the perpetrator or apparent reason for homicides. Homicide remains a rare cause of death in England and Wales, even after the standard ONS addition of adjourned inquest deaths or 'probable homicides' as in this paper. Nevertheless, it is now one of the ten leading causes in young men and women.[2]

There have been increases in deaths attributed to drug abuse/dependence in both males and females. This is related to an increase during the 1990s in deaths involving opiates, with a peak in 2000.[20] The change in distribution of deaths from poisoning from being mainly suicides to having a more mixed distribution of intents is probably related to a variety of factors, including the reduction in suicides from motor vehicle exhaust gas poisoning, as well as from drug poisoning, with drugs such as antidepressants and paracetamol, and the increase in deaths from drug abuse/dependence referred to above. There may also have been a shift in the way that coroners use verdicts, with some deaths that would in the past have been given a verdict of accident or 'open', being specified instead as drug abuse/dependence.

This article has demonstrated how using the ICE matrix can reveal patterns of injury and poisoning mortality which are not easily visible using traditional tabulations based on ICD shortlists. The overall patterns and trends in deaths from poisoning are obscured by the traditional method of tabulating them in different intent categories. Transport crashes, in contrast, are not underestimated because they are almost all coded as unintentional.

Including osteoporosis (M80–M81) and fracture with no external cause specified (X59 with secondary cause S72) increases deaths classed as falls from about 3,000 to around 6,500. This shows that the traditional ICD codes for examining falls in ICD-10 underestimate falls in England and Wales by about half. The Mortality Reference Group (MRG) of the World Health Organisation proposes to introduce new codes in a future update of ICD-10 which would allow deaths from fractures with the cause unspecified to be coded to X59.0, with the code X59.9 being used for other deaths currently coded to X59 (exposure to unspecified factor).[13] X59.0 would then be equivalent to E887 in ICD-9. This would allow these deaths to be more easily grouped with deaths from falls for analysis purposes.

In England and Wales, deaths from poisoning are seriously underestimated unless we include deaths coded to mental and behavioural disorders due to psychoactive substance use. The MRG has recommended changes to coding guidance in ICD-10, so that deaths from acute 'intoxication' or toxicity of drugs would be coded to poisoning, in chapter XX, instead of the F10–F19 codes in the mental and behavioural chapter.

Making these changes to falls and poisoning means that, in 2004, falls were the most common mechanism of injury, followed by poisoning, then transport incidents. This is different to the traditional picture of injury mortality in England and Wales, where transport is often seen as the most common mechanism of injury.[10] The demotion of transport to third commonest mechanism of deaths from external causes reflects both the dramatic real decline in transport-related deaths during this period, and the grouping of deaths from other mechanisms across intent categories. In 2004, falls and fractures accounted for nearly twice as many deaths as poisoning and more than two and a half times as many as transport.

Usually ONS combines deaths from suicide and undetermined intent to give an overall estimate of suicides. This is because in England and Wales, it has been customary to assume that most injuries and poisonings of undetermined intent are cases where the harm was self-inflicted but there was insufficient evidence to prove that the deceased deliberately intended to kill themselves.[15] We have kept these two intents separate in this article to show the different patterns of mechanism across each. These patterns may of course be because the mechanism used may well influence whether or not a suicide verdict is given in particular cases. For example, it may be felt easier to establish intent for deaths from hanging (included in suffocation in this article) than for deaths from poisoning or drowning.

One limitation of this analysis is that mechanisms common in homicides will be underestimated due to the large number which have no mechanism allocated to them. More detailed analysis of homicides can be done using a special extract from the mortality database, but even so, only a small percentage have information on the mechanism of death.[21] The Home Office does publish information on method of homicide – the most common method in 2004/05 was stabbing with a sharp instrument (29 per cent),[22] which ties in with the most common mechanism in the mortality data being cutting and piercing injuries.

This example, and the general increase in injury deaths with an unspecified mechanism, highlights issues of data quality. To be useful, injury and poisoning mortality data should be based on accurate and specific information about the circumstances around the death, collected at death registration. The coroner has a key role in supply of good quality information to inform policy on injury and poisoning prevention measures. Doctors too play a role in certifying deaths from fractures, but often do not include information on how the fracture was sustained. Lack of information, or imprecise information, can lead to bias in reporting for some injury deaths. Homicides are clearly affected by missing information, as the analysis in this paper has shown. An increasing proportion of deaths involving fractures in the elderly are certified by doctors, who have not traditionally been taught to specify the external causes that led to injury. Additional training and prompts may be needed to improve the quality of information available about these deaths for prevention. For injury and poisoning mortality data to be useful for

policy formulation, they must also be timely. Deaths from injury and poisoning are often subject to delays in registration, which can mean that numbers in the annual occurrences datasets used in this article for 1993 onwards may be less complete for some causes.[23]

Key findings

- Overall injury and poisoning mortality rates have declined since 1979 for both males and females. For both sexes, declines were greatest during the 1980s and early 1990s
- Overall rates were significantly higher for males than for females and were highest in the elderly of both sexes throughout the period 1979–2004, and have risen since the mid 1990s in this age group.
- In 2004, falls and fractures were the most common mechanism of injury mortality, followed by poisoning and transport. This is due to the inclusion of deaths from drug abuse/dependence with deaths from poisoning and deaths from osteoporosis and fracture with external cause unspecified with deaths from falls.
- There was a large decline in transport death rates, from 176 per million for males and 58 per million in females in 1979 to 79 per million and 21 per million respectively in 2004.
- For both sexes, death rates for falls and fractures declined to the mid 1990s but have increased in more recent years.
- There have been increases in death rates for drug abuse/dependence in both males and females and homicide rates have increased among males since 1979.

References

1.   Office for National Statistics (2005) *Mortality statistics: cause. Review of the Registrar General on deaths by cause, sex and age in England and Wales, 2004. Series DH2 no. 31*, Office for National Statistics: London.

2.   Griffiths C, Rooney C and Brock A (2005) Leading causes of death in England and Wales – how should we group causes? *Health Statistics Quarterly* **28**, 6–17. When using the ranking list which presents cancers by site and accidents by mechanism, selected by ONS for routine publication of the leading causes of death.

3.   Office for National Statistics (2006) Report: Deaths related to drug poisoning: England and Wales 2000-2004. *Health Statistics Quarterly* **29**, 69–76.

4.   National Center for Health Statistics (2004) Deaths: injuries, 2001. *National Vital Statistics Reports* Volume **52** (21), 87.

5.   McLoughlin E, Annest J L, Fingerhut L A *et al* (1997). *Recommended framework for presenting injury mortality data.* Morbidity and Mortality Weekly Report. Centers for Disease Control and Prevention. **46** (no. RR–14).

6.   www.cdc.gov/nchs/about/otheract/ice/matrix10.htm

7.   www.cdc.gov/nchs/about/otheract/ice/matrix.htm

8.   Smith G S (2000) Chapter 20, International comparisons of drowning mortality: The value of multiple cause data. in, *Proceedings of the International Collaborative Effort on Injury Statistics*, Volume III, Washington DC: 2nd Symposium, [June 1999]. April 2000. www.cdc.gov/nchs/about/otheract/ice/pro-iii.htm

9.   Fingerhut L A, Cox C S and Warner M (1998) International comparative analysis of injury mortality. Findings from the ICE on injury statistics. *Advance Data* No. **303**. National Center for Health Statistics.

10. Office for National Statistics (2005) Annual Update: Mortality statistics 2003: injury and poisoning. *Health Statistics Quarterly* **27**, 68–73.

11. Office for National Statistics (2006) Annual Update: Mortality statistics 2004: injury and poisoning. *Health Statistics Quarterly* **31**, 98–103.

12. Christophersen O, Rooney C and Kelly S (1998) Drug-related mortality: methods and trends. *Population Trends* **93**, 29–37.

13. Griffiths C and Rooney C (2003) The effect of the introduction of ICD-10 on trends in mortality from injury and poisoning in England and Wales. *Health Statistics Quarterly* **19**, 10–21.

14. Office for National Statistics (2006) *Mortality statistics: injury and poisoning. Review of the Registrar General on deaths attributed to injury and poisoning in England and Wales, 2004. Series DH4 no. 28.* Office for National Statistics: London.

15. Brock A and Griffiths C (2003) Trends in suicide by method in England and Wales, 1979–2001. *Health Statistics Quarterly* **20**, 7–18.

16. Waterhouse J, Muir C, Correa P and Powell J (eds) (1976) *Cancer incidence in five continents, vol III (IARC Scientific Publications No. 15.* International Agency for Research on Cancer: Lyon.

17. Office for National Statistics. *Population Estimates for England and Wales.* Available at: www.statistics.gov.uk/statbase/Product.asp?vlnk=601

18. Department for Transport. Think Road Safety. www.thinkroadsafety. gov.uk/campaigns/seatbelts/seatbelts.htm

19. Office of the Deputy Prime Minister (2006) *Fire statistics, United Kingdom, 2004.* Office of the Deputy Prime Minister: London.

20. Morgan O, Griffiths C, Toson B *et al* (2006) Trends in deaths related to drug misuse in England and Wales, 1993 to 2004. *Health Statistics Quarterly* **31**, 23–27.

21. Rooney C and Devis T (1999) Recent trends in deaths from homicide in England and Wales. *Health Statistics Quarterly* **03**, 5–13.

22. Coleman K and Cotton J (2006) Chapter 2, Homicide, in Coleman K, Hird C and Povey D (2006) *Violent Crime Overview, Homicide and Gun Crime 2004/2005. (Supplementary Volume to Crime in England and Wales 2004/2005)*, 48–70. Home Office: London.

23. Devis T and Rooney C (1997) The time taken to register a death. Population Trends **88**, 48–55.

Appendix A Codes used in this analysis

ICD-10 codes

Mechanism	Intent							All intents
	Unintentional	Suicide	Undetermined	Homicide and probable homicide	Legal intervention / war	Mental and behavioural disorders due to psychoactive substance use (Drug abuse/dependence)	Osteoporosis	
Cut/pierce	W25–W29, W45	X78	Y28	X99	Y35.4	–	–	W25–W29, W45, X78, X99, Y28, Y35.4
Drowning	W65–W74	X71	Y21	X92	–	–	–	W65–W74, X71, X92, Y21
Fall and fracture[1]	W00–W19, X59 with secondary cause S72	X80	Y30	Y01	–	–	M80–M81	M80–M81, W00–W19, X59 (with secondary cause S72) X80, Y01, Y30
Fire/flame, hot object/substance	X00–X19	X76–X77	Y26–Y27	X97–X98	Y36.3	–	–	X00–X19, X76–X77, X97–X98, Y26–Y27, Y36.3
Firearm	W32–W34	X72–X74	Y22–Y24	X93–X95	Y35.0	–	–	W32–W34, X72–X74, X93–X95, Y22–Y24, Y35.0
Machinery	W24, W30–W31	–	–	–	–	–	–	W24, W30–W31
Transport	V01–V99	X82	Y32	Y03	Y36.1	–	–	V01–V99, X82, Y03, Y32, Y36.1
Natural/environmental	W42–W43, W53–W64, W92–W99, X20–X39, X51–X57	–	–	–	–	–	–	W42–W43, W53–W64, W92–W99, X20–X39, X51–X57
Overexertion	X50	–	–	–	–	–	–	X50
Poisoning[2]	X40–X49	X60–X69	Y10–Y19	X85–X90	Y35.2	F10–F19	–	F10–F19, X40–X49, X60–X69, X85–X90, Y10–Y19, Y35.2
Struck by, against	W20–W22, W50–W52	X79	Y29	Y00, Y04	Y35.3	–	–	W20–W22, W50–W52, X79, Y00, Y04, Y29, Y35.3
Suffocation	W75–W84	X70	Y20	X91	–	–	–	W75–W84, X70, X91, Y20
Other specified	W23, W35–W41, W44, W49, W85–W91, X58, Y85, Y86	X75, X81, X83, Y87.0	Y25, Y31, Y33 (excl. Y33.9), Y87.2	X96, Y02, Y05–Y08, Y87.1	Y35(.1,.5,.6), Y36(.0, .2, .4–.8), Y89(.0,.1)	–	–	W23, W35–W41, W44, W49, W85–W91, X58, X75, X81, X83, X96, Y02, Y05–Y08, Y25, Y31, Y33 (excl. Y33.9), Y35(.1,.5,.6), Y36(.0, .2, .4–.8), Y85–Y86, Y87.0–Y87.2, Y89(.0,.1)
Unspecified	X59 (excl. X59 with secondary cause S72)	X84	Y34, Y89.9	Y09, Y33.9	Y35.7, Y36.9	–	–	X59 (excl X59 with secondary cause S72), X84, Y09, Y33.9, Y34, Y35.7, Y36.9, Y89.9
All mechanisms[3]	V01–X59, Y85–Y86*	X60–X84, Y87.0	Y10–Y34 (excl. Y33.9), Y87.2, Y89.9	X85–Y09, Y33.9, Y87.1	Y35–Y36, Y89(.0–.1)	F10–F19	M80–M81	F10–F19, M80–M81, V01–Y36, Y85–Y87, Y89

Changes from the traditional ICD-10 matrix:[6]

1 Fall and fracture includes deaths due to osteoporosis (M80–M81). Fall and fracture with unintentional intent includes deaths coded to exposure to unspecified factor with fracture of the femur as the secondary cause (X59 with S72).

2 Poisonings include those deaths coded to mental and behavioural disorders due to psychoactive substance use (F10–F19).

3 Undetermined intent excludes deaths coded to Y33.9. These have been added to homicide with unspecified mechanism.

Note: deaths attributed to complications of medical and surgical care (Y40–Y84) and sequelae with surgical and medical care as external cause (Y88) are not included in this table.

* This differs from the ICD grouping for accidents, which is V01–X59 only.

ICD-9 codes

Mechanism	Intent							All intents
	Unintentional	Suicide	Undetermined	Homicide and probable homicide	Legal intervention / war	Mental and behavioural disorders due to psychoactive substance use (Drug abuse/ dependence)	Osteoporosis	
Cut/pierce	E920	E956	E986	E966	E974	–	–	E920, E956, E966, E974, E986
Drowning	E830, E832, E910	E954	E984	E964	–	–	–	E830, E832, E910, E954, E964, E984
Fall and fracture[1]	E880–E888	E957	E987	E968.1	–	–	733.0	733.0, E880–E888, E957, E968.1, E987
Fire/flame, hot object/substance	E890–E899, E924	E958.1, .2, .7	E988.1, .2, .7	E961, E968.0, .3	–	–	–	E890–E899, E924, E958.1, .2, .7, E961, E968.0, .3, E988.1, .2, .7
Firearm	E922	E955.0–.4	E985.0–.4	E965.0–.4	E970	–	–	E922, E955.0–.4, E965.0–.4, E970, E985.0–.4
Machinery	E919	–	–	–	–	–	–	E919
Transport	E800–E829, E831, E833–E845	E958.5–E958.6	E988.5–E988.6	–	–	–	–	E800–E829, E831, E833–E845, E958.5–E958.6, E988.5–E988.6
Natural/environmental	E900–E909, E928.0–2	E958.3	E988.3	–	–	–	–	E900–E909, E928.0–2, E958.3, E988.3
Overexertion	E927	–	–	–	–	–	–	E927
Poisoning[2]	E850–E869	E950–E952	E980–E982	E962	E972	291–292, 303–305	–	291–292, 303–305, E850–E869, E950–E952, E962, E972, E980–E982
Struck by, against	E916–E917	–	–	E960.0, E968.2	E973, E975	–	–	E916–E917, E960.0, E968.2, E973, E975
Suffocation	E911–E913	E953	E983	E963	–	–	–	E911–E913, E953, E963, E983
Other specified	E846–E848, E914–E915, E918, E921, E923, E925–E926, E928.8, E929.0–5, E929.8	E955.5–.9, E958.0, .4, .8, E959	E985.5, E988.0, .4, E989	E960.1, E965.5–.9, E967, E968.4, .8, E969	E971, E977–E978, E990–E996, E997.0–.2, .8, E998, E999	–	–	E846–E848, E914–E915, E918, E921, E923, E925–E926, E928.8, E929.0–5, E929.8, E955.5–.9, E958.0, .4, .8, E959, E960.1, E965.5–.9, E967, E968.4, .8, E969, E971, E977–E978, E985.5, E988.0, .4, E989, E990–E996, E997.0–.2, .8, E998, E999
Unspecified	E928.9, E929.9	E958.9	E988.9	E968.9, E988.8	E976, E997.9	–	–	E928.9, E929.9, E958.9, E968.9, E976, E988.8, E988.9, E997.9
All mechanisms[3]	E800–E869, E880–E929	E950–E959	E980–E989 (excl. E988.8)	E960–E969, E988.8	E970–E978, E990–E999	291–292, 303–305	733.0	291–292, 303–305, 733.0, E800–E869, E880–E929, E950–E999

Changes from the traditional ICD-9 matrix:[7]

1 Fall and fracture includes deaths due to osteoporosis (733.0). Fall and fracture with unintentional intent includes deaths coded to fracture, cause unspecified (E887).
2 Poisonings include those deaths coded to mental and behavioural disorders (291–292, 303–305).
3 Undetermined intent excludes deaths coded to E988.8. These have been added to homicide with unspecified mechanism.

Note: the following causes are not included in this table:
■ Misadventures to patients during surgical and medical care (E870–E876)
■ Surgical and medical procedures as the cause of abnormal reaction of patient or later complication, without mention of misadventure at the time of procedure (E878–E879)
■ Drugs, medicaments and biological substances causing adverse effects in therapeutic use (E930–E949)

Mortality by deprivation and cause of death in England and Wales, 1999-2003

Ester Romeri, Allan Baker and Clare Griffiths

Office for National Statistics

Introduction

The link between poverty and health is well established,[1-3] and many studies have also shown a clear relationship between deprivation and death rates, with more deprived areas having worse mortality than the less deprived.[4-7]

Some studies have also considered the relationship between deprivation and mortality in the English regions and Wales, to attempt to determine whether socio-economic factors can explain the geographical differences in death rates which have been consistently identified over the last 150 years.[8-10]

Other studies have also considered whether the gradients of increasing mortality with deprivation seen in all causes of death combined, are still present when cause-specific death rates are considered.[8,11,12]

ONS and its predecessor organisations have a long history of reporting on geographical inequalities in mortality, originally through the annual reports of the Registrar General dating back to 1837, and also via Decennial Supplements to these reports. The most recent of these supplements, *Geographic Variations in Health*, examined variations in the relationship between deprivation and mortality in the countries of Great Britain and the English regions for all deaths, and selected causes.[13]

This analysis found that for both sexes there was a strong positive relationship between deprivation and death rates for all causes combined, ischaemic heart disease and lung cancer, while suicides and deaths from all cancers, stroke, and accidents showed a rather weaker relationship. There were also geographical differences in death rates

The relationship between deprivation and mortality is long established and many studies report higher death rates in more deprived areas. This article examines recent patterns of mortality and deprivation and illustrates these for leading causes of death. Results are considered by age group, sex and region. Mortality rates increased with deprivation for both sexes but the relationship was generally stronger for males. The strongest positive relationships with deprivation were mostly found for smoking-related causes. Those living in the least deprived areas had similar mortality rates, independent of region. There was more geographical variation in mortality for those in the most deprived areas with highest rates generally in the north.

between populations with similar levels of deprivation, with areas in the north generally having higher mortality than those in the south.

This article continues the ONS tradition of regular reporting on socio-economic and geographical inequalities in mortality. Analysis has been undertaken to examine the relationship between deprivation and leading causes of death in England and Wales using mortality data from 1999–2003, and to consider how this relationship varies across the English regions and Wales. The association between deprivation and mortality is also examined by sex and age group.

Methods

Cause of death

The causes selected for analysis were based on the leading causes of death in England and Wales. These were defined in a recent article which presented several alternative definitions based on different methods of grouping causes of death together.[14] For this analysis a definition of leading causes was selected where cancers are included by site but all accidents are grouped together. Cancers were examined separately because research has shown that relationships with deprivation and geographical distributions can vary greatly according to site.[15, 16] The standard ONS ranking list of leading causes examines accidents by type but for this analysis all accidents were grouped together because of the smaller number of deaths in this category.

Lists of the ten leading causes, based on numbers of deaths in England and Wales, were produced for males and females for all ages and those aged 15–64. Causes were included in this analysis if they were among the top ten for either sex or either age group.

Two of these leading causes of death have been excluded from this article (suicide and injury/poisoning of undetermined intent, and cirrhosis & other diseases of the liver). The relationship between suicide and deprivation has already been examined in an article in *Health Statistics Quarterly* 31.[17] An analysis of trends and geographical variations in alcohol-related deaths (which include deaths from liver cirrhosis) is planned for a future *Health Statistics Quarterly* article which will also include a deprivation analysis.

From 1979 to 2000 ONS coded causes of death using the Ninth Revision of the International Classification of Diseases (ICD-9) but in 2001 the Tenth Revision (ICD-10) was introduced. This marked the biggest change in mortality coding in England and Wales in over 50 years. The change in revision means that data for many causes of death are not comparable before and after 2001. The impact of the change has been examined using bridgecoded data for 1999 (deaths that were coded using both ICD-9 and ICD-10). Comparability ratios based on these data have been reported.[18]

For this analysis deaths over a five year period from 1999–2003 were included. This provided data two years either side of 2001, the census year for which deprivation scores were available. As this period included years when deaths were coded using both ICD-9 and ICD-10 there was a potential for discontinuity. The results of the bridgecoding study were used to identify the causes of death for which data were not comparable between revisions. For these causes, deaths were selected using ICD-10 only, for a four-year period from the bridgecoded data for 1999 and then annual mortality files from 2001 to 2003. There were two causes where the change in ICD revision did not have an impact – ischaemic heart disease and accidents.

Records were selected using the final underlying cause of death from annual files of deaths registered in each calendar year. The causes of death examined, and their ICD-9 and ICD-10 codes, are presented in Box One.

Box one

Cause of death	ICD-9	ICD-10
All cancers (malignant neoplasms –MN)		C00–C97
MN of oesophagus		C15
Colorectal cancer:		
MN of colon, rectosigmoid junction,		
rectum and anus		C18–C21
Lung cancer:		
MN of trachea, bronchus and lung		C33–C34
MN of female breast		C50
MN of ovary		C56
MN of prostate		C61
MN of lymphoid, haematopoietic		
and related tissue		C81–C96
Dementia and Alzheimer's Disease		F01, F03 & G30
All circulatory diseases		I00–I99
Ischaemic heart disease	410-414	I20-I25
Stroke (cerebrovascular diseases)		I60–I69
All respiratory diseases		J00–J99
Accidents	E800–E928 (excluding E870–E879)	V01–X59

Carstairs deprivation scores

In the 1980s Vera Carstairs and Russell Morris developed an index designed to be used for health analysis which measured relative material deprivation in small areas.[4] The first set of Carstairs scores were based on results from the 1981 Census and were subsequently updated following the 1991 Census.

Carstairs deprivation scores have now also been calculated by ONS using four data items from the 2001 Census –overcrowding, no car ownership, residents unemployed or in Social Class IV and V. (As the National Statistics Socio-Economic Classification replaced Social Class in the 2001 Census the closest equivalents to classes IV and V were actually used.) The calculation of these scores was described in an article in *Health Statistics Quarterly* 31, which also illustrated the geographical distribution of deprivation in 2001.[19] The 2001 Carstairs scores for wards in England and Wales are available on the National Statistics website: www.statistics.gov.uk/statbase/Product.asp?vlnk=14068

The article in Health Statistics Quarterly 31 also considered the conceptual and practical considerations which helped determine the choice of deprivation index for this analysis. When used for health analysis different deprivation indices have shown a high degree of correlation.[20,21] Carstairs was selected for this analysis because the index has been used in previous ONS studies,[13,15,22] as well as having widespread usage in much health research.[23-27] Carstairs scores could also be calculated at ward-level for which population estimates were available.

For this study, deaths were assigned to the same boundaries as the Carstairs scores (2001 Census Standard Table wards) using the May 2005 National Statistics Postcode Directory. Wards in the City of London and Isles of Scilly were aggregated to local authority level and so 8,797 areas were included in the analysis.

Ward Carstairs scores were ranked from least deprived to most deprived and then divided into fifths (quintiles), tenths (deciles) and twentieths, based on ward population size, so that each deprivation category contained approximately the same number of people. Each deprivation twentieth therefore represents five per cent of the population of England and Wales, while the quintiles and deciles represent 20 and 10 per cent of the population respectively. Each ward was thus assigned to one of five deprivation quintiles, one of ten deprivation deciles and one of 20 deprivation twentieths. Mortality data for each ward were aggregated according to these categories.

Populations

The Carstairs scores were divided into quintiles, deciles and twentieths using 2001 experimental population estimates for wards.[28] When these populations were aggregated to deprivation quintiles considerable variation across the English regions and Wales was seen. In London, for example, 42 per cent of the population in 2001 lived in the most deprived fifth of wards while in the South West only 4 per cent lived in this most deprived quintile (Figure 1). The South East and East of England also had less than 10 per cent of their population living in the most deprived fifth of wards. While almost two-fifths of the population of the South East lived in the least deprived quintile of wards, in the North East and London fewer than one in ten people lived in these areas. The East Midlands was the region with a distribution closest to the England and Wales average with around twenty per cent of its population in each deprivation quintile.

One result of these variations is that mortality rates in some quintiles in some regions are based on much smaller populations and numbers of deaths than in others, e.g. Quintile 5 in the South West. This also results in confidence intervals sometimes varying considerably in width for different deprivation quintiles within the same region.

For the calculation of mortality rates the 2001 ward population estimates were aggregated to deprivation twentieths, deciles and quintiles. The 2001 figures were multiplied by five to provide person years at risk for the calculation of mortality rates for 1999–2003. For cause-specific rates for 1999 and 2001–2003 the populations were multiplied by four.

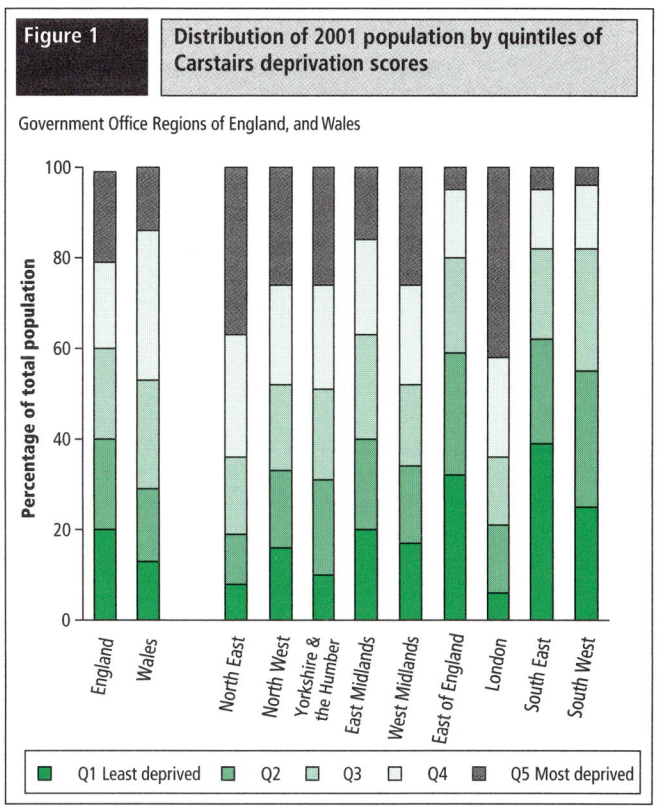

Figure 1 | **Distribution of 2001 population by quintiles of Carstairs deprivation scores**

Government Office Regions of England, and Wales

Q1 Least deprived ■ Q2 ■ Q3 ■ Q4 □ Q5 Most deprived ■

Mortality rates

Directly age-standardised mortality rates were calculated for all the analyses presented in this article. Direct age-standardisation takes into account differences in the age structures of populations meaning that comparisons can be made over time, between areas and between the sexes. Rates in this article were standardised using the European Standard Population.

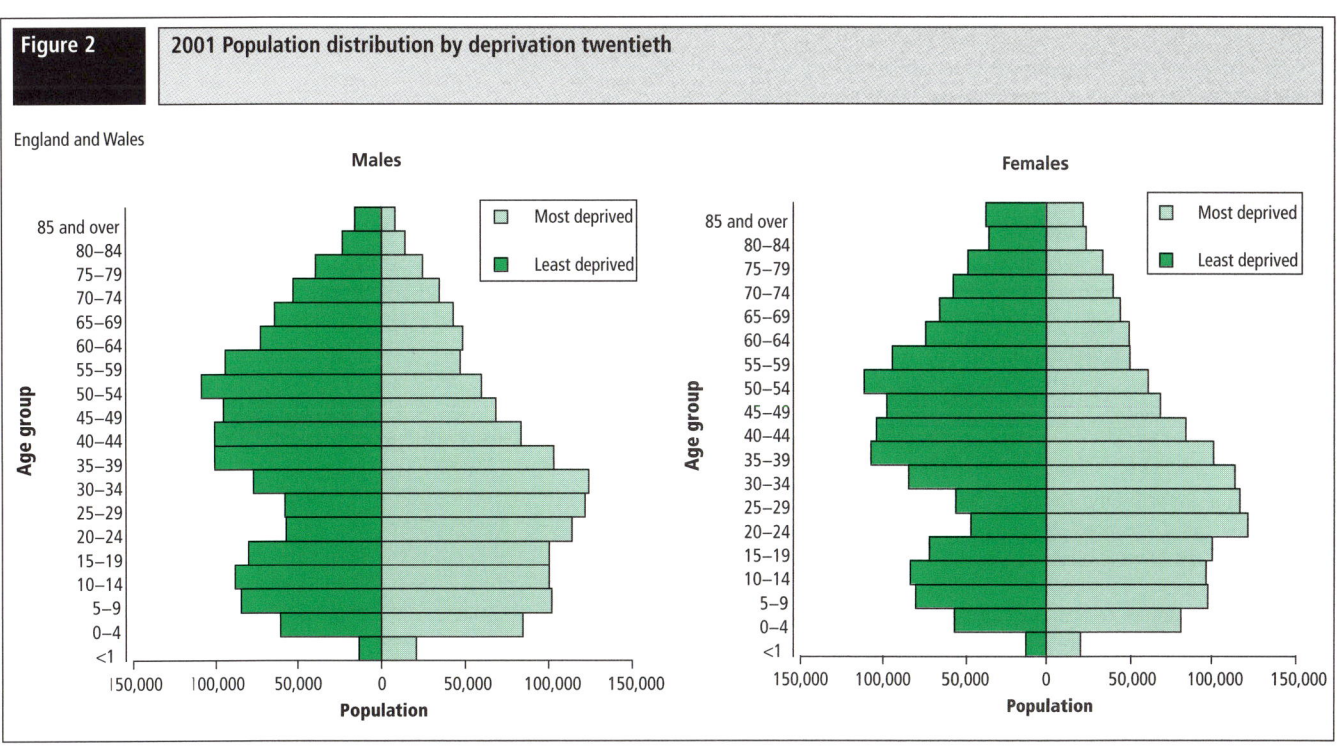

Figure 2 | **2001 Population distribution by deprivation twentieth**

England and Wales

The importance of age-standardising in this analysis can be seen from Figure 2, which illustrates the age structures of the most deprived and least deprived twentieths of the population. The total population of each of these deprivation categories is similar (around 2.6 million) but their age structures are very different, with the most deprived wards having a much younger age distribution. For males, in every age group before age 40 the most deprived wards have a larger population than the least deprived. This pattern reverses from age 40. The picture for females is similar although the least deprived wards have the larger population from age group 35–39 onwards.

Age groups

For all the causes of death analysed, the relationship between deprivation and mortality was considered at all ages. As previous research has shown that deprivation has a stronger relationship with death rates at younger ages than on the elderly,[6,7,9] many of the causes were also analysed for the age group 15–64 (which was also consistent with earlier ONS analysis[13]). For some causes, where there are only a small proportion of deaths under age 65 (such as prostate cancer and Alzheimer's disease and dementia), the analysis was restricted to deaths at all ages. For deaths from all circulatory diseases and all cancers, where there are government targets to reduce mortality rates in those aged under 75, results were also calculated for the age group 0–74.

Results presented

Results for all of the age ranges examined (all ages, 15–64, 0–74) are reported only for all causes combined. For specific causes results are included only for selected age groups. Results for England and Wales are presented for all the causes analysed but figures for the English regions and Wales are only included for selected causes. All results calculated in the analysis have however been made available on the National Statistics website at: www.statistics.gov.uk/

Confidence intervals (at the 95 per cent level) were calculated for each death rate and these are also available on the website. Results are presented using deprivation twentieths for England and Wales, and deprivation deciles and quintiles for the English regions and Wales.

Ratios are reported to indicate differentials between mortality rates in the most deprived and least deprived areas. These were calculated by dividing the death rate in the highest deprivation category (most deprived) by the death rate for the lowest category (least deprived).

Comparisons with earlier data

The Decennial Supplement, *Geographic Variations in Health*, included a deprivation analysis which looked at the relationship between selected causes of death in Great Britain in 1991–1993 with Carstairs scores based on data from the 1991 Census.[13] Only the age group 15–64 was examined. Results were presented for Great Britain using deprivation twentieths and for England, Wales, Scotland and the English regions using deprivation quintiles.

Although this article has examined the causes of death included in the Decennial Supplement, for the same age group, the two sets of results cannot be directly compared to see if there have been absolute changes in mortality rates for deprivation categories. This is because:

1. The Carstairs scores are based on results from two different censuses. As the scores measure relative deprivation at each census they cannot be used to measure absolute changes in deprivation.

2. A deprivation index which was comparable across the countries of the UK was not available in 2001. Analysis for this article was therefore restricted to England and Wales. Results for England and Wales for 1999–2003 cannot be compared with figures for Great Britain for 1991–1993, especially as death rates in Scotland are generally much higher than in the other countries of the UK.

3. The method of aggregating wards into deprivation twentieths and quintiles was not the same in 2001 as in 1991. In the earlier analysis each twentieth or quintile of deprivation was based on 5 or 20 per cent of the total number of wards. In 2001 each deprivation twentieth or quintile instead represents 5 or 20 per cent of the total population of England and Wales. Both methods are valid but we considered that the interpretation of results is more straightforward using the latter approach. This results in each deprivation category in England and Wales having an equal population. The alternative approach creates deprivation categories with equal numbers of wards but varying sizes of population.

4. Cause-specific results will be affected by the change in classification from ICD-9 to ICD-10 in 2001.

Although the geographical distribution of deprived wards was very similar between 1991 and 2001, some wards will have changed deprivation category between these time points and there were also many boundary changes to the wards used in each census.

Results: All causes of death combined

England and Wales

For both sexes it is clear that increasing deprivation is associated with higher mortality rates. For deaths at all ages male mortality rates showed a clear linear relationship with deprivation (Figure 3a). As deprivation increased mortality rates were higher (each twentieth represented a rise in mortality rates of between 13 and 60 deaths per 100,000 population). The increases became steeper with the most deprived areas. The death rate among the 5 per cent of the population living in the most deprived wards was 1.7 times higher than for the 5 per cent living in the least deprived areas (1,113 compared to 651 deaths per 100,000 population).

For females, the death rate was 1.5 times higher for those in the most deprived wards compared to those in the least deprived (706 and 479 deaths per 100,000 population respectively) (Figure 3a). The relationship was not quite as straightforward as for males as mortality rates in the least deprived areas remained more similar and did not always increase between deprivation twentieths. As with males the biggest increases in death rates were in the most deprived wards (deprivation twentieths 19 and 20).

In the age group 15–64 the relationship between mortality rates and deprivation was even more pronounced than for all ages (Figure 3b). For men there was still a strong positive relationship with rates, which increased particularly sharply in the most deprived areas. Men in the most deprived twentieth of wards had a death rate which, at 543 deaths per 100,000 population, was 2.8 times higher than the rate in the least deprived wards (196 deaths per 100,000). For women the relationship with deprivation was also stronger at ages 15–64 than at all ages. Rates were higher in each successive deprivation twentieth with steepest increases in the more deprived areas. The death rate for women in the most deprived wards was 2.1 times the rate in the least deprived wards (280 and 132 deaths per 100,000 respectively).

Although absolute comparisons of rates for 1999–2003 with those previously published by ONS for 1991–1993 cannot be made, the relative pattern of the relationship between mortality and deprivation appeared generally similar between the two time periods.

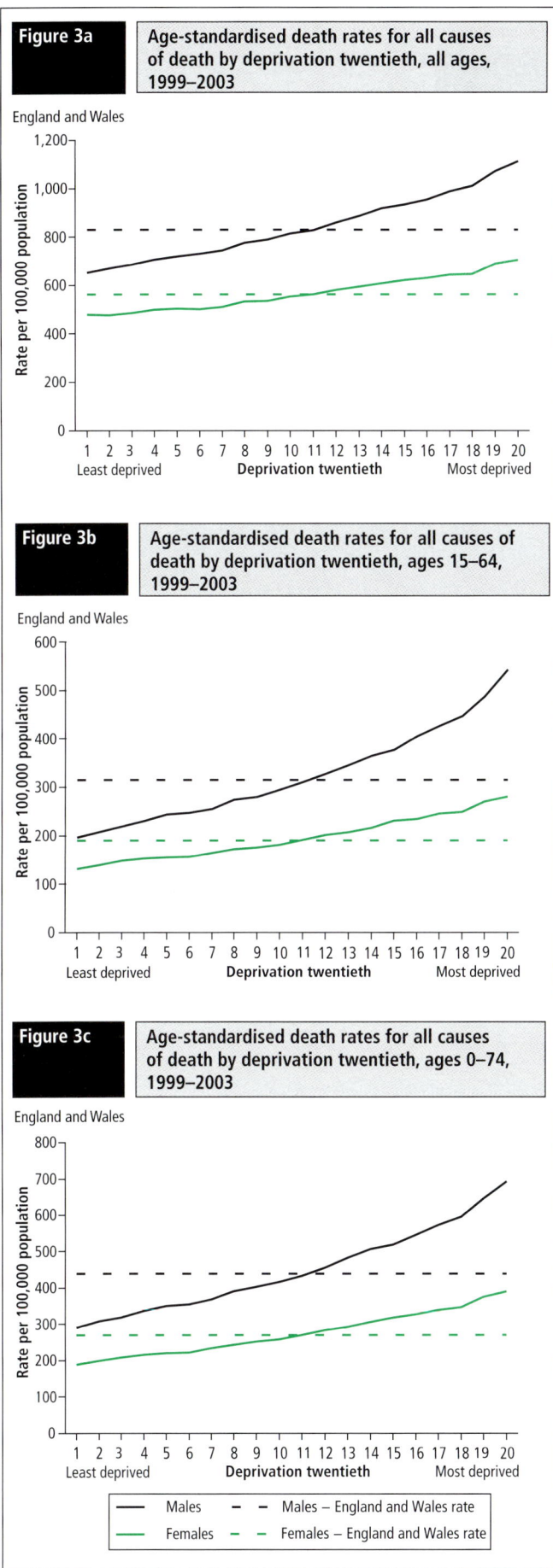

Figure 3a

Age-standardised death rates for all causes of death by deprivation twentieth, all ages, 1999–2003

England and Wales

Figure 3b

Age-standardised death rates for all causes of death by deprivation twentieth, ages 15–64, 1999–2003

England and Wales

Figure 3c

Age-standardised death rates for all causes of death by deprivation twentieth, ages 0–74, 1999–2003

England and Wales

— Males   – – Males – England and Wales rate
— Females – – Females – England and Wales rate

The results for the age group 0–74 (Figure 3c) appear as a slightly attenuated version of those for ages 15–64. The ratio between death rates in the most and least deprived wards was also 2.1 for females, but was slightly less for males (2.4 rather than 2.8).

The results presented in Figure 3 also show that differences in mortality rates between the sexes are greater in more deprived areas than in less deprived areas. In the age group 15–64, for example, the death rate for men in the most deprived twentieth was almost twice the rate for women. In the least deprived twentieth the death rate for men was only one and a half times higher than the rate for women.

English regions and Wales

To compare differences in mortality by deprivation to differences in mortality by geographical region, death rates for Government Office Regions in England, and for Wales, were calculated for 1999–2003. In Figure 4a these rates are presented ranked in order of male mortality rates. Male rates for all ages were lowest in the South West and highest in the North East (748 and 935 deaths per 100,000 population respectively). These areas also had the lowest and highest rates for females – 510 and 634 deaths per 100,000. The South East and East of England also had low mortality rates and rates in the North West were almost as high as in the North East.

The results for these ten areas can be compared to death rates calculated for ten deprivation categories. Male all age death rates for all causes ranged from 660 deaths per 100,000 population for the tenth of the population living in the least deprived wards to 1,092 per 100,000 for the ten per cent in the most deprived wards (Figure 4b). For females, death rates by deprivation decile ranged from 479 to 697 per 100,000 population. These differences were therefore greater than those seen in the geographical variation between the English regions and Wales. For males, the death rate in the region with the highest mortality was 1.3 times higher than in the region with the lowest death rate, but the rate for the tenth of the population living in the most deprived wards was 1.7 times higher than the rate for the tenth of the population living in the least deprived wards. The rate for females in the region with the highest mortality was 1.2 times higher than in the region with the lowest rate, while the rate in the most deprived deprivation decile was 1.5 times higher than in the least deprived.

Differences in mortality rates between the sexes were also more pronounced in the results for deprivation deciles than in those for regions. For all causes combined, male all age death rates were around one and a half times higher than female death rates in all the English regions and Wales (ratios ranged from 1.47 to 1.50). With the deprivation deciles the ratio between male and female death rates increased with deprivation. Ratios ranged from 1.38 in Decile 1 to 1.57 in Decile 10.

For males, each English region and Wales had a similar pattern with a strong gradient of rising all age mortality rates with increasing deprivation (Figure 5). Rates in the least deprived fifth of wards varied relatively little between areas (from 649 deaths per 100,000 population in the South West to 712 deaths per 100,000 in the North West). There was more variation in death rates in the most deprived areas (Quintile 5): the North West and London had the highest and lowest rates (1,156 and 959 deaths per 100,000 respectively).

Geographical patterns for females were broadly similar to those for males, with increasing mortality rates with increasing deprivation (Figure 5). As with males, there was relatively little geographical variation in death rates among those living in the least deprived wards but in the most deprived wards rates varied more, ranging from 605 deaths per 100,000 in London to 756 deaths per 100,000 in the North West.

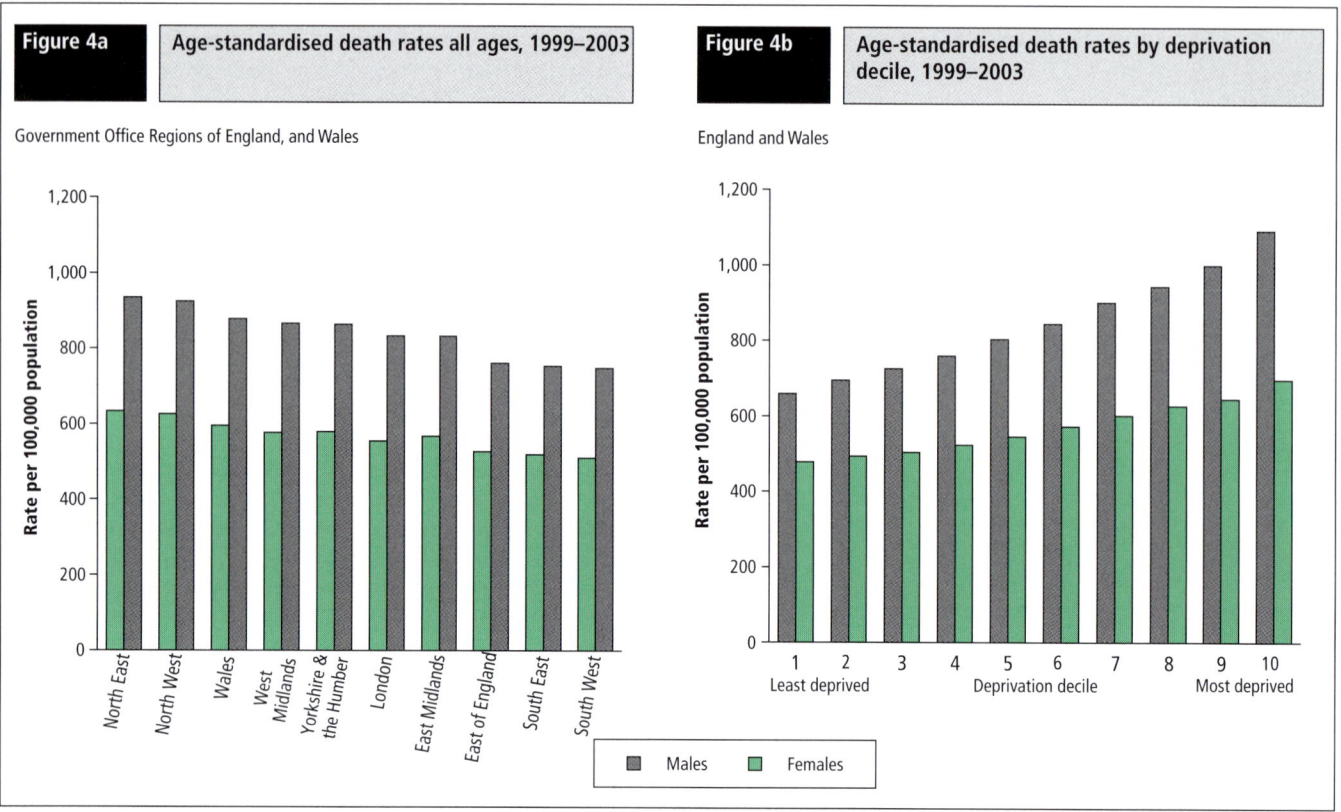

Figure 4a — Age-standardised death rates all ages, 1999–2003

Government Office Regions of England, and Wales

Figure 4b — Age-standardised death rates by deprivation decile, 1999–2003

England and Wales

■ Males   ■ Females

The North West had the highest death rates in every deprivation category for both sexes. The North East and Wales had the next highest death rates in the most deprived two quintiles for both sexes. London had the lowest death rates for both sexes in Quintiles 3, 4 and 5.

These geographical patterns are not completely consistent with the familiar north/south divide in mortality rates seen in Figure 4a. The North West and North East generally did have the highest mortality rates in the more deprived quintiles but in the least deprived quintile there was far

Figure 5 — Age-standardised death rates, all causes by sex and deprivation quintile, all ages, 1999–2003

Government Office Regions of England, and Wales

Males

Females

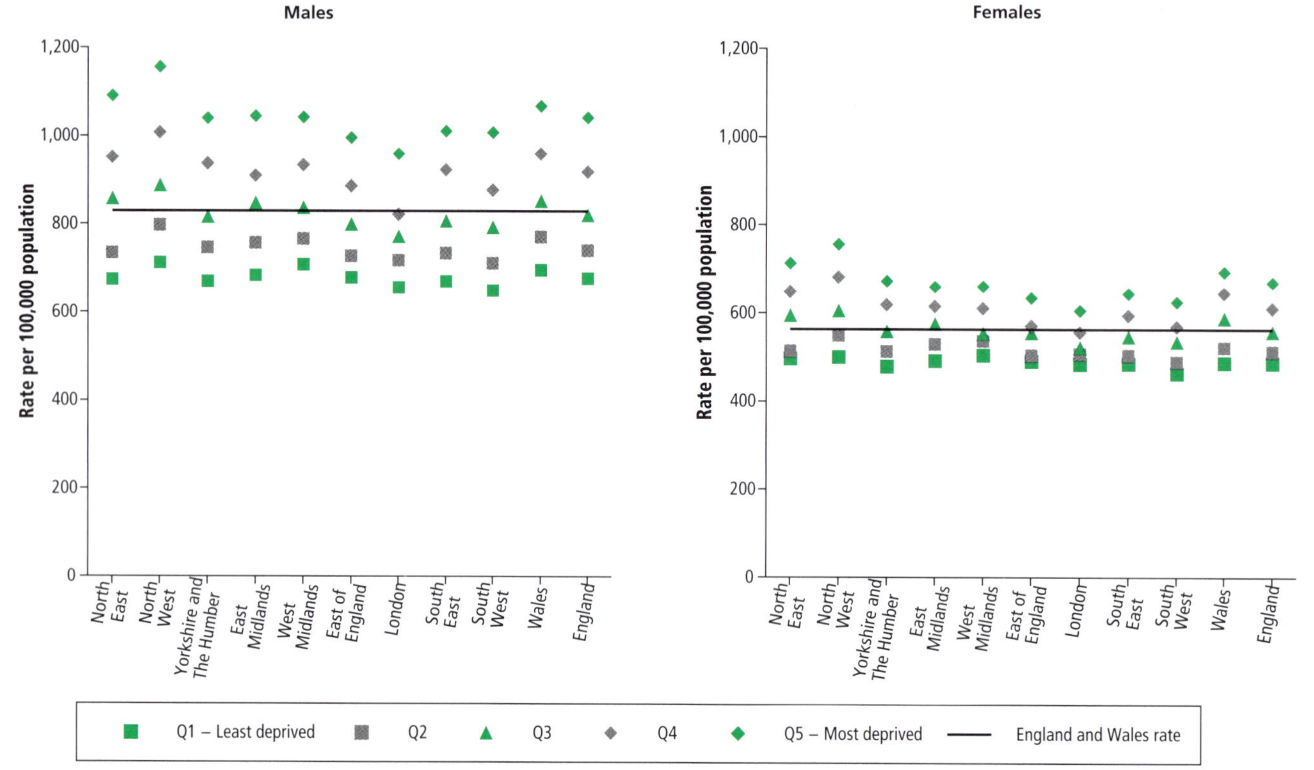

■ Q1 – Least deprived   ■ Q2   ▲ Q3   ◆ Q4   ◆ Q5 – Most deprived   — England and Wales rate

less geographical variation and rates in these regions were similar to, or even lower than, rates in other areas.

Results are particularly interesting for London as for both sexes it had the lowest, or almost the lowest, death rates in each deprivation quintile of all the English regions and Wales. Overall mortality rates though, as illustrated in Figure 4a, show that death rates in London were higher than in the other southern regions of England: the South East, South West and East of England. This pattern differs from earlier ONS results for 1991–1993.[13] In that period male all cause death rates for the age group 15–64 were higher in London for Quintile 5 than in the South East, South West and East of England. Female rates in all four regions in Quintile 5 were similar. In 1999–2003 death rates in London for those aged 15–64 were lower than in all other regions for both sexes in the three most deprived deprivation quintiles.

Results: All Circulatory Diseases

Mortality rates for all circulatory diseases were calculated for all three age groups but are presented here for 0- to 74-year-olds only. This is the age range used in the Government target to reduce circulatory disease death rates by two-fifths by 2010.[29]

In England and Wales there was a strong positive relationship between circulatory disease death rates and deprivation for both males and females (Figure 6 and Table 1). For both sexes the gradients increased particularly sharply in the most deprived areas (deprivation twentieths 19 and 20). For females, the death rate in the most deprived twentieth was almost three times higher than in the least deprived twentieth. For males the rate was 2.7 times higher.

The relationship between mortality and deprivation was also seen in the results for English regions and Wales. For both sexes, all areas had death rates from circulatory diseases which increased with deprivation (Table 2). For females, death rates in Quintile 5 were more than double

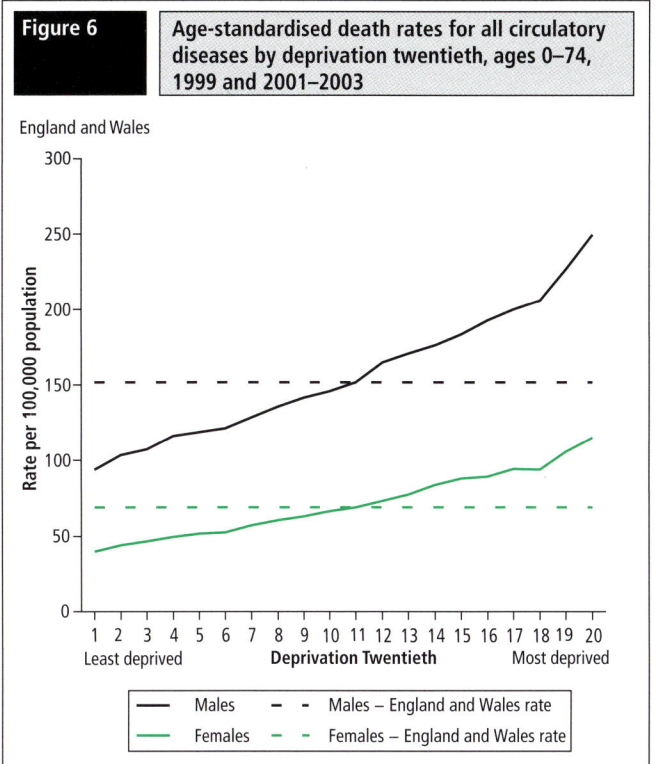

Figure 6   **Age-standardised death rates for all circulatory diseases by deprivation twentieth, ages 0–74, 1999 and 2001–2003**

rates in Quintile 1 in every English region and Wales. This was also the case for males, except in Wales and the East of England where the ratios between rates in the most and least deprived quintiles were both 1.9.

Regional patterns were similar to those for all causes, with more variation in rates in Quintile 5 than in Quintile 1. The lowest rates for each quintile were generally in London while the highest rates, at least for the more deprived quintiles, were in Wales, the North East and North West.

Table 1   **Age-standardised death rates for circulatory diseases by deprivation twentieth, sex and age group, 1999–2003**

England and Wales   Rate per 100,000 population

	Deprivation twentieth																				England and Wales rate	Ratio[3]
	Least deprived																Most deprived					
	1	2	3	4	5	6	7	8	9	10	11	12	13	14	15	16	17	18	19	20		
All circulatory diseases, ages 0–74[1]																						
Males	93.7	103.6	107.5	116.2	118.9	121.5	128.6	135.6	141.5	145.8	151.7	164.8	171.1	176.5	183.7	192.7	200.3	205.9	226.9	249.8	152	2.7
Females	39.8	43.9	46.6	49.6	51.6	52.2	56.9	60.3	62.8	66.3	68.7	73.2	77.5	83.6	88.1	89.4	94.1	94.0	105.9	115.0	68.8	2.9
Ischaemic heart disease, ages 15–64[2]																						
Males	35.4	40.4	42.3	48.1	48.5	50.1	52.1	57.7	60.4	62.2	66.5	73.6	74.6	80.2	82.7	89.8	93.3	97.5	108.1	123.4	66.5	3.5
Females	6.7	8.1	10.0	10.8	10.8	10.8	12.6	13.4	14.5	15.4	17.5	19.1	18.9	21.5	24.0	25.0	26.4	26.7	33.0	36.9	17.1	5.5
Stroke, all ages[1]																						
Males	62.5	62.3	60.8	63.9	63.2	64.6	65.9	66.1	67.0	69.2	71.6	71.4	71.6	71.7	74.8	76.3	77.3	77.9	84.2	91.4	69.9	1.5
Females	61.3	57.8	59.9	60.2	59.9	60.2	57.1	61.6	60.8	62.5	63.0	64.2	63.5	64.9	67.2	66.5	64.6	65.3	70.3	69.3	62.7	1.1
Stroke, ages 15–64[1]																						
Males	7.9	8.8	8.7	9.2	10.0	10.6	11.2	11.8	11.0	13.0	13.0	14.3	14.3	14.7	16.2	18.6	19.3	19.1	22.8	28.7	13.6	3.6
Females	6.4	6.3	7.3	8.0	7.4	8.2	8.5	9.6	9.9	9.8	10.4	10.0	11.2	12.2	14.1	14.0	14.3	15.3	17.4	16.8	10.5	2.6

1. 1999 and 2001–2003.
2. 1999–2003.
3. Ratio between rates in most deprived and least deprived deprivation twentieths.

Table 2	Age-standardised death rates for all circulatory diseases and ischaemic heart disease by deprivation quintile, sex and age group, 1999–2003

Government Office Regions of England, and Wales

Rate per 100,000 population

	Males						Females					
	All circulatory diseases, ages 0–74[1]					Ratio[3]	All circulatory diseases, ages 0–74[1]					Ratio[3]
	1	2	3	4	5		1	2	3	4	5	
North East	98.5	126.3	154.8	183.1	223.2	2.3	48.3	57.6	73.0	87.7	109.0	2.3
North West	116.5	144.6	168.1	203.1	250.6	2.2	49.0	64.3	77.8	96.0	116.9	2.4
Yorkshire and the Humber	109.2	125.3	153.4	179.2	214.3	2.0	45.3	55.5	67.0	86.0	98.1	2.2
East Midlands	107.0	131.3	153.4	181.1	219.0	2.0	48.0	57.1	69.1	88.8	102.6	2.1
West Midlands	109.7	130.3	155.0	184.9	223.0	2.0	46.6	57.7	68.1	86.1	103.4	2.2
East of England	106.0	120.2	141.2	167.6	201.2	1.9	44.7	52.4	64.0	73.1	92.3	2.1
London	99.9	118.4	137.1	159.0	200.8	2.0	41.1	53.9	61.0	73.2	88.2	2.1
South East	100.9	123.3	146.3	176.7	210.4	2.1	43.7	54.0	65.3	82.6	93.2	2.1
South West	97.0	114.0	138.8	168.3	206.8	2.1	40.9	49.3	61.8	73.4	96.6	2.4
Wales	118.9	144.5	169.2	193.6	222.5	1.9	48.8	58.0	75.0	91.4	112.2	2.3
England	104.6	125.1	149.4	179.5	219.3	2.1	44.8	55.0	67.1	83.9	101.0	2.3
England and Wales rate	152.0						68.8					

	Ischaemic heart disease, ages 15–64[2]					Ratio[3]	Ischaemic heart disease, ages 15–64[2]					Ratio[3]
	1	2	3	4	5		1	2	3	4	5	
North East	41.5	52.8	70.0	83.6	109.1	2.6	11.0	12.1	17.9	22.8	33.1	3.0
North West	47.4	62.3	72.2	93.9	124.3	2.6	10.0	14.7	19.8	27.1	37.8	3.8
Yorkshire and the Humber	45.8	53.4	69.0	83.2	105.2	2.3	9.6	11.9	17.5	24.4	29.6	3.1
East Midlands	42.4	53.8	65.3	82.9	107.5	2.5	10.2	11.8	17.2	24.0	33.8	3.3
West Midlands	43.1	51.6	69.0	82.2	109.6	2.5	9.3	11.8	16.1	24.1	32.8	3.5
East of England	43.0	47.9	61.4	75.8	91.3	2.1	8.8	11.3	15.3	18.1	20.1	2.3
London	35.8	48.5	56.5	67.4	89.9	2.5	7.7	10.6	13.2	16.1	24.0	3.1
South East	37.8	50.4	63.8	80.8	95.4	2.5	8.2	12.3	15.4	21.1	25.4	3.1
South West	39.1	47.9	62.8	76.5	88.0	2.3	7.2	10.6	15.5	17.8	29.1	4.0
Wales	48.2	60.3	69.1	87.4	111.7	2.3	11.3	12.3	19.6	24.6	35.9	3.2
England	41.2	51.6	65.3	81.1	104.4	2.5	8.8	11.9	16.4	22.1	30.2	3.4
England and Wales rate	66.5						17.1					

1. 1999 and 2001–2003.
2. 1999–2003.
3. Ratio between rates in most deprived and least deprived deprivation quintiles.

Ischaemic heart disease

Death rates for ischaemic heart disease also had a strong positive association with deprivation, which is especially evident in the age group 15–64 (Table 1). As with deaths from all causes and from all circulatory diseases, the gradient of increase in mortality rates with deprivation was particularly steep in the most deprived tenth of the population (deprivation twentieths 19 and 20).

For women aged 15–64, the death rate from ischaemic heart disease in the most deprived wards was 37 per 100,000 population. This was five and a half times higher than the rate in the least deprived wards, however that was from a relatively low base-line of seven deaths per 100,000. The rate for men was three and a half times higher in the most deprived areas.

In all regions, mortality rates for men in Quintile 5 were more than double the rates in Quintile 1, with the biggest ratios in the North East and North West where rates were 2.6 times higher (Table 2). For women, the lowest rate in the most deprived wards was in the East of England (20 deaths per 100,000). This area had the lowest ratio between rates in Quintiles 5 and 1 (2.3). Rates were highest in Quintile 5 in the North West (38 per 100,000) but the ratio between highest and lowest was greatest in the South West where the ischaemic heart disease death rate for 15- to 64-year-olds was four times higher in Quintile 5 than in Quintile 1.

Stroke

There was a positive association between death rates from stroke and deprivation in England and Wales, although for females the relationship was rather weak at all ages (Table 1). For males, all age death rates increased particularly steeply with the most deprived areas – deprivation twentieths 19 and 20. The death rate from stroke was 1.5 times higher in the most deprived wards compared to the least deprived. For females, death rates actually fell between the 19th and 20th twentieths, although not significantly. The ratio between rates for females in the most and least deprived wards was 1.1.

The relationship between death rates from stroke and deprivation was stronger in the younger age group, 15–64 (Table 1). The male rate for the most deprived wards was over three and a half times higher than that for the least deprived wards. For females the difference was over two and a half times.

Regional results are not presented for deaths from stroke but all regions had a clear gradient of increasing mortality rates with increasing deprivation.

Results: All cancers

As with circulatory diseases there is a Government target to reduce deaths rates from cancer among the under 75s (by a fifth by 2010),[29] and rates for ages 0–74 are presented here. Rates from cancer increased with deprivation for both males and females (Figure 7 and Table 3). Although rates in the most deprived twentieth were slightly lower than in deprivation category 19 for both sexes, these differences were not significant. The death rate was 1.7 times higher in the most deprived wards for males than in the least deprived wards. The ratio for females was 1.4.

All of the English regions and Wales had cancer mortality rates which increased with deprivation. As with the results for England and Wales, ratios between highest and lowest rates were greater for males than females. For males in the North East and North West, death rates in Quintile 5 were 1.7 times greater than in Quintile 1 (Table 4). In London though the ratio was only 1.4. For females in London and the East of England, rates in Quintile 5 were only 1.2 times higher than in Quintile 1 (Table 4). As with males the biggest differences were in the two northern regions of England where rates were 1.5 times higher in the most deprived wards compared to the least deprived.

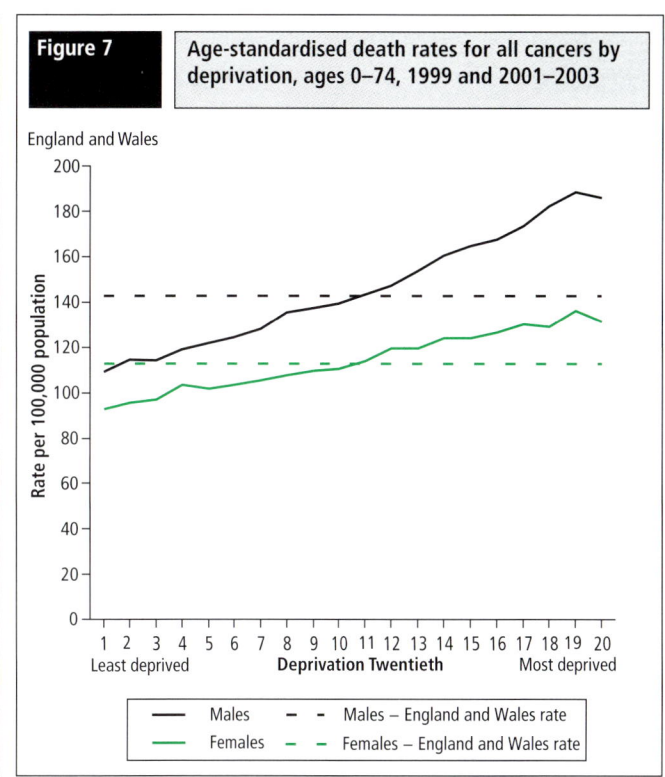

Figure 7

Age-standardised death rates for all cancers by deprivation, ages 0–74, 1999 and 2001–2003

England and Wales

| | | Males | — — Males – England and Wales rate |
| | | Females | — — Females – England and Wales rate |

Table 3

Age-standardised death rates for cancers by deprivation twentieth, sex and age group, 1999 and 2001–2003

England and Wales   Rate per 100,000 population

	Deprivation twentieth																				England and Wales rate	Ratio[1]
	Least deprived																	Most deprived				
	1	2	3	4	5	6	7	8	9	10	11	12	13	14	15	16	17	18	19	20		
All cancers, ages 0–74																						
Males	109.1	114.6	114.4	119.1	122.0	124.5	128.1	135.5	137.5	139.5	143.5	147.4	153.7	160.5	164.7	167.7	173.5	182.2	188.6	185.9	142.7	1.7
Females	92.9	95.7	97.1	103.6	102.0	103.5	105.5	107.7	109.9	110.6	114.0	119.8	119.6	124.1	124.2	126.6	130.5	129.3	136.3	131.4	112.8	1.4
Cancer of the oesophagus, all ages																						
Males	10.1	11.0	11.5	11.4	12.1	12.5	13.2	12.8	11.9	13.0	13.6	14.5	14.6	14.2	14.6	14.8	15.5	14.8	15.5	13.6	13.1	1.3
Females	4.0	4.3	4.4	4.0	4.5	4.9	4.8	5.3	4.7	5.0	5.4	5.9	5.6	5.5	5.6	5.2	6.0	5.2	5.9	5.4	5.0	1.4
Colorectal cancer, all ages																						
Males	21.8	22.6	22.1	22.5	22.7	24.2	22.5	23.1	24.0	25.4	25.0	24.5	25.8	26.4	26.5	26.7	26.7	27.2	27.7	25.3	24.4	1.2
Females	14.4	14.1	15.0	15.1	14.7	14.6	15.4	15.2	15.4	14.6	15.3	15.8	15.4	15.2	15.3	15.4	15.1	15.4	15.3	14.6	15.1	1.0
Lung cancer, all ages																						
Males	34.8	37.3	39.7	43.0	43.5	44.7	47.8	51.3	54.4	54.7	58.1	60.2	62.5	68.3	71.4	72.6	77.4	83.0	87.2	89.0	57.1	2.6
Females	17.1	17.8	18.5	20.7	21.0	22.2	23.6	24.5	25.7	26.0	28.4	30.3	31.0	35.3	34.9	38.0	41.3	41.9	47.6	44.6	28.6	2.6
Lung cancer, ages 15–64																						
Males	11.8	14.3	13.5	16.4	16.7	17.6	17.8	21.2	21.9	23.4	24.6	27.0	26.9	29.4	31.0	33.4	34.8	38.8	42.3	43.1	24.1	3.7
Females	7.2	8.1	8.6	10.7	10.3	10.9	11.5	12.4	12.5	13.2	14.6	15.9	16.4	18.9	17.8	21.3	23.0	23.4	26.6	22.8	14.6	3.2
Breast cancer, all ages																						
Females	30.6	30.3	30.8	32.9	30.1	30.4	30.7	31.8	30.2	30.5	30.5	32.2	29.9	30.3	32.1	29.6	30.9	29.7	30.1	29.1	30.7	1.0
Ovarian cancer, all ages																						
Females	10.8	10.8	11.0	11.4	11.7	11.5	11.5	11.0	11.1	12.0	11.4	11.0	11.1	11.7	11.1	11.3	10.6	10.1	9.8	9.6	11.1	0.9
Prostate cancer, all ages																						
Males	29.2	28.8	28.7	28.0	27.8	28.4	26.8	28.2	28.7	28.0	26.8	27.5	27.5	27.3	27.4	25.1	26.0	25.9	25.9	25.8	27.5	0.9
Cancer of lymphoid, haematopoietic and related tissue, ages 15–64																						
Males	8.6	8.9	8.6	8.8	9.2	8.7	9.0	9.6	9.7	8.7	8.7	9.4	10.5	10.3	10.5	9.7	9.9	10.8	10.8	11.3	9.5	1.3
Females	5.5	6.1	5.1	6.1	5.7	5.4	6.7	6.9	5.8	6.1	6.3	6.7	6.7	6.1	6.6	6.1	6.4	7.1	6.6	7.1	6.2	1.3

1. Ratio between rates in most deprived and least deprived deprivation twentieths.

| Table 4 | Age-standardised death rates for all cancers and lung cancer by deprivation quintile, sex and age group, 1999 and 2001–2003 |

Government Office Regions of England, and Wales

Rate per 100,000 population

	Males						Females					
	All cancers, ages 0–74					Ratio[1]	All cancers, ages 0–74					Ratio[1]
	1	2	3	4	5		1	2	3	4	5	
North East	117.7	138.9	154.5	174.4	205.2	1.7	97.5	106.7	116.8	129.5	142.4	1.5
North West	121.8	135.6	153.7	179.3	205.2	1.7	100.6	110.8	122.5	133.2	151.7	1.5
Yorkshire and the Humber	117.0	129.7	142.6	172.8	181.6	1.6	93.4	104.3	115.3	125.0	134.4	1.4
East Midlands	109.5	123.3	139.5	157.0	177.5	1.6	96.6	105.1	111.6	122.9	131.1	1.4
West Midlands	114.1	126.4	143.0	160.4	178.7	1.6	95.5	102.7	111.2	122.0	122.8	1.3
East of England	112.8	125.0	137.5	148.8	166.5	1.5	97.4	105.4	111.5	115.2	116.1	1.2
London	111.6	127.8	132.7	140.1	161.2	1.4	97.2	103.9	108.8	110.8	117.5	1.2
South East	115.5	124.6	143.1	160.5	174.3	1.5	98.2	104.2	114.1	127.8	130.2	1.3
South West	110.2	125.9	135.5	153.5	175.7	1.6	94.1	101.5	110.2	114.6	130.6	1.4
Wales	110.4	127.7	143.2	161.9	190.2	1.7	100.9	103.9	113.6	131.8	139.4	1.4
England	114.4	127.4	141.8	161.5	181.8	1.6	97.1	104.7	113.5	122.7	131.4	1.4
England and Wales rate	142.7						112.8					

	Lung cancer, ages 15–64					Ratio[1]	Lung cancer, ages 15–64					Ratio[1]
	1	2	3	4	5		1	2	3	4	5	
North East	11.2	19.5	26.0	29.5	48.6	4.3	8.5	12.1	15.5	23.0	33.2	3.9
North West	15.8	21.5	28.0	35.9	47.4	3.0	8.5	12.3	16.3	22.9	31.5	3.7
Yorkshire and the Humber	13.7	19.9	26.8	36.9	40.7	3.0	9.6	11.8	17.2	21.3	26.5	2.8
East Midlands	11.1	17.2	22.0	29.5	36.7	3.3	8.3	10.6	13.0	18.0	24.9	3.0
West Midlands	14.1	17.6	25.6	30.6	38.3	2.7	8.3	9.6	12.2	16.4	19.9	2.4
East of England	13.9	16.6	23.9	24.2	34.1	2.5	9.0	12.2	15.3	14.8	17.5	1.9
London	12.9	18.7	22.1	23.8	31.6	2.4	9.0	11.8	11.6	14.9	16.2	1.8
South East	14.7	18.9	23.2	33.2	42.4	2.9	8.5	11.4	14.0	18.7	23.6	2.8
South West	13.3	16.1	20.5	26.7	38.6	2.9	8.3	10.1	12.0	15.4	24.2	2.9
Wales	13.7	17.5	25.7	26.2	37.2	2.7	9.1	11.1	13.5	18.7	26.1	2.9
England	14.0	18.3	24.1	30.6	39.6	2.8	8.6	11.3	14.1	18.6	23.9	2.8
England and Wales rate	24.1						14.6					

1. Ratio between rates in most deprived and least deprived deprivation quintiles.

Cancer of the oesophagus

Although death rates from cancer of the oesophagus generally increased with deprivation the pattern was not as clear as for deaths from all causes or from all cancers (Table 3). For all ages, and for both sexes, rates in the most deprived twentieths were higher than in the least deprived twentieths but rates did not increase consistently with deprivation.

Colorectal cancer

There was no apparent relationship between female death rates from colorectal cancer and deprivation (Table 3). All age female rates were around 14–15 deaths per 100,000 population in each deprivation twentieth. This pattern was also similar for the 15–64 age group.

Male death rates did increase with deprivation and although these increments were not consistent across deprivation categories, the all age rate in the most deprived wards was 1.2 times higher than that in the least deprived wards (Table 3).

Lung cancer

Unlike some of the other cancers analysed, lung cancer death rates showed a clear positive association with deprivation (Table 3). The rates for men aged 15–64 generally increased with each deprivation twentieth with particularly big increases in the most deprived categories. The rate in the most deprived twentieth was 3.7 times higher than the rate in the least deprived twentieth. For women, the gradient of increasing lung cancer rates with deprivation was almost as strong as for men, although

rates did decrease between deprivation categories 19 and 20. The rate for the most deprived wards was 3.2 times higher than that in the least deprived wards. As the rate was highest in the 19th deprivation category though, the ratio of rates between this twentieth and the least deprived areas was the same as for men (3.7). Ratios between highest and lowest rates were the same (2.6) for both sexes for all ages (Table 3).

All of the English regions and Wales also had a clear pattern of increasing lung cancer death rates with deprivation for both sexes (Table 4). As with all causes and all cancers there was relatively little geographical variation in death rates in the least deprived wards. London and the North East were the areas with the lowest and highest rates for men in Quintile 5 for ages 15–64: 31.6 and 48.6 deaths per 100,000 respectively. The North East consequently had a rate which was 4.3 times higher in Quintile 5 than in Quintile 1, while in London the ratio between highest and lowest was 2.4. The same pattern was also seen for women: the lung cancer death rate in Quintile 5 was 1.8 times that in Quintile 1 in London. In the North East the rate for the most deprived areas was 3.9 times higher than that for the least deprived wards.

Female breast cancer

There was no relationship between deprivation and death rates for female breast cancer (Table 3). For all ages, rates ranged from 29 to 33 deaths per 100,000 but there were almost no significant differences between deprivation twentieths. There was also no relationship at younger ages, 15–64, nor in the English regions and Wales (data not shown).

The fact that there was no relationship between death rates and deprivation does not however mean that there is no relationship between breast cancer incidence and socio-economic circumstances. This is discussed later in this article in the section, 'Comparisons with other studies'.

Cancer of the ovary

Death rates for ovarian cancer showed no relationship with deprivation (Table 3). Although rates in the most deprived twentieths were slightly lower than in the least deprived categories these differences were not significant. Death rates for those aged 15–64 also showed no relationship with deprivation.

Prostate cancer

Death rates from prostate cancer show a slight inverse relationship with deprivation as the all age rate in the most deprived twentieth was statistically significantly lower than in the least deprived twentieth – 25.8 and 29.2 deaths per 100,000 respectively (Table 3).

As with breast cancer, incidence of prostate cancer, and mortality resulting from it, have different relationships with deprivation (see discussion in section on 'Comparisons with other studies').

Cancer of lymphoid, haematopoietic and related tissue

At younger ages a small positive relationship between deprivation and deaths from these cancers was seen (Table 3). For both sexes, death rates for those aged 15–64 did not increase consistently with deprivation but there was an upward gradient. For both men and women rates in the 20th deprivation category were 1.3 times higher than in the least deprived

category. Death rates for all ages though showed a less clear relationship with deprivation.

Results for other leading causes

Dementia and Alzheimer's disease

Death rates from Dementia and Alzheimer's disease showed no relationship with deprivation (Table 5). Deaths were only analysed for all ages and although rates varied between deprivation categories most of these variations were not significantly different.

Respiratory disease

Death rates from respiratory diseases for those aged 15–64 increased with each deprivation twentieth (Table 5). In this age group the death rate for men in the most deprived wards was over five times higher than the rate in the least deprived wards (40.5 and 7.9 deaths per 100,000 respectively). The rate for women was almost four times higher in the 20th deprivation category compared to the least deprived wards. This relationship was attenuated at all ages, but for both sexes rates in the most deprived wards were around double those rates in the least deprived.

Respiratory disease rates for the 15–64 age group increased with each deprivation quintile in each English region and Wales for both sexes. The male rate in Quintile 5 in the North East was five times the rate in Quintile 1 but in London the rate was only 2.8 times higher in Quintile 5 (Table 6). There was similar variation for females: the death rate in London for the most deprived wards was 2.3 times higher than the least deprived. In the North West though the rate in Quintile 5 was 4.8 times higher than the rate in Quintile 1.

| Table 5 | Age-standardised death rates for selected causes by deprivation twentieth, sex and age group, 1999–2003 |

England and Wales · Rate per 100,000 population

	Deprivation twentieth																				England and Wales rate	Ratio[3]
	Least deprived																			Most deprived		
	1	2	3	4	5	6	7	8	9	10	11	12	13	14	15	16	17	18	19	20		
Alzheimer's disease and dementia, all ages[1]																						
Males	15.3	15.0	14.4	15.8	14.3	15.4	14.0	15.8	13.8	17.3	15.7	15.9	15.8	16.2	13.4	16.2	17.2	16.0	17.5	15.6	15.5	1.0
Females	21.0	18.5	19.4	18.8	18.6	17.1	17.2	18.7	16.8	20.7	18.2	18.7	18.6	19.6	16.7	18.9	18.5	17.6	19.8	18.4	18.6	0.9
Respiratory diseases, ages 15–64[1]																						
Males	7.9	8.2	9.9	9.4	10.9	11.2	12.0	14.7	15.0	16.0	17.7	17.9	20.7	22.2	23.4	26.2	28.6	32.5	36.7	40.5	18.0	5.1
Females	6.4	6.4	6.6	6.7	8.6	7.4	9.7	10.2	11.6	11.2	12.8	14.6	14.6	17.0	17.6	18.8	20.2	21.7	22.7	25.2	12.8	3.9
Accidents, ages 15–64[2]																						
Males	18.2	18.4	20.4	20.4	20.6	19.1	19.5	19.2	18.3	20.0	21.5	20.7	23.2	23.4	22.4	25.4	26.2	25.5	28.9	29.6	21.8	1.6
Females	5.3	5.9	6.7	5.5	5.2	6.1	6.0	5.7	5.7	5.6	6.1	6.5	7.1	6.6	6.8	7.5	7.4	7.3	8.0	7.8	6.3	1.5

1. 1999 and 2001–2003.
2. 1999–2003.
3. Ratio between rates in most deprived and least deprived deprivation twentieths.

| Table 6 | Age-standardised death rates for respiratory diseases and accidents by deprivation quintile, sex, ages 15–64,1999–2003 |

Government Office Regions of England, and Wales

Rate per 100,000 population

	Males						Females					
	Respiratory diseases[1]					Ratio[3]	Respiratory diseases[1]					Ratio[3]
	1	2	3	4	5		1	2	3	4	5	
North East	117.7	138.9	154.5	174.4	205.2	1.7	97.5	106.7	116.8	129.5	142.4	1.5
North East	7.5	8.4	18.8	20.7	37.3	5.0	5.8	9.8	11.9	18.1	25.1	4.3
North West	9.6	13.5	19.3	25.4	43.3	4.5	6.2	10.9	15.5	20.9	29.8	4.8
Yorkshire and the Humber	7.6	11.9	16.6	24.4	29.8	3.9	6.6	9.1	12.0	18.2	22.1	3.3
East Midlands	10.0	12.8	16.2	22.1	35.8	3.6	7.2	8.7	15.4	18.9	23.4	3.3
West Midlands	8.2	13.1	15.4	23.6	32.9	4.0	6.3	7.8	10.0	16.4	22.3	3.5
East of England	8.2	11.7	15.6	22.3	31.7	3.9	5.8	7.9	12.5	14.7	21.7	3.7
London	10.8	12.8	17.4	20.2	30.7	2.8	7.1	9.1	9.9	12.6	16.0	2.3
South East	9.2	11.9	16.0	28.1	34.3	3.7	7.4	10.1	13.8	16.2	21.2	2.9
South West	7.7	11.7	15.8	20.3	35.2	4.6	5.5	7.8	10.5	12.4	22.5	4.1
Wales	9.4	11.9	16.6	22.0	27.0	2.9	5.2	8.8	12.4	19.2	23.7	4.6
England	8.8	12.2	16.6	23.2	34.6	3.9	6.5	9.0	12.5	16.7	22.2	3.4
England and Wales rate	18.0						12.8					

	Males					
	Accidents[2]					Ratio[3]
	1	2	3	4	5	
North East	13.1	13.8	16.5	20.5	25.1	1.9
North West	19.9	18.8	22.3	27.0	35.7	1.8
Yorkshire and the Humber	19.3	21.4	19.4	23.1	27.1	1.4
East Midlands	22.1	23.0	24.0	25.9	30.5	1.4
West Midlands	19.6	19.0	18.7	22.4	24.9	1.3
East of England	21.2	22.6	22.7	26.7	34.1	1.6
London	13.0	13.5	13.9	16.7	22.5	1.7
South East	18.6	20.0	20.0	23.0	27.1	1.5
South West	19.5	19.2	20.0	25.8	34.5	1.8
Wales	18.8	23.1	24.4	30.7	40.6	2.2
England	19.4	19.4	19.8	22.9	27.0	1.4
England and Wales rate	21.8					

1. 1999 and 2001–2003.
2. 1999–2003.
3. Ratio between rates in most deprived and least deprived deprivation quintile.

Accidents

Death rates from accidents increased with deprivation, particularly for men in the age group 15–64 (Table 5). Rates remained relatively stable until the 10th deprivation category but by the most deprived twentieth the rate was 1.6 times higher than that in the least deprived wards. Death rates for women, which were much lower than for men, appeared to have a weaker association with deprivation and are therefore not presented.

Although all areas had higher death rates for males aged 15–64 in Quintile 5 than Quintile 1 patterns were not as clear as for all causes of death (Table 6). Some regions, such as the North West and the West Midlands, had rates in Quintile 2 which were lower than Quintile 1. Unlike all causes combined, where there was little variation in death rates in the least deprived quintile, for accidents there was considerable regional variation in all quintiles. In Quintile 1 rates ranged from 13.0 deaths per 100,000 population in London to 22.1 deaths per 100,000 in the East Midlands. The rate in Quintile 5 in London (22.5 deaths per 100,000) was only slightly higher than the rate in Quintile 1 in the East Midlands. The highest rate in the most deprived quintile was in Wales (40.6 deaths per 100,000).

The more variable nature of these results could be at least partly due to the relatively small number of deaths involved.

Discussion

Summary of main findings

The results presented here reflect those reported in many earlier studies: that people living in more deprived areas have higher mortality rates than those living in less deprived areas. In this analysis this was true for both sexes and for all of the age ranges considered – all ages, 15–64 and 0–74. The all age death rate for males living in the most deprived wards in England and Wales was 1.7 times higher than for males living in the least deprived wards. The female death rate was 1.5 times higher in the most deprived areas than in the least deprived.

The relationship between deprivation and mortality rates was more pronounced at younger ages than for all ages. The death rate for men aged 15–64 in the most deprived wards was 2.8 times the rate in the least deprived wards. The death rate for women in the same age range in the most deprived areas was 2.1 times the rate for those in the least deprived areas.

Of the leading causes of death, mortality rates for both sexes clearly increased with deprivation for circulatory diseases, ischaemic heart disease, stroke, all cancers, lung cancer, respiratory diseases, and accidents. The gradients of increase differed between causes though. The association with deprivation was less clear for deaths from colorectal cancer and cancers of the oesophagus and lymphoid, haematopoietic and related tissue. Death rates from dementia and Alzheimer's disease and ovarian, breast and prostate cancer either had no association with deprivation or the relationship was slightly inverse.

For deaths from all causes, the relationship between deprivation and mortality rates was stronger for males than females. For deaths from ischaemic heart disease and all circulatory diseases though the gradients of increasing mortality with deprivation were steeper for women. The difference in mortality rates between the sexes generally also increased with deprivation.

For causes where the national results showed a clear gradient of increasing mortality with deprivation this relationship was also observed in the regions of England and Wales. There were however geographical differences in mortality rates between deprivation quintiles. Death rates for those living in the least deprived wards in Quintile 1 showed relatively little variation compared to the more deprived quintiles. Thus the 20 per cent of the population in the least deprived wards of England and Wales tended to have similar mortality rates no matter in which region they were living.

Regional variation increased with deprivation and death rates for the most deprived wards in Quintile 5 were generally highest in the North East and North West. These areas had the biggest differences in mortality rates between the least and most deprived wards. London often had the lowest mortality rates in each deprivation quintile.

The difference in mortality rates between deprivation categories was greater than the geographical variation between rates in the nine English regions and Wales. Death rates for the tenth of the population living in the most deprived wards were 1.7 times higher for males, and 1.5 times higher for females, than rates for the tenth of the population living in the least deprived wards. The ratios between the regions with the highest and lowest mortality rates were 1.3 for males and 1.2 for females.

Comparisons with other studies

The results reported here generally reflect previous studies which have reported that mortality in more deprived areas is higher than in less deprived areas. The reasons for this have been the subject of much debate, particularly regarding whether deprived areas have higher mortality simply because of the characteristics of the people who live in them, or whether there is an effect of geography over and above the socio-economic condition of the population. It has been reported that the clear positive relationship between mortality and area deprivation disappears, at least for men, once allowance has been made for individual socio-economic circumstances.[30] High mortality thus appears to be the result of personal not community disadvantage. It was later noted though that this study allowed for individual socio-economic factors which were essentially the same as those used to construct the area based deprivation measure, so that there were inevitable strong correlations between the two.[31] It has been argued that area deprivation has an effect on mortality which is independent of personal deprivation as areas can be disadvantaged by factors such as access to transport, shops and leisure facilities and may suffer from environmental pollution and social disorganisation.[31]

Like ours, many studies have shown that the association between deprivation and all cause mortality rates is stronger for males than females[5,6,8,32] and it has been suggested that this may indicate that deprivation could be a stronger proxy for health risk behaviour in men than in women.[5] Our analysis found that while the pattern for many of the leading causes was similar to all causes combined, the reverse was true for ischaemic heart disease and all circulatory diseases. For these causes

the gradients of increasing mortality with deprivation were steeper for females than males. This finding was consistent with previous studies,[8,13] and although the reasons for it remain unclear, explanations may lie in the different underlying factors which most affect male and female mortality.

For deaths from all cancers the relationship between mortality and deprivation appeared stronger for males although it has been observed that this effect is partly a result of the distribution of deaths by cancer site between the sexes.[13] For males, lung cancer deaths (which are highly associated with deprivation) make up a higher proportion of all cancers than for females. Deaths from breast cancer, which have no relationship with deprivation, make up a high proportion of all female cancer deaths. The strong positive correlation between lung cancer mortality and deprivation is mirrored in the reported relationship between lung cancer incidence and deprivation.[15] The same is not true for some of the other cancers analysed however. Female breast cancer incidence shows a clear inverse relationship with deprivation. It has been reported that incidence is about 30 per cent higher in the least deprived areas compared to the most deprived.[15] While there appears to be no clear relationship between mortality from breast cancer and deprivation, it has been consistently found that survival rates are higher for women from less deprived areas than for women from more deprived areas.[22] The same is true for prostate cancer where incidence rates have been reported which are 45 per cent higher in the least deprived areas compared to the most deprived.[15] We found though only a rather weak inverse relationship between prostate cancer mortality rates and deprivation.

Our analysis also reflects previous studies which have shown that the effects of deprivation on mortality are seen more clearly at younger ages and are attenuated at older ages.[6,7,9] It has been suggested that this could partly be the result of migration patterns in the elderly, for example when sick people move to nursing homes.[9] Life expectancy figures for wards, published by ONS, have shown that the presence of nursing homes or similar 'medical and care' communal establishments can have a great impact on mortality in small populations.[33] Relatively low life expectancy results were found in some of the least deprived wards where a large proportion of their population had been resident in 'medical and care' communal establishments.

Our study found that the variation in mortality between deprivation deciles was greater than inequalities in death rates between the nine English regions and Wales. This finding is consistent with another recent study in England and Wales.[7] The geographical patterns of mortality by deprivation we identified did not consistently follow the 'north/south' divide in overall mortality illustrated in Figure 4a. While the highest rates in the most deprived quintiles were generally in the northern regions of England, London often had the lowest mortality rates in each deprivation quintile. This was despite the capital having overall mortality rates which were higher than in the other southern regions of England. This appears to be the result of London having such a large proportion of its population living in the most deprived areas. In 2001, 42 per cent of Londoners were resident in wards which were among the fifth of areas in England and Wales with the worst deprivation scores. As this quintile has the highest death rates, overall mortality in London was reduced to a level below that of the other southern regions. This suggests that deprivation therefore at least partly explains the regional pattern of mortality in England and Wales.

Other studies have also reported mortality rates for London that were relatively low in relation to levels of deprivation,[32,34,35] although this effect was not apparent in the analysis undertaken by ONS for 1991–1993.[13] It has been suggested that deprivation indices may tend to overestimate disadvantage in London[35] and our results could support this. It may also indicate that Carstairs scores are a poorer measure of deprivation in London in 2001 than they had been in earlier censuses. The Carstairs index includes car ownership in its measure of deprivation and it has been suggested that this is less likely to be an indicator of low income in central London (where public transport is highly developed) than in rural areas, where car ownership may be essential for everyday life.[34] Other reasons have been proposed as to why mortality might be low in London relative to deprivation, including a selection process which leads to healthier people being concentrated in the capital.[35] It has also been suggested that there might be a migration effect with old people in ill health leaving London while young healthy people are attracted to the capital by its cultural and financial resources.[32]

Mortality rates in the most deprived areas were generally highest in the North East and North West regions, which other studies have also reported.[8,13] An analysis which used the ONS Longitudinal Study reported that long-term disadvantage was an important predictor of mortality in all English regions and Wales but that the gradients were steeper in the north than the south.[10]

While many studies have described the relationship between deprivation and mortality, fewer have attempted to explain the underlying reasons for the resulting inequalities. One paper that did attempt to address why mortality is higher in poorer areas of England and Wales estimated that of the excess deaths in the most deprived local authorities, about 85 per cent were due to smoking-related diseases.[9] From our analysis of the leading causes of death it is clear that smoking plays a key role in the relationship between deprivation and mortality. Lung cancer, for example, which has a clear association with smoking had death rates which strongly correlated with deprivation. Some deaths from ischaemic heart disease and stroke are also attributed to smoking (particularly at younger ages) as are proportions of deaths from pneumonia and chronic obstructive lung disease (included in the all respiratory disease category).[36] We also found a positive relationship with deprivation for mortality rates from these causes. Causes which have no reported link with smoking, such as cancers of the breast, ovary and prostate[15] either had mortality rates which did not increase with deprivation or the relationship was slightly inverse.

Limitations

A limitation of all studies which consider mortality using an area based deprivation score, rather than an individual based measure such as Social Class or income, is that the results are subject to the 'ecological fallacy', i.e. the assumption that the population within an area shares the same environmental characteristics. Not everyone who lives in a deprived area is deprived however and not all deprived people live in deprived places. Ecological studies such as this one still have a valid role however in adding to the understanding of health inequalities. It has been argued that ecological information is not a substitute for individual data but provides a means for '…testing for the combined effects of compositional and contextual influences.'[37]

Carstairs and Morris acknowledged that the deprivation scores they had developed were subject to the ecological fallacy but they argued that for an outcome such as mortality, there is an area effect in addition to an individual effect, as measured, for example, by Social Class.[20] They also pointed out that Social Class categories are not themselves homogenous, and are likely to contain people with widely differing occupations and incomes.

The possible limitations of the Carstairs scores for measuring deprivation in London have been noted above but it has also been argued that the index is less valid in rural areas because the experience of deprivation in rural areas is different to urban areas.[35] It has also been reported that rural areas have more heterogeneous populations than urban areas.[38] Thus the effect of deprived people in poor health in rural areas tends to be masked by less deprived healthier people living in the same area.[38]

The analysis we have undertaken was based on the ward of usual residence at the time of death. Migration effects, especially in the elderly, may however mean that people die in areas which may differ substantially from where they lived earlier in life. Such life course effects cannot be accounted for in an analysis like this, nor can the effects of disadvantage in early life which, it has been reported, may be important in predicting mortality from some causes.[39]

The choice of deprivation indicator and means of measuring mortality may also produce different results when considering the relationship between the two. When used for health analysis, different deprivation indices have shown a high degree of correlation[20,21] but cause specific mortality patterns have been shown to depend on the choice of deprivation index,[11] especially when measures of material deprivation were compared to indicators of social fragmentation.

Mortality rates have been reported here using directly age-standardised rates, standardised using the European Standard Population. Age-standardisation was essential as the age structures of the population of the most and least deprived areas were so different (Figure 2). The choice of method, or of the weights used in direct standardisation, may however influence results. As such substantial differences between deprivation categories were reported for many of the leading causes of death it is unlikely though that using a different method of reporting would have radically altered the underlying patterns we have illustrated.

The association between mortality and deprivation has been reported in this article by the presentation of death rates for individual deprivation categories (twentieths for England and Wales and deciles and quintiles for English regions and Wales). This allows the relationship with mortality to be considered across the whole spectrum of deprivation. Ratios have also been presented to indicate differentials between most and least deprived areas, but these may appear more extreme for those causes where mortality rates were low. Other reporting methods, such as correlation coefficients, could be used to give a summary of the gradients of mortality rates by deprivation.

For the results for England and Wales each of the twenty deprivation categories has approximately the same population. In the results for quintiles within English regions and Wales however, population sizes vary between deprivation categories (as illustrated in Figure 1). This means that death rates may be based on very different sized populations, both within region by deprivation quintile, and between regions for equivalent deprivation categories. Confidence intervals have been calculated for these rates (published on the National Statistics website), and can be used to assess whether differences between rates are statistically significant. Other reporting methods, such as the relative slope index of inequality,[40] which takes into account variations in population size of the deprivation categories, could be considered for the future reporting of inequalities in mortality rates.

Carstairs scores have now been calculated using data from three successive censuses. Results in this article indicate that the 2001 index continues to be an effective means of measuring the relationship between deprivation and mortality at national level. Some of the regional results however may indicate that alternative variables should be considered to effectively measure recent material deprivation. Other deprivation indices could be used to examine inequalities in mortality, including the Indices of Multiple Deprivation, if the conceptual and practical challenges their use presents can be overcome.[19]

The question of how much deprivation explains the regional variations in mortality, which have existed for so long in England and Wales, has not been addressed in this study and this debate is likely to continue. A modelling approach could be used to explore the interaction between region and deprivation using more formal statistical methods. This study has added to the existing literature on the relationship between mortality and deprivation by illustrating recent patterns for the leading causes of death, at both national and regional levels. How these patterns have changed over time, and whether the relationship between deprivation and cause-specific death rates has worsened or improved in recent years, however currently remains unexamined.

Key findings

- People living in more deprived areas had higher mortality rates than those living in less deprived areas. The all age death rate for males in the most deprived wards in England and Wales was 1.7 times higher than that in the least deprived wards. The female death rate was 1.5 times higher.

- The relationship between deprivation and death rates was stronger at younger ages than for all ages. The death rate for men aged 15-64 in the most deprived wards was 2.8 times the rate in the least deprived wards. For women the rate was 2.1 times higher.

- Mortality rates for both sexes increased with deprivation for all circulatory diseases, ischaemic heart disease, stroke, all cancers, lung cancer, respiratory diseases, and accidents. The relationship with deprivation was less clear for deaths from colorectal cancer and cancers of the oesophagus and lymphoid, haematopoietic and related tissue. Death rates from dementia and Alzheimer's disease and ovarian, breast and prostate cancer either had no correlation with deprivation or the relationship was slightly inverse.

- For all causes of death combined, male mortality rates were higher than for females and this difference between the sexes increased with increasing deprivation.

- The 20 per cent of the population living in the least deprived wards of England and Wales tended to have similar mortality rates no matter in which region they were living.

- Death rates for those living in the most deprived fifth of wards were generally highest in the North East and North West. These areas had the biggest differences in mortality rates between the least and most deprived wards. London often had the lowest mortality rates in each deprivation quintile.

- The difference in mortality rates between deprivation deciles was greater than the geographical variation in death rates between the nine English regions and Wales.

References

1. Department of Health (2004) *Choosing Health*, TSO: London.
2. Acheson D (1998) *Independent Inquiry into Inequalities in Health*, TSO: London
3. Townsend P, Davidson N and Whitehead M (1992) I*nequalities in Health: The Black Report; The Health Divide*, Penguin Books: London.
4. Carstairs V and Morris R (1989) Deprivation and mortality: an alternative to social class? *Community Medicine* **11**(3), 210–219.
5. Raleigh V S and Kiri V A (1997) Life expectancy in England: variations and trends by gender, health authority, and level of deprivation. *Journal of Epidemiology and Community Health* **51**, 649–658.
6. Drever F and Whitehead M (1995) Mortality in regions and local authority districts in the 1990s: exploring the relationship with deprivation. *Population Trends* **82**, 19–25.
7. Woods LM, Rachet B, Riga M, Stone N, Shah A and Coleman M P (2005) Geographical variation in life expectancy at birth in England and Wales is largely explained by deprivation. J*ournal of Epidemiology and Community Health* **59**, 115–120.
8. Eames M, Ben-Shlomo Y and Marmot M G (1993) Social deprivation and premature mortality: regional comparison across England. *British Medical Journal* **307,** 1097–1102.
9. Law M R and Morris J K (1998) Why is mortality higher in poorer areas and in more northern areas of England and Wales? *Journal of Epidemiology and Community Health* **52**, 344–352.
10. Reid A and Harding S (2000) An examination of persisting disadvantage and mortality in the regions using the Longitudinal Study. *Health Statistics Quarterly* **6**, 7–13.
11. Davey Smith G, Whitley E, Dorling D and Gunnell D (2001) Area based measures of social and economic circumstances: cause specific mortality patterns depend on the choice of index. Journal of *Epidemiology and Community Health* **55**, 149–150.
12. Benach J, Yasui Y, Borrell C, Sáez and Pasarin MI (2001) Material deprivation and leading causes of death by gender: evidence from a nationwide small area study. *Journal of Epidemiology and Community Health* **55**, 239–245.
13. Uren Z and Fitzpatrick J (2001) Chapter 11: Analysis of mortality by deprivation and cause of death, in Griffiths C and Fitzpatrick J (eds.) *Geographic Variations in Health* (DS No 16), TSO: London.
14. Griffiths C, Rooney C and Brock A (2005) Leading causes of death in England and Wales – how should we group them? *Health Statistics Quarterly* **28**, 6–17.
15. Quinn M, Wood H, Cooper N and Rowan S (eds.) (2005) *Cancer Atlas of the United Kingdom and Ireland 1991–2000.* Studies on Medical and Population Subjects No 68, Palgrave Macmillan: Basingstoke.
16. Fitzpatrick J, Griffiths C, Kelleher M and McEvoy S (2001) Chapter 10: Descriptive analysis of geographic variations in adult mortality by cause of death, in Griffiths C and Fitzpatrick J (eds.) *Geographic Variations in Health* (DS No 16), TSO: London.
17. Brock A, Baker A, Griffiths C, Jackson G, Fegan G and Marshall D (2006) Suicide trends and geographical variations in the United Kingdom, 1991–2004. *Health Statistics Quarterly* **31**, 6–22.
18. Office for National Statistics (2002) Results of the ICD-10 bridge coding study, England and Wales, 1999. *Health Statistics Quarterly* **14**, 75–83.
19. Morgan O and Baker A (2006) Measuring deprivation in England and Wales using 2001 Carstairs scores. *Health Statistics Quarterly* **31**, 28–33.
20. Morris R and Carstairs V (1991) Which deprivation? A comparison of selected deprivation indexes. *Journal of Public Health Medicine* **13**(4), 318–326.

21. Hoare J (2003) Comparison of area-based inequality measures and disease morbidity in England, 1994-1998. *Health Statistics Quarterly* **18**, 18–24.

22. Coleman M, Babb P, Damiecki P *et al* (1999) *Cancer Survival Trends in England and Wales, 1971-1995: deprivation and NHS Regions.* Studies on Medical and Population Subjects No 61, TSO: London

23. Boyle P, Norman P and Rees P (2002) Does migration exaggerate the relationship between deprivation and limiting long-term illness? A Scottish analysis. *Social Science and Medicine* **55**, 21–31.

24. Morrison A, Stone DH, Redpath A, Campbell H and Norrie J (1999) Trend analysis of socioeconomic differentials in deaths from injury in childhood in Scotland, 1981–95. *British Medical Journal* **318** (7183), 567–568.

25. Weich S, Twigg L, Holt G, Lewis G and Jones K (2003) Contextual risk factors for the common mental disorders in Britain: a multilevel investigation of the effects of place. *Journal of Epidemiology and Community Health* **57**, 616–621.

26. Boyle P, Exeter D, Feng Z and Flowerdew R (2005) Suicide gap among young adults in Scotland: population study. *British Medical Journal* **330,** 175–176.

27 Evans J M M, Newton R W, Ruta D A, MacDonald T M and Morris A D (2000) Socio-economic status, obesity and prevalence of Type 1 and Type 2 diabetes mellitus. *Diabetic Medicine* **17** (6), 478–480.

28. Office for National Statistics. Ward population estimates for England and Wales, mid-2001 and mid-2002 (experimental statistics) Available at: www.statistics.gov.uk/statbase/Product.asp?vlnk=13893 Accessed 23rd May 2006.

29. Department of Health (1999) *Saving Lives: Our Healthier Nation,* TSO: London.

30. Sloggett A and Joshi H (1994) Higher advantage in deprived areas: community or personal disadvantage? *British Medical Journal* **309**, 1470–1474.

31. Davey Smith G, Hart C, Watt G, Hole D and Hawthorne V (1998) Individual social class, area-based deprivation, cardiovascular disease risk factors, and mortality: the Renfrew and Paisley study. *Journal of Epidemiology and Community Health* **52**, 399–405.

32. Doran T, Drever F and Whitehead M (2006) Health underachievement and overachievement in English local authorities. *Journal of Epidemiology and Community Health* **60**, 686–693.

33. Office for National Statistics. Life expectancy at birth for wards in England and Wales (experimental statistics). Available at: www.statistics.gov.uk/statbase/Product.asp?vlnk=14466 Accessed 8th September 2006.

34. Mays N and Chinn S (1989) Relation between all cause standardised mortality ratios and two indices of deprivation at regional and district level in England. *Journal of Epidemiology and Community Health* **43**(2), 191–199.

35. Haynes R and Gale S (1999) Mortality, long-term illness and deprivation in rural and metropolitan wards of England and Wales. *Health & Place* **5**, 301–312.

36. Twigg L, Moon G and Walker S (2004) *The smoking epidemic in England,* Health Development Agency.

37. Curtis S and Rees Jones I (1998) Is there a place for geography in the analysis of health inequality? *Sociology of Health and Illness* **20**(5), 645–672.

38. Haynes R and Gale S (2000) Deprivation and poor health in rural areas: inequalities hidden by averages. *Health & Place* **6**(4), 275–285.

39. Leon DA and Davey Smith G (2000) Infant mortality, stomach cancer, stroke, and coronary heart disease: ecological analysis. *British Medical Journal* **320**, 1705–1706.

40. Kunst A E and Mackenbach JP (1995) *Measuring socioeconomic inequalities in health,* World Health Organization Regional Office for Europe: Copenahagen.

Time and generational trends in smoking among men and women in Great Britain, 1972–2004/05

Melissa Davy

Office for National Statistics

Introduction

Smoking is the largest single cause of preventable deaths in the UK. It accounts for one in five of all deaths and is the main avoidable risk factor for coronary heart disease and cancer.[1] Smoking not only affects the health of the smoker, but also people around them through passive smoking.[2] The Government is committed to reducing levels of smoking, and has set targets to reduce the prevalence of cigarette smoking among adults in England from 28 per cent in 1996 to 21 per cent by 2010.[3] Various policies have been introduced to try to reduce smoking, including health education campaigns, restrictions on cigarette advertising, increasing tobacco tax, regulating the contents of tobacco products and the labelling of packaging, and the introduction of NHS 'stop smoking' services and Nicotine Replacement Therapy.

This article increases our knowledge on generational changes in levels of cigarette smoking in Great Britain and may help to predict future trends in smoking behaviour when considered alongside other factors such as impact of government policy. It describes trends in cigarette smoking over time, examines how prevalence by age has changed over the last four decades, and then examines cohort trends in smoking and heavy smoking. The cohort analysis focuses on trends for men, while commenting on similarities and differences for women. This article builds on previous pseudo-cohort analyses of the General Household Survey (GHS)[4, 5] but uses eight more years of data and analyses heavy smoking for the first time.

This article examines General Household Survey data from 1972 to 2004/05. It describes trends in cigarette smoking over time, observes how prevalence by age has changed over the last four decades, then examines pseudo-cohort trends in cigarette smoking for both men and women in Great Britain. The findings show that, for men, there were generational reductions in smoking prevalence, and when this trend began to slow, a trend for generational reductions in heavy smoking started. The remaining smokers were less likely to smoke 20 or more cigarettes than those in previous cohorts. However both these trends have now stopped, suggesting the levels of cigarette consumption we are observing today among men may be maintained in future generations if these patterns continue.

The cohort trends for current smoking among women are similar to those for men, with three main exceptions. First, for women there is no cohort effect for those born before the mid-1920s. Second, the prevalence rates of smoking tend to be lower for women than men for most ages or cohorts. Third, the cohort effect does not appear to have stopped for those born since the mid-1960s.

Data

This article primarily analyses data from the GHS in order to get a better picture of how smoking prevalence has changed since the 1970s. The GHS is a large government survey of households in Great Britain. It is the preferred government source of data on smoking prevalence and is used to monitor progress towards their cigarette smoking targets.[6] Questions about smoking behaviour were included in the GHS from 1972 to 1975, in alternate years from 1976 to 1998, and in every year from 2000 onwards. The question wording has remained consistent. The questions were asked of all people aged 16 and over in the household, with a self-completion form offered to those aged 16 or 17.

The analysis of GHS data in this article describes cigarette smoking only and does not look at other less common forms of tobacco consumption such as cigars, pipes or snuff. Cigarette smokers are defined as those who answered yes to the question, 'Do you smoke cigarettes at all nowadays?' The prevalence of heavy smoking (those smoking, on average, 20 or more cigarettes a day) is also examined. Changes in the prevalence of heavy smoking in the population can result from changes in smoking prevalence overall, from changes in heavy smoking rates among smokers, or from a combination of these two factors. Therefore this analysis describes heavy smoking among smokers, instead of among the whole population, so that these factors can be separated.

GHS smoking data are considered a reliable source. However it is likely that the GHS underestimates both the prevalence of smoking and the number of cigarettes consumed. In terms of prevalence, under-reporting is most likely to occur among young people. Underestimates of consumption are likely to occur in all age groups, due to smokers rounding down the number of cigarettes they smoke to the nearest multiple of ten. When considering trends in smoking, it is usually assumed that rates of under-reporting remain constant over time. However as smoking has become less socially acceptable, some people may be less likely to admit how much they smoke, or to admit to smoking at all.[6]

In 2000, item non-response weighting was introduced on the GHS to reduce bias in survey estimates.[7] Weights were calculated from 1998 onwards. It is likely that non-respondents differ systematically from respondents in their characteristics, which could result in the survey estimates not representing the true population figures. The weighting attempts to compensate for this by matching respondent to non-respondents with similar survey characteristics, and then weighting accordingly. The effect of weighting on the smoking data is minimal, for example in 1998 it only increased the overall reported prevalence of cigarette smoking by one percentage point. Nonetheless, it has been applied to all analysis in this article.

Tobacco and cigarette use over time

The GHS first asked questions about smoking in 1972, but it is useful to look also at other data showing earlier trends in tobacco and cigarette use. Smoking in Great Britain began among men. Tobacco use by men was well established before the 20th century and consumption increased until the 1940s, with the exception of a slight fall at the end of the First World War. Since the Second World War, tobacco consumption has fallen. At the beginning of the 20th century cigarettes only accounted for one-sixth of all tobacco consumed by men, but cigarette use rapidly increased in the first half of the 20th century so that by the 1940s, 80 per cent of tobacco consumed by men was in the form of cigarettes. The mid-1960s saw a peak in the average number of cigarettes smoked by men after which there has been a decline.[8]

Tobacco use by women has always been nearly exclusively in the form of cigarettes. In the mid-1920s tobacco companies started targeting women in their advertising campaigns after which cigarette consumption among women steadily increased up to the late 1970s, before starting to decline.[8]

GHS data (Figure 1) show that the proportion of people smoking cigarettes has fallen throughout the period from the early 1970s to 2004/05, but that the rate of decline has been gradually slowing. The proportion of male and female smokers who smoke 20 or more cigarettes per day (heavy smokers) has also decreased since peaking in 1976, declining from 55 per cent to 33 per cent in 2004/05 for male smokers, and from 40 percent to 27 per cent for female smokers (Figure 2). Therefore the total proportion of heavy smokers among the population will have reduced both as a result of smoking prevalence falling, and a decline in heavy smoking among smokers.

Figure 1 | **Percentage of cigarette smokers at the time of interview by year**

Great Britain

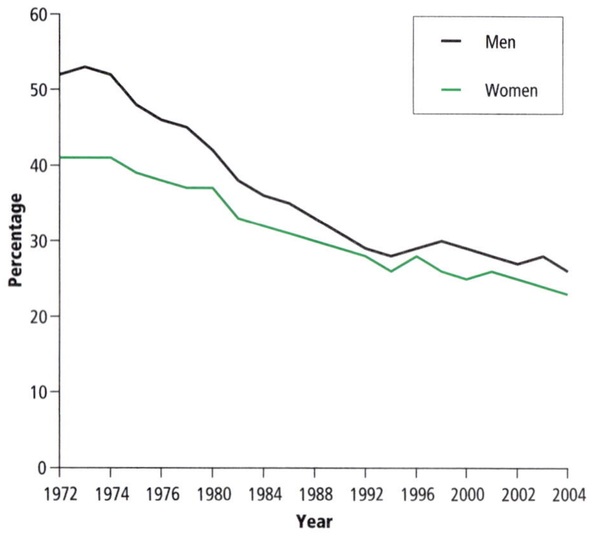

Source: General Household Survey, 1972-2004/05
Note: Before 1988, survey data were collected over calendar years. From 1988 onwards, data were collected over financial years.

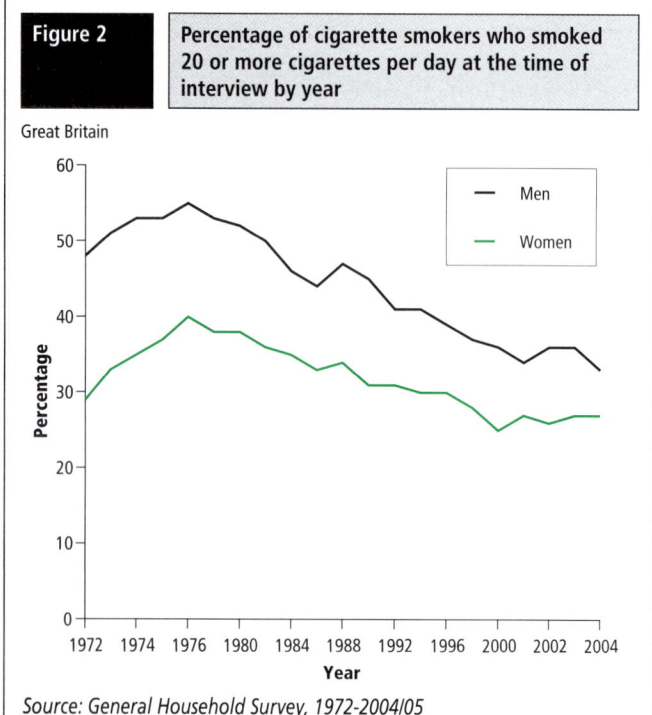

Figure 2 | **Percentage of cigarette smokers who smoked 20 or more cigarettes per day at the time of interview by year**

Great Britain

Source: General Household Survey, 1972-2004/05
Note: Before 1988, survey data were collected over calendar years. From 1988 onwards, data were collected over financial years.

Men have always been more likely than women to smoke cigarettes, but the difference in prevalence has virtually disappeared in recent years. In 1972, 52 per cent of men smoked, compared with 41 per cent of women, whereas in 2004, 26 per cent of men smoked compared with 23 per cent of women.

Cigarette smoking by age

Prevalence of cigarette smoking is related to age, but to a varying extent over time. Figure 3 and Figure 4 show the percentage of male and female cigarette smokers at the time of interview by age from four different decades: the 1970s, 1980s, 1990s and the first half of the 2000s. The data are pooled from all the available years of data for each of the decades. The graphs have been adjusted to account for the differential death rates between smokers and non-smokers (Appendix A). Without this adjustment the percentage who smoked would decline in the older age groups because, on average, smokers die before non-smokers and therefore, out of those who are alive, a smaller percentage smoke.

A consistent finding across all decades, for both men and women, is that the proportion smoking sharply increased during the teenage years as young people started taking up the habit.

For men, data from the 1970s shows that smoking peaked at just over 50 per cent, and then remained around that level at all ages (Figure 3). In the 1980s there was a similar pattern, except that a smaller proportion of people started smoking, with the percentage smoking plateauing at around 40 per cent. However data from the 1990s shows a different pattern. After an initial peak at about 40 per cent, there was a gradual decline in the proportion smoking, so by the age of 50 only 30 per cent were smokers. This suggests that male smokers were giving up the habit. This trend is also apparent using data from the first half of this decade, except that the percentage of young men who took up smoking peaks at a lower level and at a later age, and the decline in the overall percentage of smokers was more sustained.

The trends for women differ from the trends for men in the 1970s and 1980s (Figure 4). In the 1970s the percentage smoking did not remain at a constant level, but increased with age peaking for women aged in their late forties and early fifties, after which there was a decline in

smoking levels. The reason why this is different for women than men, is because cigarette use among women started later than among men. In the 1980s smoking remained fairly constant at around 40 per cent, but again declines for women aged 60 or older. In 1990s and 2000s the general pattern of smoking by age for women is fairly similar to the pattern for men, although in 2000s women peak at a lower level.

As with smoking prevalence, heavy smoking among smokers also exhibits differential age patterns over time. Pooled data for each of the four decades (the 1970s, 1980s, 1990s and the first half of the 2000s) show different patterns for heavy smoking by age. For both men and women, the age at which the largest proportion smoke increased over time, peaking at a later age with each subsequent decade.

Cigarette smoking by pseudo-birth cohort

Each line in Figure 3 and Figure 4 presents the age effects on smoking in a snapshot of time. The lines do not represent the smoking patterns that happen to someone during their life course. In fact, if you wanted to track someone over their life, the 20-year-olds in the 1970s data would then be represented by the 30-year-olds in the 1980s data, the 40-year-olds in the 1990s data, and so on. It is therefore useful to examine the data by the date when someone was born.

Members of a birth cohort are people who were born in a defined time period (such as between the years 1981 and 1985) and are therefore about the same age at any moment in time. A birth cohort can be tracked over time to see how smoking patterns change as the cohort ages. Examining the data in this way can help to indicate whether changes in smoking prevalence are solely due to age effects, or period effects, or whether it is due to birth cohort effects, which is an interaction between both age and period effects.

A traditional way of tracking a cohort over time is to use panel data, where the information on the same individual, such as their smoking status, is obtained at different points over their lifetime so that changes can be seen as the individuals age. However, there is no single source of longitudinal data in Great Britain which both contains a reliable smoking measurement and covers a range of birth cohorts. Instead the GHS has been used to generate pseudo-birth cohorts.

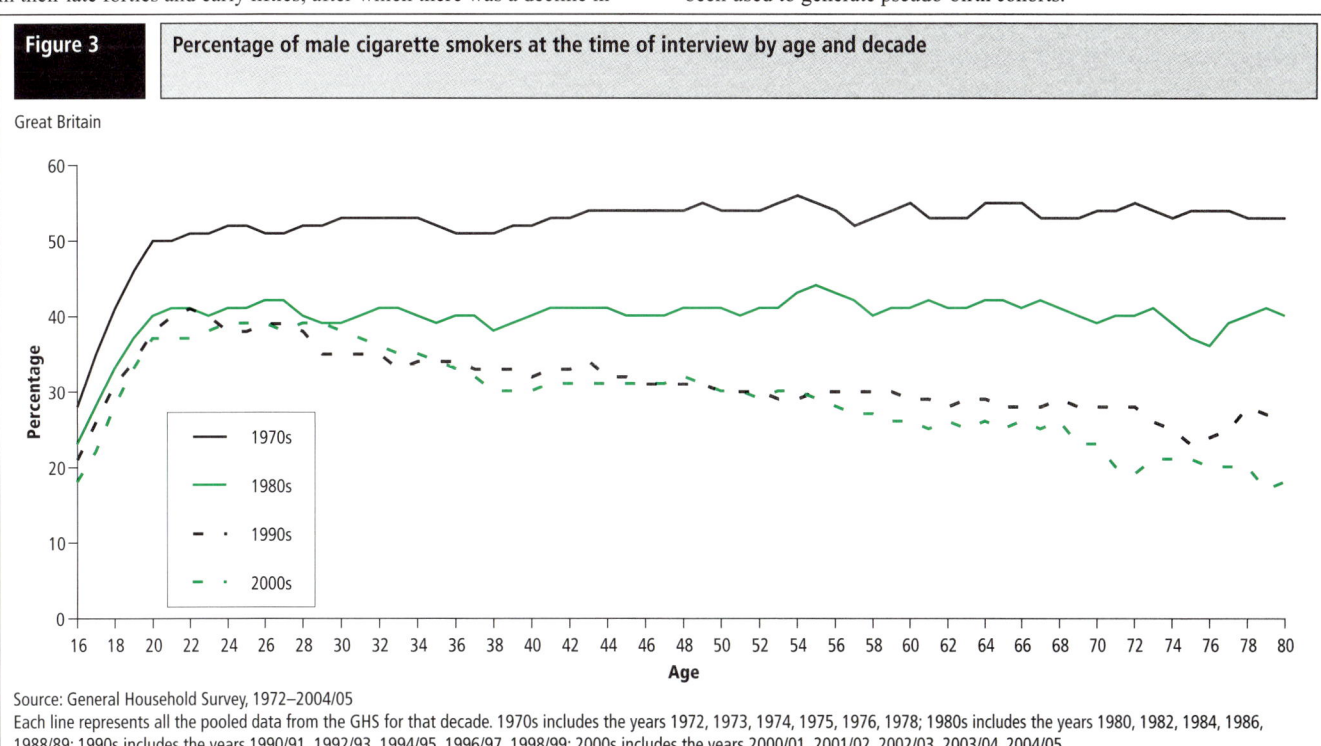

Figure 3   Percentage of male cigarette smokers at the time of interview by age and decade

Great Britain

Legend:
— 1970s
— 1980s
— · 1990s
— · 2000s

Source: General Household Survey, 1972–2004/05
Each line represents all the pooled data from the GHS for that decade. 1970s includes the years 1972, 1973, 1974, 1975, 1976, 1978; 1980s includes the years 1980, 1982, 1984, 1986, 1988/89; 1990s includes the years 1990/91, 1992/93, 1994/95, 1996/97, 1998/99; 2000s includes the years 2000/01, 2001/02, 2002/03, 2003/04, 2004/05.
Note: All data points are based on three-year moving averages with the exception of data for 16 year olds which are not averaged as there is no data available for 15 year olds.
Data has been adjusted to account for differential death rates (Appendix A).

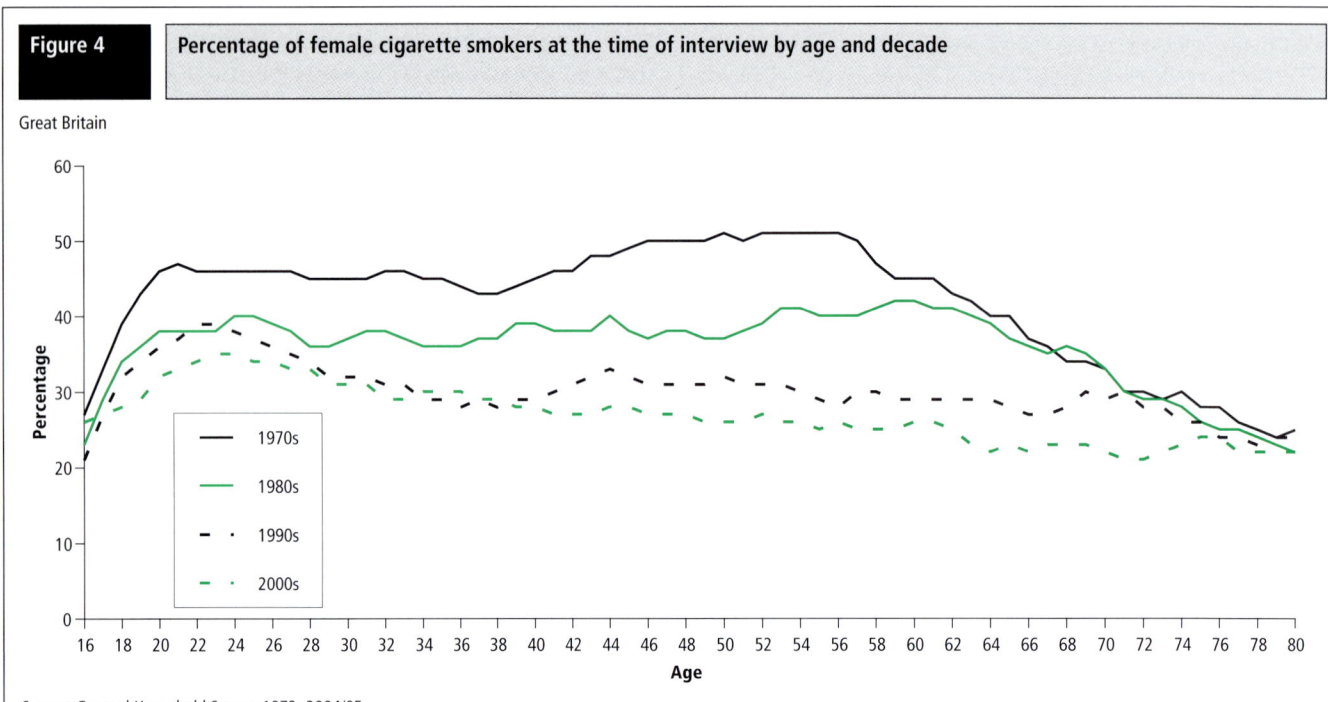

Figure 4 Percentage of female cigarette smokers at the time of interview by age and decade

Great Britain

Legend:
- 1970s
- 1980s
- - · 1990s
- - · 2000s

Source: General Household Survey, 1972–2004/05
Each line represents all the pooled data from the GHS for that decade. 1970s includes the years 1972, 1973, 1974, 1975, 1976, 1978; 1980s includes the years 1980, 1982, 1984, 1986, 1988/89; 1990s includes the years 1990/91, 1992/93, 1994/95, 1996/97, 1998/99; 2000s includes the years 2000/01, 2001/02, 2002/03, 2003/04, 2004/05.
Note: All data points are based on three-year moving averages with the exception of data for 16 year olds which are not averaged as there is no data available for 15 year olds.
Data has been adjusted to account for differential death rates (Appendix A).

Pseudo-cohort analyses track the average experiences of people who were born in the same time period. Unlike conventional longitudinal analyses, the same individuals are not tracked from year to year. As the GHS is a cross-sectional survey, the average experiences of respondents in a given survey year are taken to represent the experiences of their particular birth cohort, at that age. For example, people aged 20–24 in the 1980 GHS survey, are taken as being representative of the birth cohort born in 1956 to 1960. The same birth cohort is then represented by those aged 21–25 in 1981, and 22–26 in 1982, and finally by those aged between 44 and 48 in 2004.

The advantages of a pseudo-cohort approach over a panel approach is that it makes use of data that are already available, and it does not suffer from the problem of non-random attrition that occurs with conventional panel data, because a new sample is drawn each survey year. Smoking data from the GHS has already been examined extensively, but linking the cross sections gives additional richness to the data and offers a greater opportunity to investigate changes over time, age and cohort.

There are also disadvantages in using pseudo-cohort analysis, as opposed to conventional cohort analysis. First, differences between groups surveyed at different points in time may be a function of variations in the nature of the samples surveyed on those occasions, whereas in true panel data, the same samples are used on each occasion. However, the GHS has a large sample size so the sample errors around the estimates are relatively small. Second, the fact that we are not tracking the same individual, and instead looking at the average experience of a cohort, limits how we can analyse the data. For example, it would be impossible to measure the duration of an event for an individual, such as length of time that they smoked. Instead the average duration for the cohort as a whole has to be measured. Nor does the data allow for examination of movement between different categories. For example if pseudo-cohort data showed no change in smoking prevalence with increasing age, this could be due to either no change in smoking habits, or due to non-smokers starting to smoke and being replaced by a corresponding number of smokers who stop.

This analysis was run on a dataset that was created by the Office for National Statistics by combining GHS data from 1972 to 2004/05. The construction of this dataset is described in detail in Uren (2006).[9] The sample was divided into five-year birth cohorts. Cohorts were followed up to the age of 80. Three-year moving averages were used to remove the effects of random fluctuations due to small sample size.

BOX one

How to 'read' a pseudo-cohort graph

A pseudo-cohort graph (for example, Figure 5) can be read as you would a normal line graph. Age is presented on the horizontal X-axis, and the percentage of the population that exhibit the characteristic of interest, in this case smoking, is presented on the vertical Y-axis. Each line represents a different birth cohort. You can therefore track each line to see how smoking patterns change with age within that particular cohort. In other words, changes within cohorts correspond to movements along each line. The slope of the line indicates the rate of change within that cohort. The vertical distance between the cohort lines represent the differences between cohorts at a certain age. If there was no difference between the cohorts then the lines would follow the same course and could not be distinguished from one another. If there was a difference between the cohorts then the lines would appear separate from each other.

The fact that this pseudo-cohort dataset contains data from 1972 to 2004/05 means that none of the cohorts are followed over their whole life. For the oldest cohorts, we do not have information about them when they were young, and for the people born most recently, the rest of their lives have yet to be lived. This censoring effect means that some cohorts cannot be directly compared with some other cohorts, which can make it difficult to distinguish whether a change is due to an age or cohort effect.

This article builds on analyses by Kemm[4] and by Evandrou and Falkingham,[5] but uses eight additional years of data (1972, 1973, 1975 and 2000/01-2004/05) and analyses heavy smoking for the first time.

The creation of pseudo-cohort graphs allows a graphic representation of the data. Box 1 describes how to interpret pseudo-cohort graphs.

Male cohort trends for smoking

Figure 5 shows pseudo-cohort trends for current cigarette smoking among men. The data have been adjusted to account for differential death rates (Appendix A).

There are two main trends in Figure 5: the cohort reduction in the proportion of smokers in the population (which is illustrated by how separate the lines are), and the rate in which people give up smoking (represented by the gradient of the line).

There are clear cohort reductions in the proportion of smokers in the population for men born before the mid-1950s; Lines G-R do not lie together, but are separate (until the tail-end of each line where they change direction and start to overlap). At a given age those in an earlier cohort were more likely to smoke than those born later. For example, over half of men born in 1931–1935 (line K) smoked at 40 years old, whereas, among men born, on average, 20 years later (in 1951–1955, line G) only about a third of 40-year-olds smoked. In fact, at every age, each cohort is significantly different from at least one other cohort. However, immediately adjacent cohorts (that is men born, on average, five years earlier or later) are not significantly different from one another, and statistical differences only emerge when comparisons are made with men born, on average, at least 15 years earlier or later (Appendix B).

However, the cohort effect slows and then stops among men born more recently (1956–1985 cohorts, lines A–F), as represented by the lines becoming less distinct from each other until they lie together and virtually follow the same path. In fact, at all ages, a similar percentage of young men in the most recent cohort (1981–1985, line A) smoked compared with men born, on average, 5, 10 or 15 years earlier.

More than half of all men born between 1896 and 1955 (lines G-R) were a smoker at some time during their lives, whereas far fewer of men born after the mid-1950s had ever smoked (with the maximum proportion smoking being 44 per cent for 20-year-olds in the 1956–1960 cohort, line F).

For most of the cohorts in Figure 5 it is not possible to know what patterns of smoking prevalence were when men in that cohort were young (because GHS data are not available before 1972). There are three possible scenarios. Kemm[4] and Evandrou and Falkingham[5] suggest the decline in smoking prevalence is due to a fall in the age at which smokers quit in successive cohorts. An alternative explanation is that, at each successive cohort, fewer people started smoking than was the case in the past. Or it could be a combination of both these factors. The 1951–1955 cohort (line G) is the first to contain data for men in their late teens and early twenties. If we compare this group of men to those born, on average, five years later (the 1956–1960 cohort, line F), we find that the reason for the drop in smoking prevalence is that fewer men start smoking. Although these data suggest the main factor is that there has been a decline in the proportion of men beginning to smoke, we cannot extrapolate this finding to previous cohorts.

For each cohort in Figure 5 an age affect can be clearly seen. There is a rapid increase in smoking prevalence for teenagers and men in their early twenties (the 1951–1985 cohorts, lines A–G), presumably as young men became smokers for the first time. However, after this initial rise, each cohort shows a decline in smoking prevalence as they aged. The gradient of the slope represents the rate in which smoking prevalence declines, which is likely to represent the rate of giving up smoking, as only a few people take up smoking once they have reached their mid-twenties.

For men born before the mid-1930s, all the cohort lines (lines K–R) follow remarkably similar gradients. For men born between the mid-1930s and the mid-1950s, the cohort lines (G–J) initially follow the same gradient as the previous cohorts, but then become less steep at the tail-end of the lines. The fact that the lines are initially parallel (with the only change being a shift to the left with each subsequent cohort) shows that smoking prevalence declined at a similar rate, or that men gave up at the same rate across the cohorts.

For men born after the mid-1950s (cohorts 1956–1985, lines A–F) there is an obvious change in the gradient. It is less steep than the previous cohorts, and is in fact similar to the slopes of the tail-ends of lines G–J. This shows that the rate of giving up has slowed. There appears to be two factors influencing this. First, there is a cohort effect, so that those born after the mid-1950s have a slower rate of smoking cessation, than those born earlier. For example, the decline is slower in the 1956–1960 cohort (line F) than for those born 15 years earlier (the 1941–1945 cohort, line

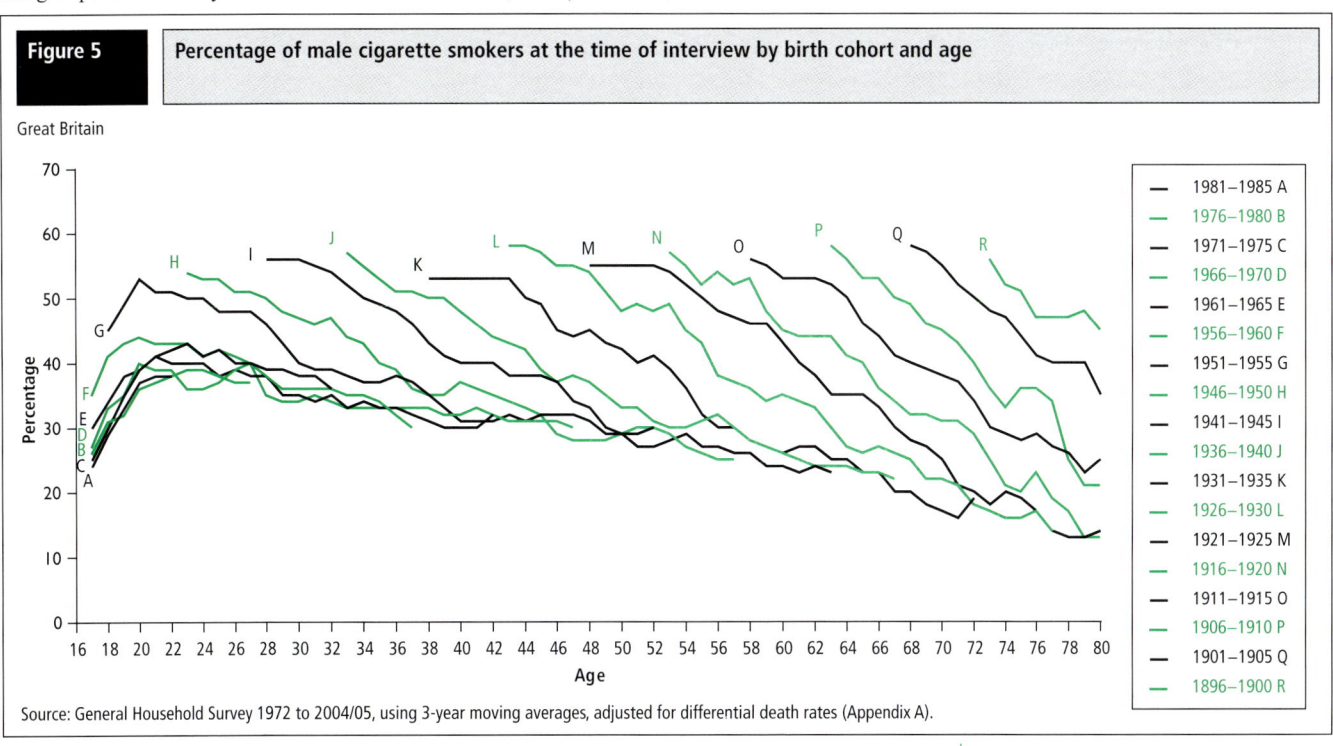

Figure 5 | Percentage of male cigarette smokers at the time of interview by birth cohort and age

Great Britain

Legend:
- 1981–1985 A
- 1976–1980 B
- 1971–1975 C
- 1966–1970 D
- 1961–1965 E
- 1956–1960 F
- 1951–1955 G
- 1946–1950 H
- 1941–1945 I
- 1936–1940 J
- 1931–1935 K
- 1926–1930 L
- 1921–1925 M
- 1916–1920 N
- 1911–1915 O
- 1906–1910 P
- 1901–1905 Q
- 1896–1900 R

Source: General Household Survey 1972 to 2004/05, using 3-year moving averages, adjusted for differential death rates (Appendix A).

I). Second, there appears to be a period effect. Earlier, the fact that the gradient becomes less steep in the tail-end of some lines was described. The age this happens gets progressively younger in subsequent cohorts: 51-year-olds in the 1941–1945 cohort, 46-year-olds in the 1946-1950 cohort and 40-year-olds in the 1951–1955 cohort. This shift in the gradient corresponds to data from the same time period, the early to mid-1990s, showing that since this time there has been a change to a slower rate of smoking cessation across all cohorts. Figure 1 shows that smoking prevalence for men levels out during this time period.

There appears to be a 'lower limit line' which most cohorts reach. This may represent the proportion of smokers who are, as yet, relatively resistant to policies aimed at discouraging people from starting smoking, or at encouraging smokers to give up. As there have been no changes in smoking patterns for the most recent cohorts it could be predicted that, if these patterns continued, these cohorts would follow the 'lower limit line', although only tentative conclusions can be drawn in predicting future trends.

Figure 5 has shown that the reduction in smoking prevalence over subsequent cohorts slows then stops for men for recent cohorts. However if we look at the amount smoked by men who remained a smoker we can see a cohort reduction in the percentage smoking 20 or more cigarettes (Figure 6). Data are presented up to the age of 50, as beyond this age no cohort effect can be seen, and are adjusted for differential death rates (Appendix A). Again the age effects can be clearly seen, with rates of heavy smoking among smokers increasing in the younger ages, and then levelling out.

It is hard to distinguish any cohort effects occurring for men born before the 1950s, but there is a reduction in heavy smoking among smokers in subsequent cohorts. So the 1946–1950 cohort (line H) averages at 56 per cent, the 1956–1960 cohort (line F) at about 46 per cent and, after an initial rise in smoking, the 1966–1970 cohort averages at around 32 per cent (line D). This trend for a reduction in the percentage of smokers to smoker of 20 or more cigarettes has not occurred in the most recent cohort.

Female cohort trends for smoking

The birth cohort trends are also clear for women and are similar to those for men. However, for women there is no cohort effect for those born before the mid-1920s. For example a woman born in 1900 would be just as likely to smoke as a woman of the same age born 20 years later. This may be because women lag behind men in the process of cigarette 'adoption, diffusion and abatement',[10] as cigarette smoking only started to become popular among women in the 1920s, about two decades later than it had done for men. It is likely that if the dataset went back another 20 years a similar pattern would be apparent for men.

For women, there are clear birth cohort trends for those born between the mid-1920s and the mid-1950s, after which the cohort effects lessen, then stop. However the pattern changes for the most recent cohort (1981–1985), in which women aged 18 or over are smoking less than previous cohorts. Although the differences only reach statistical significance when compared with women born in 1970 or earlier, this does not mean that there is not a real change. Where clear cohort trends do exist it is generally the case that a cohort is not significantly different from the previous two cohorts.

Women show similar cohort trends to men for heavy smoking among the remaining smokers, although the prevalence of heavy smoking is much lower for women.

Conclusion

Re-examining GHS smoking data using pseudo-cohort analysis gives us a better understanding of trends in smoking, than we get from the cross-sectional data alone, and allows for the examination of cohort, age and period effects.

The proportion of men and women in Great Britain who smoke cigarettes has decreased with subsequent generations. At every age, people are smoking less than the previous generation (with the exception of women born before the mid-1920s). The reduction in smoking prevalence is **not**

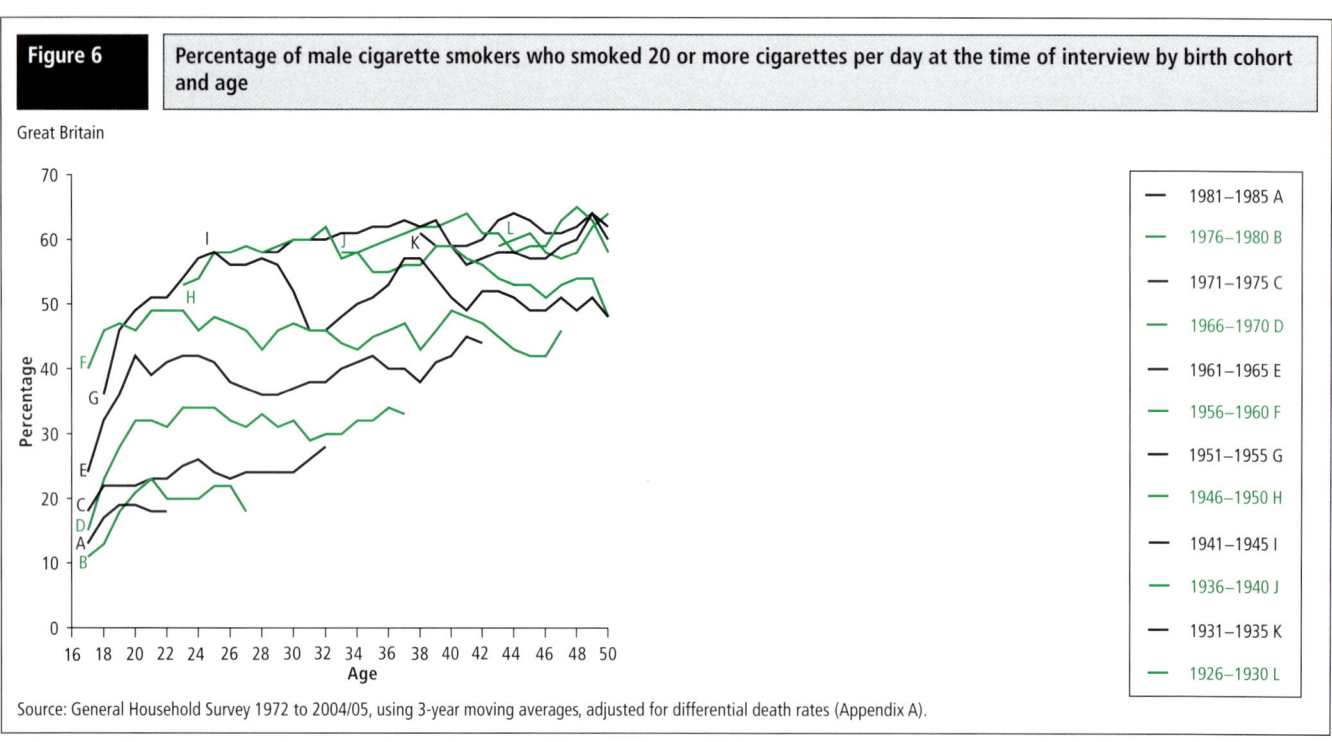

Figure 6 | **Percentage of male cigarette smokers who smoked 20 or more cigarettes per day at the time of interview by birth cohort and age**

Great Britain

—	1981–1985 A
—	1976–1980 B
—	1971–1975 C
—	1966–1970 D
—	1961–1965 E
—	1956–1960 F
—	1951–1955 G
—	1946–1950 H
—	1941–1945 I
—	1936–1940 J
—	1931–1935 K
—	1926–1930 L

Source: General Household Survey 1972 to 2004/05, using 3-year moving averages, adjusted for differential death rates (Appendix A).

due to established smokers giving up more rapidly, but is either due to fewer young people starting to smoke, or due to smokers starting to give up at a younger age, or a combination of these two factors.

Although men born since the mid-1950s were smoking less than men born earlier, this trend slows and then stops. In the most recent cohorts, fewer men were starting to smoke but were then giving up at a slower rate than in the past. The data suggest that for men the cohort effects on smoking have stopped and that smoking habits are becoming more stable. It might be that there is a 'lower limit line' which represents smokers who are, as yet, relatively resistant to policies aimed at stopping people starting smoking, or encouraging smokers to give up. As there have been no changes in smoking patterns for the most recent cohorts it could be predicted that, if these patterns continued, these cohorts may follow the 'lower limit line', although only tentative conclusions can be drawn in predicting future trends.

The cohort trends for current smoking among women are similar to those for men, with three main exceptions. First, for women there is no cohort effect for those born before the mid-1920s. Second, the prevalence rates of smoking tend to be lower for women than men for most ages or cohorts. Third, for men the cohort effect appears to have stopped for those born since the mid-1960s. However, the pattern for women changes with those born between 1981 and 1985, who, from the age of 18, were less likely to be a smoker than women in the previous cohorts.

For both men and women, smokers born since the 1960s were less likely to smoke 20 or more cigarettes per day than smokers were in the past. The data presented in this article suggests that the overall number of cigarettes consumed in Great Britain has been constantly falling. First the prevalence of smokers reduces with subsequent cohorts. Second, once this first trend has slowed, those who remained smokers were less likely to be heavy smokers compared with previous cohorts. However this cohort reduction in heavy smoking among smokers may now have stopped.

It is very difficult to make future predictions, however the data suggest that, if current trends continued, the levels of cigarette consumption that we are observing today among men in Great Britain would be maintained in future generations. However, forthcoming and future policy changes may well have an effect on trends in cigarette consumption.

Key findings

- At any age, men and women in Great Britain are smoking less than the previous generation (with the exception of women born before the mid-1920s).

- The reduction in smoking prevalence is not due to established smokers giving up more rapidly, but is due to either fewer young people starting to smoke, or to smokers giving up at a younger age, or a combination of these two factors.

- For men born since the mid-1960s the cohort effects on smoking have stopped and smoking habits have become more stable.

- For both men and women, smokers born since the 1960s were less likely to smoke 20 or more cigarettes per day than smokers were in the past. However this cohort effect may have now have stopped.

- It is very difficult to make future predictions, however the data suggest that, if current trends continued, the levels of cigarette consumption that we are observing today among men in Great Britain would be maintained in future generations.

References

1. Department of Health (1998) *Smoking kills – a White Paper on tobacco*. TSO: London.
2. Donaldson L (2002) *Chief Medical Officer's Annual Report*. TSO London.
3. Department of Health (2004) Spending Review 2004 Public Service Agreement. Available at: www.dh.gov.uk/AboutUs/HowDHWorks/ ServiceStandardsAndCommitments/DHPublicServiceAgreement/ PublicServiceAgreementArticle/fs/en?CONTENT_ ID=4106188&chk=zYiEVM
4. Kemm J R (2001) A birth cohort analysis of smoking by adults in Great Britain 1974–1998. *Journal of Public Health Medicine*, **23(4)**, 306–311.
5. Evandrou M and Falkingham J (2002) Smoking behaviour and socio-economic status: a cohort analysis, 1974–1998, *Health Statistics Quarterly* **14**, 30–39.
6. Goddard and Green (2005) *Smoking and drinking among adults 2004*. Available at: www.statistics.gov.uk/statbase/Product. asp?vlnk=5756
7. Walker A, Maher J, Coulthard M, Goddard E and Thomas M (2001) *Living in Britain: Results from the 2000 General Household Survey*. TSO: London. Also available at www.statistics.gov.uk/lib2000/ Section177.html
8. Doll R, Darby S and Whitley E (1997) Chapter 9 – Trends in mortality from smoking-related diseases, in ONS (ed.) *Health of Adult Britain 1841–1994*, Volume 1, TSO Office: London.
9. Uren Z (2006) The GHS Pseudo Cohort Dataset (GHSPCD): Introduction and Methodology. Survey Methodology Bulletin, **59**, 25–37. Available at: www.statistics.gov.uk/cci/article.asp?ID=1637
10. Pampel F C (2001) Cigarette Diffusion and Sex Differences in Smoking. *Journal of Health and Social Behaviour* **42**, 388–404.

Appendix A

How to account for differential death rates with increasing age

Smoking prevalence decreases with age for the older age groups. For example, in pooled GHS data from the 1970s the percentage smoking decreases for those aged in their mid-fifties (Figure A, unadjusted line). Why is this? One explanation is that smokers die before non-smokers, and therefore, out of those who are alive, a smaller percent smoke.

Richard Doll's 50 year study of male British doctors gives differential survival curves for smokers compared with non-smokers.[A] I have used the survival curve from age 35 for those born in 1900–1930 to calculate the percentage smoking you would expect, if no one changed their habits, due to these differential death rates between smokers and non-smokers. Data can then be adjusted to account for the differential death rates.

Doll's study looks at one specific sub group (male doctors) and compares non-smokers with smokers within that sub-group. I am using this data and applying it to other groups. This relies on the assumption that the differential death rates from smoking related diseases will be similar among other sub-groups (for example women and non-manual groups) an assumption which has been argued by Marang-van de Mheen, Davey Smith and Hart.[B]

Box A works through an example for one data point. The formula presented was entered into excel and used to calculate the adjusted figures for all ages above the age of 35, and then the data was plotted (Figure A, adjusted line). In the 1970s the decline in smoking prevalence is completely accounted for by the fact that more smokers than non-smokers have died.

Adjusting the pseudo-cohort charts

The added complication of adjusting the cohort graphs is that the youngest age groups for some cohorts is older than 35. The calculations using Doll's survival curve use data on the percentage that smoked at age 35. However, using our knowledge of differential death rates we are able to predict what percentage would have been smoking at age 35 from the proportion that are smoking at an older age.

Box A

Worked example to account for differential death rates with increasing age

This example uses pooled data for the 1970s for males. Differential death rates are calculated for men age 70.

P = Prevalence of smoking for those aged 35 from the GHS data = 0.52
1-P = Prevalence of non-smoking for those aged 35 from the GHS data = 0.48
S = proportion of smokers alive at 70 = 0.58 (taken from Doll's survival curve)
N = proportion of non-smokers alive at 70 = 0.81 (taken from Doll's survival curve)

Therefore the percentage of smokers (once differential death rates have been accounted for) is smokers surviving divided by the total surviving:

$$= \frac{P \times S}{(P \times S) + ((1-P) \times N)}$$

$$= \frac{0.52 \times 0.58}{((0.52 \times 0.58) + (0.48 \times 0.81))}$$

$$= 0.43$$

That is to say, if 52 per cent smoked at aged 35 and smokers and non-smokers died at the rates expected from Doll's survival curve then you would expect the percentage of non-smokers to fall to 43 per cent at age 70, even if there was no change in smoking habit. The actual figure at age 70 from the GHS data is 45 per cent.

We can then adjust the GHS data to account for this differential death rate. We do this by taking the actual data at 35 and dividing by this adjusted figure.

$$\frac{0.52}{0.45} = 1.19$$

We can then times this actual data by this adjusted figure.
0.45 x 1.19 = 0.54.
Therefore the adjusted figure is 54 per cent.

(Note: All figures from the GHS data are based on three-year moving average as the data points fluctuate from one age to the next. The exception is data for 16-year-olds which are not averaged as there is no data available for 15-year-olds.)

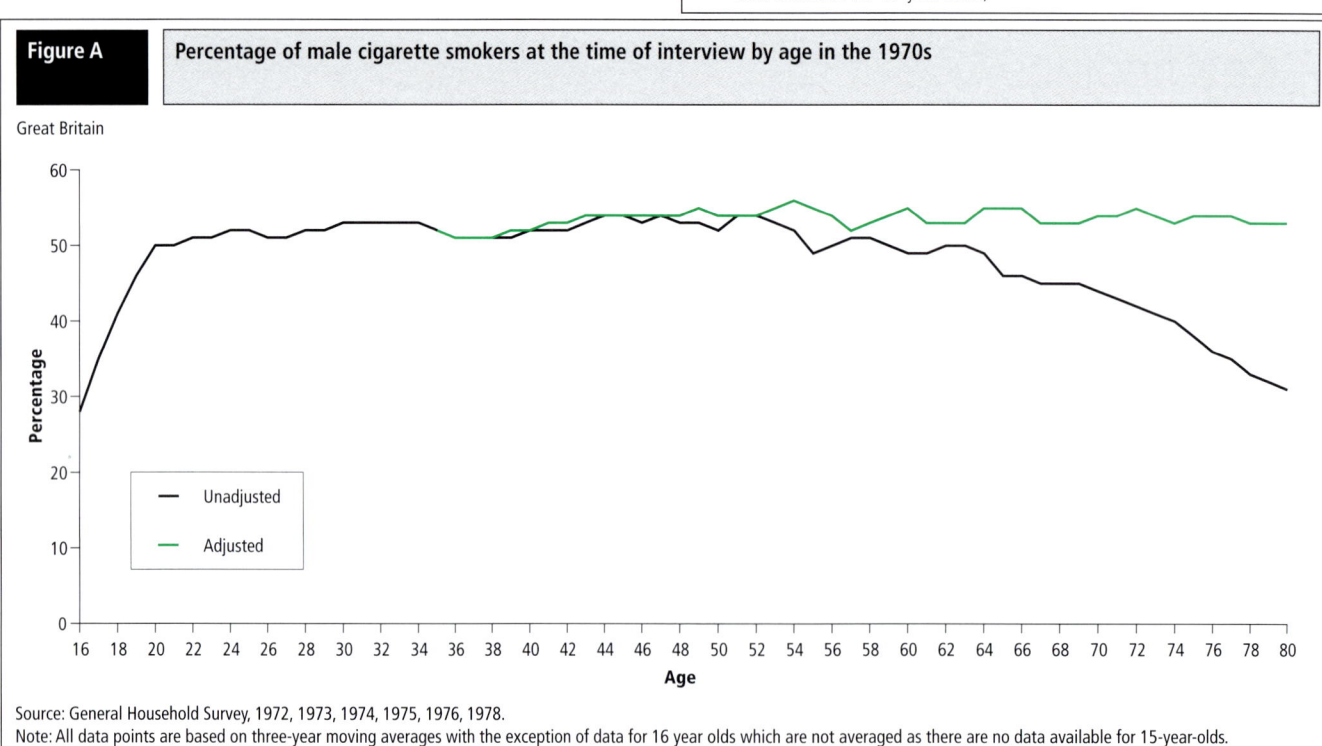

Figure A Percentage of male cigarette smokers at the time of interview by age in the 1970s

Great Britain

Source: General Household Survey, 1972, 1973, 1974, 1975, 1976, 1978.
Note: All data points are based on three-year moving averages with the exception of data for 16 year olds which are not averaged as there are no data available for 15-year-olds.

Adjusting for heavy smoking

The methods described above were used to adjust Figure 6. Ideally, we would have used a survival curve which compared death rates for those smoking 20 or more cigarettes a day with death rates for non-smokers. However this data is not easily available.

There will therefore be a slight underestimate of the effects of differential death rates as heavy smokers have a higher mortality rate than current smokers.

However, we do not predict the underestimate to be substantial. Table 3 from Doll *et al* presents the relative risks of mortality for smokers versus non-smokers for men aged 60 and over who were born in the 20th century.[A] (Note that these figures look at mortality rates for men age 60 and over, rather than 35 or over as used in the survival curve.) Compared with lifelong non-smokers the relative risk for current smokers is 2.19, for those smoking 15–24 cigarettes per day it is 2.17 and for those smoking 25 or more cigarettes it is 2.16. From these figures we would predict that the difference between current smokers and those smoking 20 or more cigarettes per day (the measure of heavy smoking used in our analysis) is minimal.

The effects of adjusting for differential death rates on Figure 6 are small as data is only presented up to the age of 50. The largest change resulting from the adjustments was a one percentage point increase.

References

A. Doll R, Peto R, Boreham J and Sutherland I (2004) Mortality in relation to smoking: 50 years' observations on male British doctors, *British Medical Journal*, **328**, 1519.
B. Marang-van de Mheen P, Davey Smith G and Hart C (2006) The health impact of smoking in manual and non-manual social class men and women: a test of the Blaxter hypothesis. *Social Science and Medicine* **48**, 1851–1856.

Appendix B

Significance testing of the pseudo-cohort graphs

95% confidence intervals were produced around each pseudo-cohort line on the graph to determine whether the differences between cohort lines were significant. If the 95% confidence intervals around two rates do not overlap then the two rates are significantly different at the 5 per cent level. If the confidence intervals overlap then it is impossible to tell whether two rates are significantly different at the 5 per cent level. For cases where this was of interest t-tests were run.

The confidence intervals and t-test calculations included a design factor, or deft, which is used to give an indication of the effect of the clustering on the reliability of estimates. These vary for males and females. We use the published GHS defts for male current smokers aged 16 and over (1.07) and for female current smokers aged 16 and over (1.13) (The defts were taken from Table C.10, GHS 2004, Appendix C www.statistics.gov.uk/statbase/Product.asp?vlnk=5756). We made the assumption that these defts would also be appropriate to use for the heavy smokers.

Socio-demographic characteristics of the healthcare workforce in England and Wales – results from the 2001 Census

Mohammed Yar, David Dix and Madhavi Bajekal

Office for National Statistics

Based on Census 2001 data, this article presents analysis of the socio-demographic characteristics of people working in the healthcare sector, focusing particularly on four key healthcare occupations: doctors, dentists, nurses and midwives. Unlike the NHS workforce statistics, which only include people directly employed by the NHS, census data also include those working in the private healthcare market and those who are self-employed. The article also examines patterns of distribution of key healthcare professions per head of population by local authority and by area deprivation.

Introduction

The system of healthcare in England and Wales is complex involving a range of organisations and occupations engaged in delivering healthcare. Healthcare is primarily provided through the publicly funded National Health Service (NHS), with limited activity also undertaken by separate services within the armed forces, prisons, and schools. In addition, healthcare is also provided by the private sector, for example by independent hospitals, nursing homes and voluntary organisations. The NHS, however, remains the dominant healthcare provider and is known to be the largest employer in Europe.

The *World Health Report 2000* underlined that the most important input of a healthcare system is human resources and that the quality of healthcare provided crucially depends upon the number and skills of the workforce.[1] The NHS Plan 2000 acknowledges this and adds: 'The biggest constraint the NHS faces today is no longer shortage of financial resources. It is shortage of human resources – the doctors, nurses, therapists and other health professionals – who keep the NHS going day in and day out.'[2] In order to meet the shortage of healthcare workers, the NHS Plan set up specific targets for increasing the number of doctors, nurses and allied heath professionals.

To support policy development, the NHS Health and Social Care Information Centre in England (and the National Assembly for Wales in Wales) conducts an annual census of the NHS workforce to gather demographic and skills information.[3-9] However, there is no similar data source for those employed in the healthcare sector outside the NHS. In order to develop policies for the future, it is important to understand the dynamics and structure of the healthcare workforce as a whole, both those within the NHS and those outside it.

Data sources that can be usefully exploited to estimate the size of the total healthcare workforce are the UK Labour Force Surveys and the UK Population Censuses. The population coverage of both these sources includes the adult population as a whole and therefore includes people working in both the public and private healthcare sectors. The annual Labour Force Survey contains detailed information on the labour market characteristics of the sampled population but, despite its relatively large sample size, it does not provide reliable estimates for a specific industry at the sub-national level (local authorities). In contrast, although the UK Population Censuses have limited information on workforce skills, they can be used to provide robust sub-national estimates by type of industry. Use of census data has the added advantage of providing a consistent metric for comparing the socio-demographic profile of the healthcare workforce against that of any other industry or the labour market as a whole.[7]

This article presents a socio-demographic profile of the healthcare workforce in England and Wales using the 2001 Census with emphasis on four key healthcare occupations: doctors (medical practitioners), dentists (dental practitioners), nurses and midwives. The wealth of information collected in the Census allows analysis of specific workforce characteristics such as the proportion of healthcare workers born overseas or the proportion of healthcare workers in industries other than the healthcare industry. Lastly, the article examines geographic variations in the distribution of key healthcare professionals and investigates their relationship with deprivation at local authority level.

Methods and data sources

The data used in this paper were tables from the 2001 Census which included questions on industry and occupation.[8] The question on industry asked for a description of the business activity of the employer to establish the type of industry worked in. Responses to the industry question were coded using a modified version of the UK Standard Industrial Classification 1992 (SIC(92)).[9] Similarly the question on occupation asked people about their job title and what they did in their main job. Responses to the occupation question were coded using the Standard Occupational Classification 2000 (SOC2000) which is also a four level hierarchical classification.[10]

In this article the workforce employed in the healthcare sector has been defined as those aged 16 to state pensionable age (65 years for men and 60 years for women) currently employed in industries relating to human health whatever their occupation (Box one). This definition therefore excludes those with a medical or allied professional occupation (eg doctors, nurses) who were not currently employed in either of the four industries.

Box one

SIC(92) industry and SOC 2000 occupations defining the healthcare sector

SIC(92) Industry	SOC 2000 Occupation
8511 Hospital activities	All occupations
8512 Medical practice activities	All occupations
8513 Dental practice activities	All occupations
8514 Other human health activities	All occupations

Note: A detailed description of the activities under each of these four headings is given in *Methodological guide to the 1992 Standard Industrial Classification of Economic Activities*[9]

The healthcare sector includes a wide range of occupations, both clinical and non-clinical, ranging from doctors and dentists to cleaners and drivers. The workforce in the sector spans all of the nine major occupational groups although it is primarily concentrated in four: Managers and Senior Officials, Professional Occupations, Associate Professional and Technical Occupations, and Personal Service Occupations. A detailed description of individual occupations and their hierarchical classification is given in *Standard Occupational Classification 2000: Volumes 1 and 2*.[10] (For the SOC2000 classification of the main healthcare occupations, see Appendix A).

Although in the 2001 Census the questions relating to industry and occupation were asked of all those aged 16–74 working in the week before the census (and all those aged 16–64 not currently in work but who last worked in 1996 or later), this article restricts workforce analysis to people aged 16 to state pensionable age (SPA) and in current employment. This was mainly because of a high level of item non-response for the occupation and industry questions in the age group SPA to 74.

In order to conform to the definition as stated, special tables were commissioned from the 2001 Census. Local authority (LA) level workforce tables were compiled according to where people worked, rather than their place of residence. At the Government Office Region (GOR) level, however, workforce tables were compiled according to where people lived. Although the LA tables were compiled differently from the GOR tables, local authority tables when aggregated closely matched the GOR tables for the key healthcare occupations.

Results

Workforce size, occupational composition and regional distribution

According to the 2001 Census, 1,439,000 people aged 16 to SPA were employed in the healthcare sector out of the total workforce of 22,932,000 in England and Wales. The healthcare sector accounted for 60 per cent of the employment in the Health and Social Work industry and 6 per cent of employment in the economy as a whole. Of the 1,439,000 healthcare workforce 1,350,000 (94 per cent) were working in England and 90,000 (6 per cent) in Wales.[11]

The healthcare sector workforce for England and Wales included 110,000 doctors (8 per cent), 20,000 dentists (1 per cent), 356,000 nurses (25 per cent) and 24,000 midwives (2 per cent). These four occupations together made up more than a third (35 per cent) of the entire healthcare sector workforce.

A substantial proportion of medical and allied professionals worked in industries outside the healthcare sector; for example 14,000 doctors (11 per cent of all doctors), 3,000 dentists (12 per cent of all dentists), 63,000 nurses (15 per cent of all nurses) and 2,000 midwives (7 per cent of all midwives) were working in industries such as education, voluntary sector, prisons and occupational health (Table A, Appendix A).

Healthcare sector employment as a proportion of total employment varied from 8 per cent in Wales to 5 per cent in the East of England. This reflects the differential nature and composition of regional economies (Table 1).

An analysis of the healthcare sector workforce by occupation shows that most of the workforce was concentrated in four major SOC 2000 occupational groups (Table 2). The largest occupational groups were 'Associate Professional and Technical Occupations' (such as nurses and midwives), 'Personal Service Occupations' (such as care assistants and home carers), 'Administrative and Secretarial Occupations' (such as medical secretaries) and 'Professional Occupations' (such as doctors

| Table 1 | Workforce[1] in Healthcare Sector and in Other Industries by Government Office Region, 2001 |

England and Wales

	Healthcare Sector		Other Industries		All Industries (=100%) (thousands)
	%	thousands	%	thousands	
North East	7	74	93	936	1,010
North West	7	198	93	2,622	2,821
Yorkshire and the Humber	7	146	93	1,979	2,125
East Midlands	6	115	94	1,750	1,865
West Midlands	6	138	94	2,126	2,264
East of England	5	135	95	2,360	2,495
London	6	191	94	3,034	3,225
South East	6	214	94	3,540	3,754
South West	6	139	94	2,065	2,204
England	6	1,350	94	20,413	21,763
Wales	8	90	92	1,061	1,150
England and Wales	6	1,439	94	21,474	22,913

1. Adults aged 16 to state pensionable age.
Source: Census 2001, Office for National Statistics

and dentists). In each of these groups the proportions of employees in the healthcare sector were higher than in All Industries. Altogether these four groups accounted for 86 per cent of the healthcare sector workforce compared with 45 per cent in All Industries.

Healthcare occupations are a combination of clinical and non-clinical occupations. Clinical occupations mostly fall in the two occupation groups 'Associate Professional and Technical Occupations' and 'Professional Occupations'. These two groups together made up half of the Healthcare workforce compared with a quarter of the workforce in All Industries. The group 'Associate Professional and Technical Occupations' accounted for 38 per cent of the total healthcare workforce of which 25 per cent were nurses and 2 per cent midwives. The other group 'Professional Occupations' accounted for 13 per cent of the workforce of which 8 per cent were doctors and 1 per cent dentists.

There was a distinct gender bias for many healthcare occupations. While 'Managers and Senior Officials' and 'Professional Occupations' were predominantly male, 'Associate Professional and Technical Occupations', 'Administrative and Secretarial Occupations' and 'Personal Service Occupations' were predominantly female.

In terms of the size of the workforce, the top five healthcare occupations were: nurses (accounting for 25 per cent of the healthcare workforce), doctors (8 per cent), care assistants and home carers (7 per cent), nursing auxiliaries and assistants (7 per cent) and receptionists (5 per cent). In two of these occupations, receptionists and care assistants and home carers, people were as likely or more to work in other industries as in the healthcare sector.

The healthcare sector workforce of 1,439,000 for England and Wales equated to 277 healthcare workers per 10,000 population.[12] For England and Wales, rates for the key healthcare workers ranged from 68 nurses to 4 dentists per 10,000 population (Table 3).

At the GOR level, Wales had the highest rates of healthcare workers per head of population (309 per 10,000 population) and the East of England the lowest (250 per 10,000). The regional distributions of key healthcare workers followed different patterns for doctors, dentists, nurses and midwives. London had the highest rates of doctors (31 per 10,000) and dentists (5) and Wales the highest rates of nurses (82) and midwives (5). At the other end of the spectrum, the East of England had the lowest rates for doctors (17), nurses (62) and midwives (4) and the East Midlands had the lowest rate for dentists (3).

Age and sex

The healthcare workforce was predominantly female. Women comprised nearly four-fifths of the healthcare workforce (Table 4). This compares with women making up less than half of the workforce in All Industries. Of the selected healthcare occupations, doctors and dentists were mostly male – nearly two-thirds of doctors and dentists were male. By contrast, nurses and midwives were predominantly female – 89 per cent of nurses

| Table 2 | Workforce[1] in Healthcare Sector and in All Industries by SOC 2000 major occupation groups and sex, 2001 |

England and Wales   Percentages

	Healthcare Sector			All Industries		
	Males	Females	All	Males	Females	All
Managers And Senior Officials	9	5	6	18	11	15
Professional Occupations	34	7	13	12	10	11
Doctors (medical practitioners)	23	4	8	1	0	1
Dentists (dental practitioners)	4	1	1	0	0	0
Associate Professional And Technical Occupations	26	41	38	14	14	14
Nurses	12	28	25	0	4	2
Midwives	0	2	2	0	0	0
Administrative and Secretarial Occupations	4	19	16	5	23	13
Receptionists	0	6	5	0	2	1
Skilled Trades Occupations	4	1	1	19	2	12
Personal Service Occupations	12	21	19	2	13	7
Nursing auxiliaries and assistants	5	7	7	0	1	1
Care assistants and home carers	4	8	7	0	4	2
Sales and Customer Service Occupations	0	0	0	4	12	8
Process; Plant and Machine Operatives	2	0	1	13	3	9
Elementary Occupations	9	5	6	12	12	12
All Occupations (=100%) (thousands)	306	1,134	1,439	12,565	10,367	22,932

1. Adults aged 16 to state pensionable age.
Source: Census 2001, Office for National Statistics

Table 3	Key healthcare workers per 10,000 population by Government Office Region, 2001

Rate per 10,000 population

	Doctors	Dentists	Nurses	Midwives	Healthcare Sector
North East	20.8	3.5	74.4	4.6	295.0
North West	20.7	3.8	74.2	5.3	294.8
Yorkshire and the Humber	21.6	3.8	72.6	4.7	293.7
East Midlands	19.0	3.0	68.5	4.7	274.9
West Midlands	18.6	3.4	66.0	4.9	262.5
East of England	17.4	3.5	61.6	4.2	250.0
London	30.8	5.0	62.5	4.2	266.3
South East	19.2	4.2	63.6	4.2	267.2
South West	20.1	4.2	70.7	4.6	281.8
England	21.2	3.9	67.5	4.6	274.7
Wales	21.1	3.7	82.2	5.5	308.6
England and Wales	21.2	3.9	68.3	4.6	276.6

Source: Census 2001, Office for National Statistics

Table 4	Workforce[1] in key healthcare occupations by sex, 2001

England and Wales

Percentages

	Persons aged 16 to SPA		
	Males	Females	All (=100%) (thousands)
Doctors	63	37	110
Dentists	62	38	20
Nurses	11	89	356
Midwives	1	99	24
Healthcare Sector	21	79	1,439
All Industries	55	45	22,932

1. Adults aged 16 to state pensionable age.
Source: Census 2001, Office for National Statistics

and 99 per cent of midwives were female. The other major occupations – receptionists, care assistants and home carers, nursing auxiliaries and assistants – were all predominantly female.

The age profile of the healthcare workforce was relatively older than that in All Industries (Figure 1). The proportion of people in the age range 35 to SPA in the healthcare workforce was 68 per cent compared with 61 per cent in All Industries. On the other hand, in the younger age groups (16 to 34), the proportion of healthcare employment was consistently lower than in All Industries. This was particularly so for the youngest age group 16 to 24 where the share of employment in the healthcare sector (7 per cent for males and 8 per cent for females) was almost half that in All Industries (13 per cent for males and 15 per cent for females).

Like the rest of the healthcare sector workforce, the vast majority of people working in key healthcare occupations were aged 25 to 54 but there were important differences particularly at the younger and older age groups. Both for males and females, the proportions of key healthcare workers at the two ends of the age distribution (16 to 24, 55 to SPA) were lower than the proportions for the healthcare sector for the same age groups. In the younger group this is likely to be due to the years of study required to enter these professions and in the older age group possibly due to the retirement age of 60 in the NHS.

The age profile of female doctors and dentists was distinctly younger than that of male practitioners. The proportions of female doctors (44 per cent) and dentists (46 per cent) in the younger age group 16–34 were higher than the equivalent male proportions (29 per cent and 26 per cent, respectively) while in the older age group 35-SPA the proportions of female doctors (56 per cent) and dentists (54 per cent) were lower than for males (71 per cent and 74 per cent, respectively). Although, overall, doctors and dentists were mostly males, in the younger age group 16–29, there were as many female doctors ((9,700) as male (9,600) and slightly more female dentists (2,100) than male (1,800).

Figure 1	Age and sex distribution of the workforce in Healthcare Sector and in All Industries, 2001

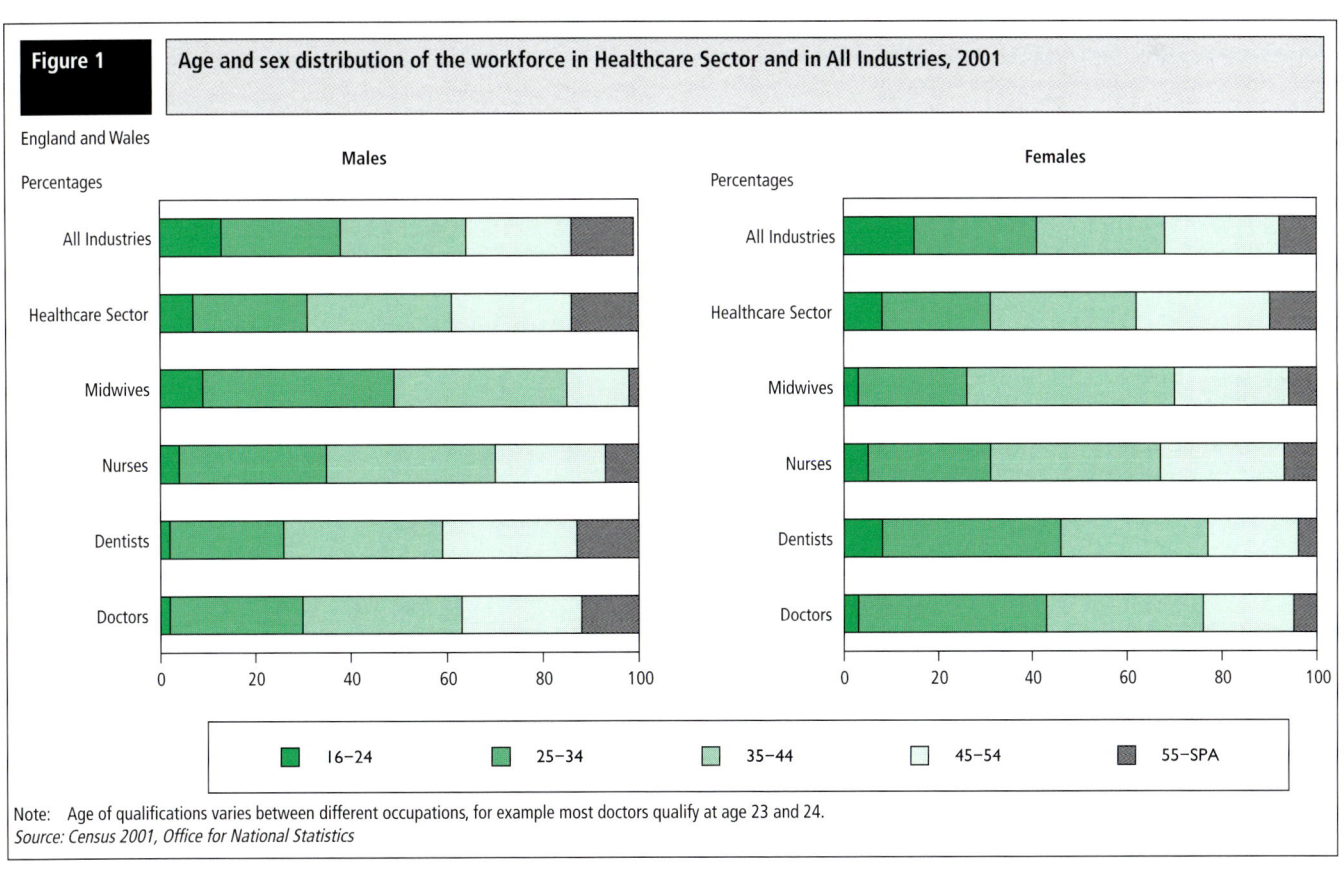

England and Wales

Note: Age of qualifications varies between different occupations, for example most doctors qualify at age 23 and 24.
Source: Census 2001, Office for National Statistics

Employment status

The level of self employment in the healthcare sector was much lower than in All Industries. The proportion of self employed people in the healthcare sector (7 per cent) was half that in All Industries (13 per cent) (Table 5). Occupations in the healthcare sector with the highest level of self-employment included doctors (general practitioners), dentists, therapists and chiropodists. In common with employment patterns in the labour market as a whole, self-employment was higher among men than among women. The self-employment rate for men (16 per cent) was about four times higher than for women (4 per cent).

Table 5	Employment status of the workforce[1] in Healthcare Sector and in All Industries by sex, 2001					

England and Wales

Percentages

	Healthcare Sector			All Industries		
	Male	Female	All	Male	Female	All
Employees	84	96	93	83	93	87
Self employed	16	4	7	17	7	13
All employed (=100%)(thousands)	305	1,134	1,439	12,565	10,367	22,932

1. Adults aged 16 to state pensionable age.
Source: Census 2001, Office for National Statistics

Part-time working (working 30 hours or less a week) was higher in the healthcare sector than in All Industries. In 2001, nearly two in five employees worked part-time in the healthcare sector compared with approximately one in four in All Industries. Similar to the employment pattern in All Industries, women in the healthcare sector were far more likely to work part time than men – nearly half of women (45 per cent) worked part time compared with one in ten men (10 per cent) (Table 6).

Among the key healthcare occupations, part-time working was higher among nurses (36 per cent) and midwives (44 per cent) than among doctors (12 per cent) and dentists (24 per cent); this may be due to the fact that these occupations are predominantly female, and in all industries women were more likely to work part-time than men. Although lower than for women, rates of part-time working were sizeable even among male healthcare workers. For example, 12 per cent of male dentists and 5 per cent of male doctors were working part-time compared with 44 per cent and 25 per cent of female dentists and doctors respectively.

Table 6	Full-time and part-time working in healthcare, 2001[1]					

England and Wales

Percentages

	Males		Females		All	
	Part-time	Full-time	Part-time	Full-time	Part-time	Full-time
Doctors	5	95	25	75	12	88
Dentists	12	88	44	56	24	76
Nurses	7	93	39	61	36	64
Midwives	25	75	44	56	44	56
Healthcare Sector	10	90	45	55	38	62
All Industries	9	91	41	59	24	76

1. Adults aged 16 to state pensionable age.
Source: Census 2001, Office for National Statistics

Ethnic Group

Ethnic minority groups were more highly represented in the healthcare sector than in All Industries. While 9 per cent of the working age population in England and Wales was non-white, 10 per cent of the healthcare sector workforce and 7 per cent of All Industries workforce were non-white. All the four main minority ethnic groups had higher representation in the healthcare sector than in All Industries (Table 7).

People from ethnic minorities tend to be concentrated in certain healthcare occupations. All the four key occupations (doctors, dentists, nurses and midwives) had higher proportions of non-white workers compared with the non-white proportion of the working age population. Compared with one in ten non-white workers in the healthcare sector as a whole, three in ten doctors and two in ten dentists were non-white. Of the minority ethnic groups, Asians made up the largest proportions of doctors (21 per cent) and dentists (14 per cent) and the Black group made up the largest proportions of nurses (5 per cent) and midwives (7 per cent). In fact, of all Asians employed in the healthcare sector, the majority were doctors; for all the other minority ethnic groups most were employed as nurses.

All regions had higher representation of non-white groups in the healthcare workforce than their proportions in the working age populations, except in Yorkshire and the Humber (Figure 2). London had the highest proportion of non-white workers (33 per cent) followed by the West Midlands (11 per cent)

Table 7	Ethnic group of the workforce[1] in Healthcare Sector, All Industries and working age population, 2001						

England and Wales

Percentages

	Doctors	Dentists	Nurses	Midwives	Healthcare Sector	All Industries	Working age population
White	70	81	89	89	90	93	91
Non-white	30	19	11	11	10	7	9
Mixed	2	1	1	1	1	1	1
Asian	21	14	2	2	4	3	5
Black	3	2	5	7	3	2	2
Chinese	4	3	3	2	2	1	1
All people (=100%)(thousands)	110	20	356	24	1,439	22,931	31,945

1. Adults aged 16 to state pensionable age.
Source: Census 2001, Office for National Statistics

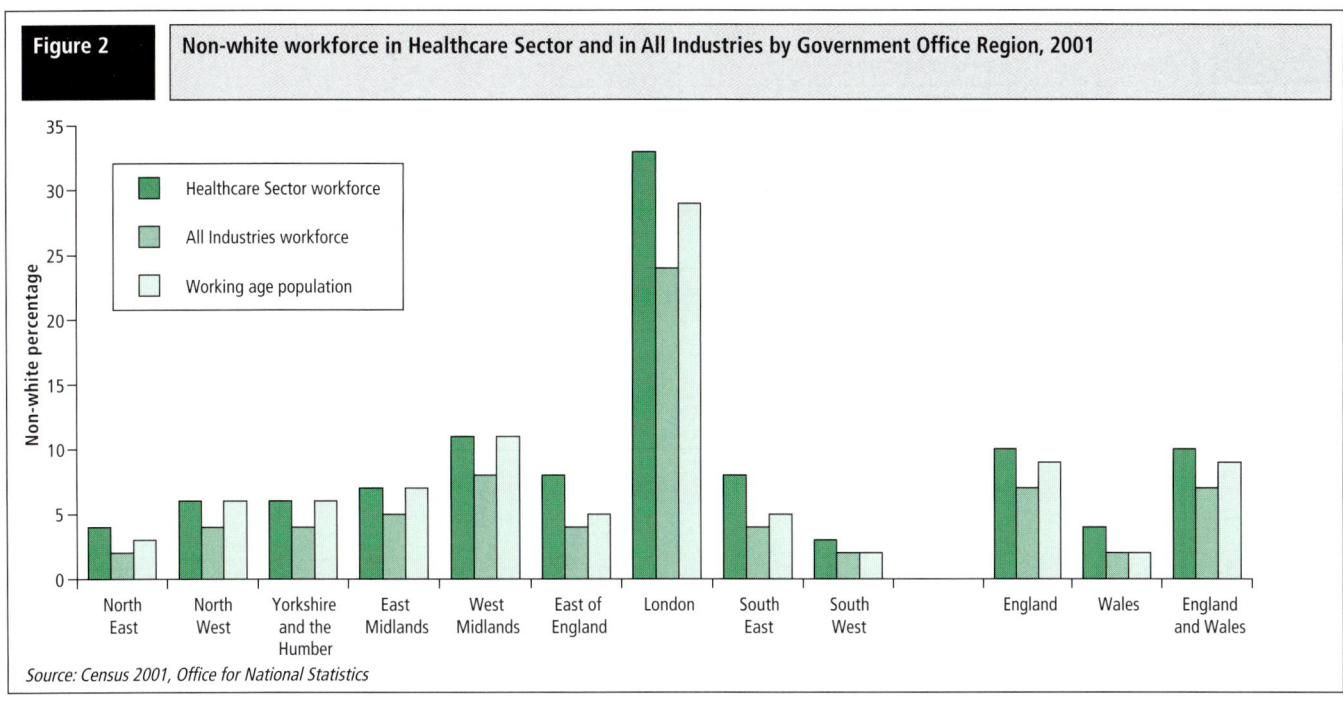

Figure 2 Non-white workforce in Healthcare Sector and in All Industries by Government Office Region, 2001

Source: Census 2001, Office for National Statistics

For the four key healthcare occupations, London had the largest proportions of non-white workers with 40 per cent of doctors, 45 per cent of dentists, 40 per cent of nurses and 46 per cent of midwives from non-white ethnic groups. This reflects the greater clustering of minority ethnic groups in London and London as the favoured destination of those immigrating to the UK. In all regions, the proportions of doctors and dentists who were non-white exceeded their equivalent share of the total working age population proportions. In most GORs, particularly in the south of the country, the proportions of non-white nurses and midwives well exceeded their equivalent proportions in the population.

Country of birth

The healthcare sector is heavily reliant on workers born overseas. Around 192,000 healthcare workers were born outside the UK, constituting 13 per cent of the entire healthcare workforce compared with 9 per cent of the workforce born overseas in the whole of the economy. The largest proportion of migrant workers came from countries in Asia, Africa and Europe (excluding UK) (3 to 4 per cent) and a further 1 per cent came from North America. For all continents, the proportion of non-UK born healthcare workers was higher than the proportions in All Industries (Table 8).

For the key healthcare occupations (doctors, dentists, nurses and midwives), the healthcare sector is even more reliant on foreign-born workers. In 2001, there were 40,000 doctors, 5,000 dentists, 58,000 nurses and 4,000 midwives born overseas. The largest proportion of foreign-born doctors and dentists came from Asia, Africa and other European countries; more than one in four doctors (28 per cent) and one in six dentists (17 per cent) were born in the developing countries of Asia and Africa. About one in six nurses (16 per cent) and midwives (16 per cent) were born overseas mostly in countries in Asia and Africa, with a much smaller proportion (2 per cent of nurses and 3 per cent of midwives) from countries in North America.

Sub-regional distribution of key healthcare workers

The broad regional distribution of key healthcare workers highlighted in an earlier section masks the much larger variations in provision per head of population found at local authority (LA) level. For example, at LA level the number of doctors per 10,000 population for Camden (102) in London was more than 20 times higher than for South Holland (5) in the East Midlands. Similarly, the rate per 10,000 population for nurses for

Table 8 Country of birth of the workforce[1] in Healthcare Sector and in All Industries, 2001

England and Wales

Percentages

	Persons aged 16 to SPA						
	Doctors	Dentists	Nurses	Midwives	Healthcare Sector	All Industries	Working age population
England and Wales	59	70	80	80	84	88	87
Rest of UK (inc. part unspecified)	5	5	3	4	3	2	2
Rest of Europe	6	5	4	4	3	3	3
Africa	8	9	4	4	3	2	2
Asia[2]	20	8	4	3	4	3	4
North America	1	1	2	3	1	1	1
South America	0	0	0	0	0	0	0
Oceania[3]	1	1	1	1	1	0	0
Other	0	0	0	0	0	0	0
All (=100%) (thousands)	110	20	356	24	1,439	22,932	31,945

1. Adults aged 16 to state pensionable age.
2. Includes Middle East, Far East and South Asia.
3. Includes Australia, New Zealand and Papua New Guinea.
Source: Census 2001, Office for National Statistics

Table 9	Local authorities with the ten highest and lowest rates of doctors and nurses (per 10,000 population), 2001

England and Wales

Local authority	Government Office Region	Doctors per 10,000 population	Local authority	Nurses per 10,000 population	Government Office Region	Nurses per 10,000 population
Areas with the highest rates			**Areas with the highest rates**			
Camden	London	102	Oxford		South East	205
Oxford	South East	84	Westminster		London	203
Westminster	London	84	Cambridge		East of England	189
Kensington and Chelsea	London	70	Camden		London	178
Cambridge	East of England	69	Newcastle upon Tyne		North East	162
Newcastle upon Tyne	North East	56	Nottingham UA		East Midlands	157
Lambeth	London	55	Norwich		East of England	154
Carrick	South West	55	Lincoln		East Midlands	150
Leicester UA	East Midlands	55	Carrick		South West	150
Hammersmith and Fulham	London	54	Exeter		South West	146
Areas with the lowest rates			**Areas with the lowest rates**			
South Derbyshire	East Midlands	6	East Northamptonshire		East Midlands	20
Ryedale	Yorkshire and the Humber	6	Tamworth		West Midlands	19
South Northamptonshire	East Midlands	5	Wokingham UA		South East	19
Cannock Chase	West Midlands	5	Rushmoor		South East	19
Maldon	East of England	5	Uttlesford		East of England	19
South Staffordshire	West Midlands	5	Three Rivers		East of England	18
Blaenau Gwent	Wales	5	South Northamptonshire		East Midlands	17
Castle Point	East of England	5	Barking and Dagenham		London	17
Swale	South East	5	Castle Point		East of England	15
South Holland	East Midlands	5	Broxbourne		East of England	14

Source: Census 2001, Office for National Statistics

Oxford (205) in the South East was 15 times higher than for Broxbourne (14) in the East of England (Table 9). In comparison, at GOR level rates for doctors varied from 31 per 10,000 for London to 17 per 10,000 for the East of England and for nurses from 82 per 10,000 for Wales to 62 per 10,000 for the East of England (Table 9).

A more detailed geographic distribution pattern of doctors and nurses for LAs is shown in Maps 1 and 2. These show local authorities categorised into five groups by rates of provision of doctors (Map 1) and nurses (Map 2) with an approximately equal number of LAs in each group (quintiles).

Local authorities with the highest level of provision of doctors and nurses were often those with major cities/ urban centres and with medical schools and teaching hospitals. By contrast local authorities with the lowest provision were mostly rural areas. It is noteworthy that only one local authority (Carrick) among the top ten local authorities with the highest rates per head of doctors and nurses was rural (Table 9). An earlier study reported similar findings on the distribution of dentists by primary care trusts.[13]

Variation in key healthcare workers by area deprivation

The relationship between levels of healthcare provision and deprivation is of policy interest when developing strategies to reduce inequalities in health. To investigate the link between healthcare provision and deprivation, two measures of area deprivation were used: the summary score of the index of multiple deprivation (IMD) and the Department of Health categorisation of LAs in England into those belonging to the relatively deprived 'Spearhead Group' or not.[14, 15] Although the IMD is also available for LAs in Wales it is calculated on a different basis to that for England. Therefore, the analysis in this section is limited to LAs in England only.

LAs were first ranked by ascending IMD score and partitioned into five groups, with approximately equal fifth population in each group. The bottom group (labelled 5) consisted of the most deprived local authorities

and the top group (1) consisted of the least deprived local authorities. Aggregating up the census counts of the LAs within each group, rates per 10,000 population of key healthcare workers were then calculated for each of the five deprivation groups.

As can be seen from Figure 3, the level of provision for doctors, nurses and midwives increases gradually with increasing deprivation. At the extremes, for the most deprived group the rates per 10,000 population of doctors (30), nurses (88) and midwives (6) were approximately two times higher than for the least deprived group (14, 47 and 3, respectively).

Figure 3	Key healthcare workers per 10,000 population by IMD deprivation quintiles, 2001

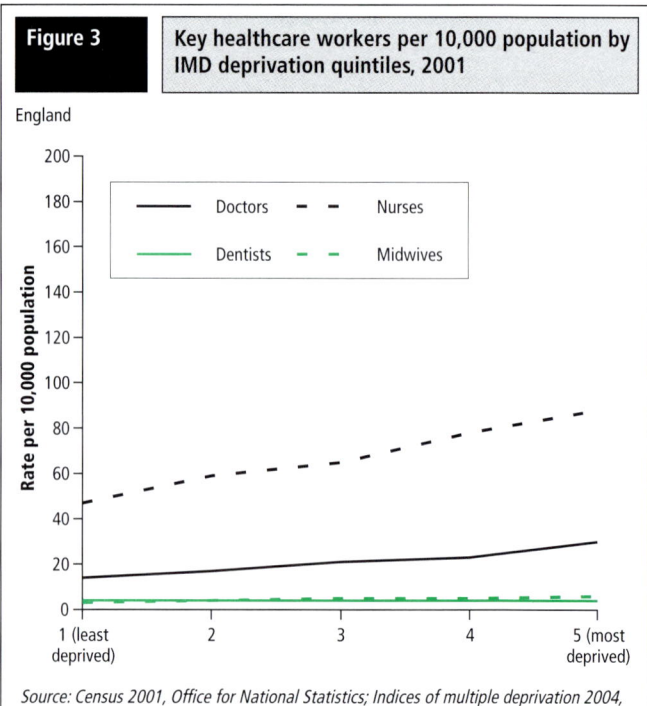

Source: Census 2001, Office for National Statistics; Indices of multiple deprivation 2004, Department of Communities and Local Government

Map 1

Number of doctors per 10,000 population by local authority, 2001

England and Wales

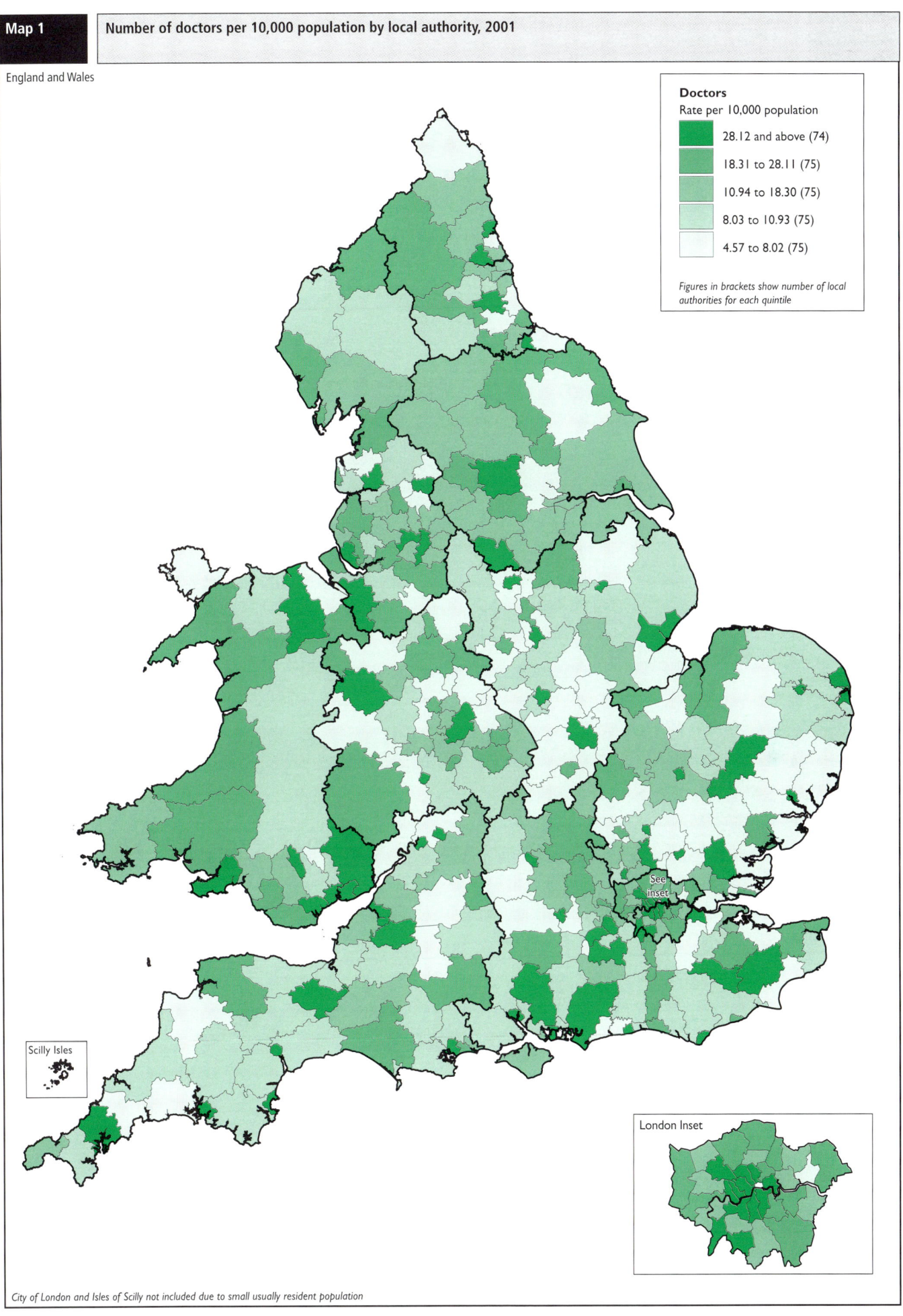

Doctors

Rate per 10,000 population

28.12 and above (74)

18.31 to 28.11 (75)

10.94 to 18.30 (75)

8.03 to 10.93 (75)

4.57 to 8.02 (75)

Figures in brackets show number of local authorities for each quintile

Scilly Isles

See Inset

London Inset

City of London and Isles of Scilly not included due to small usually resident population

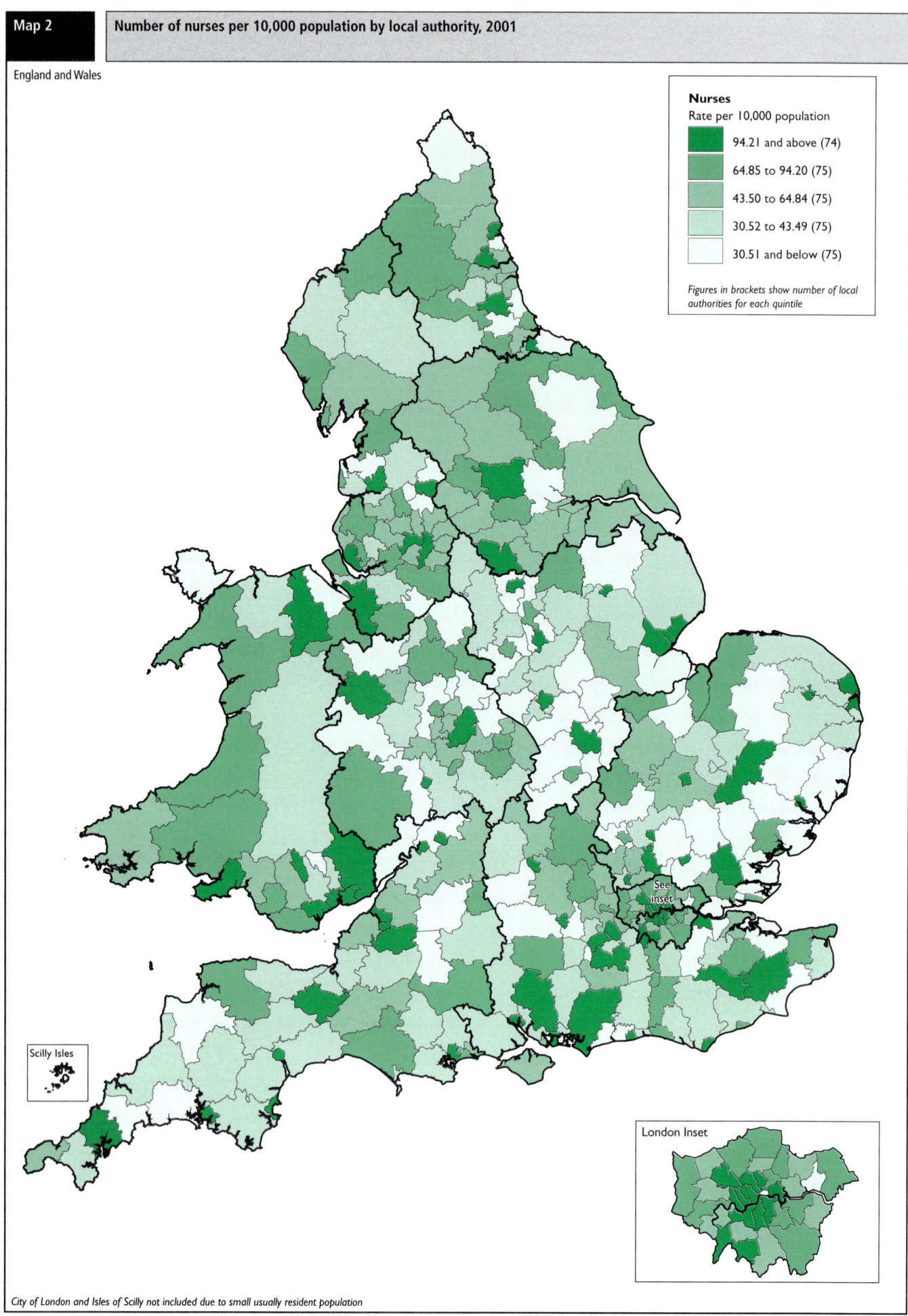

Map 2

Number of nurses per 10,000 population by local authority, 2001

England and Wales

Nurses
Rate per 10,000 population

94.21 and above (74)

64.85 to 94.20 (75)

43.50 to 64.84 (75)

30.52 to 43.49 (75)

30.51 and below (75)

Figures in brackets show number of local authorities for each quintile

See inset

Scilly Isles

London Inset

City of London and Isles of Scilly not included due to small usually resident population

Similarly, rates of key healthcare workers per 10,000 population were compared between the Spearhead Group and non-Spearhead Group of LAs. It was found that the rates for doctors, nurses and midwives were higher for the Spearhead Group than for the non-Spearhead Group. However, the distribution of dentists did not follow this pattern; rates for dentists were more or less uniform across all IMD groups and between the Spearhead and non-Spearhead Group.

The higher provision per head of population of doctors, nurses and midwives in the most deprived LAs can be explained through an analysis of the breakdown of the healthcare sector into its component industries (hospital activities, medical practice activities, dental practice activities, other human health activities). The largest proportion of the healthcare workforce was engaged in hospital activities (68 per cent) and hospitals are almost entirely located in urban population centres which score highly on the measures of deprivation. By contrast local authorities with fewer hospitals (typically rural areas) have fewer healthcare workers per capita on average and do not score highly on the deprivation index.

In comparison, dentists mostly work in Dental Practice Activities providing general dental services which are based in the community (primary care) and are spread more evenly. As a result they show a more uniform pattern of distribution than that found for the other key healthcare workers.

The relationship between deprivation and the provision of primary health and dental services was further investigated by studying the distribution of doctors recorded as employed in 'medical practice activities' and dentists working in 'dental practice activities'. These categories provide the closest approximation to doctors and dentists working in primary care. It was found that the rates for doctors and dentists in these selected sub-industries in the Spearhead Group were similar to the rates in the non-Spearhead Group. Similarly, the extent of variation in the distribution of primary care doctors and dentists was small on the basis of IMD quintiles. The number of doctors per capita in the most deprived group of LAs (7.5 per 10,000) was only slightly higher than for the least deprived group (6.9); and the number of dentists were similar in the top (3.8) and bottom quintiles (3.7). These findings suggest that, at least at the level of local authorities, the distribution of primary care doctors, dentists, nurses and midwives across deprivation categories was fairly uniform.

Comparison between the 2001 Census and the NHS workforce censuses

The Department of Health annually conducts three separate censuses of NHS staff:

- non-medical staff (staff excluding doctors and dentists) employed in hospital and community health services (HCHS)
- medical staff (doctors and dentists) employed in HCHS
- staff employed in general medical practice (e.g. GPs, nurses, receptionists etc)

These censuses are employer based and include people employed by strategic health authorities, primary care trusts, NHS Trusts and other statutory authorities. Similar censuses of NHS staff in Wales are conducted by the National Assembly for Wales. These censuses do not cover dentists employed in general dental services that are enumerated separately by the Dental Practice Board for England and Wales with data supplied by the Primary Care Trusts.

Using the NHS data for September 2000 and 2001, the NHS workforce as at 29 April 2001 (the 2001 Census day) was estimated using simple interpolation. A comparison of the 2001 Census healthcare workforce

(employees and self employed) and the NHS workforce is shown in Table 10. As expected, the overall NHS count of the workforce was lower than the 2001 Census count (by about 13 per cent). This must partly be because the 2001 Census count was more comprehensive as it included those working in private healthcare, self employed people, agency staff and those employed in outsourced activities, and other staffing categories (e.g dental nurses and receptionists in general dental services) not covered in the NHS data. However, some of the differences between the two counts are likely to be due to differences in timing, definitions and quality of returns.

Table 10	Comparison between the 2001 Census and the NHS workforce counts

England and Wales

	Census 2001 (thousands)	NHS (thousands)[1–4]	% Difference
Doctors	110	100	*9.2*
Dentists	20	23	*-14.9*
Nurses and midwives	380	370	*2.6*
All occupations	1,439	1,249	*13.2*

1. NHS totals for doctors are 'all doctors' including general practitioners.
2. NHS totals for dentists cover those employed in hospital and community health services, general dental services and personal dental services.
3. NHS total for nurses and midwives is for qualified nursing staff including GP practice nurses. In England it excludes students on training courses and in Wales it includes these.
4. NHS total for all occupations covers headcounts for hospital and community health services (including GP and practice staff) and dentists in general dental services.
Sources: For Census data, Office for National Statistics; for NHS data, Health and Social Care Information Centre (HSCIC), Dental Practice Board and National Assembly for Wales

For the key healthcare occupations, the count differences between the sources were relatively small, except for doctors where the Census count was 9.2 per cent higher than the NHS count. For dentists, on the other hand, the NHS workforce count was higher than the 2001 Census count by about 3,000 (15 per cent difference). Further analysis showed that the total number of dentists recorded in the 2001 Census (All Industries) was 23,112 which was only 0.8 per cent lower than the NHS count of 23,306. It is possible that this discrepancy was partly because of difficulties in assigning occupation to industry in the 2001 Census when key items of information on the census returns were not completed. In a related context, differences were noted when comparing the LFS and the 2001 Census workforce data sets, for example higher estimates noted from the Census for the occupation group 'Managers and senior officials' and lower for the group 'Professional occupations' than the LFS estimates.[16]

Discussion

The 2001 Census has provided useful additional insight into the structure and socio-demographic characteristics of the healthcare workforce. In particular it has enabled the study of the relative size of the healthcare sector compared to All Industries; its age, gender, ethnic group and country of birth distributions. At the local authority level, there was no evidence of lower provision of doctors (primary and secondary care combined) and dentists in deprived areas; in fact rates per head of population of doctors, nurses and midwives were the highest in the most deprived areas.

The size of the healthcare sector workforce as enumerated in the 2001 Census was considerably higher than the NHS workforce size (including general dentists). There are a number of possible reasons for the discrepancies between the two data sources including differences in definitions and coverage. Firstly, the NHS data derive from employer based surveys and covers the NHS only. It specifically excludes independent and voluntary sectors and those working in outsourced activities such as catering and cleaning. Secondly, the NHS data uses the occupation coding scheme which is internal to its management and administration and is different from the SOC 2000 classification used in the 2001 Census.[17] Although there are some similarities between the two types of classifications in general there is no direct correspondence between them.

According to the *World Health Report* 2000, human resources for healthcare are 'the stock of all individuals engaged in promoting, protecting or improving the health of population'.[1] Such an inclusive definition includes not only health professionals but also a range of other occupations such as drivers, cleaners and managers. This article has used a standard industrial classification based definition of the healthcare sector. Although this definition covers major healthcare providers such as the NHS and independent hospitals, it does not include healthcare workers working in other industries such as retail and education. The measurement of the workforce according to this definition helps to address issues such as the role of health in the economy and to assess total expenditure on healthcare (health accounts). However, the measurement of the healthcare workforce according to the broader definition presents challenging problems. It raises serious issues such as 'what constitutes a healthcare worker?' Similar problems were noted in an earlier study that analysed the social care workforce.[18]

Key findings

- In 2001, the healthcare sector in England and Wales employed 1,439,000 people of working age including 110,000 doctors, 20,000 dentists, 356,000 nurses and 24,000 midwives. This corresponds to 277 healthcare workers per 10,000 population and 21 doctors, 4 dentists, 68 nurses and 5 midwives per 10,000 population.

- The healthcare workforce was predominantly female - women made up 79 per cent of the total workforce. Overall, 62 per cent of doctors and dentists were male; but amongst those aged under 30 years, there were as many female as male doctors and slightly more female dentists.

- The healthcare sector was reliant on workers born overseas particularly in clinical occupations. Compared with 13 per cent of the total healthcare workforce born outside the UK, the proportions of doctors (36 per cent), dentists (25 per cent), nurses and midwives (16 per cent) born abroad were significantly higher.

Acknowledgements

The authors would like to express their gratitude to many colleagues at the Department of Health, Health and Social Care Information Centre and the National Assembly for Wales, in particular to Debbie Mellor, Guy Cross and Vivien Trew for many helpful discussions and providing the NHS workforce census data for this article.

References

1. World Health Organisation (2000) *World Health report 2000 – Health Systems: Improving Performance.* Available at www.who. int/whr/2000/en/

2. Department of Health (2000) *The NHS Plan – a plan for investment, a plan for reform.* Available at www.dh.gov.uk/ PublicationsAndStatistics/Publications/PublicationsPolicyAndGuid- ance/PublicationsPolicyAndGuidanceArticle/fs/en?CONTENT_ ID=4002960&chk=07GL5R

3. Health and Social Care Information Centre (2006) *NHS workforce: summary statistics for 1994–2005 and detailed results from September 2005 census and trend analysis from 1994-2005.* Available at www.ic.nhs.uk/pubs/wfdecade2005censustrends

4. Health and Social Care Information Centre (2006) General & Personal Medical Services in England: 1995–2005. Available at www.ic.nhs.uk/pubs/nhsstaff/gpbulletinpdf/file

5. National Assembly for Wales (2006) *Health Statistics Wales 2005.* Available at. www.wales.gov.uk/keypubstatisticsforwales/content/ publication/health/2004/hsw2005/hsw2005-e.htm

6. Sutherland A (2001) The NHS workforce: who they are, where they are (and where they are not). Proceedings Statistics Users' Annual Conference, 2001, Imac Research.

7. Gupta N, Diallo K *et al* (2003) Assessing human resources for health: what can be learned from labour force surveys. Human Resources for Health 2003, 1:5. Available at www.human-resources- health.com/content/1/1/5)

8. Office for National Statistics (2001) Census 2001 – England household form H1. Available at www.statistics.gov.uk/census2001/ census_form.asp

9. Office for National Statistics (1996) *Methodological guide to the 1992 Standard Industrial Classification of Economic Activities,* HMSO: London. Also available at www.statistics.gov.uk/methods_ quality/sic/default.asp

10. Office for National Statistics (2000) *Standard Occupational Classification 2000: Volumes 1 and 2*, TSO: London. Also available at www.statistics.gov.uk/methods_quality/ns_sec/soc2000.asp

11. Numbers were rounded to the nearest thousand and percentages to the nearest integer. As a result individual categories may not add up to the totals.

12. Rates of healthcare workers per 10,000 population were also calculated using two other denominators. These were, (i) the revised mid-year population (MYE) estimates 2001 (September 2004 release), and (ii) MYEs weighted for differences in the age profile of LAs using age- weights as specified in the NHS resource allocation formula (Resource Allocation: Weighted Capitation Formula, Department of Health, 2005). There was minimal difference in rates or ranking of LAs using the three alternative population bases. In this article we have used the Census 2001 population counts as the denominator for the calculation of rates.

13. Boulos M N K and Phillipps GP (2004) Is NHS dentistry in crisis? 'Traffic light' maps of dentists distribution in England and Wales. *International Journal of Health Geographics*, 3:10.

14. The IMD 2004 deprivation index (average IMD score) is a weighted score of seven domains of deprivation namely income deprivation, employment deprivation, health deprivation and disability, education, skills and training deprivation, barriers to housing and Services, living environment deprivation and Crime. The IMD 2004 are available at www.communities.gov.uk/index.asp?id=1159207

15. The Spearhead Group consists of local authorities lying in the 'worst' fifth of LAs for at least three out of five selected health deprivation indicators: IMD average score, male life expectancy at birth, female life expectancy at birth, cancer mortality rate for under 75 and circulatory disease mortality rate for under 75. In total, there are 70 local authorities in the Spearhead Group and the Department of Health especially targets these local authorities when developing policies and actions to reduce health inequalities between areas.

16. Heap D (2005) Comparison of 2001 Census and Labour Force Survey labour market indicators. *Labour Market Trends* **113**, no 1, 33–48.

17. Department of Health (2004) *National Health Service Occupational Code Manual* version 4.

18. Simon A and Owen C (2005) Using the Labour Force Survey to map the care workforce. *Labour Market Trends*, May 2005.

Appendix A

Industry classification in the 2001 Census

The 2001 Census responses to the industry question were coded using
a modified version of the UK Standard Industrial Classification 1992
(SIC(92)) which is a four level hierarchical classification.[A] At the highest
level, the modified SIC(92) was identical with SIC (92) having 17
categories known as sections, denoted by letters A to Q. At the lowest level,
the modified SIC(92) was a combination of 2nd, 3rd and 4th level SIC(92)
categories having 191 categories in total. The healthcare sector forms part
of the main industry 'N Health and Social Work' which comprises seven
subcategories at the most detailed level. The subcategories chosen to define
the healthcare sector in this article were those relating to human health
(Box one main text). Specifically, it excluded the following sub-categories:

852   Veterinary activities
853   Social work activities
850   Health and social work not otherwise specified

Occupational coding in the 2001 Census

Responses to the occupation question were coded using the Standard
Occupational Classification 2000 (SOC2000). The SOC2000 is also
a four level hierarchical classification. At the highest level it has 9
categories known as major groups and at the most detailed level it has
353 categories known as unit groups.[B] Most of the healthcare occupations
are classified under four major groups:

Managers and senior officials
Professional occupations
Associate professional and technical occupations
Personal service occupations

Table A (overleaf) shows people employed in the healthcare sector and in
All Industries by SOC 2000 major and selected unit groups.

References

A. Office for National Statistics (1996) *Methodological guide to the
    1992 Standard Industrial Classification of Economic Activities*,
    HMSO: London. Also available at. www.statistics.gov.uk/methods_
    quality/sic/default.asp

B. Office for National Statistics (2000) *Standard Occupational
    Classification 2000: Volumes 1 and 2*, TSO: London. Also available
    at www.statistics.gov.uk/methods_quality/ns_sec/soc2000.asp

| Table A | Workforce[1] in Healthcare Sector and in All Industries by SOC 2000 occupations, 2001 |

England and Wales

		Healthcare Sector[2]			All Industries		
		Males	Females	All	Males	Females	All
1.	**Managers And Senior Officials**	**26,327**	**54,979**	**81,306**	**2,321,603**	**1,157,310**	**3,478,913**
1181	Hospital and health service managers	7,633	17,254	24,887	17,252	24,233	41,485
1183	Healthcare practice managers	1,804	13,712	15,516	1,873	13,866	15,739
2.	**Professional Occupations**	**102,649**	**80,004**	**182,653**	**1,523,238**	**1,047,916**	**2,571,154**
2211	Doctors (medical practitioners)	69,010	41,380	110,390	78,348	46,246	124,594
2212	Psychologists	2,059	5,073	7,132	3,780	8,918	12,698
2213	Pharmacists/pharmacologists	1,249	3,157	4,406	8,833	10,096	18,929
2214	Ophthalmic opticians	560	632	1,192	4,634	4,464	9,098
2215	Dentists (dental practitioners)	12,619	7,675	20,294	14,698	8,428	23,126
3.	**Associate Professional And Technical Occupations**	**78,416**	**463,686**	**542,102**	**1,697,881**	**1,490,768**	**3,188,649**
3211	Nurses	37,431	318,214	355,645	47,142	371,686	418,828
3212	Midwives	159	23,967	24,126	199	25,864	26,063
3213	Paramedics	5,869	1,442	7,311	6,416	1,608	8,024
3214	Medical radiographers	2,158	12,098	14,256	2,506	12,944	15,450
3215	Chiropodists	1,996	5,208	7,204	2,674	6,453	9,127
3216	Dispensing opticians	125	194	319	1,762	2,661	4,423
3217	Pharmaceutical dispensers	474	5,666	6,140	1,475	15,497	16,972
3218	Medical and dental technicians	5,539	8,059	13,598	12,176	10,175	22,351
3221	Physiotherapists	2,753	17,559	20,312	3,423	19,575	22,998
3222	Occupational therapists	811	10,830	11,641	1,222	14,865	16,087
3223	Speech and language therapists	151	5,712	5,863	209	7,191	7,400
3567	Occupational hygienists and safety officers (health and safety)	385	301	686	15,634	4,645	20,279
3568	Environmental health officers	155	144	299	5,605	2,914	8,519
4.	**Administrative and Secretarial Occupations**	**13,012**	**217,728**	**230,740**	**677,992**	**2,352,145**	**3,030,137**
4211	Medical secretaries	324	36,895	37,219	523	40,329	40,852
4216	Receptionists	862	69,360	70,222	10,292	198,700	208,992
5.	**Skilled Trades Occupations**	**13,592**	**7,133**	**20,725**	**2,446,561**	**239,974**	**2,686,535**
6.	**Personal Service Occupations**	**36,430**	**242,178**	**278,608**	**252,783**	**1,319,799**	**1,572,582**
6111	Nursing auxiliaries and assistants	14,434	81,462	95,896	19,078	97,204	116,282
6112	Ambulance staff (excluding paramedics)	7,851	3,842	11,693	9,826	4,514	14,340
6113	Dental nurses	319	28,314	28,633	400	29,114	29,514
6115	Care assistants and home carers	10,870	95,544	106,414	55,260	421212	476,472
7.	**Sales and Customer Service Occupations**	**1,094**	**5,355**	**6,449**	**511,414**	**1,2403,29**	**1,751,743**
8.	**Process; Plant and Machine Operatives**	**7,265**	**4973**	**12,238**	**1,646,321**	**323,950**	**1,970,271**
9.	**Elementary Occupations**	**26,833**	**57,806**	**84,639**	**1,486,841**	**1,194,930**	**2,681,771**
9221	Hospital porters	10,544	609	11,153	11,592	655	12,247
	All Occupations	**305,618**	**1,133,842**	**1,439,460**	**12,564,634**	**10,367,121**	**22,931,755**

1. Adults aged 16 to state pensionable age.
2. Healthcare Sector comprises the sub-industries 'Hospital activities', 'Medical practice activities', 'Dental practice activities' and 'Other human health activities'
Source: Census 2001, Office for National Statistics

Tables

			Page
Notes to tables			59

StatBase®

Health Statistics Quarterly tables are now available on StatBase® which can be accessed via our website www.statistics.gov.uk

Symbols

    ..   not available

    :   not applicable

    -     nil or less than half the final digit shown

    blank not yet available

Notes to tables

Time series
For most tables, years start at 1971 and then continue at five-year intervals until 1991. Individual years are shown thereafter. If a year is not present the data are not available.

United Kingdom
The United Kingdom comprises England, Wales, Scotland and Northern Ireland. The Channel Islands and the Isle of Man are not part of the United Kingdom.

Population
The estimated resident population of an area includes all people who usually live there, whatever their nationality. Members of HM and US Armed Forces in England and Wales are included on residential basis wherever possible. HM Forces stationed outside England and Wales are not included. Students are taken to be resident at their term time addresses.

Further information on population estimates can be found on the National Statistics website at www.statistics.gov.uk/popest

Live births
For England and Wales, figures relate to numbers occurring in a period; for Scotland and Northern Ireland, figures relate to those registered in a period. See also Note on page 63 of *Population Trends* 67.

Perinatal mortality
In October 1992 the legal definition of a stillbirth was changed, from a baby born dead after 28 completed weeks of gestation or more, to one born dead after 24 completed weeks of gestation or more.

Period expectation of life
The life tables on which these expectations are based use death rates for the given period to describe mortality levels for each year. Each individual year shown is based on a three-year period, so that for instance 1986 represents 1985–87. More details can be found at www.gad.gov.uk/life_tables/interim_life_tables.htm

Deaths
Figures for England and Wales relate to the number of deaths registered in each year up to 1992, and the number occurring in each year from 1993, though provisional figures are registrations. Figures for both Scotland and Northern Ireland relate to the number of deaths registered in each year.

Coding cause of death
Between 1 January 1984 and 31 December 1992, ONS applied its own interpretation of the International Classification of Diseases Section Rule 3 in the coding of deaths where terminal events and other 'modes of dying' such as cardiac arrest, cardiac failure, certain thrombembolic disorders, and unspecified pneumonia and bronchopneumonia, were

stated by the certifier to be the underlying cause of death and other major pathology appeared on the certificate. In these cases ONS Rule 3 allowed the terminal event to be considered a direct sequel to the major pathology and that primary condition was selected as the underlying cause of death. Prior to 1984 and between 1 January 1993 and 31 December 2000, such certificates were coded to the terminal event. National Statistics also introduced automated coding of cause of death in 1993, which may also affect comparisons of deaths by cause from 1993. Further details can be found in the annual volumes Mortality statistics: Cause 1984, Series DH2 no. 11, and Mortality statistics: Cause 1993 (revised) and 1994, Series DH2 no. 21.

From 1 January 2001, under ICD-10, Rule 3 has again been changed – for details see the article in Health Statistics Quarterly no. 13. This has resulted in a fall in the death rates from respiratory diseases, notably pneumonia, and consequently slight rises in the rates for other causes eg. strokes. For details of the major changes between ICD-9 and ICD-10, see the articles in Health Statistics Quarterly 08, 13 and 14.

Age-standardised mortality rates
Directly age-standardised rates make allowances for changes in the age structure of the population. The age-standardised rate for a particular condition is that which would have occurred if the observed age-specific rates for the condition had applied in a given standard population. Tables 2.2 and 6.3 use the European Standard Population. This is a hypothetical population standard which is the same for both males and females allowing standardised rates to be compared for each sex, and between males and females.

Abortions
Figures relate to numbers occurring in a period.

Calculating quarterly rates
The denominators used for calculating quarterly rates for births, conceptions and abortions have been produced from mid-year population estimates and projections by linear interpolation.

Marriages and divorces
Marriages are tabulated according to date of solemnisation. Divorces are tabulated according to date of decree absolute. In Scotland a small number of late divorces from previous years are added to the current year. The term 'divorces' includes decrees of nullity. The fact that a marriage or divorce has taken place in England, Wales, Scotland or Northern Ireland does not necessarily mean that either of the parties is resident there.

Sources
Figures for Scotland and Northern Ireland have been provided by the General Register Office for Scotland and the Northern Ireland Statistics and Research Agency respectively.

Rounding
All figures are rounded independently; constituent parts may not add to totals. Generally numbers and rates per 1,000 population are rounded to one decimal place (eg 123.4); where appropriate, for small figures (below 10.0), two decimal places are given (eg 7.62). Figures which are provisional or estimated are given in less detail (eg 123 or 7.6 respectively) if their reliability does not justify giving the standard amount of detail. Where figures need to be treated with particular caution, an explanation is given as a footnote.

Latest figures
Figures for the latest quarters and years may be provisional and will be updated in future issues when later information becomes available. Where figures are not yet available, cells are left blank.

Table 1.1	Population and vital rates: international

Selected countries
Numbers (thousands)/Rates per thousand

Year	United Kingdom	Austria	Belgium	Cyprus[1]	Czech Republic	Denmark	Estonia	Finland	France	Germany[2]	Greece[3]	Hungary	Irish Republic
Population (thousands)													
1971	55,928	7,501	9,673	..	9,810	4,963	1,369	4,612	51,251	78,313	8,831	10,370	2,992
1976	56,216	7,566	9,818	498	10,094	5,073	1,435	4,726	52,909	78,337	9,167	10,590	3,238
1981	56,357	7,569	9,859	515	10,293	5,121	1,482	4,800	54,182	78,408	9,729	10,712	3,443
1986	56,684	7,588	9,862	545	10,340	5,120	1,534	4,918	55,547	77,720	9,967	10,631	3,543
1991	57,439	7,813	9,979	587	10,309	5,154	1,566	5,014	57,055	79,984	10,247	10,346	3,526
1996	58,164	7,953	10,160	661[10]	10,321	5,260	1,470	5,117	58,030	81,900	10,480	10,190	3,630
1997	58,314	7,965	10,180	670[10]	10,300	5,275	1,460	5,140	58,610	82,060	10,500	10,150	3,660
1998	58,475	7,980	10,200	679[10]	10,290	5,295	1,450	5,147	58,400	82,030	10,520	10,110	3,700
1999	58,684	7,990	10,230	686[10]	10,280	5,330	1,440	5,170	58,620	82,060	10,530	10,070	3,740
2000	58,886	8,010	10,250	694[10]	10,270	5,340	1,372	5,180	58,900	82,180	10,008	10,020	3,790
2001	59,113	8,040	10,290	701[10]	10,220	5,360	1,360	5,190	59,190	82,350	10,020	10,190	3,840
2002	59,322	8,080	10,330	710[10]	10,206	5,370	1,361	5,200	59,490	82,490	10,988	10,160	3,920
2003	59,554	8,120	10,380	721[10]	10,203	5,390	1,350	5,210	59,770	82,530	11,018	10,130	3,980
2004	59,834	8,170	10,396	730[10]	10,212	5,400	1,351 [P]	5,230	60,200	82,500	11,041	10,117	4,028
2005	60,209	8,207[16,P]	10,446[16,P]	749[10]	10,240[16,P]	5,411[16,P]	1,350[16,P]	5,250[16,P]	60,380[16,P]	82,470[16,P]	11,076[16,P]	10,097[16,P]	4,130[16,P]
Population changes (per 1,000 per annum)													
1971–76	1.0	1.7	3.0	..	5.8	4.4	9.6	4.9	6.5	0.1	7.6	4.2	16.4
1976–81	0.5	0.1	0.8	6.8	3.9	1.9	6.6	3.1	4.8	0.2	12.3	2.3	12.7
1981–86	1.2	0.5	0.1	11.7	0.9	0.0	7.0	4.9	5.0	− 1.8	4.9	− 1.5	5.8
1986–91	2.7	5.9	2.4	15.4	− 0.6	1.3	4.2	3.9	5.4	5.8	5.6	− 5.4	− 1.0
1991–96	2.5	3.6	3.6	25.2	0.1	4.1	−12.4	3.8	3.4	4.8	4.5	− 3.0	4.3
1997–98	2.8	1.9	2.0	13.4	− 1.0	3.8	− 6.8	1.4	− 3.6	− 0.4	1.9	− 3.9	10.9
1998–99	3.6	1.3	2.9	10.3	− 1.0	6.6	−16.9	4.5	3.8	− 0.4	1.0	− 4.0	10.8
1999–2000	3.4	2.5	2.0	11.7	− 1.0	1.9	−47.2	1.9	4.8	1.5	−49.6	− 5.0	13.4
2000–01	3.9	3.7	3.9	10.1	− 4.9	3.7	− 8.7	1.9	4.9	2.1	1.0	17.0	13.2
2001–02	3.5	5.0	3.9	12.8	− 2.0	1.9	0.0	1.9	5.1	1.7	96.8	− 2.9	20.8
2002–03	3.9	5.0	4.8	15.5	0.0	3.7	− 7.4	1.9	4.7	0.5	2.7	− 3.0	15.3
2003–04	4.7	6.2	1.5	12.5	1.2	1.9	0.7	3.8	7.2	− 0.4	1.9	− 1.3	12.1
2004–05	6.3	4.4	4.8	26.0	2.7	2.0	− 0.7	3.8	3.0	− 0.4	3.2	− 2.0	25.3
Live birth rate (per 1,000 population per annum)													
1971–75	14.1	13.3	13.4	17.7	17.8	14.6	15.4	13.1	16.0	10.5	15.8	16.1	22.2
1976–80	12.5	11.5	12.5	19.0	17.1	12.0	15.0	13.6	14.1	10.5	15.6	15.8	21.3
1981–85	12.9	12.0	12.0	20.2	13.5	10.2	15.6	13.4	14.2	10.7	13.3	12.3	19.2
1986–90	13.7	11.6	12.1	18.8	12.7	11.5	15.5	12.7	13.8	9.8	10.6	11.8	15.8
1991–95	13.2	11.8	12.0	16.9	11.1	13.1	10.7	12.9	12.7	10.9	9.9	11.7	14.0
1996	12.6	11.0	11.5	14.5	8.8	12.9	9.0	11.8	12.6	9.7	9.6	10.3	13.9
1997	12.5	10.4	11.4	13.9	8.8	12.8	8.7	11.5	12.4	9.9	9.7	9.9	14.4
1998	12.3	10.1	11.2	13.1	8.8	12.5	8.4	11.1	12.6	9.7	9.6	9.6	14.5
1999	11.9	9.8	11.1	12.4	8.7	12.4	8.7	11.1	12.7	9.4	11.0	9.4	14.2
2000	11.5	9.8	11.2	12.2	8.8	12.6	9.6	11.0	13.2	9.3	11.7	9.7	14.3
2001	11.3	9.4	11.1	11.6	8.9	12.2	9.3	10.8	13.0	8.9	10.2	9.5	15.1
2002	11.3	9.7	11.2	11.1	9.6	11.9	9.6	10.7	12.8	8.7	9.5	9.5	15.5
2003	11.7	9.5	11.1	11.2	9.2	12.0	9.6	10.9	12.7	8.6	9.5	9.3	15.4
2004	12.1	9.7	11.2	11.3	9.6	11.9	10.4	11.4	..	8.6	..	9.4	15.3
2005	12.0[P]	9.5[P]	..	10.9	10.0 [P]	11.9 [P]	..	11.0 [P]	..	..	..	..	14.8
Death rate (per 1,000 population per annum)													
1971–75	11.8	12.6	12.1	9.9	12.4	10.1	11.1	9.5	10.7	12.3	8.6	11.9	11.0
1976–80	11.9	12.3	11.6	10.4	12.5	10.5	12.1	9.3	10.2	12.2	8.8	12.9	10.2
1981–85	11.7	12.0	11.4	10.0	12.8	11.1	12.3	9.3	10.1	12.0	9.0	13.7	9.4
1986–90	11.4	11.1	10.8	10.2	12.4	11.5	11.9	9.8	9.5	11.6	9.3	13.5	9.1
1991–95	11.1	10.4	10.4	9.0	11.6	11.9	13.9	9.8	9.1	10.8	9.5	14.3	8.8
1996	10.9	10.0	10.3	8.5	10.9	11.6	12.9	9.6	9.2	10.8	9.6	14.0	8.7
1997	10.8	9.8	10.2	8.8	10.9	11.3	12.7	9.6	9.0	10.5	9.5	13.7	8.6
1998	10.8	9.7	10.3	8.0	10.6	11.0	13.4	9.6	9.2	10.4	9.8	13.9	8.5
1999	10.8	9.8	10.3	7.4	10.7	11.1	12.8	9.6	9.2	10.3	10.3	14.2	8.5
2000	10.3	9.6	10.2	7.7	10.6	10.9	13.4	9.5	9.1	10.2	10.2	13.5	8.2
2001	10.2	9.3	10.1	6.9	10.5	10.9	13.6	9.4	9.0	10.1	10.1	13.0	7.9
2002	10.2	9.4	10.2	7.3	10.6	10.9	13.5	9.5	9.2	10.2	10.2	13.1	7.5
2003	10.3	9.5	..	7.2	10.9	10.7	13.4	9.4	9.4	10.3	10.3	13.4	7.2
2004	9.7	9.1	9.8	7.1	10.5	10.3	13.2	9.1	8.4	10.0	..	13.1	7.0
2005	9.7 [P]	9.1 [P]	..	7.2	10.6 [P]	10.2 [P]	..	9.1 [P]	..	..	..	..	6.6

Note:
Estimated population (mid-year), live birth and death rates up to the latest available data, as given in the *United Nations Demographic Yearbook (2003 Edn)*, *United Nations Monthly Bulletin of Statistics (Sept 2006)*, and the *Eurostat Yearbook 2005 (Sept 2006)*.

1 Republic of Cyprus - Greek Cypriot controlled area only
2 Including former GDR throughout.
3 Greece - Mid-year population excludes armed forces stationed outside the country but include alien forces stationed in the area.
4 Portugal - including the Azores and Madeira islands.
5 Spain - Including the Balearic and Canary Islands.
6 The European Union consists of 25 member countries (EU25) - 1 May 2004 (10 new member countries).
7 Including the Indian held part of Jammu and Kashmir, the final status of which has not yet been determined.

8 Rates are based on births to or deaths of Japanese nationals only.
9 USA - Excluding armed forces overseas and civillian citizens absent from the country for extended periods.
10 Indicates population estimates of uncertain reliability.
11 Figures were updated taking into account the results of the 2002 All Russian Population Census.
12 Mid-year estimates have been adjusted for under-enumeration.
13 For statistical purposes the data for China do not include those for the Hong Kong SAR, Macao SAR and Taiwan province of China. Data for the period 1996 to 2000 have been adjusted on the basis of the Population Census of 2000. Data from 2001 to 2004 have been estimated on the basis of the annual national sample surveys of Population Changes. Estimate of uncertain reliability.
14 Includes Hong Kong.
15 Rate is for 1990-1995.
16 As at 1 January.
p provisional

Table 1.1 continued	Population and vital rates: international													

Selected countries   Numbers (thousands)/Rates per thousand

Year	United Kingdom	Italy	Latvia	Lithuania	Luxem-bourg	Malta	Nether-lands	Poland	Portugal[4]	Slovakia	Slovenia	Spain[5]	Sweden	EU-25[6]
Population (thousands)														
1971	55,928	54,073	2,366	3,160	342	330	13,194	32,800	8,644	4,540	1,732	34,216	8,098	..
1976	56,216	55,718	2,465	3,315	361	330	13,774	34,360	9,356	4,764	1,809	36,118	8,222	420,258
1981	56,357	56,502	2,515	3,422	365	322	14,247	35,902	9,851	4,996	1,910	37,741	8,320	428,563
1986	56,684	56,596	2,588	3,560	368	344	14,572	37,456	10,011	5,179	1,975	38,536	8,370	433,555
1991	57,439	56,751	2,662	3,742	387	358	15,070	38,245	9,871	5,283	2,002	38,920	8,617	440,927
1996	58,164	57,380	2,460	3,615	420	380	15,530	38,620	10,060	5,368	1,990	39,430	8,838	447,522
1997	58,314	57,520	2,430	3,580	416	380	15,610	38,650	10,090	5,379	1,987	39,520	8,845	448,785
1998	58,475	57,590	2,410	3,550	430	390	15,710	38,670	10,130	5,388	1,985	39,650	8,848	449,121
1999	58,684	57,650	2,390	3,520	427	390	15,810	38,650	10,170	5,393	1,978	39,840	8,860	449,994
2000	58,886	57,760	2,370	3,512	440	389	15,910	38,260	10,230	5,399	1,988	40,170	8,870	450,287
2001	59,113	57,950	2,364	3,480	440	390	16,050	38,250	10,290	5,379	1,990	40,610	8,900	452,043
2002	59,322	57,160	2,340	3,470	450	390	16,150	38,230	10,370	5,379	2,000	41,200	8,920	453,772
2003	59,554	57,610	2,332	3,460	450	400	16,220	38,200	10,440	5,379	2,000	41,870 P	8,960	455,764
2004	59,834	58,170	2,310	3,440	450	400	16,270	38,180	10,500 P	5,380	2,000	42,345	8,990	457,645
2005	60,209	58,640[16,P]	2,310[16,P]	3,410[16,P]	460[16,P]	403[16,P]	16,310[16,P]	38,174[16,P]	10,410[16,P]	5,390[16,P]	2,000[16,P]	43,430[16,P]	9,030[16,P]	459,981 P
Population changes (per 1,000 per annum)														
1971–76	1.0	6.1	8.4	9.8	10.7	0.0	8.8	9.5	16.5	9.9	8.9	11.1	3.1	..
1976–81	0.5	2.8	4.1	6.5	2.5	– 4.8	6.9	9.0	10.6	9.7	11.2	9.0	2.4	4.0
1981–86	1.2	0.3	5.8	8.1	1.8	13.7	4.6	8.7	3.2	7.3	6.8	4.2	1.2	2.3
1986–91	2.7	0.5	5.7	10.2	10.2	8.1	6.8	4.2	–2.8	4.0	2.7	2.0	5.9	3.4
1991–96	2.5	2.2	–12.8	– 1.7	17.0	8.4	4.6	2.0	3.8	3.4	–1.1	2.6	1.2	3.0
1997–98	2.8	1.2	– 8.2	– 8.4	33.7	26.3	6.4	0.5	4.0	1.5	–1.0	3.3	0.3	0.7
1998–99	3.6	1.0	– 8.3	– 8.5	– 0.7	0.0	6.4	– 0.5	3.9	0.7	–3.5	4.8	1.4	1.9
1999–2000	3.4	1.9	– 8.4	– 2.3	30.4	– 2.6	6.3	–10.1	5.9	0.9	5.1	8.3	1.1	0.7
2000–01	3.9	3.3	– 4.2	– 9.1	0.0	2.6	8.8	– 0.3	5.9	–3.7	1.0	11.0	3.4	3.9
2001–02	3.5	– 13.6	– 8.5	– 2.9	22.7	0.0	6.2	– 0.5	–7.8	0.0	5.0	14.5	2.2	3.8
2002–03	3.9	7.9	– 4.3	– 2.9	0.0	25.6	4.3	– 0.8	6.8	0.0	0.0	16.3	4.5	4.4
2003–04	4.7	9.7	– 8.6	– 5.8	0.0	0.0	3.1	– 0.5	5.7	0.0	0.0	11.3	3.3	4.3
2004–05	6.3	8.1	– 0.0	– 8.7	22.2	7.5	2.5	– 0.2	–8.6	1.9	0.0	25.6	4.4	5.1
Live birth rate (per 1,000 population per annum)														
1971–75	14.1	16.0	14.4	16.4	11.6	17.5	14.9	17.9	20.3	19.7	16.4	19.2	13.5	..
1976–80	12.5	12.6	13.9	15.4	11.2	17.0	12.6	19.3	17.9	20.3	16.3	17.1	11.6	..
1981–85	12.9	10.6	15.2	16.0	11.6	15.3	12.2	19.0	14.5	18.0	14.2	12.8	11.3	..
1986–90	13.7	9.8	15.3	15.8	12.2	16.0	12.8	15.5	11.9	15.8	12.3	10.8	13.2	..
1991–95	13.2	9.6	10.8	13.1	13.3	14.0	12.8	12.9	11.4	13.3	10.0	9.8	13.3	..
1996	12.6	9.2	7.9	10.5	13.7	13.5	12.2	11.1	11.1	11.2	9.4	9.2	10.8	10.8
1997	12.5	9.4	7.6	10.2	13.1	13.1	12.3	10.7	11.4	11.0	9.1	9.4	10.2	10.7
1998	12.3	9.3	7.5	10.4	12.7	12.2	12.7	10.2	11.4	10.7	9.0	9.3	10.1	10.5
1999	11.9	9.1	8.1	10.3	13.0	11.3	12.7	10.2	11.4	10.4	8.8	9.5	10.0	10.5
2000	11.5	9.4	8.5	9.8	13.1	11.1	13.0	9.9	11.6	10.2	9.1	9.9	10.2	10.6
2001	11.3	9.2	8.3	9.1	12.4	10.0	12.6	9.6	11.0	9.5	8.8	10.0	10.3	10.4
2002	11.3	9.4	8.6	8.7	12.0	9.8	12.5	9.3	11.0	9.5	8.8	.10.2	10.7	10.3
2003	11.7	9.4	9.0	8.9	11.8	9.8	12.3	9.2	10.8	9.6	8.7	10.5	11.1	..
2004	12.1	9.7	8.8	8.9	11.8	..	11.9	9.3	10.4	10.0	9.0	10.6	11.2	..
2005	12.1	..	9.4 P	..	11.8	..	11.5	..	..	..	..	10.7	..	..
Death rate (per 1,000 population per annum)														
1971–75	11.8	9.8	11.6	9.0	12.2	9.0	8.3	8.4	11.0	9.4	10.0	8.5	10.5	..
1976–80	11.9	9.7	12.6	10.1	11.5	9.0	8.1	9.2	10.1	9.8	9.8	8.0	10.9	..
1981–85	11.7	9.5	12.8	10.6	11.2	8.2	8.3	9.6	9.6	10.1	10.3	7.7	11.0	..
1986–90	11.4	9.4	12.4	10.3	10.5	7.4	8.5	10.0	9.6	10.1	9.6	8.2	11.1	..
1991–95	11.1	9.7	14.8	12.0	9.8	7.6	8.8	10.2	10.4	9.9	9.7	8.7	10.9	..
1996	10.9	9.6	13.8	11.6	9.4	7.4	8.9	10.0	10.8	9.8	9.4	8.9	10.6	10.1
1997	10.8	9.8	13.8	11.1	9.4	7.7	8.7	9.8	10.6	9.7	9.5	8.9	10.5	10.0
1998	10.8	10.0	14.2	11.5	9.2	8.1	8.8	9.7	10.7	9.9	9.6	9.2	10.5	10.0
1999	10.8	9.9	13.7	11.4	8.8	8.1	8.9	9.9	10.6	9.7	9.5	9.3	10.7	10.0
2000	10.3	9.7	13.6	11.1	8.6	7.7	8.8	9.6	10.3	9.8	9.3	9.0	10.5	9.8
2001	10.2	9.6	14.0	11.6	8.4	7.6	8.7	9.5	10.2	9.7	9.3	8.9	10.5	9.7
2002	10.2	9.8	13.9	11.8	8.4	7.8	8.8	9.4	10.2	9.6	9.4	8.9	10.6	9.8
2003	10.3	10.2	13.9	11.9	9.0	7.7	8.7	9.6	10.4	9.7	9.7	9.2	10.4	..
2004	9.7	9.4	13.9	12.0	7.6	..	8.4	9.5	9.7	9.6	9.3	8.2	10.1	..
2005	9.7 P	..	14.2 P	..	8.0	..	8.4 P	..	..	..	..	8.9	8.9	..

See notes on first page of table.

Table 1.1 continued	Population and vital rates: international									

Selected countries   Numbers (thousands)/Rates per thousand

Year	United Kingdom	EU–25[6]	Russian Federation	Australia	Canada	New Zealand	China	India[7]	Japan[8]	USA[9]
Population (thousands)										
1971	55,928	..	130,934	13,067	22,026	2,899	852,290 [13]	551,311	105,145	207,661
1976	56,216	420,258	135,027	14,033	23,517	3,163	937,170 [13]	617,248	113,094	218,035
1981	56,357	428,563	139,225	14,923	24,900	3,195	1,008,460 [13]	675,185	117,902	229,958
1986	56,684	433,555	144,154	16,018	26,204	3,317	1,086,733 [13]	767,199	121,672	240,680
1991	57,439	440,927	148,245	17,284	28,031	3,477	1,170,100 [13]	851,897	123,964	252,639
1996	58,164	447,552	148,160[11]	18,311[12]	29,610[12]	3,730	1,217,550 [13]	941,580 [10]	125,761	265,463
1997	58,314	448,785	147,920[11]	18,524[12]	29,910[12]	3,780	1,230,080 [13]	959,800 [10]	126,065	268,008
1998	58,475	449,121	147,670[11]	18,710[12]	30,160[12]	3,820	1,248,100 [13]	978,080 [10]	126,400	270,300
1999	58,684	449,994	147,210[11]	18,930[12]	30,490[12]	3,840	1,252,740 [13]	996,430 [10]	126,630	272,691
2000	58,886	450,287	146,600[11]	19,150[12]	30,770[12]	3,860	1,262,650 [13]	1,014,820 [10]	126,840	282,190
2001	59,113	452,043	145,976[11]	19,410[12]	31,110[12]	3,850	1,271,850 [13]	1,033,325 [10]	127,130	285,110
2002	59,322	453,772	145,306 [11]	19,640[12]	31,410[12]	3,940	1,280,400 [13]	1,050,640 [10]	127,400	287,980
2003	59,554	455,764	144,566 [11]	19,870[12]	31,630[12]	4,010	1,288,400 [13]	1,068,210 [10]	127,650	290,850
2004	59,834	457,645	143,820 [11]	20,110[12]	31,950[12]	4,060	1,296,080 [13]	1,085,600 [10]	126,670	293,660
2005	60.209	459,981[P]	143,500 [11]	..	32,270[12,P]	4,100 [P]	..	1,097,000 [10]	..	296,410
Population changes (per 1,000 per annum)										
1971–76	1.0	..	6.3	14.8	13.5	18.2	19.9	23.9	15.1	10.0
1976–81	0.5	4.0	6.2	12.7	11.8	2.0	15.2	18.8	8.5	10.9
1981–86	1.2	2.3	7.1	14.7	10.5	7.6	15.5	27.3	6.4	9.3
1986–91	2.6	3.4	5.7	15.8	13.9	9.6	15.3	22.1	3.8	9.9
1991–96	2.5	3.0	−0.7	11.9	11.3	15.1	10.3	21.1	2.9	10.2
1997–98	2.8	0.7	− 4.1	10.0	8.4	10.6	3.7	19.0	2.7	8.8
1998–99	3.6	1.9	− 2.6	11.8	10.9	5.2	7.9	18.8	1.8	34.8
1999–2000	3.4	0.7	− 2.9	11.6	9.2	5.2	7.3	18.5	1.7	10.3
2000–01	3.9	3.9	2.9	13.6	11.0	− 2.6	7.3	18.2	2.3	10.3
2001–02	3.5	3.8	− 4.6	11.8	9.6	23.4	6.7	16.8	2.1	10.1
2002–03	3.9	4.4	− 5.1	11.7	7.0	17.8	6.2	16.7	2.0	10.0
2003–04	4.7	4.3	− 5.2	12.1	10.1	12.5	6.0	16.3	0.2	9.7
2004–05	6.3	5.1	− 2.2	..	10.0	9.9	..	10.5	..	9.4
Live birth rate (per 1,000 population per annum)										
1971–75	14.1	..	..	18.8	15.9	20.4	27.2	35.6	18.6	15.3
1976–80	12.5	..	..	15.7	15.5	16.8	18.6	33.4	14.9	15.2
1981–85	12.9	..	..	15.6	15.1	15.8	19.2	..	12.6	15.7
1986–90	13.7	..	..	15.1	14.8	17.1	..	..	10.6	16.0
1991–95	13.2	..	10.2	..	..	..	18.5 [15]	..	..	..
1996	12.6	10.8	8.8	13.9	12.3	15.4	9.8	27.3	9.6	14.7
1997	12.5	10.7	8.6	13.6	11.6	15.4	9.1 [14]	..	9.5	14.5
1998	12.3	10.5	8.7	13.3	11.3	14.5	8.1 [14]	26.2	9.5	14.6
1999	11.9	10.5	8.3	13.1	11.1	14.9	7.8 [14]	26.0	9.3	14.5
2000	11.5	10.6	8.6	13.0	10.7	14.7	8.1 [14]	25.8	9.4	14.7
2001	11.3	10.4	9.0	12.7	10.8	14.4	7.2 [14]	25.4	9.2	14.1
2002	11.3	10.3	9.6	12.8	10.5	13.7	7.1 [14]	25.0	9.1	13.9
2003	11.7	..	10.2	12.6	10.5	14.0	6.9 [14]	24.8	8.8	14.1
2004	12.1	..	10.5	12.7	..	14.3	7.2 [14]	..	8.7	..
2005	12.1	..	..	12.9	..	..	..	..	..	..
Death rate (per 1,000 population per annum)										
1971–75	11.8	..	..	8.2	7.4	8.4	7.3	15.5	6.4	9.1
1976–80	11.9	..	..	7.6	7.2	8.2	6.6	13.8	6.1	8.7
1981–85	11.7	..	..	7.3	7.0	8.1	6.7	..	6.1	8.6
1986–90	11.4	..	..	7.2	7.3	8.2	..	..	6.4	8.7
1991–95	11.1	..	13.7	..	..	..	..	..	..	..
1996	10.9	10.1	14.1	7.0	7.2	7.6	5.0	8.9	7.1	8.7
1997	10.8	10.0	13.7	7.0	7.2	7.3	4.9 [14]	..	7.2	8.6
1998	10.8	10.0	13.5	6.8	7.2	6.9	5.0 [14]	9.0	7.4	8.6
1999	10.8	10.0	14.6	6.8	7.2	7.3	5.0 [14]	8.7	7.8	8.8
2000	10.3	9.8	15.2	6.7	7.1	6.9	5.1 [14]	8.5	7.6	8.7
2001	10.2	9.7	15.4	6.6	7.1	7.2	5.0 [14]	8.4	7.6	8.5
2002	10.2	9.8	16.1	6.8	7.1	7.1	5.0 [14]	8.1	7.7	8.5
2003	10.3	..	16.4	6.7	7.2	7.0	5.4 [14]	8.0	8.0	8.4
2004	9.7	..	16.0	6.6	..	7.0	5.3 [14]	..	8.1	..
2005	9.7 [P]	..	..	6.4	..	..	..	..	..	..

See notes on first page of table.

Table 1.2	Population: national

Constituent countries of the United Kingdom

Numbers (thousands) and percentage age distribution

Mid-year	United Kingdom	Great Britain	England and Wales	England	Wales	Scotland	Northern Ireland
Estimates							
1971	55,928	54,388	49,152	46,412	2,740	5,236	1,540
1976	56,216	54,693	49,459	46,660	2,799	5,233	1,524
1981	56,357	54,815	49,634	46,821	2,813	5,180	1,543
1986	56,684	55,110	49,999	47,188	2,811	5,112	1,574
1991	57,439	55,831	50,748	47,875	2,873	5,083	1,607
1993	57,714	56,078	50,986	48,102	2,884	5,092	1,636
1994	57,862	56,218	51,116	48,229	2,887	5,102	1,644
1995	58,025	56,376	51,272	48,383	2,889	5,104	1,649
1996	58,164	56,503	51,410	48,519	2,891	5,092	1,662
1997	58,314	56,643	51,560	48,665	2,895	5,083	1,671
1998	58,475	56,797	51,720	48,821	2,900	5,077	1,678
1999	58,684	57,005	51,933	49,033	2,901	5,072	1,679
2000	58,886	57,203	52,140	49,233	2,907	5,063	1,683
2001	59,113	57,424	52,360	49,450	2,910	5,064	1,689
2002	59,322	57,625	52,570	49,647	2,923	5,055	1,697
2003	59,554	57,851	52,794	49,856	2,938	5,057	1,703
2004	59,834	58,124	53,046	50,093	2,952	5,078	1,710
2005	60,209	58,485	53,390	50,432	2,959	5,095	1,724
2005 by age group **(percentages)**							
0–4	5.7	5.7	5.7	5.7	5.4	5.2	6.4
5–15	13.6	13.5	13.6	13.5	13.8	13.0	15.7
16–44	40.2	40.2	40.3	40.4	37.5	39.6	41.3
45–64M/59F	21.8	21.9	21.8	21.7	22.8	23.0	20.4
65M/60F–74	11.0	11.1	11.0	10.9	12.1	11.7	10.0
75 and over	7.6	7.7	7.7	7.7	8.4	7.4	6.3
Projections[1]							
2006	60,533	58,800	53,691	50,714	2,977	5,108	1,733
2011	61,892	60,124	55,005	51,967	3,037	5,120	1,767
2016	63,304	61,504	56,378	53,276	3,102	5,126	1,800
2021	64,727	62,897	57,770	54,605	3,165	5,127	1,830
2021 by age groups **(percentages)**							
0–4	5.6	5.6	5.6	5.6	5.3	5.0	5.9
5–15	12.0	12.0	12.1	12.1	11.8	11.2	13.0
16–44	36.8	36.8	36.9	37.1	34.7	35.0	37.2
45–64[2]	25.9	25.9	25.8	25.8	25.9	27.6	25.6
65–74[2]	10.2	10.2	10.1	10.0	11.6	11.3	9.5
75 and over	9.5	9.5	9.5	9.4	10.6	10.0	8.6

Note: Figures may not add exactly due to rounding.

1   National projections based on mid-2004 population estimates.

2   Between 2010 and 2020, state retirement age will change from 65 years for men and 60 years for women to 65 years for both sexes.

Tel no. for all queries relating to population estimates - 01329 813318

Table 1.3	Population: subnational

Government Office Regions of England

Numbers (thousands) and percentage age distribution

Mid-year	North East	North West	Yorkshire and The Humber	East Midlands	West Midlands	East	London	South East	South West
Estimates									
1971	2,679	7,108	4,902	3,652	5,146	4,454	7,529	6,830	4,112
1976	2,671	7,043	4,924	3,774	5,178	4,672	7,089	7,029	4,280
1981	2,636	6,940	4,918	3,853	5,187	4,854	6,806	7,245	4,381
1986	2,594	6,833	4,884	3,908	5,180	4,999	6,774	7,468	4,548
1991	2,587	6,843	4,936	4,011	5,230	5,121	6,829	7,629	4,688
1993	2,594	6,847	4,954	4,056	5,246	5,154	6,844	7,673	4,734
1994	2,589	6,839	4,960	4,072	5,249	5,178	6,874	7,712	4,757
1995	2,583	6,828	4,961	4,092	5,257	5,206	6,913	7,763	4,782
1996	2,576	6,810	4,961	4,108	5,263	5,233	6,974	7,800	4,793
1997	2,568	6,794	4,958	4,120	5,262	5,267	7,015	7,853	4,827
1998	2,561	6,792	4,958	4,133	5,271	5,302	7,065	7,889	4,849
1999	2,550	6,773	4,956	4,152	5,272	5,339	7,154	7,955	4,881
2000	2,543	6,774	4,959	4,168	5,270	5,375	7,237	7,991	4,917
2001	2,540	6,773	4,977	4,190	5,281	5,400	7,322	8,023	4,943
2002	2,538	6,783	4,993	4,223	5,304	5,422	7,371	8,044	4,968
2003	2,539	6,805	5,009	4,252	5,320	5,463	7,388	8,080	4,999
2004	2,545	6,827	5,039	4,280	5,334	5,491	7,429	8,110	5,038
2005	2,558	6,846	5,064	4,306	5,365	5,542	7,518	8,164	5,068
2005 by age group **(percentages)**									
0–4	*5.3*	*5.6*	*5.7*	*5.5*	*5.9*	*5.7*	*6.6*	*5.6*	*5.1*
5–15	*13.3*	*13.9*	*13.8*	*13.6*	*14.0*	*13.7*	*12.7*	*13.7*	*13.2*
16–44	*39.2*	*39.5*	*39.7*	*39.2*	*39.3*	*38.5*	*48.9*	*39.0*	*36.9*
45–64M/59F	*22.8*	*22.1*	*22.0*	*22.6*	*21.8*	*22.4*	*18.1*	*22.4*	*23.0*
65M/60F–74	*11.8*	*11.3*	*11.2*	*11.3*	*11.3*	*11.4*	*8.1*	*11.1*	*12.4*
75 and over	*7.7*	*7.5*	*7.7*	*7.8*	*7.7*	*8.1*	*5.7*	*8.2*	*9.4*
Projections[1]									
2005	2,550	6,852	5,074	4,309	5,356	5,532	7,522	8,162	5,078
2009	2,563	6,926	5,189	4,409	5,420	5,666	7,762	8,320	5,210
2014	2,581	7,028	5,332	4,531	5,504	5,830	8,049	8,518	5,373
2019	2,603	7,141	5,478	4,655	5,594	6,000	8,332	8,734	5,543
2024	2,624	7,247	5,617	4,774	5,680	6,164	8,587	8,953	5,712
2029	2,638	7,331	5,738	4,874	5,749	6,308	8,807	9,150	5,863
2029 by age group **(percentages)**									
0–4	*5.0*	*5.3*	*5.4*	*5.0*	*5.6*	*5.2*	*6.4*	*5.3*	*4.7*
5–15	*11.6*	*12.2*	*12.1*	*11.7*	*12.6*	*12.0*	*12.0*	*12.1*	*11.2*
16–44	*35.1*	*35.7*	*36.2*	*34.1*	*35.3*	*33.8*	*44.9*	*35.1*	*32.7*
45–64[2]	*24.4*	*24.5*	*24.3*	*25.0*	*24.2*	*24.9*	*23.5*	*24.7*	*25.0*
65–74[2]	*12.0*	*11.1*	*10.9*	*11.7*	*10.7*	*11.4*	*7.0*	*10.8*	*12.4*
75 and over	*11.9*	*11.2*	*11.1*	*12.4*	*11.7*	*12.7*	*6.2*	*12.0*	*14.0*

Note: Figures may not add exactly due to rounding.

1   These projections are based on the mid-2004 population estimates and are consistent with the 2004-based national projections produced by the Government Actuary's Department and presented in Table 1.2.

2   Between 2010 and 2020, state retirement age will change from 65 years for men and 60 years for women to 65 years for both sexes.

Tel no. for all queries relating to population estimates:- 01329 813318.

Table 1.4	Population: age and sex

Constituent countries of the United Kingdom

Numbers (thousands)

Mid-year	All ages	Under 1	1–4	5–14	15–24	25–34	35–44	45–59	60–64	65–74	75–84	85–89	90 and over	Under 16	16–64/59	65/60 and over
United Kingdom																
Persons																
1981	56,357	730	2,726	8,147	9,019	8,010	6,774	9,540	2,935	5,195	2,677	..	..	12,543	33,780	10,035
1986	56,684	748	2,886	7,143	9,200	8,007	7,711	9,212	3,069	5,020	2,971	716	..	11,645	34,725	10,313
1991	57,439	790	3,077	7,141	8,168	8,898	7,918	9,500	2,888	5,067	3,119	626	248	11,685	35,197	10,557
1996	58,164	719	3,019	7,544	7,231	9,131	7,958	10,553	2,785	5,066	3,129	711	317	12,018	35,498	10,649
1998	58,475	713	2,930	7,649	7,079	8,948	8,285	10,767	2,835	4,979	3,211	736	344	12,013	35,746	10,717
1999	58,684	704	2,896	7,684	7,090	8,795	8,474	10,887	2,877	4,948	3,230	746	354	12,011	35,928	10,745
2000	58,886	682	2,869	7,652	7,139	8,646	8,678	11,011	2,900	4,940	3,249	755	364	11,959	36,138	10,788
2001	59,113	663	2,819	7,624	7,261	8,475	8,846	11,168	2,884	4,947	3,296	753	377	11,863	36,406	10,845
2002	59,322	661	2,753	7,601	7,403	8,256	9,002	11,316	2,890	4,969	3,345	739	388	11,783	36,622	10,916
2003	59,554	679	2,703	7,542	7,575	8,070	9,108	11,424	2,943	5,005	3,401	706	399	11,712	36,828	11,014
2004	59,834	705	2,684	7,477	7,720	7,937	9,192	11,517	3,021	5,033	3,435	703	409	11,646	37,064	11,125
2005	60,209	716	2,712	7,382	7,871	7,897	9,246	11,624	3,114	5,048	3,424	756	419	11,598	37,368	11,244
Males																
1981	27.412	374	1,400	4,184	4,596	4,035	3,409	4,711	1,376	2,264	922	..	..	6,439	17,646	3,327
1986	27,542	384	1,478	3,664	4,663	4,022	3,864	4,572	1,463	2,206	1,060	166	..	5,968	18,142	3,432
1991	27,909	403	1,572	3,655	4,146	4,432	3,949	4,732	1,390	2,272	1,146	166	46	5,976	18,303	3,630
1996	28,287	369	1,547	3,857	3,652	4,540	3,954	5,244	1,360	2,311	1,187	201	65	6,148	18,375	3,764
1998	28,458	365	1,503	3,916	3,570	4,444	4,109	5,342	1,388	2,293	1,240	215	73	6,151	18,486	3,821
1999	28,578	361	1,485	3,934	3,577	4,367	4,200	5,400	1,409	2,289	1,259	221	77	6,152	18,582	3,845
2000	28,690	350	1,469	3,920	3,606	4,292	4,298	5,457	1,420	2,294	1,278	225	81	6,128	18,685	3,878
2001	28,832	338	1,445	3,906	3,672	4,215	4,382	5,534	1,412	2,308	1,308	227	85	6,077	18,827	3,928
2002	28,963	339	1,409	3,895	3,754	4,107	4,460	5,604	1,414	2,327	1,339	226	89	6,037	18,945	3,982
2003	29,108	349	1,384	3,864	3,850	4,018	4,514	5,653	1,439	2,354	1,371	219	94	6,002	19,068	4,038
2004	29,271	361	1,375	3,833	3,933	3,954	4,553	5,694	1,476	2,374	1,394	224	99	5,970	19,210	4,091
2005	29,479	367	1,389	3,785	4,018	3,933	4,579	5,746	1,519	2,389	1,403	248	103	5,946	19,390	4,143
Females																
1981	28,946	356	1,327	3,963	4,423	3,975	3,365	4,829	1,559	2,931	1,756	..	..	6,104	16,134	6,708
1986	29,142	364	1,408	3,480	4,538	3,985	3,847	4,639	1,606	2,814	1,911	550	..	5,678	16,583	6,881
1991	29,530	387	1,505	3,487	4,021	4,466	3,968	4,769	1,498	2,795	1,972	460	202	5,709	16,894	6,927
1996	29,877	350	1,472	3,687	3,579	4,591	4,005	5,309	1,426	2,755	1,942	509	252	5,870	17,123	6,885
1998	30,017	348	1,427	3,733	3,509	4,504	4,176	5,425	1,447	2,686	1,971	521	271	5,861	17,260	6,895
1999	30,106	343	1,412	3,750	3,513	4,428	4,273	5,487	1,468	2,659	1,971	525	277	5,859	17,346	6,900
2000	30,196	333	1,399	3,732	3,533	4,353	4,380	5,554	1,481	2,646	1,971	530	283	5,832	17,453	6,911
2001	30,281	324	1,375	3,718	3,589	4,260	4,465	5,634	1,473	2,640	1,987	526	292	5,786	17,579	6,917
2002	30,359	323	1,344	3,706	3,649	4,149	4,542	5,712	1,476	2,641	2,006	512	299	5,747	17,677	6,934
2003	30,446	331	1,319	3,677	3,725	4,052	4,594	5,771	1,504	2,651	2,030	486	305	5,710	17,760	6,976
2004	30,563	343	1,309	3,644	3,787	3,983	4,640	5,823	1,545	2,659	2,041	478	310	5,676	17,854	7,034
2005	30,730	349	1,323	3,597	3,853	3,964	4,667	5,878	1,595	2,659	2,022	508	316	5,652	17,978	7,100
England and Wales																
Persons																
1981	49,634	634	2,372	7,085	7,873	7,086	5,996	8,433	2,607	4,619	2,388	383	157	10,910	29,796	8,928
1986	49,999	654	2,522	6,226	8,061	7,052	6,856	8,136	2,725	4,470	2,655	461	182	10,161	30,647	9,190
1991	50,748	698	2,713	6,248	7,165	7,862	7,022	8,407	2,553	4,506	2,790	561	223	10,247	31,100	9,400
1996	51,410	637	2,668	6,636	6,336	8,076	7,017	9,363	2,457	4,496	2,801	639	285	10,584	31,353	9,474
1998	51,720	631	2,594	6,740	6,212	7,925	7,304	9,552	2,503	4,411	2,875	661	311	10,599	31,591	9,530
1999	51,933	625	2,566	6,779	6,228	7,800	7,475	9,656	2,542	4,381	2,891	671	319	10,608	31,771	9,554
2000	52,140	607	2,544	6,757	6,275	7,682	7,661	9,764	2,564	4,372	2,907	680	328	10,572	31,977	9,591
2001	52,360	589	2,502	6,740	6,387	7,536	7,816	9,898	2,549	4,377	2,947	677	340	10,495	32,226	9,639
2002	52,570	589	2,445	6,726	6,520	7,349	7,962	10,027	2,553	4,395	2,990	664	351	10,435	32,435	9,700
2003	52,794	606	2,402	6,677	6,681	7,190	8,062	10,116	2,599	4,427	3,039	634	360	10,381	32,627	9,786
2004	53,046	629	2,388	6,621	6,817	7,073	8,140	10,188	2,669	4,451	3,067	633	370	10,327	32,837	9,882
2005	53,390	639	2,413	6,537	6,959	7,039	8,195	10,272	2,757	4,463	3,056	681	379	10,287	33,114	9,989
Males																
1981	24,160	324	1,218	3,639	4,011	3,569	3,024	4,178	1,227	2,020	825	94	32	5,601	15,589	2,970
1986	24,311	335	1,292	3,194	4,083	3,542	3,438	4,053	1,302	1,972	951	115	35	5,208	16,031	3,072
1991	24,681	356	1,385	3,198	3,638	3,920	3,504	4,199	1,234	2,027	1,029	150	42	5,240	16,193	3,248
1996	25,030	327	1,368	3,393	3,202	4,020	3,489	4,659	1,205	2,059	1,067	182	59	5,416	16,247	3,367
1998	25,201	323	1,331	3,451	3,135	3,942	3,627	4,744	1,230	2,041	1,115	194	66	5,428	16,355	3,417
1999	25,323	321	1,315	3,471	3,144	3,880	3,711	4,793	1,250	2,036	1,132	200	70	5,434	16,452	3,437
2000	25,438	311	1,303	3,462	3,172	3,823	3,802	4,842	1,259	2,040	1,148	204	73	5,416	16,556	3,466
2001	25,574	301	1,281	3,453	3,231	3,758	3,881	4,907	1,252	2,052	1,175	206	77	5,376	16,688	3,510
2002	25,702	302	1,251	3,446	3,307	3,664	3,955	4,967	1,253	2,069	1,203	205	81	5,346	16,799	3,557
2003	25,841	311	1,230	3,422	3,394	3,588	4,006	5,008	1,274	2,092	1,231	199	85	5,320	16,914	3,607
2004	25,988	322	1,223	3,395	3,473	3,531	4,043	5,040	1,307	2,109	1,251	203	90	5,294	17,041	3,653
2005	26,179	327	1,236	3,352	3.553	3,511	4,070	5,082	1,347	2.122	1.259	225	94	5,275	17,205	3,699
Females																
1981	25,474	310	1,154	3,446	3,863	3,517	2,972	4,255	1,380	2,599	1,564	289	126	5,309	14,207	5,958
1986	25,687	319	1,231	3,032	3,978	3,509	3,418	4,083	1,422	2,498	1,704	346	148	4,953	14,616	6,118
1991	26,067	342	1,328	3,050	3,527	3,943	3,517	4,208	1,319	2,479	1,761	411	181	5,007	14,908	6,152
1996	26,381	310	1,300	3,243	3,134	4,056	3,528	4,704	1,252	2,437	1,734	457	227	5,168	15,106	6,107
1998	26,519	308	1,264	3,289	3,077	3,983	3,677	4,808	1,272	2,370	1,760	467	244	5,171	15,235	6,113
1999	26,610	305	1,251	3,308	3,083	3,920	3,763	4,863	1,292	2,345	1,759	472	249	5,175	15,318	6,117
2000	26,702	296	1,241	3,296	3,103	3,859	3,859	4,923	1,304	2,332	1,758	476	255	5,155	15,421	6,126
2001	26,786	288	1,220	3,287	3,156	3,778	3,935	4,992	1,297	2,326	1,771	471	263	5,119	15,538	6,129
2002	26,868	287	1,194	3,280	3,214	3,684	4,007	5,059	1,300	2,326	1,787	460	270	5,090	15,635	6,143
2003	26,953	295	1,172	3,256	3,286	3,602	4,056	5,108	1,325	2,335	1,808	436	275	5,061	15,714	6,179
2004	27,057	307	1,164	3,226	3,344	3,542	4,098	5,148	1,362	2,341	1,816	429	280	5,033	15,796	6,229
2005	27,211	312	1,177	3,185	3,406	3,528	4,124	5,190	1,410	2,342	1,798	456	285	5,013	15,909	6,290

Note: Figures may not add exactly due to rounding.

Tel no. for all enquiries relating to population estimates:- 01329 813318

Table 1.4 continued	Population: age and sex

Constituent countries of the United Kingdom

Numbers (thousands)

Mid-year	All ages	Under 1	1–4	5–14	15–24	25–34	35–44	45–59	60–64	65–74	75–84	85–89	90 and over	Under 16	16–64/59	65/60 and over
England																
Persons																
1981	46,821	598	2,235	6,678	7,440	6,703	5,663	7,948	2,449	4,347	2,249	362	149	10,285	28,133	8,403
1986	47,188	618	2,380	5,869	7,623	6,682	6,478	7,672	2,559	4,199	2,501	435	172	9,583	28,962	8,643
1991	47,875	660	2,560	5,885	6,772	7,460	6,633	7,920	2,399	4,222	2,626	529	210	9,658	29,390	8,827
1996	48,519	603	2,523	6,255	5,985	7,667	6,638	8,822	2,310	4,217	2,631	602	269	9,985	29,639	8,895
1998	48,821	598	2,453	6,356	5,869	7,524	6,915	8,999	2,353	4,140	2,698	623	293	10,003	29,868	8,950
1999	49,033	592	2,427	6,394	5,881	7,412	7,079	9,097	2,391	4,114	2,713	632	301	10,014	30,044	8,975
2000	49,233	575	2,406	6,375	5,923	7,304	7,257	9,199	2,411	4,107	2,727	641	309	9,980	30,243	9,010
2001	49,450	558	2,366	6,359	6,032	7,171	7,407	9,327	2,395	4,113	2,764	638	321	9,908	30,487	9,055
2002	49,647	558	2,312	6,345	6,155	6,993	7,548	9,448	2,397	4,130	2,804	625	331	9,853	30,683	9,111
2003	49,856	575	2,273	6,300	6,304	6,843	7,643	9,533	2,438	4,159	2,852	596	340	9,804	30,862	9,190
2004	50,093	597	2,260	6,247	6,432	6,732	7,718	9,600	2,503	4,181	2,879	594	349	9,754	31,059	9,280
2005	50,432	606	2,287	6,169	6,570	6,701	7,772	9,682	2,586	4,191	2,870	640	357	9,721	31,330	9,381
Males																
1981	22,795	306	1,147	3,430	3,790	3,377	2,856	3,938	1,154	1,902	777	89	30	5,280	14,717	2,798
1986	22,949	317	1,219	3,010	3,862	3,357	3,249	3,822	1,224	1,853	897	108	33	4,911	15,147	2,891
1991	23,291	336	1,307	3,011	3,439	3,721	3,311	3,957	1,159	1,900	970	141	39	4,938	15,302	3,050
1996	23,629	309	1,294	3,198	3,023	3,818	3,302	4,390	1,133	1,932	1,003	172	55	5,110	15,358	3,161
1998	23,794	306	1,258	3,254	2,960	3,743	3,436	4,470	1,157	1,916	1,047	183	62	5,123	15,462	3,209
1999	23,916	304	1,243	3,274	2,969	3,689	3,517	4,516	1,176	1,913	1,063	188	66	5,129	15,558	3,229
2000	24,030	294	1,232	3,266	2,995	3,638	3,604	4,562	1,184	1,917	1,078	192	69	5,113	15,661	3,256
2001	24,166	285	1,212	3,257	3,053	3,580	3,681	4,624	1,176	1,928	1,103	194	73	5,075	15,793	3,298
2002	24,288	286	1,183	3,251	3,123	3,492	3,753	4,682	1,176	1,944	1,128	193	77	5,047	15,899	3,342
2003	24,415	295	1,164	3,228	3,204	3,418	3,802	4,721	1,195	1,965	1,156	187	80	5,024	16,003	3,388
2004	24,554	306	1,158	3,203	3,278	3,364	3,837	4,752	1,225	1,981	1,175	191	85	5,000	16.122	3,431
2005	24,741	311	1,171	3,164	3,355	3,346	3,866	4,792	1,263	1,992	1,182	212	89	4,984	16,283	3,474
Females																
1981	24,026	292	1,088	3,248	3,650	3,327	2,807	4,009	1,295	2,445	1,472	273	119	5,004	13,416	5,605
1986	24,239	301	1,161	2,859	3,761	3,325	3,229	3,850	1,335	2,346	1,604	326	140	4,672	13,815	5,752
1991	24,584	324	1,253	2,873	3,333	3,739	3,322	3,964	1,239	2,323	1,656	388	171	4,720	14,088	5,777
1996	24,890	293	1,229	3,056	2,961	3,849	3,336	4,432	1,177	2,286	1,628	430	214	4,876	14,281	5,734
1998	25,027	292	1,195	3,102	2,908	3,781	3,479	4,529	1,196	2,224	1,651	440	230	4,880	14,406	5,741
1999	25,117	288	1,183	3,121	2,912	3,724	3,562	4,581	1,215	2,201	1,650	444	235	4,885	14,486	5,746
2000	25,203	281	1,174	3,109	2,928	3,667	3,653	4,637	1,227	2,190	1,649	448	240	4,867	14,582	5,755
2001	25,284	273	1,154	3,102	2,979	3,591	3,726	4,702	1,219	2,185	1,661	444	248	4,834	14,694	5,757
2002	25,358	272	1,129	3,095	3,031	3,501	3,795	4,766	1,220	2,186	1,676	433	254	4,806	14,783	5,769
2003	25,441	280	1,109	3,072	3,100	3,424	3,841	4,812	1,243	2,194	1,696	409	260	4,780	14,859	5,802
2004	25,539	291	1,103	3,044	3,155	3,368	3,881	4,849	1,278	2,200	1,704	403	264	4,754	14,936	5,849
2005	25,691	296	1,116	3,005	3,215	3,356	3,907	4,890	1,322	2,200	1,688	428	269	4,737	15,048	5,906
Wales																
Persons																
1981	2,813	36	136	407	434	383	333	485	158	272	139	21	8	626	1,663	525
1986	2,811	37	143	357	438	369	378	464	166	271	154	26	10	578	1,686	547
1991	2,873	38	153	363	393	402	389	486	154	284	164	32	13	589	1,711	573
1996	2,891	34	146	381	352	409	379	541	147	279	170	37	17	598	1,714	578
1998	2,900	34	141	384	343	401	390	553	150	271	177	38	18	596	1,723	581
1999	2,901	33	139	385	347	388	395	559	151	267	178	39	18	594	1,727	580
2000	2,907	32	138	383	352	378	403	565	152	265	180	39	19	591	1,734	581
2001	2,910	32	136	382	356	365	409	572	154	264	183	39	20	587	1,739	584
2002	2,923	30	132	380	366	356	415	579	156	265	185	39	20	582	1,752	589
2003	2,938	31	129	377	377	347	418	583	161	268	187	38	20	577	1,765	596
2004	2,952	32	127	374	385	341	422	588	166	270	188	39	21	572	1,778	602
2005	2,959	32	127	368	389	338	422	590	171	272	186	42	21	567	1,783	609
Males																
1981	1,365	18	70	209	221	193	168	240	73	118	48	5	2	321	871	173
1986	1,362	19	73	184	221	186	190	231	79	119	54	7	2	297	885	181
1991	1,391	20	78	186	199	199	194	242	74	128	60	8	2	302	891	198
1996	1,401	17	74	195	179	203	187	269	72	128	64	10	3	306	890	206
1998	1,407	17	72	197	174	199	192	274	73	125	68	11	4	305	894	208
1999	1,408	17	72	198	176	192	194	277	74	124	69	11	4	305	895	208
2000	1,408	16	71	196	177	185	198	280	75	124	71	12	4	303	895	210
2001	1,409	16	69	196	179	178	200	283	75	124	73	12	4	301	895	212
2002	1,414	16	68	195	183	172	202	286	77	125	74	12	5	299	900	215
2003	1,426	16	66	194	191	170	204	287	79	127	75	12	5	297	911	219
2004	1,434	16	66	192	196	167	206	289	82	128	76	12	5	294	918	222
2005	1,438	17	65	189	199	165	205	290	84	130	77	13	5	291	922	225
Females																
1981	1,448	18	66	199	213	190	165	246	85	154	91	16	6	305	791	352
1986	1,449	18	70	173	217	184	188	233	87	152	100	20	8	282	801	366
1991	1,482	19	75	177	194	203	195	244	80	156	104	24	10	288	820	375
1996	1,490	16	71	186	173	206	192	272	75	151	106	27	13	293	825	373
1998	1,492	16	69	187	169	202	198	278	76	146	109	27	14	290	829	373
1999	1,493	16	68	187	171	196	201	282	77	144	109	27	15	289	832	371
2000	1,499	15	67	186	175	192	206	285	77	142	109	28	15	288	840	371
2001	1,502	15	66	186	177	187	209	289	78	141	110	27	15	286	844	372
2002	1,509	15	65	185	182	183	212	293	80	140	111	27	16	283	852	374
2003	1,512	15	63	184	186	178	214	296	82	141	112	26	16	281	855	377
2004	1,518	15	62	182	189	174	216	299	85	142	112	26	16	278	859	380
2005	1,521	16	61	180	190	172	217	300	88	142	110	28	16	276	861	384

See notes on first page of table.

Table 1.4 continued	Population: age and sex

Constituent countries of the United Kingdom · Numbers (thousands)

Mid-year	All ages	Under 1	1–4	5–14	15–24	25–34	35–44	45–59	60–64	65–74	75–84	85–89	90 and over	Under 16	16–64/59	65/60 and over
Scotland																
Persons																
1981	5,180	69	249	780	875	724	603	880	260	460	232	35	14	1,188	3,110	882
1986	5,112	66	257	656	863	739	665	849	273	435	252	42	15	1,061	3,161	890
1991	5,083	66	258	634	746	795	696	853	265	441	259	51	19	1,021	3,151	912
1996	5,092	59	252	643	651	798	722	925	259	448	256	57	24	1,019	3,151	922
1998	5,077	58	239	644	628	766	749	941	261	445	262	59	26	1,003	3,145	929
1999	5,072	56	234	643	625	743	762	951	262	444	265	59	27	995	3,144	933
2000	5,063	53	230	636	628	717	774	962	263	445	267	59	28	985	3,141	937
2001	5,064	52	224	629	633	696	782	979	262	447	272	59	29	970	3,150	944
2002	5,055	51	217	622	639	669	788	993	262	449	276	58	30	955	3,150	950
2003	5,057	52	212	614	648	648	793	1,008	265	452	281	55	31	943	3,156	958
2004	5,078	54	210	609	653	635	796	1,025	270	455	286	54	31	935	3,175	968
2005	5,095	54	211	600	659	629	794	1,042	273	457	286	59	32	929	3,191	975
Males																
1981	2,495	35	128	400	445	364	298	424	118	194	77	8	3	610	1,603	282
1986	2,462	34	131	336	438	371	331	410	127	184	86	10	3	543	1,636	283
1991	2,445	34	132	324	377	394	345	415	124	192	91	13	3	522	1,623	299
1996	2,447	30	128	328	327	392	355	454	122	198	93	15	5	521	1,616	310
1998	2,439	30	122	329	315	374	367	463	124	198	96	16	5	513	1,610	316
1999	2,437	29	120	329	313	362	372	469	125	198	98	16	6	510	1,609	318
2000	2,432	28	118	326	315	347	377	474	125	199	100	17	6	505	1,606	322
2001	2,434	26	115	322	319	337	379	483	125	200	103	17	6	497	1,610	327
2002	2,432	26	111	319	324	325	382	490	125	202	106	17	7	489	1,612	331
2003	2,435	26	108	314	329	315	383	496	126	204	108	16	7	483	1,616	336
2004	2,446	28	107	312	332	310	384	503	129	207	111	16	7	479	1,627	341
2005	2,456	28	107	307	335	309	382	511	131	208	112	18	7	476	1,635	345
Females																
1981	2,685	33	121	380	430	359	305	456	142	265	155	27	11	579	1,506	600
1986	2,649	32	126	320	424	368	334	439	146	250	166	32	12	518	1,525	606
1991	2,639	32	126	309	369	402	351	437	141	249	168	38	16	499	1,528	612
1996	2,645	28	123	315	324	406	367	470	137	250	164	42	20	498	1,535	612
1998	2,638	28	116	315	313	392	382	478	137	248	166	43	21	490	1,535	614
1999	2,635	27	114	314	312	381	390	483	138	246	166	43	22	486	1,535	614
2000	2,631	26	112	310	313	369	397	488	138	246	166	43	22	480	1,535	616
2001	2,630	26	109	307	314	359	403	496	137	246	169	43	23	473	1,540	617
2002	2,623	25	106	303	315	344	406	504	137	247	171	41	23	466	1,538	619
2003	2,623	25	104	300	318	332	410	512	139	248	173	39	24	460	1,540	622
2004	2,632	26	103	297	321	325	412	521	141	248	175	38	24	457	1,549	627
2005	2,639	26	103	293	324	320	411	531	142	249	174	41	25	453	1,556	630
Northern Ireland																
Persons																
1981	1,543	27	106	282	271	200	175	227	68	116	57	..	..	444	874	224
1986	1,574	28	107	261	277	217	190	227	71	115	64	16	..	423	917	234
1991	1,607	26	106	260	256	240	200	241	70	121	69	14	6	417	945	246
1996	1,662	24	99	266	244	257	220	266	70	123	72	15	7	415	993	253
1998	1,678	24	97	264	239	257	231	275	71	122	74	16	7	411	1,010	257
1999	1,679	23	96	262	237	252	237	279	73	122	75	16	7	408	1,014	258
2000	1,683	22	95	259	237	247	243	284	73	123	75	16	7	403	1,020	259
2001	1,689	22	93	255	240	243	248	290	74	123	77	16	7	397	1,030	262
2002	1,697	22	91	253	243	238	251	296	75	125	79	16	7	393	1,037	266
2003	1,703	21	89	251	246	233	254	301	78	126	81	16	8	388	1,044	271
2004	1,710	22	87	248	250	229	256	305	81	127	82	16	8	383	1,052	275
2005	1,724	23	88	245	253	228	257	310	84	128	83	16	9	381	1,064	280
Males																
1981	757	14	54	145	140	102	87	109	32	50	21	..	..	228	454	75
1986	768	14	55	134	142	109	95	110	33	50	23	4	..	217	474	77
1991	783	13	54	133	131	119	100	118	32	53	26	4	1	213	487	83
1996	810	12	51	136	124	128	109	131	33	54	27	4	1	212	511	87
1998	819	12	50	135	121	128	114	135	34	54	28	5	2	211	520	89
1999	818	12	49	134	119	125	117	138	35	54	29	5	2	209	521	89
2000	820	11	49	133	120	122	119	141	35	55	29	5	2	207	524	90
2001	824	11	48	131	122	120	122	144	35	56	30	5	2	204	529	92
2002	829	11	47	130	124	117	123	147	36	56	31	5	2	202	534	94
2003	833	11	46	129	126	115	124	149	38	58	31	5	2	199	538	95
2004	836	11	45	127	128	113	125	151	39	58	32	5	2	197	542	97
2005	844	12	45	126	130	113	126	153	41	59	32	5	2	196	550	99
Females																
1981	786	13	52	137	130	98	88	118	37	66	37	..	..	216	420	150
1986	805	13	52	127	135	107	96	118	38	65	41	12	..	206	442	157
1991	824	13	52	127	125	121	100	123	38	67	44	10	4	203	458	163
1996	851	11	49	130	120	129	110	135	37	69	45	11	6	203	482	167
1998	859	12	47	129	118	129	117	139	37	68	46	11	6	201	490	168
1999	861	11	47	128	117	127	120	141	38	68	46	11	6	199	493	169
2000	862	11	46	126	118	125	124	143	38	68	46	11	6	196	497	169
2001	865	10	45	124	119	123	126	146	38	68	47	11	6	193	501	170
2002	868	11	44	123	119	120	128	149	39	68	48	11	6	191	504	173
2003	870	10	43	122	120	118	129	152	40	68	49	11	6	189	506	175
2004	874	11	42	121	122	116	130	154	42	69	50	11	6	187	509	178
2005	880	11	43	119	123	115	131	157	43	69	50	11	7	186	514	181

See notes on first page of table.

Table 1.5	Population: age, sex and legal marital status

England and Wales   Numbers (thousands)

Mid-year	Total population	Males					Females				
		Single	Married	Divorced	Widowed	Total	Single	Married	Divorced	Widowed	Total
Aged											
16 and over											
1971	36,818	4,173	12,522	187	682	17,563	3,583	12,566	296	2,810	19,255
1976	37,486	4,369	12,511	376	686	17,941	3,597	12,538	533	2,877	19,545
1981	38,724	5,013	12,238	611	698	18,559	4,114	12,284	828	2,939	20,165
1986[1]	39,837	5,625	11,867	917	695	19,103	4,617	12,000	1,165	2,953	20,734
1991	40,501	5,891	11,636	1,187	727	19,441	4,817	11,833	1,459	2,951	21,060
1996	40,827	6,225	11,310	1,346	733	19,614	5,168	11,433	1,730	2,881	21,212
1997	40,966	6,337	11,240	1,379	734	19,690	5,288	11,353	1,781	2,855	21,276
1998	41,121	6,450	11,183	1,405	735	19,773	5,406	11,284	1,827	2,832	21,349
1999	41,325	6,582	11,143	1,433	732	19,890	5,526	11,235	1,875	2,800	21,435
2000	41,569	6,721	11,113	1,456	731	20,022	5,650	11,199	1,927	2,772	21,547
2001	41,865	6,894	11,090	1,482	733	20,198	5,798	11,150	1,975	2,745	21,667
2002	42,135	7,076	11,015	1,535	731	20,357	5,961	11,073	2,035	2,709	21,778
2003	42,413	7,261	10,940	1,590	728	20,520	6,128	11,000	2,096	2,668	21,892
2004	42,719	7,461	10,863	1,644	726	20,694	6,306	10,935	2,156	2,628	22,025
16–19											
1971	2,666	1,327	34	0	0	1,362	1,163	142	0	0	1,305
1976	2,901	1,454	28	0	0	1,482	1,289	129	0	0	1,419
1981	3,310	1,675	20	0	0	1,694	1,523	93	0	0	1,616
1986[1]	3,131	1,587	10	0	0	1,596	1,484	49	1	0	1,535
1991	2,665	1,358	8	0	0	1,366	1,267	32	0	0	1,300
1996	2,402	1,209	6	0	0	1,216	1,164	21	0	0	1,186
1997	2,478	1,246	6	0	0	1,253	1,203	20	1	1	1,225
1998	2,532	1,274	6	1	0	1,281	1,230	20	1	1	1,251
1999	2,543	1,280	6	1	1	1,288	1,234	20	1	1	1,255
2000	2,523	1,276	6	1	1	1,283	1,221	18	1	1	1,240
2001	2,567	1,304	5	1	1	1,312	1,237	16	1	1	1,255
2002	2,633	1,347	4	1	1	1,353	1,266	13	1	1	1,280
2003	2,702	1,386	4	1	1	1,391	1,299	12	0	1	1,311
2004	2,770	1,423	3	0	0	1,427	1,332	11	0	0	1,343
20–24											
1971	3,773	1,211	689	3	0	1,904	745	1,113	9	2	1,869
1976	3,395	1,167	557	4	0	1,728	725	925	16	2	1,667
1981	3,744	1,420	466	10	1	1,896	1,007	811	27	2	1,847
1986[1]	4,171	1,768	317	14	0	2,099	1,383	657	32	1	2,072
1991	3,911	1,717	242	12	0	1,971	1,421	490	29	1	1,941
1996	3,291	1,538	117	3	0	1,658	1,361	260	11	1	1,633
1997	3,141	1,479	99	3	0	1,580	1,325	225	9	1	1,561
1998	3,047	1,442	86	2	0	1,530	1,306	201	8	1	1,517
1999	3,047	1,449	78	2	0	1,530	1,320	188	8	1	1,517
2000	3,088	1,470	74	3	0	1,548	1,352	180	8	1	1,540
2001	3,157	1,501	74	3	1	1,579	1,390	178	8	1	1,578
2002	3,211	1,534	69	3	1	1,607	1,428	166	8	1	1,604
2003	3,283	1,573	69	3	1	1,646	1,466	161	8	1	1,637
2004	3,358	1,621	67	3	1	1,692	1,499	156	8	2	1,665
25–29											
1971	3,267	431	1,206	16	1	1,654	215	1,367	29	4	1,614
1976	3,758	533	1,326	39	2	1,900	267	1,522	65	5	1,859
1981	3,372	588	1,057	54	1	1,700	331	1,247	89	4	1,671
1986[1]	3,713	835	949	79	1	1,863	527	1,207	113	4	1,850
1991	4,154	1,132	856	82	1	2,071	800	1,158	123	2	2,083
1996	3,950	1,273	650	46	1	1,970	977	906	93	3	1,980
1997	3,877	1,294	595	42	1	1,932	1,012	844	85	3	1,945
1998	3,789	1,304	544	38	1	1,887	1,039	783	77	3	1,902
1999	3,687	1,304	497	34	1	1,836	1,051	725	72	3	1,851
2000	3,605	1,305	459	31	1	1,796	1,065	677	65	3	1,810
2001	3,487	1,293	420	28	1	1,742	1,059	625	58	3	1,745
2002	3,348	1,276	371	26	1	1,674	1,052	567	52	3	1,674
2003	3,262	1,271	337	25	1	1,634	1,053	524	49	2	1,628
2004	3,260	1,292	318	24	1	1,635	1,080	497	47	2	1,625

1 The estimates by marital status for 1986 are based on the original mid-2001 population estimates, and are subject to further revision.

Table 1.5 continued	Population: age, sex and legal marital status									

England and Wales   Numbers (thousands)

Mid-year	Total population	Males					Females				
		Single	Married	Divorced	Widowed	Total	Single	Married	Divorced	Widowed	Total
30–34											
1971	2,897	206	1,244	23	3	1,475	111	1,269	34	8	1,422
1976	3,220	236	1,338	55	3	1,632	118	1,388	75	8	1,588
1981	3,715	318	1,451	97	3	1,869	165	1,544	129	9	1,846
1986[1]	3,338	355	1,197	124	2	1,679	206	1,293	154	6	1,660
1991	3,708	520	1,172	155	2	1,849	335	1,330	189	5	1,859
1996	4,126	776	1,135	138	2	2,050	551	1,316	201	7	2,076
1997	4,151	817	1,111	133	2	2,064	589	1,293	198	7	2,088
1998	4,136	848	1,078	127	3	2,056	621	1,259	193	7	2,081
1999	4,113	877	1,043	121	3	2,044	651	1,223	188	7	2,069
2000	4,076	904	1,007	114	2	2,027	679	1,182	181	7	2,049
2001	4,050	934	971	108	2	2,016	711	1,142	174	7	2,033
2002	4,000	961	921	105	2	1,990	743	1,094	167	6	2,010
2003	3,928	981	868	102	2	1,954	767	1,043	159	6	1,974
2004	3,813	987	811	97	2	1,897	777	985	149	5	1,916
35–44											
1971	5,736	317	2,513	48	13	2,891	201	2,529	66	48	2,845
1976	5,608	286	2,442	104	12	2,843	167	2,427	129	42	2,765
1981	5,996	316	2,519	178	12	3,024	170	2,540	222	41	2,972
1986[1]	6,856	396	2,738	293	12	3,438	213	2,815	350	39	3,418
1991	7,022	477	2,632	384	11	3,504	280	2,760	444	34	3,517
1996	7,017	653	2,426	398	12	3,489	427	2,568	497	36	3,528
1997	7,155	708	2,433	403	12	3,556	472	2,580	511	36	3,599
1998	7,304	768	2,442	405	13	3,627	522	2,596	523	36	3,677
1999	7,475	832	2,459	408	13	3,711	577	2,617	533	37	3,763
2000	7,661	899	2,481	410	12	3,802	635	2,640	547	37	3,859
2001	7,816	963	2,494	411	12	3,881	692	2,649	558	36	3,935
2002	7,962	1,031	2,489	424	12	3,955	751	2,650	571	35	4,007
2003	8,062	1,089	2,471	435	12	4,006	805	2,634	583	34	4,056
2004	8,140	1,142	2,445	444	11	4,043	858	2,614	593	32	4,098
45–64											
1971	11,887	502	4,995	81	173	5,751	569	4,709	125	733	6,136
1976	11,484	496	4,787	141	160	5,583	462	4,568	188	683	5,901
1981	11,040	480	4,560	218	147	5,405	386	4,358	271	620	5,635
1986[1]	10,860	461	4,422	331	141	5,355	327	4,220	388	570	5,505
1991	10,960	456	4,394	456	127	5,433	292	4,211	521	503	5,527
1996	11,820	528	4,587	628	121	5,864	318	4,466	732	440	5,956
1997	11,927	545	4,593	656	120	5,914	328	4,486	770	430	6,014
1998	12,055	565	4,608	681	121	5,974	340	4,512	807	422	6,080
1999	12,198	589	4,627	706	121	6,043	355	4,541	844	415	6,155
2000	12,328	615	4,638	727	121	6,101	372	4,564	881	410	6,227
2001	12,447	644	4,647	747	121	6,159	391	4,578	918	401	6,289
2002	12,580	671	4,649	780	120	6,220	413	4,596	960	391	6,359
2003	12,715	702	4,647	815	118	6,283	437	4,613	1,002	380	6,433
2004	12,857	736	4,644	850	117	6,347	465	4,628	1,045	371	6,510
65 and over											
1971	6,592	179	1,840	17	492	2,527	580	1,437	32	2,016	4,065
1976	7,119	197	2,033	33	510	2,773	569	1,579	60	2,138	4,347
1981	7,548	216	2,167	54	534	2,971	533	1,692	90	2,263	4,578
1986[1]	7,768	223	2,234	76	539	3,072	477	1,759	127	2,333	4,696
1991	8,080	231	2,332	99	586	3,248	422	1,853	152	2,405	4,832
1996	8,221	247	2,390	134	597	3,367	369	1,897	196	2,393	4,854
1997	8,237	248	2,404	143	597	3,391	358	1,904	207	2,377	4,845
1998	8,258	250	2,418	152	597	3,417	348	1,913	218	2,362	4,841
1999	8,262	251	2,431	161	594	3,437	338	1,922	230	2,336	4,825
2000	8,287	252	2,449	171	593	3,466	327	1,938	243	2,313	4,821
2001	8,342	254	2,478	183	595	3,510	318	1,960	259	2,295	4,832
2002	8,400	256	2,511	197	595	3,557	308	1,987	276	2,272	4,843
2003	8,461	258	2,544	211	594	3,607	301	2,015	294	2,244	4,854
2004	8,520	259	2,575	225	593	3,653	293	2,044	314	2,216	4,867

| Table 2.1 | Vital statistics summary |

Constituent countries of the United Kingdom | Numbers (thousands) and rates

Year and quarter	All live births		Live births outside marriage		Marriages		Divorces		Deaths		Infant mortality[5]		Neonatal mortality[6]		Perinatal mortality[7]	
	Number	Rate[1]	Number	Rate[2]	Number	Rate[3]	Number	Rate[4]	Number	Rate[1]	Number	Rate[2]	Number	Rate[2]	Number	Rate[8]
United Kingdom																
1976	675.5	12.0	61.1	90	406.0	..	135.4	..	680.8	12.1	9.79	14.5	6.68	9.9	12.25	18.0
1981	730.7	13.0	91.3	125	397.8	49.4	156.4	11.3	658.0	11.7	8.16	11.2	4.93	6.7	8.79	12.0
1986	754.8	13.3	154.3	204	393.9	..	168.2	..	660.7	11.7	7.18	9.5	4.00	5.3	7.31	9.6
1991	792.3	13.8	236.1	298	349.7	..	173.5	..	646.2	11.2	5.82	7.4	3.46	4.4	6.45	8.1
1996	733.2	12.6	260.4	355	317.5	..	171.7	..	636.0	10.9	4.50	6.1	3.00	4.1	6.41	8.7
1999	700.0	11.9	271.6	388	301.1	..	158.7	..	632.1	10.8	4.05	5.8	2.73	3.9	5.79	8.2
2000	679.0	11.5	268.1	395	305.9	..	154.6	..	608.4	10.3	3.79	5.6	2.63	3.9	5.56	8.1
2001	669.1	11.3	268.0	401	286.1	..	156.8	..	602.3	10.2	3.66	5.5	2.43	3.6	5.39	8.0
2002	668.8	11.3	271.7	406	293.0	..	160.5	..	606.2	10.2	3.50	5.2	2.36	3.5	5.57	8.3
2003	695.6	11.7	288.5	415	308.6	..	166.7	..	612.0	10.3	3.69	5.3	2.53	3.6	5.96	8.5
2004	716.0	12.0	302.6	423	312.2[p]	..	167.1	..	583.1	9.7	3.61	5.0	2.46	3.4	6.00	8.3
2005	722.6[p]	12.0[p]	310.2[p]	429[p]	..	..	155.1[p]	..	582.7[p]	9.7[p]	3.68[p]	5.1[p]	2.53[p]	3.5[p]	5.82[p]	8.0[p]
2004 March	174.3	11.7	73.6	422	39.7[p]	..	43.1	..	159.7	10.7	0.97	5.5	0.64	3.7	1.51	8.6
June	176.2	11.8	73.2	415	85.7[p]	..	41.5	..	139.3	9.4	0.84	4.8	0.59	3.4	1.48	8.3
Sept	185.1	12.3	78.5	424	128.8[p]	..	42.3	..	135.1	9.0	0.90	4.9	0.64	3.5	1.59	8.5
Dec	180.4	12.0	77.3	429	57.9[p]	..	40.2	..	149.0	9.9	0.90	5.0	0.58	3.2	1.43	7.9
2005 March	173.2[p]	11.7[p]	74.5[p]	430[p]	..	..	39.4	..	165.1[p]	11.1[p]	0.95[p]	5.5[p]	0.64[p]	3.7[p]	1.39[p]	8.0[p]
June	179.0[p]	11.9[p]	75.0[p]	419[p]	..	..	40.0	..	141.1[p]	9.5[p]	0.93[p]	5.2[p]	0.64[p]	3.6[p]	1.53[p]	8.5[p]
Sept	190.3[p]	12.5[p]	82.5[p]	434[p]	..	..	38.9	..	130.9[p]	8.7[p]	0.91[p]	4.8[p]	0.66[p]	3.5[p]	1.49[p]	7.8[p]
Dec	180.1[p]	11.9[p]	78.2[p]	434[p]	..	..	36.7	..	145.5[p]	9.7[p]	0.90[p]	5.0[p]	0.59[p]	3.3[p]	1.42[p]	7.8[p]
2006 March	178.9[p]	12.0[p]	77.4[p]	433[p]	..	..	..	..	159.7[p]	10.8[p]	0.90[p]	5.0[p]	0.61[p]	3.4[p]	1.38[p]	7.6[p]
June	185.1[p]	12.3[p]	79.9[p]	431[p]	..	..	..	..	141.1[p]	9.4[p]	0.93[p]	5.0[p]	0.65[p]	3.5[p]	1.44[p]	7.7[p]
England and Wales																
1976	584.3	11.8	53.8	92	358.6	57.7	126.7	10.1	598.5	12.1	8.34	14.3	5.66	9.7	10.45	17.7
1981	634.5	12.8	81.0	128	352.0	49.6	145.7	11.9	577.9	11.6	7.02	11.1	4.23	6.7	7.56	11.8
1986	661.0	13.2	141.3	214	347.9	43.6	153.9	12.9	581.2	11.6	6.31	9.6	3.49	5.3	6.37	9.6
1991	699.2	13.8	211.3	302	306.8	36.0	158.7	13.5	570.0	11.2	5.16	7.4	3.05	4.4	5.65	8.0
1996	649.5	12.6	232.7	358	279.0	30.9	157.1	13.8	560.1	10.9	3.99	6.1	2.68	4.1	5.62	8.6
1999	621.9	12.0	241.9	389	263.5	27.8	144.6	12.9	556.1	10.7	3.62	5.8	2.44	3.9	5.14	8.2
2000	604.4	11.6	238.6	395	268.0	27.8	141.1	12.7	535.7	10.3	3.38	5.6	2.34	3.9	4.96	8.2
2001	594.6	11.4	238.1	400	249.2	25.4	143.8	12.9	530.4	10.1	3.24	5.4	2.14	3.6	4.76	8.0
2002	596.1	11.3	242.0	406	255.6	25.6	147.7	13.4	533.5	10.1	3.13	5.2	2.13	3.6	4.99	8.3
2003	621.5	11.8	257.2	414	270.1	26.4	153.5	14.0	538.3	10.2	3.31	5.3	2.26	3.6	5.36	8.6
2004	639.7	12.1	269.7	422	270.7[p]	25.9[p]	153.4[p]	14.1	512.5	9.7	3.22	5.0	2.21	3.5	5.39	8.4
2005	645.8	12.1	276.5	428	..	..	141.8[p]	13.0[p]	512.7	9.7	3.26	5.0	2.23[p]	3.4[p]	5.21[p]	8.0[p]
2004 March	155.2	11.8	65.2	421	35.0[p]	13.5[p]	39.5	14.6	140.5	10.7	0.87	5.6	0.58	3.8	1.34	8.6
June	157.4	11.9	65.2	414	74.6[p]	28.7[p]	38.1	14.0	122.1	9.3	0.74	4.7	0.52	3.3	1.31	8.3
Sept	165.4	12.4	70.2	424	112.6[p]	42.8[p]	39.0	14.2	118.6	8.9	0.80	4.8	0.57	3.5	1.43	8.6
Dec	161.7	12.1	69.1	427	49.5[p]	18.8[p]	36.9	13.5	131.3	9.8	0.81	5.0	0.53	3.3	1.30	8.0
2005 March	154.3	11.7	66.3	430	..	..	36.2	13.5[p]	145.7	11.0	0.85	5.5	0.57[p]	3.7[p]	1.25[p]	8.0[p]
June	159.8	12.0	66.6	417	..	..	36.5	13.4[p]	123.8	9.4	0.82	5.2	0.56[p]	3.5[p]	1.35[p]	8.4[p]
Sept	170.2	12.6	73.7	433	..	..	35.6	13.0[p]	114.7	8.6	0.79	4.6	0.57[p]	3.4[p]	1.34[p]	7.8[p]
Dec	161.7	12.0	69.9	433	..	..	33.4	12.2[p]	128.5	9.6	0.80	4.9	0.52[p]	3.2[p]	1.28[p]	7.9[p]
2006 March	159.5[p]	12.0[p]	68.7[p]	431[p]	..	..	34.2[p]	12.7[p]	140.8[p]	10.7[p]	0.82[p]	5.2[p]	0.55[p]	3.5[p]	1.25[p]	7.8[p]
June	165.3[p]	12.3[p]	71.0[p]	430[p]	..	..	..	..	123.6[p]	9.3[p]	0.84[p]	5.1[p]	0.58[p]	3.5[p]	1.31[p]	7.9[p]
England																
1976	550.4	11.8	50.8	92	339.0	..	..	..	560.3	12.0	7.83	14.2	5.32	9.7	9.81	17.6
1981	598.2	12.8	76.9	129	332.2	..	..	..	541.0	11.6	6.50	10.9	3.93	6.6	7.04	11.7
1986	623.6	13.2	133.5	214	328.4	..	146.0	..	544.5	11.6	5.92	9.5	3.27	5.2	5.98	9.5
1991	660.8	13.7	198.9	301	290.1	..	150.1	..	534.0	11.2	4.86	7.3	2.87	4.3	5.33	8.0
1996	614.2	12.7	218.2	355	264.2	..	148.7	..	524.0	10.8	3.74	6.1	2.53	4.1	5.36	8.7
1999	589.5	12.0	226.7	385	249.5	..	137.0	..	519.6	10.8	3.38	5.7	2.29	3.9	4.86	8.2
2000	572.8	11.7	223.8	391	253.8	..	133.9	..	501.0	10.2	3.18	5.6	2.21	3.9	4.69	8.2
2001	563.7	11.4	223.3	396	236.2	..	136.4	..	496.1	10.0	3.04	5.4	2.02	3.6	4.51	8.0
2002	565.7	11.4	227.0	401	242.1	..	140.2	..	499.1	10.1	2.97	5.2	2.02	3.6	4.75	8.3
2003	589.9	11.8	241.4	409	255.6	..	145.8	..	503.4	10.1	3.14	5.3	2.15	3.7	5.09	8.6
2004	607.2	12.1	253.1	417	255.9[p]	..	145.5	..	479.2	9.6	3.03	5.0	2.09	3.4	5.10	8.4
2005	613.0	12.2	259.4	423	..	..	134.6[p]	..	479.4	9.6	3.10	5.0	2.12[p]	3.5[p]	4.92[p]	8.0[p]
2004 March	147.3	11.8	61.2	416	33.3[p]	..	37.4	..	131.4	10.6	0.82	5.5	0.55	3.7	1.26	8.5
June	149.6	12.0	61.3	410	70.6[p]	..	36.0	..	114.2	9.2	0.69	4.6	0.49	3.3	1.25	8.3
Sept	156.9	12.5	65.8	420	106.2[p]	..	36.9	..	110.8	8.8	0.74	4.7	0.53	3.4	1.35	8.6
Dec	153.3	12.2	64.7	422	46.8[p]	..	35.1	..	122.9	9.8	0.78	5.1	0.52	3.4	1.24	8.1
2005 March	146.4	11.8	62.1	424	..	..	34.4	..	136.2	10.9	0.81	5.6	0.54[p]	3.7[p]	1.18[p]	8.0[p]
June	151.8	12.1	62.5	412	..	..	34.7	..	115.7	9.3	0.78	5.1	0.53[p]	3.5[p]	1.28[p]	8.4[p]
Sept	161.4	12.7	69.1	428	..	..	33.8	..	107.3	8.5	0.75	4.7	0.55[p]	3.4[p]	1.27[p]	7.8[p]
Dec	153.4	12.1	65.6	428	..	..	31.7	..	120.3	9.6	0.75	4.9	0.50[p]	3.3[p]	1.18[p]	7.7[p]
2006 March	151.3[p]	12.1[p]	64.4[p]	426[p]	..	..	32.4[p]	..	131.8[p]	10.6[p]	0.79[p]	5.2[p]	0.54[p]	3.6[p]	1.19[p]	7.8[p]
June	157.0[p]	12.4[p]	66.7[p]	425[p]	..	..	..	..	115.7[p]	9.2[p]	0.79[p]	5.1[p]	0.55[p]	3.5[p]	1.25[p]	7.9[p]

Note: Death figures for England and Wales represent the number of deaths registered in each year up to 1992, and the number of deaths occurring in each year from 1993 to 2005. Provisional death figures for 2006 relate to registrations.
Birth and death figures for England and also for Wales each exclude events for persons usually resident outside England and Wales. These events are, however, included in the totals for England and Wales combined, and for the United Kingdom.
From 1981 births to non-resident mothers in Northern Ireland are excluded from the figures for Northern Ireland, and for the United Kingdom.

Birth rates for 2006 are based on the 2004-based population projections for 2006. Marriage and divorce rates in England and Wales for 1986 have been calculated using the interim revised marital status estimates (based on the original mid-2001 estimates) and are subject to further revision..
Marriage and divorce rates in England and Wales for 2005 are based on 2004 marital status estimates. Marriage and divorce rates in Scotland for 2006 are based on 2005 marital status estimates.

Perinatal mortality figures for 2003 and 2004 have been revised in HSQ31 to include stillbirths data notified to ONS too late to be included in the original statistics.

Table 2.1 continued — Vital statistics summary

Constituent countries of the United Kingdom

Numbers (thousands) and rates

Year and quarter	All live births		Live births outside marriage		Marriages		Divorces		Deaths		Infant mortality[5]		Neonatal mortality[6]		Perinatal mortality[7]	
	Number	Rate[1]	Number	Rate[2]	Number	Rate[3]	Number	Rate[4]	Number	Rate[1]	Number	Rate[2]	Number	Rate[2]	Number	Rate[8]
Wales																
1976	33.4	11.9	2.9	86	19.5	..	..	..	36.3	13.0	0.46	13.7	0.32	9.6	0.64	19.0
1981	35.8	12.7	4.0	112	19.8	..	..	..	35.0	12.4	0.45	12.6	0.29	8.1	0.51	14.1
1986	37.0	13.1	7.8	211	19.5	..	7.9	..	34.7	12.3	0.35	9.5	0.21	5.6	0.38	10.3
1991	38.1	13.3	12.3	323	16.6	..	8.6	..	34.1	11.9	0.25	6.6	0.16	4.1	0.30	7.9
1996	34.9	12.1	14.4	412	14.8	..	8.4	..	34.6	12.0	0.20	5.6	0.13	3.6	0.26	7.5
1999	32.1	11.1	14.8	461	14.0	..	7.5	..	35.0	12.1	0.20	6.1	0.13	4.0	0.25	7.7
2000	31.3	10.8	14.8	472	14.1	..	7.2	..	33.3	11.5	0.17	5.3	0.11	3.5	0.23	7.2
2001	30.6	10.5	14.8	483	13.0	..	7.4	..	33.0	11.3	0.16	5.4	0.11	3.5	0.23	7.5
2002	30.2	10.3	15.0	497	13.5	..	7.6	..	33.2	11.3	0.14	4.5	0.10	3.2	0.24	7.7
2003	31.4	10.7	15.8	503	14.5	..	7.7	..	33.7	11.5	0.13	4.3	0.10	3.1	0.24	7.6
2004	32.3	10.9	16.6	513	14.8p	..	7.9p	..	32.1	10.9	0.16	4.9	0.10	3.1	0.26	8.0
2005	32.6	11.0	17.1	524	..	..	7.2	..	32.1	10.9	0.13	4.1	0.09p	2.9p	0.24p	7.4p
2004 March	7.8	10.6	4.0	514	1.7p	..	2.0	..	8.8	12.0	0.05	5.9	0.03	3.9	0.08	9.8
June	7.8	10.6	3.9	500	4.0p	..	2.0	..	7.6	10.4	0.04	4.9	0.02	3.1	0.06	7.5
Sept	8.4	11.4	4.3	512	6.4p	..	2.1	..	7.5	10.1	0.04	4.9	0.03	3.7	0.07	7.8
Dec	8.3	11.2	4.4	523	2.7p	..	1.8	..	8.1	11.0	0.03	3.8	0.02	1.8	0.06	6.8
2005 March	7.8	10.7	4.1	529	..	..	1.8	..	9.3	12.6	0.03	4.2	0.02p	3.1p	0.06p	7.7p
June	7.9	10.7	4.0	510	..	..	1.8	..	7.8	10.6	0.03	4.2	0.03p	3.2p	0.06p	7.9p
Sept	8.7	11.6	4.6	530	..	..	1.8	..	7.1	9.6	0.03	3.3	0.02p	2.8p	0.06p	7.0p
Dec	8.2	11.0	4.3	527	..	..	1.8	..	7.9	10.7	0.04	4.6	0.02p	2.6p	0.06p	6.8p
2006 March	8.1p	11.1p	4.2p	520p	..	..	1.8p	..	8.7p	11.9p	0.03p	3.1p	0.02p	2.0p	0.06p	6.9p
June	8.3p	11.1p	4.3p	523p	..	..	..	..	7.6p	10.3p	0.03p	4.1p	0.02p	2.4p	0.05p	6.3p
Scotland																
1976	64.9	12.5	6.0	93	37.5	53.8	8.1	6.5	65.3	12.5	0.96	14.8	0.67	10.3	1.20	18.3
1981	69.1	13.4	8.5	122	36.2	47.5	9.9	8.0	63.8	12.3	0.78	11.3	0.47	6.9	0.81	11.6
1986	65.8	12.9	13.6	206	35.8	42.9	12.8	10.7	63.5	12.4	0.58	8.8	0.34	5.2	0.67	10.2
1991	67.0	13.2	19.5	291	33.8	39.0	12.4	10.6	61.0	12.0	0.47	7.1	0.29	4.6	0.58	8.6
1996	59.3	11.6	21.4	360	30.2	33.2	12.3	10.9	60.7	11.9	0.37	6.2	0.23	3.9	0.55	9.2
1999	55.1	10.9	22.7	412	29.9	31.5	11.9	10.9	60.3	11.9	0.28	5.0	0.18	3.3	0.42	7.6
2000	53.1	10.5	22.6	426	30.4	31.6	11.1	10.3	57.8	11.4	0.31	5.7	0.21	4.0	0.45	8.4
2001	52.5	10.4	22.8	433	29.6	31.0	10.6	9.7	57.4	11.3	0.29	5.5	0.20	3.8	0.45	8.5
2002	51.3	10.1	22.5	440	29.8	30.8	10.8	10.0	58.1	11.5	0.27	5.3	0.16	3.2	0.39	7.6
2003	52.4	10.4	23.9	455	30.8	31.3	10.1	10.2	58.5	11.6	0.27	5.1	0.18	3.4	0.42	8.0
2004	54.0	10.6	25.2	467	32.2	32.2	11.2	10.5	56.2	11.1	0.27	4.9	0.17	3.1	0.44	8.1
2005	54.4	10.7	25.6	471	30.9	30.3	10.9	10.3	55.7	11.0	0.28	5.2	0.19	3.5	0.42	7.7
2004 March	13.5	10.7	6.4	472	3.9	15.6	2.9	10.9	15.3	12.2	0.06	4.6	0.04	2.7	0.13	9.2
June	13.3	10.5	6.1	459	8.7	35.1	2.8	10.5	13.6	10.7	0.07	5.1	0.05	3.6	0.11	8.4
Sept	13.8	10.8	6.4	462	12.7	50.6	2.7	10.2	13.1	10.2	0.07	5.3	0.05	3.4	0.11	7.8
Dec	13.3	10.4	6.3	475	6.8	27.3	2.8	10.4	14.2	11.1	0.06	4.7	0.03	2.6	0.09	6.9
2005 March	13.4	10.6	6.2	464	3.8	15.3	2.6	10.0	15.6	12.4	0.07	5.0	0.04	3.3	0.09	7.0
June	13.6	10.7	6.4	472	8.6	34.0	2.8	10.7	13.7	10.8	0.07	5.1	0.05	3.4	0.13	9.2
Sept	14.2	11.1	6.7	471	12.3	48.0	2.7	10.1	12.8	10.0	0.08	5.6	0.06	3.9	0.11	7.6
Dec	13.2	10.3	6.3	477	6.1	23.7	2.8	10.3	13.6	10.7	0.07	5.2	0.05	3.4	0.10	7.1
2006 March	13.6p	10.8p	6.6p	487p	3.5p	13.9p	2.6p	9.7p	14.9p	11.8p	0.05p	3.7p	0.03p	2.4p	0.09p	6.8p
June	14.0p	11.0p	6.7p	475p	8.3p	32.8p	3.0p	11.3p	13.9p	11.0p	0.07p	5.0p	0.05p	3.3p	0.09p	6.4p
Northern Ireland																
1976	26.4	17.3	1.3	50	9.9	..	0.6	..	17.0	11.2	0.48	18.3	0.35	13.3	0.59	22.3
1981	27.2	17.6	1.9	70	9.6	45.4	1.4	4.2	16.3	10.6	0.36	13.2	0.23	8.3	0.42	15.3
1986	28.0	17.8	3.6	128	10.2	..	1.5	..	16.1	10.3	0.36	13.2	0.23	8.3	0.42	15.3
1991	26.0	16.2	5.3	203	9.2	..	2.3	..	15.1	9.4	0.19	7.4	0.12	4.6	0.22	8.4
1996	24.4	14.7	6.3	260	8.3	..	2.3	..	15.2	9.2	0.14	5.8	0.09	3.7	0.23	9.4
1999	23.0	13.7	7.0	303	7.6	..	2.3	..	15.7	9.3	0.15	6.4	0.11	4.8	0.23	10.0
2000	21.5	12.8	6.8	318	7.6	..	2.4	..	14.9	8.9	0.11	5.1	0.08	3.8	0.15	7.3
2001	22.0	13.0	7.1	325	7.3	..	2.4	..	14.5	8.6	0.13	6.1	0.10	4.5	0.19	8.5
2002	21.4	12.6	7.2	335	7.6	..	2.2	..	14.6	8.6	0.10	4.7	0.07	3.5	0.19	8.9
2003	21.6	12.7	7.4	344	7.8	..	2.3	..	14.5	8.5	0.11	5.3	0.09	4.0	0.18	8.1
2004	22.3	13.0	7.7	345	8.3	..	2.5	..	14.4	8.4	0.12	5.5	0.08	3.7	0.18	8.2
2005	22.3p	13.0p	8.1p	363p	..	..	..	..	14.2p	8.3p	0.14p	6.3p	0.11p	5.1p	0.18p	8.1p
2004 March	5.7	13.3	2.0	352	0.8	..	7.7	..	3.9	9.1	0.03	5.5	0.02	3.5	0.05	7.9
June	5.4	12.7	1.8	337	2.4	..	6.5	..	3.6	8.4	0.03	5.9	0.02	4.4	0.05	9.5
Sept	5.8	13.5	2.0	339	3.5	..	5.5	..	3.4	8.0	0.04	6.0	0.02	4.1	0.05	8.3
Dec	5.4	12.7	1.9	353	1.6	..	5.5	..	3.5	8.1	0.02	4.4	0.02	2.8	0.04	7.0
2005 March	5.5p	13.0p	2.0p	363p	0.9	..	5.9	..	3.8p	8.9p	0.03p	5.2p	0.02p	4.3p	0.05p	8.8p
June	5.7p	13.3p	2.0p	359p	2.2	..	6.8	..	3.7p	8.6p	0.04p	7.2p	0.03p	5.6p	0.04p	8.4p
Sept	5.9p	13.7p	2.0p	358p	3.5	..	5.5	..	3.4p	7.8p	0.04p	6.6p	0.03p	5.6p	0.04p	7.2p
Dec	5.2p	11.9p	1.9p	373p	1.4	..	5.4	..	3.4p	7.9p	0.03p	6.0p	0.02p	4.6p	0.04p	7.9p
2006 March	5.8p	13.6p	2.2p	370p	..	..	..	..	4.0p	9.5p	0.03p	5.3p	0.02p	3.3p	0.04p	6.8p
June	5.8p	13.3p	2.2p	381p	..	..	..	..	3.6p	8.4p	0.03p	4.7p	0.02p	3.6p	0.04p	6.9p

See notes opposite.
1 Per 1,000 population of all ages.
2 Per 1,000 live births.
3 Persons marrying per 1,000 unmarried population aged 16 and over.
4 Persons divorcing per 1,000 married population.
5 Deaths under 1 year.

6 Deaths under 4 weeks.
7 Stillbirths and deaths under 1 week.
8 Per 1,000 live births and stillbirths.
p provisional.

Table 2.2	Key demographic and health indicators

Constituent countries of the United Kingdom

Numbers (thousands), rates, percentages, mean age

	Population	Live births	Deaths	Dependency ratio Children[1]	Dependency ratio Elderly[2]	TFR[3]	Standardised mean age of mother at birth (years)[4]	Unstand-ardised mean age of mother at birth (years)[5]	Outside marriage as percentage of total live births	Age-standardised mortality rate[6]	Period expectation of life at birth Males	Period expectation of life at birth Females	Infant mortality rate[7]
United Kingdom													
1976	56,216.1	675.5	680.8	42.1	29.5	1.74	..	26.4	9.0	10,486	..	..	14.5
1981	56,357.5	730.7	658.0	37.1	29.7	1.82	27.0	26.8	12.5	9,506	70.8	76.8	11.2
1986	56,683.8	754.8	660.7	33.5	29.7	1.78	27.4	27.0	21.4	8,914	71.9	77.7	9.5
1991	57,438.7	792.3	646.2	33.2	30.0	1.82	27.7	27.7	29.8	8,168	73.2	78.7	7.4
1996	58,164.4	733.2	636.0	33.9	30.0	1.73	28.2	28.6	35.5	7,584	74.3	79.4	6.1
1999	58,684.4	700.0	632.1	33.4	29.9	1.68	28.4	28.9	38.8	7,318	75.0	79.9	5.8
2000	58,886.1	679.0	608.4	33.1	29.9	1.64	28.5	29.1	39.5	6,974	75.4	80.2	5.6
2001	59,113.5	669.1	602.3	32.6	29.8	1.63	28.6	29.2	40.1	6,807	75.7	80.4	5.5
2002	59,321.7	668.8	606.2	32.2	29.8	1.64	28.7	29.3	40.6	6,765	75.9	80.5	5.2
2003	59,553.8	695.6	612.0	31.8	29.9	1.71	28.8	29.4	41.5	6,757	76.3	80.7	5.3
2004	59,834.3	716.0	583.1	31.4	30.0	1.77	28.9	29.4	42.3	6,390	..	..	5.0
2005	60,209.5	722.6ᵖ	582.7ᵖ	31.0	30.1	1.79ᵖ	29.1	29.5	42.9	6,259ᵖ	..	..	5.1ᵖ
England													
1976	46,659.9	550.4	560.3	41.4	29.7	1.70	..	26.4	9.2	10,271	..	..	14.2
1981	46,820.8	598.2	541.0	36.4	29.9	1.79	..	26.8	12.9	9,298	71.1	77.0	10.9
1986	47,187.6	623.6	544.5	33.1	29.8	1.76	27.4	27.0	21.4	8,725	72.2	77.9	9.5
1991	47,875.0	660.8	534.0	32.9	30.0	1.81	27.7	27.7	30.1	8,017	73.4	78.9	7.3
1996	48,519.1	614.2	524.0	33.7	30.0	1.73	28.2	28.7	35.5	7,414	74.5	79.6	6.1
1999	49,032.9	589.5	519.6	33.3	29.9	1.69	28.4	29.0	38.5	7,138	75.3	80.1	5.7
2000	49,233.3	572.8	501.0	33.0	29.8	1.65	28.5	29.2	39.1	6,821	75.7	80.4	5.6
2001	49,449.7	563.7	496.1	32.5	29.7	1.63	28.6	29.3	39.6	6,650	76.0	80.6	5.4
2002	49,646.9	565.7	499.1	32.1	29.7	1.65	28.7	29.4	40.1	6,603	76.2	80.7	5.2
2003	49,855.7	589.9	503.4	31.8	29.8	1.73	28.9	29.4	40.9	6,602	76.6	80.9	5.3
2004	50,093.1	607.2	479.2	31.4	29.9	1.78	29.0	29.5	41.7	6,232	..	..	5.0
2005	50,431.7	613.0	479.4	31.0	29.9	1.80	29.1	29.5	42.3	6,110	..	..	5.0
Wales													
1976	2,799.3	33.4	36.3	42.0	30.9	1.78	..	26.0	8.7	10,858	..	..	13.7
1981	2,813.5	35.8	35.0	37.6	31.6	1.87	..	26.6	11.2	9,846	70.4	76.4	12.6
1986	2,810.9	37.0	34.7	34.3	32.5	1.86	26.9	26.5	21.1	9,043	71.6	77.5	9.5
1991	2,873.0	38.1	34.1	34.4	33.5	1.88	27.1	27.0	32.3	8,149	73.1	78.8	6.6
1996	2,891.3	34.9	34.6	34.9	33.7	1.81	27.5	27.8	41.2	7,758	73.9	79.1	5.6
1999	2,900.6	32.1	35.0	34.4	33.6	1.72	27.6	28.1	46.1	7,637	74.7	79.6	6.1
2000	2,906.9	31.3	33.3	34.1	33.5	1.68	27.7	28.2	47.2	7,180	74.9	79.8	5.3
2001	2,910.2	30.6	33.0	33.7	33.6	1.66	27.8	28.3	48.3	7,017	75.4	80.1	5.4
2002	2,923.4	30.2	33.2	33.2	33.6	1.63	28.0	28.4	49.7	6,951	75.7	80.2	4.5
2003	2,938.0	31.4	33.7	32.7	33.7	1.71	28.1	28.5	50.3	6,980	76.0	80.4	4.3
2004	2,952.5	32.3	32.3	32.2	33.9	1.77	28.2	28.5	51.3	6,582	..	..	4.9
2005	2,958.6	32.6	32.2	32.1	34.1	1.79	28.4	28.5	52.4	6,434	..	..	4.1
Scotland													
1976	5,233.4	64.9	65.3	44.7	28.4	1.79	..	26.0	9.3	11,675	..	..	14.8
1981	5,180.2	69.1	63.8	38.2	28.4	1.84	..	26.3	12.2	10,849	69.1	75.3	11.3
1986	5,111.8	65.8	63.5	33.6	28.1	1.67	27.1	26.6	20.6	10,120	70.2	76.2	8.8
1991	5,083.3	67.0	61.0	32.4	28.9	1.69	27.5	27.4	29.1	9,216	71.4	77.1	7.1
1996	5,092.2	59.3	60.7	32.3	29.2	1.56	28.0	28.5	36.0	8,791	72.2	77.9	6.2
1999	5,072.0	55.1	60.3	31.7	29.7	1.51	28.3	28.9	41.2	8,493	72.8	78.4	5.0
2000	5,062.9	53.1	57.8	31.4	29.8	1.48	28.4	29.0	42.6	8,082	73.1	78.6	5.7
2001	5,064.2	52.5	57.4	30.8	30.0	1.49	28.5	29.2	43.3	7,930	73.3	78.8	5.5
2002	5,054.8	51.3	58.1	30.3	30.2	1.48	28.6	29.2	44.0	7,955	73.5	78.9	5.3
2003	5,057.4	52.4	58.5	29.9	30.3	1.54	28.7	29.3	45.5	7,922	73.8	79.1	5.1
2004	5,078.4	54.0	56.2	29.5	30.5	1.60	28.9	29.4	46.7	7,536	74.2ᵖ	79.3ᵖ	4.9
2005	5,094.8	54.4	55.7	29.1	30.6	1.62	29.0	29.5	47.1	7,349	..	..	5.2
Northern Ireland													
1976	1,523.5	26.4	17.0	56.1	25.3	2.68	..	27.4	5.0	11,746	..	..	18.3
1981	1,543.0	27.2	16.3	50.6	25.3	2.59	28.1	27.5	7.0	10,567	69.2	75.5	13.2
1986	1,573.5	28.0	16.1	46.1	25.5	2.45	28.1	27.5	12.8	10,071	70.9	77.1	13.2
1991	1,607.3	26.0	15.1	44.1	26.1	2.16	28.3	28.0	20.3	8,303	72.6	78.4	7.4
1996	1,661.8	24.4	15.2	41.8	25.5	1.95	28.7	28.8	26.0	7,742	73.8	79.2	5.8
1999	1,679.0	23.0	15.7	40.2	25.5	1.86	28.8	29.0	30.3	7,699	74.5	79.6	6.4
2000	1,682.9	21.5	14.9	39.5	25.4	1.75	29.0	29.2	31.8	7,279	74.8	79.8	5.1
2001	1,689.3	22.0	14.5	38.6	25.5	1.80	29.1	29.4	32.5	6,976	75.2	80.1	6.1
2002	1,696.6	21.4	14.6	37.9	25.7	1.77	29.2	29.5	33.5	6,930	75.6	80.4	4.7
2003	1,702.6	21.6	14.5	37.2	25.9	1.81	29.2	29.5	34.4	6,744	75.8	80.6	5.3
2004	1,710.3	22.3	14.4	36.4	26.2	1.87	29.4	29.7	34.5	6,609	..	..	5.5
2005	1,724.4	22.3ᵖ	14.2ᵖ	35.8	26.3	1.87ᵖ	29.5	29.7	36.3	6,418ᵖ	..	..	6.3ᵖ

Notes: Death figures for England and Wales represent the number of deaths registered in each year up to 1992, and the number of deaths occurring in each year from 1993 to 2005. Births and death figures for England and also for Wales each exclude events for persons usually resident outside England and Wales. These events are, however, included in the totals for England and Wales combined, and for the United Kingdom. From 1981 births to non-resident mothers in Northern Ireland are excluded from the figures for Northern Ireland, and for the United Kingdom.

1 Percentage of children under 16 to working population (males 16–64 and females 16–59).
2 Percentage of males 65 and over and females 60 and over to working population (males 16–64 and females 16–59).

3 TFR (total fertility rate) is the number of children that would be born to a woman if current patterns of fertility persisted throughout her childbearing life. It is sometimes called the TPFR (total period fertility rate).
4 Standardised to take account of the age structure of the population.
5 Unstandardised and therefore takes no account of the age structure of the population.
6 Per million population. The age-standardised mortality rate makes allowances for changes in the age structure of the population. See Notes to tables.
7 Deaths at age under one year per 1,000 live births.

p provisional

Table 3.1 — Live births: age of mother

England and Wales — Numbers (thousands), rates, mean age and TFRs

Year and quarter	All ages	Under 20	20–24	25–29	30–34	35–39	40 and over	Mean[1] age (years)	All ages	Under 20	20–24	25–29	30–34	35–39	40 and over	Mean[2] age (years)	TFR[3]
	Total live births (numbers)								Age-specific fertility rates[4]								
1961	811.3	59.8	249.8	248.5	152.3	77.5	23.3	27.6	89.2	37.3	172.6	176.9	103.1	48.1	15.0	27.4	2.77
1964(max)	876.0	76.7	276.1	270.7	153.5	75.4	23.6	27.2	92.9	42.5	181.6	187.3	107.7	49.8	13.7	27.3	2.93
1966	849.8	86.7	285.8	253.7	136.4	67.0	20.1	26.8	90.5	47.7	176.0	174.0	97.3	45.3	12.5	27.1	2.75
1971	783.2	82.6	285.7	247.2	109.6	45.2	12.7	26.2	83.5	50.6	152.9	153.2	77.1	32.8	8.7	26.6	2.37
1976	584.3	57.9	182.2	220.7	90.8	26.1	6.5	26.4	60.4	32.2	109.3	118.7	57.2	18.6	4.8	26.5	1.71
1977(min)	569.3	54.5	174.5	207.9	100.8	25.5	6.0	26.5	58.1	29.4	103.7	117.5	58.6	18.2	4.4	26.6	1.66
1981	634.5	56.6	194.5	215.8	126.6	34.2	6.9	26.8	61.3	28.1	105.3	129.1	68.6	21.7	4.9	27.0	1.79
1986	661.0	57.4	192.1	229.0	129.5	45.5	7.6	27.0	60.6	30.1	92.7	123.8	78.0	24.6	4.8	27.4	1.77
1991	699.2	52.4	173.4	248.7	161.3	53.6	9.8	27.7	63.6	33.0	89.3	119.4	86.7	32.1	5.3	27.7	1.82
1992	689.7	47.9	163.3	244.8	166.8	56.7	10.2	27.9	63.6	31.7	86.1	117.6	87.4	33.4	5.8	27.8	1.80
1993	673.5	45.1	152.0	236.0	171.1	58.8	10.5	28.1	62.7	30.9	82.5	114.4	87.4	34.1	6.2	27.9	1.76
1994	664.7	42.0	140.2	229.1	179.6	63.1	10.7	28.4	62.0	28.9	79.0	112.2	89.4	35.8	6.4	28.1	1.75
1995	648.1	41.9	130.7	217.4	181.2	65.5	11.3	28.5	60.5	28.5	76.4	108.4	88.3	36.3	6.8	28.2	1.72
1996	649.5	44.7	125.7	211.1	186.4	69.5	12.1	28.6	60.6	29.7	77.0	106.6	89.8	37.5	7.2	28.2	1.74
1997	643.1	46.4	118.6	202.8	187.5	74.9	12.9	28.8	60.0	30.2	76.0	104.3	89.8	39.4	7.6	28.3	1.73
1998	635.9	48.3	113.5	193.1	188.5	78.9	13.6	28.9	59.2	30.9	74.9	101.5	90.6	40.4	7.9	28.3	1.72
1999	621.9	48.4	110.7	181.9	185.3	81.3	14.3	29.0	57.8	30.9	73.0	98.3	89.6	40.6	8.1	28.4	1.70
2000	604.4	45.8	107.7	170.7	180.1	85.0	15.1	29.1	55.9	29.3	70.0	94.3	87.9	41.4	8.3	28.5	1.65
2001	594.6	44.2	108.8	159.9	178.9	86.5	16.3	29.2	54.7	28.0	69.0	91.7	88.0	41.5	8.8	28.6	1.63
2002	596.1	43.5	110.9	153.4	180.5	90.5	17.3	29.3	54.7	27.0	69.2	91.6	89.8	43.0	9.1	28.7	1.65
2003	621.5	44.2	116.6	156.9	187.2	97.4	19.1	29.4	56.8	26.8	71.2	96.4	94.8	46.4	9.8	28.8	1.73
2004	639.7	45.1	121.1	160.0	190.6	102.2	20.8	29.4	58.2	26.9	72.7	98.4	99.4	48.9	10.4	28.9	1.78
2005	645.8	44.8	122.1	164.3	188.2	104.1	22.2	29.5	58.4	26.3	71.7	98.8	100.9	50.3	10.8	29.0	1.80
2002 March	143.3	10.5	26.5	37.4	43.2	21.6	4.1	29.3	53.3	26	67	91	87	42	9	28.7	1.61
June	147.2	10.4	26.7	37.9	45.5	22.4	4.3	29.4	54.1	26	67	91	91	43	9	28.8	1.63
Sept	155.0	11.4	28.9	39.9	46.9	23.4	4.5	29.3	56.4	28	72	95	93	44	9	28.7	1.70
Dec	150.6	11.2	28.8	38.2	45.0	23.0	4.5	29.3	54.8	28	71	91	89	44	9	28.7	1.65
2003 March	147.4	10.9	27.9	37.5	44.0	22.6	4.6	29.3	54.6	27	69	93	90	44	10	28.8	1.66
June	155.1	10.7	28.5	39.3	47.4	24.5	4.7	29.5	56.9	26	70	97	96	47	10	28.9	1.73
Sept	162.8	11.5	30.5	41.0	49.3	25.6	5.0	29.4	59.0	28	74	100	99	48	10	28.9	1.79
Dec	156.0	11.2	29.7	39.1	46.5	24.6	4.8	29.4	56.6	27	72	95	94	47	10	28.8	1.72
2004 March	155.2	11.0	29.3	38.7	46.6	24.7	4.9	29.4	56.8	27	71	96	98	47	10	28.9	1.74
June	157.4	10.7	29.3	39.4	47.7	25.2	5.0	29.5	57.6	26	71	97	100	49	10	29.0	1.77
Sept	165.4	11.7	31.4	41.6	49.0	26.3	5.4	29.4	59.9	28	75	102	102	50	11	28.9	1.84
Dec	161.7	11.6	31.1	40.3	47.2	26.0	5.5	29.4	58.6	28	74	99	98	49	11	28.9	1.80
2005 March	154.3	10.9	29.3	38.9	45.0	24.7	5.4	29.5	56.6	26	70	95	98	48	11	29.0	1.74
June	159.8	10.7	29.6	40.3	47.5	26.2	5.4	29.5	57.9	25	70	97	102	51	11	29.1	1.78
Sept	170.2	11.9	32.5	43.7	49.4	26.9	5.7	29.4	61.1	28	76	104	105	52	11	29.0	1.88
Dec	161.7	11.3	30.7	41.4	46.3	26.3	5.7	29.4	58.0	27	72	99	99	50	11	29.0	1.79
2006 March[5]	159.5[p]	11.1[p]	30.5[p]	40.6[p]	45.2[p]	26.3[p]	5.7[p]	29.5[p]	58.4[p]	26[p]	72[p]	96[p]	102[p]	52[p]	11[p]	29.1[p]	1.80[p]
June	165.3[p]	11.3[p]	31.1[p]	42.7[p]	47.4[p]	27.0[p]	5.9[p]	29.5[p]	59.8	27[p]	72[p]	100[p]	106[p]	53[p]	11[p]	29.1[p]	1.85[p]

Notes: The rates for women of all ages, under 20, and 40 and over are based upon the populations of women aged 15–44, 15–19, and 40–44 respectively.
1 Unstandardised and therefore takes no account of the age structure of the population.
2 Standardised to take account of the age structure of the population. This measure is more appropriate for use when analysing trends or making comparisons between different geographies.
3 TFR (total fertility rate) is the number of children that would be born to a woman if current patterns of fertility persisted throughout her childbearing life. It is sometimes called the TPFR (total period fertility rate).
4 Births per 1,000 women in the age-group; all quarterly age-specific fertility rates are adjusted for days in the quarter. They are not adjusted for seasonality.
5 Birth rates for 2006 are based on the 2004-based population projections for 2006.
p provisional

Table 3.2 — Live births outside marriage: age of mother and type of registration

England and Wales

Numbers (thousands), mean age and percentages

Year and quarter	Age of mother at birth — Live births outside marriage (numbers)							Mean[1] age (years)	Age of mother at birth — Percentage of total live births in age-group							Registration[2] — As a percentage of all births outside marriage		
	All ages	Under 20	20–24	25–29	30–34	35–39	40 and over		All ages	Under 20	20–24	25–29	30–34	35–39	40 and over	Joint Same[3] address	Joint Different[3] addresses	Sole
1971	65.7	21.6	22.0	11.5	6.2	3.2	1.1	23.7	8.4	26.1	7.7	4.7	5.7	7.0	9.0	45.5		54.5
1976	53.8	19.8	16.6	9.7	4.7	2.3	0.7	23.3	9.2	34.2	9.1	4.4	5.2	8.6	10.1	51.0		49.0
1981	81.0	26.4	28.8	14.3	7.9	1.3	0.9	23.4	12.8	46.7	14.8	6.6	6.2	3.9	12.5	58.2		41.8
1986	141.3	39.6	54.1	27.7	13.1	5.7	1.1	23.8	21.4	69.0	28.2	12.1	10.1	12.6	14.7	46.6	19.6	33.8
1991	211.3	43.4	77.8	52.4	25.7	9.8	2.1	24.8	30.2	82.9	44.9	21.1	16.0	18.3	21.3	54.6	19.8	25.6
1992	215.2	40.1	77.1	55.9	28.9	10.9	2.3	25.2	31.2	83.7	47.2	22.8	17.3	19.3	22.9	55.4	20.7	23.9
1993	216.5	38.2	75.0	57.5	31.4	11.9	2.5	25.5	32.2	84.8	49.4	24.4	18.4	20.2	23.5	54.8	22.0	23.2
1994	215.5	35.9	71.0	58.5	34.0	13.4	2.7	25.8	32.4	85.5	50.6	25.5	18.9	21.2	25.2	57.5	19.8	22.7
1995	219.9	36.3	69.7	59.6	37.0	14.4	3.0	26.0	33.9	86.6	53.3	27.4	20.4	22.0	26.2	58.1	20.1	21.8
1996	232.7	39.3	71.1	62.3	40.5	16.2	3.2	26.1	35.8	88.0	56.5	29.5	21.7	23.4	26.7	58.1	19.9	21.9
1997	238.2	41.1	69.5	63.4	42.2	18.2	3.7	26.2	37.0	88.7	58.6	31.3	22.5	24.3	28.6	59.5	19.3	21.2
1998	240.6	43.0	67.8	62.4	43.9	19.6	3.9	26.3	37.8	89.1	59.7	32.3	23.3	24.8	29.0	60.9	18.3	20.8
1999	241.9	43.0	67.5	61.2	45.0	20.8	4.3	26.4	38.9	89.0	61.0	33.6	24.3	25.6	30.2	61.8	18.2	19.9
2000	238.6	41.1	67.5	59.1	43.9	22.3	4.7	26.5	39.5	89.7	62.6	34.6	24.4	26.2	31.0	62.7	18.2	19.2
2001	238.1	39.5	68.1	56.8	45.2	23.3	5.1	26.7	40.0	89.5	62.6	35.5	25.3	26.9	31.6	63.2	18.4	18.4
2002	242.0	38.9	70.2	55.8	46.4	25.1	5.6	26.8	40.6	89.5	63.3	36.4	25.7	27.7	32.2	63.7	18.5	17.8
2003	257.2	39.9	75.7	58.2	49.2	27.8	6.4	26.9	41.4	90.2	64.9	37.1	26.3	28.5	33.3	63.5	19.0	17.4
2004	269.7	41.0	79.8	61.4	50.7	29.7	7.1	27.0	42.2	91.0	65.9	38.4	26.6	29.0	34.0	63.6	19.6	16.8
2005	276.5	41.2	82.1	64.4	50.8	30.3	7.7	27.0	42.8	91.8	67.2	39.2	27.0	29.1	34.8	63.5	20.2	16.3
2002 March	58.0	9.4	16.7	13.6	10.9	6.0	1.3	26.8	40.5	89.4	63.0	36.4	25.4	27.7	31.5	63.2	18.5	18.3
June	58.3	9.3	16.6	13.5	11.4	6.1	1.4	26.8	39.6	89.4	62.2	35.6	25.0	27.2	31.7	64.2	18.2	17.7
Sept	63.4	10.2	18.4	14.6	12.3	6.5	1.5	26.8	40.9	89.3	63.8	36.6	26.1	27.9	32.7	63.9	18.5	17.5
Dec	62.3	10.0	18.4	14.1	11.9	6.5	1.5	26.8	41.4	89.7	64.1	36.9	26.4	28.0	32.8	63.3	18.9	17.8
2003 March	61.0	9.8	18.0	13.9	11.6	6.3	1.5	26.8	41.4	90.1	64.5	37.0	26.9	29.1	33.3	63.0	18.9	18.1
June	62.8	9.6	18.3	14.2	12.2	6.9	1.6	27.0	40.5	90.0	64.0	36.2	25.7	28.3	33.7	64.0	18.5	17.4
Sept	67.6	10.3	20.0	15.3	13.0	7.3	1.7	26.9	41.5	90.2	65.6	38.3	26.4	28.6	33.3	63.7	19.3	18.0
Dec	65.8	10.2	19.5	14.9	12.5	7.3	1.6	26.9	42.2	90.4	65.6	38.0	27.7	29.5	32.9	63.3	19.4	17.4
2004 March	65.2	10.1	19.3	14.8	12.5	7.0	1.7	26.9	42.0	91.2	65.8	38.2	26.8	28.2	34.3	63.1	19.4	17.4
June	65.2	9.8	19.1	14.9	12.5	7.3	1.7	27.0	41.4	91.0	65.1	37.7	26.2	28.8	34.5	63.9	19.5	16.6
Sept	70.2	10.7	20.7	16.1	13.0	7.9	1.8	27.0	42.4	91.2	66.1	38.6	26.5	30.0	33.5	63.7	19.7	16.6
Dec	69.1	10.6	20.7	15.7	12.7	7.5	1.9	26.9	42.7	90.6	66.6	39.0	27.0	29.0	33.9	63.6	19.8	16.6
2005 March	66.3	10.1	19.6	15.2	12.2	7.3	1.9	27.0	43.0	92.0	67.0	39.0	27.1	29.6	35.2	63.1	20.3	16.6
June	66.6	9.8	19.7	15.4	12.5	7.4	1.8	27.0	41.7	91.2	66.5	38.2	26.4	28.1	33.5	63.7	19.8	16.5
Sept	73.7	10.9	22.1	17.3	13.4	7.9	2.1	26.9	43.3	92.0	68.0	39.6	27.2	29.3	35.7	63.7	20.3	16.0
Dec	69.9	10.4	20.7	16.5	12.6	7.7	2.0	27.0	43.2	92.1	67.4	39.8	27.3	29.5	34.8	63.5	20.3	16.2
2006 March[p]	68.4	10.3	20.7	16.0	11.9	7.5	2.0	26.9	43.1	93.2	68.0	39.4	26.5	28.9	34.6	63.1	20.9	16.0
June[p]	71.0	10.5	21.2	16.8	12.7	7.8	2.0	27.0	43.0	92.6	68.1	39.4	26.8	28.9	34.9	63.8	20.6	15.6

1 Unstandardised and therefore takes no account of the age structure of the population.
2 Births outside marriage can be registered by both the mother and father (joint) or by the mother alone (sole).
3 Usual address(es) of parents.
p provisional

Table 4.1 — Conceptions: age of woman at conception

England and Wales (residents)
Numbers (thousands) and rates; and percentage terminated by abortion

Year and quarter	All ages	\multicolumn{8}{c}{Age of woman at conception}

Year and quarter	All ages	Under 16	Under 18	Under 20	20–24	25–29	30–34	35–39	40 and over
(a) numbers (thousands)									
1991	853.7	7.5	40.1	101.6	233.3	281.5	167.5	57.6	12.1
1996	816.9	8.9	43.5	94.9	179.8	252.6	200.0	75.5	14.1
1999	774.0	7.9	42.0	98.8	157.6	218.5	197.1	86.0	16.0
2000	767.0	8.1	41.3	97.7	159.0	209.3	195.3	88.7	17.0
2001	763.7	7.9	41.0	96.0	161.6	199.3	196.7	92.2	17.8
2002	787.0	7.9	42.0	97.1	167.8	199.4	204.3	98.9	19.6
2003	806.8	8.0	42.2	98.6	175.3	199.8	209.0	103.1	20.9
2004	826.8	7.6	42.2	101.3	181.3	205.1	209.6	106.8	22.8
2002 March	191.6	1.9	10.3	24.1	41.3	48.8	49.0	23.7	4.6
June	190.4	2.0	10.5	24.2	40.7	48.2	48.8	23.8	4.8
Sept	197.4	2.0	10.2	23.4	41.4	50.2	52.4	25.2	4.9
Dec	207.6	2.0	11.0	25.4	44.4	52.3	54.2	26.2	5.2
2003 March	198.2	1.9	10.5	24.5	42.9	49.4	51.2	25.2	4.9
June	198.5	2.1	10.8	24.7	43.2	49.1	51.1	25.2	5.2
Sept	200.1	2.0	10.2	23.7	43.1	49.3	52.8	26.1	5.2
Dec	210.0	2.0	10.7	25.7	46.1	52.0	54.0	26.7	5.6
2004 March	207.9	2.0	10.9	26.2	45.9	51.1	52.6	26.6	5.6
June	200.1	1.9	10.6	25.0	43.7	49.3	50.4	25.9	5.7
Sept	203.6	1.8	10.0	24.0	44.1	50.7	52.7	26.6	5.6
Dec	215.2	1.9	10.8	26.1	47.7	54.0	54.0	27.6	5.8
2005 March[p]	204.2	1.9	10.4	25.0	45.3	50.7	51.0	26.5	5.7
June[1p]	204.3	2.0	10.4	24.9	44.8	50.4	50.2	26.7	5.8
Sept[1p]	209.7	2.0	10.4	25.1	45.1	52.6	52.5	27.2	6.0
(b) rates (conceptions per thousand women in age group)									
1991	77.7	8.9	44.6	64.1	120.2	135.1	90.1	34.4	6.6
1996	76.2	9.5	46.3	63.2	110.1	127.6	96.3	40.7	8.4
1999	71.9	8.3	45.1	63.1	103.9	118.0	95.3	42.9	9.1
2000	70.9	8.3	43.9	62.5	103.2	115.7	95.3	43.2	9.4
2001	70.3	8.0	42.7	60.8	102.5	114.2	96.7	44.3	9.6
2002	72.2	7.9	42.8	60.3	104.6	119.1	101.6	47.0	10.3
2003	73.7	8.0	42.3	59.8	107.1	122.8	105.9	49.1	10.7
2004	75.3	7.5	41.7	60.3	108.9	126.2	109.4	51.0	11.4
2002 March	71.3	7.7	42.9	61.3	105.1	116.4	98.4	45.8	9.9
June	70.1	8.1	42.9	60.4	101.9	114.8	97.1	45.5	10.2
Sept	71.8	7.7	41.2	57.5	102.1	119.4	103.5	47.6	10.2
Dec	75.4	8.0	44.1	62.1	108.9	125.1	107.6	49.4	10.7
2003 March	73.5	7.8	42.8	60.8	107.2	121.8	104.5	48.6	10.3
June	72.8	8.3	43.3	60.3	106.1	120.6	103.5	48.0	10.8
Sept	72.5	7.9	40.5	56.8	104.2	120.2	106.4	49.3	10.5
Dec	76.0	7.8	42.5	61.4	110.9	126.8	109.7	50.5	11.2
2004 March	76.2	7.8	43.4	63.1	111.5	126.3	109.1	51.1	11.4
June	73.3	7.7	42.1	60.1	105.8	122.1	105.3	49.8	11.5
Sept	73.7	7.1	39.2	56.8	105.0	123.6	109.8	50.6	11.1
Dec	77.8	7.4	42.4	61.6	113.0	131.1	113.2	52.8	11.4
2005 March[p]	75.1	7.6	41.4	60.1	108.9	124.7	109.7	51.7	11.4
June[1p]	74.2	8.0	41.1	59.0	106.0	122.0	107.6	51.6	11.4
Sept[1p]	75.2	7.8	40.3	58.5	105.0	125.1	112.2	52.1	11.5
(c) percentage terminated by abortion									
1991	19.4	51.1	39.9	34.5	22.2	13.4	13.7	22.0	41.6
1996	20.8	49.2	40.0	36.2	25.7	15.6	14.1	21.2	37.6
1999	22.6	52.6	43.0	38.6	28.5	17.5	14.7	21.2	37.0
2000	22.7	54.0	44.2	39.3	29.2	17.7	14.5	20.5	35.4
2001	23.2	55.8	45.7	40.4	29.7	18.4	14.6	20.4	34.6
2002	22.5	55.6	45.3	39.9	28.8	17.9	13.9	19.5	34.6
2003	22.5	57.4	45.7	40.2	29.0	17.9	13.6	18.9	34.7
2004	22.4	57.2	45.6	40.1	28.9	18.2	13.2	18.3	33.0
2002 March	22.9	54.3	44.9	40.2	29.4	18.1	14.1	19.8	35.1
June	22.9	55.5	45.0	39.4	28.9	18.4	14.5	20.1	34.8
Sept	21.6	56.1	45.0	39.4	27.8	17.3	13.2	18.7	34.2
Dec	22.6	56.4	46.3	40.7	29.0	17.8	13.9	19.4	34.5
2003 March	22.8	58.9	46.1	40.2	29.5	17.9	13.8	19.7	34.5
June	23.1	58.3	46.2	40.9	29.3	18.4	14.2	19.2	36.1
Sept	21.6	56.9	45.3	39.5	28.0	17.1	13.0	18.0	33.8
Dec	22.5	55.7	45.0	40.3	29.0	18.1	13.5	18.5	34.5
2004 March	22.7	58.2	45.7	40.2	29.4	18.5	13.4	18.2	32.9
June	23.0	57.2	46.3	40.8	29.2	18.6	13.7	19.2	33.5
Sept	21.9	56.8	45.8	40.0	28.4	17.9	12.8	17.8	33.0
Dec	22.0	56.3	44.5	39.3	28.6	17.8	13.0	18.2	32.5
2005 March[p]	22.4	57.3	47.2	41.0	29.1	18.0	13.1	17.9	32.5
June[1p]	22.7	57.0	46.1	40.6	29.2	18.8	14.1	18.0	34.0
Sept[1p]	21.5	56.1	45.6	39.4	27.8	17.7	12.8	17.4	32.4

Notes: Conception figures are estimates derived from birth registrations and abortion notifications.
Rates for women of all ages, under 16, under 18, under 20 and 40 and over are based on the population of women aged 15–44, 13–15, 15–17, 15–19 and 40–44 respectively.
For a quarterly analysis of conceptions to women under 18 for local authority areas see the National Statistics website, www.statistics.gov.uk
1 Figures for conceptions by age for the June and September quarters of 2005 exclude maternities where the mother's age was not recorded.
p provisional

Table 4.2 — Abortions: residents and non-residents; age and gestation (residents only)

England and Wales | Numbers (thousands) and rates; and percentages for gestation weeks

Numbers (thousands)

Year and quarter	All[1] women	Residents[1]	Non-[1] residents	Under 16	16–19	20–24	25–29	30–34	35–44	45 and over	Under 9	9–12	13–19	20 and over
1976	129.7	101.9	27.8	3.4	24.0	23.6	19.3	14.6	14.7	0.5	24.8	55.8	15.0	1.1
1981	162.5	128.6	33.9	3.5	31.4	34.3	21.9	18.7	17.6	0.6	31.0	53.4	13.5	1.3
1986	172.3	147.6	24.7	3.9	33.8	45.3	28.7	18.0	17.5	0.4	33.4	53.8	11.5	1.4
1991	179.5	167.4	12.1	3.2	31.1	52.7	38.6	23.4	17.9	0.4	35.2	52.9	10.6	1.2
1996	177.5	167.9	9.6	3.6	28.8	46.4	39.3	28.2	21.1	0.4	40.0	48.7	10.1	1.3
1997	179.7	170.1	9.6	3.4	29.9	45.0	40.2	28.9	22.3	0.5	41.2	47.9	9.6	1.2
1998	187.4	177.9	9.5	3.8	33.2	45.8	40.4	30.4	23.8	0.5	41.4	47.6	9.7	1.3
1999	183.2	173.7	9.5	3.6	32.8	45.0	38.5	29.1	24.1	0.5	42.5	46.5	9.5	1.4
2000	185.4	175.5	9.8	3.7	33.2	47.1	37.9	28.7	24.4	0.5	43.3	45.0	10.3	1.5
2001	186.3	176.4	9.9	3.7	33.4	48.3	36.5	28.8	25.2	0.5	42.8	45.0	10.6	1.6
2002	185.4	175.9	9.5	3.7	33.0	48.4	35.8	28.5	26.0	0.5	42.2	45.2	11.0	1.6
2003	190.7	181.6	9.1	4.0	34.2	51.1	36.0	28.7	26.9	0.5	43.6	43.7	11.1	1.6
2004[4]	194.5	185.7	8.8	3.8	35.5	52.8	37.8	28.1	27.3	0.5	46.2	41.5	10.8	1.6
2005	194.4	186.4	7.9	3.8	35.3	53.3	38.3	27.8	27.2	0.6	53.6	35.7	9.3	1.4
2001 March	47.8	45.3	2.5	0.9	8.7	12.4	9.4	7.3	6.4	0.1	40.5	46.3	11.6	1.5
June	46.6	44.1	2.5	0.9	8.3	12.1	9.1	7.2	6.3	0.1	42.0	45.8	10.6	1.6
Sept	46.2	43.8	2.4	1.0	8.2	11.8	9.1	7.3	6.3	0.1	43.1	44.7	10.6	1.5
Dec	45.6	43.3	2.4	0.9	8.2	11.9	8.9	7.0	6.2	0.1	45.7	43.1	9.7	1.6
2002 March	47.6	45.2	2.5	0.9	8.6	12.6	9.2	7.3	6.5	0.1	38.9	47.4	12.0	1.6
June	45.9	43.5	2.5	0.9	8.2	12.0	8.9	7.0	6.4	0.1	40.0	46.4	11.8	1.8
Sept	46.5	44.1	2.4	1.0	8.2	11.9	8.9	7.3	6.6	0.1	42.9	45.1	10.4	1.6
Dec	45.3	43.2	2.1	0.9	8.0	11.9	8.8	6.9	6.5	0.1	47.0	41.8	9.7	1.5
2003 March	50.0	47.6	2.4	1.0	9.1	13.4	9.4	7.5	7.0	0.1	40.9	45.3	12.2	1.6
June	47.7	45.4	2.3	1.0	8.5	12.7	9.1	7.2	6.7	0.1	42.5	44.4	11.4	1.6
Sept	47.7	44.8	2.3	1.0	8.3	12.5	8.9	7.2	6.7	0.1	43.3	43.9	11.2	1.5
Dec	46.0	43.9	2.1	0.9	8.3	12.5	8.6	6.9	6.5	0.1	47.7	41.0	9.6	1.7
2004[4] March	51.1	48.7	2.4	1.0	9.4	13.9	9.8	7.5	7.0	0.1	41.7	44.5	12.1	1.7
June	48.9	46.6	2.3	1.0	8.9	13.3	9.5	6.9	6.9	0.1	43.6	43.3	11.2	1.8
Sept	48.4	46.3	2.1	1.0	8.9	13.0	9.4	7.0	6.9	0.1	47.8	40.5	10.3	1.4
Dec	46.1	44.2	1.9	1.0	8.4	12.6	9.1	6.6	6.5	0.1	52.0	37.2	9.5	1.3
2005 March	50.1	47.9	2.1	0.9	9.1	13.9	9.7	7.2	7.0	0.1	47.2	40.4	11.0	1.4
June	50.1	48.0	2.1	1.0	9.2	13.9	9.9	7.1	6.9	0.1	53.8	35.6	9.2	1.4
Sept	47.0	45.1	1.9	1.0	8.5	12.7	9.3	6.9	6.7	0.1	56.5	33.6	8.5	1.3
Dec	47.2	45.3	1.8	0.9	8.6	12.9	9.5	6.7	6.7	0.1	57.2	32.9	8.3	1.5
2006 March[p]	51.6	49.6	2.0	1.0	9.6	14.3	10.2	7.1	7.1	0.2	50.3	37.6	10.5	1.6
June[p]	50.3	48.4	1.9	1.0	9.2	13.8	10.1	7.1	6.9	0.2	53.3	35.6	9.5	1.6

Rates (per thousand women residents)

Year and quarter	ASR[3] (women 15–44)	Crude rate[2] (women 15–44)	Non-resident	Under 16	16–19	20–24	25–29	30–34	35–44	45 and over
1976	10.2	10.5	:	2.9	16.9	14.2	10.4	9.2	5.3	0.3
1981	11.9	12.4	:	3.0	19.4	18.6	13.1	10.1	5.9	0.4
1986	13.0	13.5	:	3.7	22.0	21.9	15.5	10.8	5.1	0.3
1991	15.0	15.2	:	3.8	24.0	27.1	18.5	12.6	5.1	0.3
1996	16.0	15.7	:	3.9	24.2	28.4	19.9	13.6	6.0	0.2
1997	16.3	15.9	:	3.7	24.4	28.8	20.7	13.8	6.2	0.3
1998	17.1	16.6	:	4.0	26.8	30.2	21.2	14.6	6.5	0.3
1999	16.8	16.2	:	3.8	26.3	29.7	20.8	14.1	6.4	0.3
2000	17.0	16.3	:	3.9	26.9	30.7	20.9	14.1	6.3	0.3
2001	17.0	16.2	:	3.7	26.6	30.6	20.9	14.2	6.4	0.3
2002	17.0	16.1	:	3.7	25.8	30.1	21.4	14.2	6.5	0.3
2003	17.5	16.6	:	3.9	26.1	31.2	22.1	14.6	6.6	0.3
2004[4]	17.8	16.9	:	3.7	26.5	31.9	23.3	14.7	6.7	0.3
2005	17.8	17.0	:	3.7	26.3	32.0	23.6	14.5	6.6	0.3
2001 March	17.5	16.7	:	3.6	27.9	31.8	21.2	14.3	6.6	0.3
June	17.0	16.2	:	3.8	26.6	30.8	20.9	14.1	6.4	0.3
Sept	16.9	16.1	:	3.9	25.9	29.9	20.9	14.4	6.4	0.3
Dec	16.7	15.9	:	3.6	26.0	30.0	20.8	13.8	6.3	0.2
2002 March	17.4	16.6	:	3.7	26.9	31.6	21.7	14.4	6.6	0.2
June	16.7	15.9	:	3.7	25.6	29.9	21.1	13.9	6.4	0.3
Sept	16.9	16.1	:	3.8	25.1	29.2	21.9	14.8	6.5	0.2
Dec	16.5	15.7	:	3.7	24.7	29.2	21.4	13.9	6.4	0.3
2003 March	18.3	17.4	:	4.0	28.0	33.0	22.9	15.1	6.9	0.3
June	17.4	16.6	:	4.0	26.1	31.1	22.3	14.5	6.6	0.3
Sept	17.2	16.4	:	4.0	25.3	30.6	21.8	14.6	6.6	0.3
Dec	16.8	16.0	:	3.7	25.2	30.4	21.1	14.2	6.4	0.3
2004[4] March	18.7	17.8	:	3.9	28.3	33.8	24.1	15.4	6.9	0.3
June	17.9	17.0	:	3.8	26.7	32.3	23.3	14.4	6.7	0.3
Sept	17.8	16.9	:	3.7	26.6	31.5	23.0	14.8	6.8	0.3
Dec	17.0	16.2	:	3.5	25.0	30.4	22.3	14.2	6.3	0.3
2005 March	18.4	17.5	:	3.7	27.0	33.5	23.8	15.2	6.8	0.3
June	18.4	17.5	:	3.8	27.2	33.3	24.1	15.3	6.7	0.3
Sept	17.3	16.4	:	3.8	25.2	30.5	22.6	14.8	6.5	0.3
Dec	17.4	16.5	:	3.6	25.4	30.9	23.0	14.4	6.5	0.3
2006 March[p]	19.0	18.1	:	3.9	28.4	34.1	24.6	15.7	6.9	0.3
June[p]	18.5	17.6	:	3.8	27.2	33.0	24.2	15.8	6.7	0.4

Notes: Rates for Under 16 and 45 and over are based on female populations aged 13–15 and 45–49 respectively.
1   Includes cases with not stated age and/or gestation week.
2   Includes incomplete forms that have been returned to practitioners.
3   Rates for all women residents age-standardised to the European population for ages 15–44.
4   Numbers and rates revised in 2006.
p   provisional

Table 5.1 — Period expectation of life at birth and selected age

Constituent countries of the United Kingdom · Years

	Males									Females							
Year	At birth	5	20	30	50	60	70	80	Year	At birth	5	20	30	50	60	70	80
United Kingdom																	
1981	70.8	66.9	52.3	42.7	24.1	16.3	10.1	5.8	1981	76.8	72.7	57.9	48.2	29.2	20.8	13.3	7.5
1986	71.9	67.8	53.2	43.6	24.9	16.8	10.5	6.0	1986	77.7	73.4	58.6	48.8	29.8	21.2	13.8	7.8
1991	73.2	68.9	54.2	44.7	26.0	17.7	11.1	6.4	1991	78.7	74.3	59.5	49.7	30.6	21.9	14.3	8.2
1996	74.3	69.8	55.1	45.6	26.9	18.5	11.6	6.6	1996	79.4	74.9	60.1	50.3	31.2	22.3	14.5	8.3
1997	74.5	70.1	55.4	45.9	27.2	18.8	11.7	6.7	1997	79.6	75.1	60.2	50.4	31.3	22.5	14.6	8.4
1998	74.8	70.3	55.6	46.1	27.4	18.9	11.9	6.7	1998	79.7	75.2	60.4	50.5	31.4	22.6	14.7	8.4
1999	75.0	70.6	55.9	46.3	27.6	19.2	12.0	6.8	1999	79.9	75.4	60.5	50.7	31.6	22.8	14.8	8.5
2000	75.4	70.9	56.2	46.6	28.0	19.5	12.3	7.0	2000	80.2	75.6	60.8	51.0	31.9	23.0	15.0	8.6
2001	75.7	71.2	56.5	46.9	28.3	19.8	12.5	7.1	2001	80.4	75.9	61.0	51.2	32.1	23.2	15.2	8.7
2002	75.9	71.5	56.7	47.2	28.5	20.0	12.6	7.2	2002	80.5	76.0	61.1	51.3	32.2	23.3	15.2	8.7
2003	76.3	71.8	57.0	47.4	28.8	20.2	12.9	7.3	2003	80.7	76.2	61.3	51.5	32.4	23.4	15.3	8.7
England and Wales																	
1981	71.0	67.1	52.5	42.9	24.3	16.4	10.1	5.8	1981	77.0	72.9	58.1	48.3	29.4	20.9	13.4	7.5
1986	72.1	68.0	53.4	43.8	25.0	16.9	10.5	6.1	1986	77.9	73.6	58.8	49.0	30.0	21.4	13.9	7.9
1991	73.4	69.1	54.4	44.8	26.1	17.8	11.2	6.4	1991	78.9	74.5	59.7	49.9	30.8	22.0	14.4	8.3
1996	74.5	70.1	55.4	45.8	27.1	18.7	11.6	6.6	1996	79.6	75.1	60.2	50.4	31.3	22.5	14.6	8.4
1997	74.8	70.3	55.6	46.1	27.4	18.9	11.8	6.7	1997	79.7	75.2	60.4	50.6	31.5	22.6	14.7	8.4
1998	75.0	70.6	55.8	46.3	27.6	19.1	11.9	6.8	1998	79.9	75.4	60.5	50.7	31.6	22.7	14.8	8.4
1999	75.3	70.8	56.1	46.5	27.8	19.3	12.1	6.9	1999	80.1	75.6	60.7	50.9	31.8	22.9	14.9	8.5
2000	75.6	71.2	56.4	46.9	28.1	19.6	12.3	7.0	2000	80.3	75.8	61.0	51.1	32.0	23.1	15.1	8.6
2001	76.0	71.5	56.7	47.2	28.5	19.9	12.6	7.1	2001	80.6	76.0	61.2	51.4	32.2	23.3	15.2	8.7
2002	76.2	71.7	57.0	47.4	28.7	20.1	12.7	7.2	2002	80.7	76.1	61.3	51.5	32.3	23.4	15.3	8.7
2003	76.5	72.0	57.3	47.7	28.9	20.4	13.0	7.3	2003	80.9	76.4	61.5	51.7	32.5	23.6	15.4	8.8
England																	
1981	71.1	67.1	52.5	42.9	24.3	16.4	10.1	5.8	1981	77.0	72.9	58.2	48.4	29.4	20.9	13.4	7.5
1986	72.2	68.1	53.4	43.8	25.1	17.0	10.6	6.1	1986	77.9	73.6	58.8	49.0	30.0	21.4	13.9	7.9
1991	73.4	69.1	54.4	44.9	26.2	17.8	11.2	6.4	1991	78.9	74.5	59.7	49.9	30.8	22.0	14.4	8.3
1996	74.5	70.1	55.4	45.9	27.1	18.7	11.7	6.6	1996	79.6	75.1	60.3	50.5	31.3	22.5	14.6	8.4
1997	74.8	70.4	55.6	46.1	27.4	18.9	11.8	6.7	1997	79.8	75.3	60.4	50.6	31.5	22.6	14.7	8.4
1998	75.0	70.6	55.9	46.3	27.6	19.1	12.0	6.8	1998	79.9	75.4	60.6	50.7	31.6	22.7	14.8	8.5
1999	75.3	70.9	56.1	46.5	27.9	19.4	12.1	6.9	1999	80.1	75.6	60.8	50.9	31.8	22.9	14.9	8.5
2000	75.7	71.2	56.5	46.9	28.2	19.6	12.4	7.0	2000	80.4	75.8	61.0	51.2	32.0	23.1	15.1	8.6
2001	76.0	71.5	56.8	47.2	28.5	19.9	12.6	7.1	2001	80.6	76.1	61.2	51.4	32.3	23.4	15.3	8.7
2002	76.2	71.8	57.0	47.4	28.7	20.1	12.8	7.2	2002	80.7	76.2	61.3	51.5	32.4	23.4	15.3	8.7
2003	76.6	72.1	57.3	47.7	29.0	20.4	13.0	7.3	2003	80.9	76.4	61.5	51.7	32.6	23.6	15.5	8.8
Wales																	
1981	70.4	66.5	51.9	42.2	23.6	15.8	9.7	5.6	1981	76.4	72.3	57.5	47.7	28.9	20.5	13.1	7.4
1986	71.6	67.5	52.8	43.2	24.6	16.6	10.3	6.0	1986	77.5	73.3	58.5	48.7	29.7	21.1	13.7	7.8
1991	73.1	68.8	54.1	44.6	25.8	17.6	11.0	6.4	1991	78.8	74.3	59.5	49.7	30.6	21.8	14.3	8.3
1996	73.9	69.4	54.7	45.3	26.6	18.2	11.3	6.4	1996	79.1	74.6	59.7	49.9	30.9	22.1	14.4	8.3
1997	74.3	69.8	55.1	45.6	26.9	18.5	11.6	6.6	1997	79.3	74.8	60.0	50.2	31.1	22.3	14.5	8.4
1998	74.4	70.0	55.2	45.8	27.1	18.6	11.6	6.6	1998	79.4	74.9	60.0	50.2	31.1	22.3	14.5	8.3
1999	74.7	70.2	55.5	46.1	27.4	18.9	11.9	6.8	1999	79.6	75.1	60.2	50.4	31.3	22.5	14.6	8.4
2000	74.9	70.5	55.8	46.3	27.6	19.1	12.0	6.8	2000	79.8	75.3	60.4	50.6	31.5	22.6	14.7	8.4
2001	75.4	70.9	56.2	46.7	28.0	19.5	12.3	7.1	2001	80.1	75.5	60.6	50.8	31.8	22.9	14.9	8.5
2002	75.7	71.1	56.3	46.9	28.2	19.7	12.4	7.1	2002	80.2	75.6	60.7	50.9	31.8	22.9	15.0	8.6
2003	76.0	71.4	56.7	47.1	28.5	20.0	12.6	7.2	2003	80.4	75.8	60.9	51.1	32.0	23.1	15.1	8.6
Scotland																	
1981	69.1	65.2	50.6	41.1	22.9	15.4	9.6	5.5	1981	75.3	71.2	56.4	46.7	27.9	19.7	12.7	7.2
1986	70.2	66.0	51.4	41.9	23.5	15.8	9.9	5.7	1986	76.2	71.9	57.1	47.3	28.4	20.1	13.0	7.5
1991	71.4	67.1	52.5	43.0	24.6	16.6	10.4	6.1	1991	77.1	72.7	57.9	48.1	29.2	20.7	13.5	7.9
1996	72.2	67.8	53.1	43.7	25.3	17.3	10.9	6.3	1996	77.9	73.3	58.5	48.8	29.8	21.2	13.8	8.0
1997	72.4	68.0	53.3	43.9	25.6	17.5	11.0	6.4	1997	78.0	73.5	58.7	48.9	30.0	21.4	13.9	8.0
1998	72.6	68.2	53.5	44.2	25.8	17.8	11.1	6.5	1998	78.2	73.6	58.8	49.0	30.1	21.4	13.9	8.0
1999	72.8	68.4	53.7	44.4	26.0	18.0	11.3	6.6	1999	78.4	73.8	59.0	49.2	30.3	21.6	14.0	8.1
2000	73.1	68.6	53.9	44.6	26.3	18.2	11.5	6.6	2000	78.6	74.0	59.2	49.4	30.5	21.8	14.1	8.1
2001	73.3	68.8	54.2	44.8	26.6	18.4	11.7	6.8	2001	78.8	74.2	59.4	49.6	30.7	22.0	14.3	8.2
2002	73.5	69.0	54.3	45.0	26.7	18.6	11.8	6.8	2002	78.9	74.3	59.5	49.7	30.8	22.1	14.4	8.2
2003	73.8	69.3	54.6	45.2	27.0	18.8	12.0	6.9	2003	79.1	74.5	59.7	49.9	30.9	22.2	14.5	8.3
2004[P]	74.2	69.7	55.0	45.6	27.3	19.1	12.2	7.0	2004[P]	79.3	74.7	59.9	50.1	31.1	22.4	14.7	8.4
Northern Ireland																	
1981	69.2	65.4	50.9	41.5	23.2	15.6	9.7	5.8	1981	75.5	71.6	56.8	47.1	28.3	20.0	12.8	7.3
1986	70.9	66.8	52.2	42.7	24.2	16.4	10.4	6.2	1986	77.1	72.9	58.1	48.3	29.3	20.8	13.4	7.8
1991	72.6	68.2	53.6	44.1	25.5	17.3	11.0	6.4	1991	78.4	74.0	59.2	49.4	30.3	21.6	14.2	8.3
1996	73.8	69.4	54.7	45.3	26.6	18.2	11.4	6.6	1996	79.2	74.7	59.9	50.0	30.9	22.1	14.4	8.4
1997	74.2	69.7	55.0	45.5	26.8	18.4	11.5	6.6	1997	79.5	75.0	60.2	50.3	31.2	22.4	14.5	8.4
1998	74.3	69.8	55.2	45.7	27.0	18.6	11.6	6.6	1998	79.5	75.0	60.2	50.4	31.2	22.4	14.5	8.2
1999	74.5	70.0	55.4	45.9	27.2	18.8	11.7	6.6	1999	79.6	75.1	60.2	50.4	31.3	22.5	14.6	8.2
2000	74.8	70.4	55.7	46.2	27.6	19.1	11.9	6.6	2000	79.8	75.2	60.4	50.6	31.5	22.6	14.6	8.2
2001	75.2	70.7	56.1	46.6	27.9	19.4	12.3	6.9	2001	80.1	75.6	60.7	50.9	31.8	22.9	14.9	8.4
2002	75.6	71.1	56.4	46.9	28.2	19.7	12.4	7.0	2002	80.4	75.9	61.0	51.2	32.0	23.1	15.1	8.5
2003	75.8	71.4	56.7	47.1	28.4	19.9	12.6	7.2	2003	80.6	76.0	61.1	51.3	32.2	23.3	15.2	8.6

Note: Figures from 1981 are calculated from the population estimates revised in the light of the 2001 Census. All figures are based on a three-year period.

P provisional.

Table 6.1	Deaths: age and sex

England and Wales

Numbers (thousands) and rates

Year and quarter	All ages	Under 1[1]	1–4	5–9	10–14	15–19	20–24	25–34	35–44	45–54	55–64	65–74	75–84	85 and over
Numbers (thousands)														
Males														
1976	300.1	4.88	0.88	0.68	0.64	1.66	1.66	3.24	5.93	20.4	52.0	98.7	80.3	29.0
1981	289.0	4.12	0.65	0.45	0.57	1.73	1.58	3.18	5.54	16.9	46.9	92.2	86.8	28.5
1986	287.9	3.72	0.57	0.33	0.38	1.43	1.75	3.10	5.77	14.4	43.6	84.4	96.2	32.2
1991	277.6	2.97	0.55	0.34	0.35	1.21	1.76	3.69	6.16	13.3	34.9	77.2	95.8	39.3
1996	268.7	2.27	0.44	0.24	0.29	0.93	1.41	4.06	5.84	13.6	30.1	71.0	90.7	47.8
1999	264.3	2.08	0.41	0.22	0.28	0.90	1.27	3.85	5.93	13.6	28.7	64.3	90.4	52.3
2000	255.5	1.89	0.34	0.22	0.28	0.87	1.22	3.76	6.05	13.4	27.9	60.6	87.1	51.9
2001	252.4	1.81	0.32	0.19	0.28	0.88	1.27	3.63	6.07	13.3	27.5	57.5	87.0	52.7
2002	253.1	1.81	0.32	0.20	0.28	0.83	1.24	3.47	6.20	12.9	27.7	56.3	88.3	53.6
2003	253.9	1.81	0.31	0.19	0.24	0.81	1.23	3.26	6.32	12.7	28.2	55.1	89.6	54.0
2004	244.1	1.79	0.29	0.17	0.26	0.78	1.15	3.10	6.19	12.2	27.0	52.5	87.3	51.3
2005p	243.3	1.87	0.28	0.16	0.25	0.75	1.11	2.89	6.14	12.1	27.3	51.0	84.8	54.7
Females														
1976	298.5	3.46	0.59	0.45	0.42	0.62	0.67	1.94	4.04	12.8	29.6	67.1	104.7	72.1
1981	288.9	2.90	0.53	0.30	0.37	0.65	0.64	1.82	3.74	10.5	27.2	62.8	103.6	73.9
1986	293.3	2.59	0.49	0.25	0.27	0.56	0.67	1.65	3.83	8.8	25.8	58.4	106.5	83.6
1991	292.5	2.19	0.44	0.25	0.22	0.46	0.64	1.73	3.70	8.4	21.3	54.2	103.3	95.7
1996	291.5	1.69	0.32	0.18	0.20	0.43	0.51	1.85	3.66	8.9	18.2	50.2	96.7	108.7
1999	291.8	1.55	0.30	0.17	0.22	0.39	0.47	1.67	3.79	9.0	18.0	45.1	93.9	117.2
2000	280.1	1.49	0.25	0.16	0.18	0.38	0.47	1.69	3.87	9.1	17.6	42.2	89.3	113.4
2001	277.9	1.43	0.27	0.19	0.18	0.38	0.47	1.59	3.77	8.9	17.6	40.5	88.8	113.9
2002	280.4	1.31	0.24	0.16	0.19	0.38	0.43	1.61	3.77	8.7	17.7	39.6	90.0	116.3
2003	284.4	1.50	0.28	0.15	0.19	0.35	0.46	1.57	3.86	8.5	18.0	39.0	92.7	117.9
2004	268.4	1.43	0.23	0.13	0.16	0.38	0.46	1.49	3.80	8.1	17.6	36.9	88.3	109.4
2005	269.4	1.39	0.22	0.13	0.18	0.37	0.46	1.42	3.73	8.1	17.8	36.0	86.4	113.2
Rates (deaths per 1,000 population in each age group)														
Males														
1976	12.5	16.2	0.65	0.34	0.31	0.88	0.96	0.92	2.09	6.97	19.6	50.3	116.4	243.2
1981	12.0	12.6	0.53	0.27	0.29	0.82	0.83	0.89	1.83	6.11	17.7	45.6	105.2	226.5
1986	11.8	11.0	0.44	0.21	0.23	0.72	0.83	0.88	1.68	5.27	16.6	42.8	101.2	215.4
1991	11.2	8.3	0.40	0.21	0.23	0.72	0.89	0.94	1.76	4.56	13.9	38.1	93.1	205.6
1996	10.7	6.8	0.32	0.14	0.18	0.60	0.85	1.01	1.67	4.06	11.9	34.5	85.0	198.8
1999	10.4	6.5	0.31	0.12	0.16	0.56	0.83	0.99	1.60	3.99	10.9	31.6	79.9	194.4
2000	10.0	6.1	0.26	0.13	0.16	0.54	0.79	0.98	1.59	3.92	10.4	29.7	75.9	187.5
2001	9.9	5.9	0.25	0.11	0.16	0.53	0.80	0.97	1.56	3.89	10.0	28.0	74.0	186.4
2002	9.8	5.9	0.25	0.12	0.16	0.49	0.77	0.95	1.57	3.85	9.7	27.2	73.4	187.5
2003	9.8	5.7	0.25	0.11	0.14	0.46	0.95	0.91	1.58	3.81	9.6	26.3	72.8	190.4
2004	9.4	5.5	0.23	0.10	0.15	0.44	0.68	0.88	1.53	3.67	9.0	24.9	69.8	175.2
2005	9.3	5.7	0.23	0.10	0.14	0.42	0.64	0.82	1.51	3.59	8.9	24.0	67.4	171.6
2003 March	10.5	6.4	0.27	0.12	0.16	0.48	0.77	0.94	1.62	3.94	10.0	27.8	72.8	214.3
June	9.4	5.5	0.24	0.09	0.12	0.45	0.74	0.92	1.60	3.78	9.2	25.4	70.2	179.1
Sept	9.0	5.2	0.19	0.11	0.14	0.52	0.79	0.93	1.57	3.63	9.1	24.6	66.1	165.9
Dec	10.3	5.8	0.29	0.13	0.13	0.39	0.69	0.84	1.52	3.91	10.0	27.7	77.0	202.8
2004 March	10.2	5.9	0.25	0.12	0.15	0.46	0.67	0.92	1.59	3.81	9.4	26.6	76.9	199.3
June	9.1	5.2	0.23	0.12	0.14	0.39	0.74	0.94	1.58	3.72	8.8	24.5	66.9	164.0
Sept	8.7	5.3	0.23	0.10	0.18	0.46	0.71	0.86	1.47	3.58	8.5	23.2	64.5	154.8
Dec	9.5	5.5	0.23	0.08	0.11	0.43	0.58	0.78	1.49	3.58	9.2	25.4	70.8	183.0
2005 March	10.5	6.2	0.26	0.09	0.17	0.46	0.71	0.88	1.56	3.83	9.7	26.6	77.3	201.2
June	9.1	5.5	0.25	0.10	0.18	0.42	0.59	0.83	1.57	3.53	8.8	23.4	65.8	162.9
Sept	8.3	5.3	0.20	0.09	0.12	0.40	0.63	0.85	1.44	3.46	8.3	22.2	59.6	146.0
Dec	9.3	5.6	0.21	0.11	0.11	0.39	0.62	0.73	1.46	3.54	8.8	24.0	66.9	176.9
2006[2] March p	10.2	5.3	0.29	0.14	0.16	0.47	0.75	0.96	1.59	3.86	9.7	25.2	74.1	205.8
June p	9.0	5.5	0.24	0.09	0.15	0.45	0.69	0.88	1.57	3.59	8.8	23.0	63.5	158.9
Females														
1976	11.8	12.2	0.46	0.24	0.21	0.35	0.40	0.56	1.46	4.30	10.1	26.0	74.6	196.6
1981	11.3	9.4	0.46	0.19	0.19	0.32	0.35	0.52	1.26	3.80	9.5	24.1	66.2	178.2
1986	11.4	8.0	0.40	0.17	0.17	0.29	0.33	0.47	1.12	3.24	9.2	23.4	62.5	169.4
1991	11.2	6.4	0.33	0.16	0.15	0.29	0.33	0.44	1.05	2.87	8.2	21.8	58.7	161.6
1996	11.0	5.3	0.25	0.10	0.12	0.29	0.31	0.46	1.04	2.63	7.1	20.6	55.8	158.9
1999	11.0	5.1	0.24	0.10	0.13	0.25	0.31	0.43	1.01	2.61	6.7	19.2	53.4	162.6
2000	10.5	5.1	0.20	0.10	0.11	0.25	0.30	0.44	1.00	2.62	6.4	18.1	50.8	155.2
2001	10.4	4.9	0.22	0.12	0.11	0.24	0.30	0.42	0.96	2.57	6.3	17.4	50.1	155.0
2002	10.4	4.5	0.20	0.10	0.11	0.24	0.27	0.44	0.94	2.54	6.0	17.0	50.4	159.4
2003	10.6	4.9	0.24	0.10	0.12	0.21	0.28	0.44	0.95	2.51	5.9	16.7	51.3	165.8
2004	9.9	4.6	0.20	0.09	0.10	0.22	0.27	0.42	0.93	2.39	5.7	15.8	48.6	154.3
2005	9.9	4.4	0.19	0.09	0.11	0.22	0.27	0.40	0.90	2.38	5.6	15.4	48.1	152.7
2003 March	11.4	5.3	0.26	0.09	0.09	0.19	0.33	0.48	1.00	2.59	6.1	17.6	54.8	184.6
June	10.0	4.8	0.24	0.09	0.17	0.22	0.25	0.43	0.90	2.58	5.8	16.1	49.3	153.6
Sept	9.6	4.5	0.20	0.12	0.10	0.21	0.30	0.43	0.97	2.38	5.6	15.3	46.8	147.6
Dec	11.2	5.2	0.26	0.09	0.10	0.24	0.25	0.40	0.94	2.49	6.2	17.8	54.3	177.5
2004 March	11.1	5.3	0.22	0.09	0.10	0.27	0.32	0.42	0.95	2.50	6.0	17.1	53.9	177.0
June	9.4	4.1	0.17	0.08	0.11	0.26	0.27	0.43	0.94	2.41	5.4	15.0	46.5	144.3
Sept	9.1	4.3	0.20	0.06	0.09	0.20	0.24	0.42	0.88	2.27	5.4	14.9	44.6	137.5
Dec	10.1	4.6	0.19	0.11	0.09	0.17	0.27	0.40	0.93	2.36	5.9	16.1	49.5	158.4
2005 March	11.6	4.8	0.22	0.09	0.13	0.20	0.32	0.46	0.95	2.57	6.0	17.3	57.0	184.7
June	9.5	4.7	0.20	0.10	0.10	0.25	0.27	0.37	0.97	2.31	5.5	15.0	46.6	144.2
Sept	8.7	3.9	0.14	0.06	0.09	0.20	0.24	0.36	0.86	2.32	5.4	13.8	42.0	129.7
Dec	9.8	4.2	0.19	0.08	0.11	0.22	0.24	0.41	0.84	2.31	5.6	15.3	46.8	152.7
2006[2] March p	11.0	5.0	0.25	0.07	0.07	0.24	0.32	0.39	1.01	2.45	6.2	16.4	51.9	180.5
June p	9.4	4.6	0.22	0.10	0.14	0.19	0.25	0.42	0.88	2.33	5.4	14.7	45.3	141.9

Note: Figures represent the numbers of deaths registered in each year up to 1992 and the numbers of deaths occurring in each year from 1993 to 2005. Provisional figures for 2006 relate to registrations.
1 Rates per 1,000 live births.
2 Death rates for 2006 are based on the 2004-based population projections for 2006.
p provisional

Table 6.2	Deaths: subnational

Government Office Regions of England									Rates
Year and quarter	North East	North West	Yorkshire and The Humber	East Midlands	West Midlands	East	London	South East	South West

Total deaths (deaths per 1,000 population of all ages)

1996	11.7	11.7	11.2	10.7	10.7	10.3	9.4	10.7	11.7
1997	11.6	11.6	11.1	10.5	10.6	10.2	9.0	10.6	11.7
1998	11.9	11.7	11.2	10.8	10.6	10.2	8.8	10.4	11.4
1999	11.6	11.5	10.9	10.7	10.7	10.3	8.7	10.5	11.6
2000	10.8	10.7	10.3	10.0	10.0	9.9	8.2	9.8	11.3
2001	11.1	11.0	10.4	10.1	10.2	9.9	7.9	9.9	11.0
2002	11.2	11.0	10.5	10.2	10.2	10.0	7.8	9.9	11.1
2003	11.3	11.0	10.5	10.3	10.4	9.9	7.8	9.9	11.2
2004	10.9	10.5	10.1	9.7	9.8	9.5	7.2	9.4	10.4
2005	10.7	10.4	9.9	9.8	9.9	9.5	7.0	9.4	10.5
2004 March	11.8	11.6	11.2	10.7	10.8	10.5	8.0	10.4	11.6
June	10.6	10.0	9.6	9.3	9.5	9.2	7.0	9.1	9.9
Sept	9.8	9.7	9.3	9.0	9.0	8.8	6.6	8.7	9.5
Dec	11.2	10.6	10.3	9.9	10.1	9.6	7.4	9.6	10.7
2005 March	12.1	12.0	11.4	11.1	11.5	10.9	8.2	10.9	12.1
June	10.6	10.0	9.6	9.5	9.5	9.2	6.8	9.1	10.2
Sept	9.5	9.2	8.8	8.6	8.8	8.4	6.3	8.3	9.3
Dec	10.7	10.3	9.9	9.9	9.8	9.5	6.9	9.4	10.4
2006[1] March[p]	11.6	11.4	10.9	11.0	11.2	10.9	7.8	10.9	11.7
June[p]	10.7	10.3	9.8	9.6	9.7	9.4	6.7	9.1	10.1

Infant mortality (deaths under 1 year per 1,000 live births)

1996	6.2	6.3	6.5	6.3	6.8	5.3	6.3	5.3	5.5
1997	5.8	6.7	6.5	5.7	7.0	4.8	5.8	5.0	5.8
1998	5.0	6.3	6.9	5.6	6.5	5.0	6.0	4.4	4.8
1999	5.6	6.5	6.3	6.0	6.9	4.6	6.0	4.8	4.7
2000	6.5	6.2	7.3	5.4	6.8	4.4	5.4	4.4	4.7
2001	5.4	5.8	5.5	4.9	6.4	4.5	6.1	4.2	5.4
2002	4.8	5.4	6.1	5.6	6.6	4.3	5.5	4.5	4.3
2003	4.9	5.9	5.7	5.9	7.4	4.5	5.4	4.2	4.1
2004	4.6	5.4	5.8	4.9	6.3	4.2	5.2	3.9	4.5
2005	4.7	5.6	6.0	4.8	6.6	4.0	5.2	3.9	4.5
2004 March	5.9	6.1	6.1	4.8	6.9	4.9	5.7	4.5	5.0
June	4.6	4.9	5.8	4.8	5.6	4.0	4.6	3.3	4.8
Sept	3.1	5.3	4.9	4.3	7.0	4.3	5.0	3.5	4.2
Dec	4.8	5.3	6.3	5.6	5.6	3.5	5.5	4.5	4.2
2005 March	4.8	6.1	6.0	7.3	7.1	4.8	5.4	3.9	5.3
June	4.8	5.4	7.0	5.1	6.4	4.2	5.7	3.4	4.4
Sept	4.8	4.8	5.4	3.4	7.5	3.7	4.7	4.0	3.6
Dec	4.5	6.1	5.6	3.8	5.6	3.3	5.0	4.4	4.9
2006 March[p]	5.4	6.0	5.4	5.9	6.6	3.8	5.5	4.3	4.2
June[p]	6.4	5.5	6.1	5.0	7.0	4.3	4.5	4.2	3.8

Neonatal mortality (deaths under 4 weeks per 1,000 live births)

1996	4.1	4.0	4.2	4.2	4.9	3.5	4.4	3.5	3.8
1997	3.7	4.3	4.4	3.7	5.0	3.3	3.7	3.4	3.9
1998	3.1	4.1	4.5	3.7	4.8	3.4	4.1	2.9	3.3
1999	4.1	4.4	4.1	4.3	4.8	3.0	4.1	3.2	3.2
2000	4.4	4.3	5.0	4.1	5.0	3.0	3.7	3.1	3.0
2001	3.5	3.8	3.2	3.4	4.4	2.9	4.1	2.9	3.7
2002	3.2	3.6	4.0	4.0	4.8	2.9	3.6	2.9	3.1
2003	3.2	4.1	4.0	4.2	5.1	3.0	3.7	2.8	2.9
2004	2.8	3.6	3.8	3.5	4.7	2.9	3.6	2.8	3.2
2005[p]	2.9	3.8	4.0	3.5	4.9	2.6	3.4	2.7	3.2
2004 March	3.7	3.5	4.0	3.5	5.3	3.4	3.9	2.7	3.8
June	3.2	3.4	4.0	3.6	4.2	3.1	3.1	2.5	2.9
Sept	1.4	3.8	3.2	3.3	5.5	3.0	3.5	2.6	3.0
Dec	2.8	3.5	4.1	3.6	3.9	2.1	3.6	3.2	3.1
2005 March[p]	3.3	3.9	4.3	5.1	4.9	2.9	3.2	2.8	3.5
June[p]	3.0	3.5	4.3	3.7	4.9	3.0	3.8	2.1	3.2
Sept[p]	2.7	3.1	3.9	2.8	5.7	2.7	3.5	2.9	2.7
Dec[p]	2.8	4.6	3.5	2.4	4.1	1.8	3.0	3.1	3.5
2006 March[p]	4.1	3.8	4.0	4.2	4.7	2.7	3.3	2.9	3.2
June[p]	4.0	3.8	4.2	3.9	5.1	3.1	3.2	2.6	2.4

Perinatal mortality (stillbirths and deaths under 1 week per 1,000 total births)

1996	9.2	8.6	8.3	8.7	10.2	7.5	9.6	7.8	7.5
1997	8.0	8.9	8.3	7.7	9.6	7.3	9.0	7.3	8.7
1998	8.2	8.7	9.2	8.0	9.3	7.4	9.0	6.8	7.3
1999	8.2	8.7	8.3	7.8	9.9	7.0	9.0	6.9	7.8
2000	8.5	8.6	9.6	7.8	9.6	7.1	9.0	6.6	6.6
2001	7.8	8.7	7.5	7.9	9.1	7.1	8.9	6.9	7.2
2002	8.1	8.5	9.0	8.5	10.0	7.5	9.3	6.9	6.8
2003[2]	7.8	9.0	9.1	9.5	10.2	7.3	9.6	7.0	7.0
2004[2]	7.9	8.4	9.4	8.1	9.6	7.6	9.3	7.0	7.2
2005[p]	7.8	8.2	9.4	7.6	9.9	6.4	8.5	6.8	6.8
2004[2] March	9.6	8.2	9.4	8.4	10.1	8.0	9.3	7.2	6.6
June	9.1	8.3	9.4	8.5	9.2	7.4	9.0	6.9	7.5
Sept	6.8	8.3	9.8	8.2	10.3	7.7	9.6	7.0	8.1
Dec	6.2	8.8	9.0	7.2	8.8	7.2	9.3	7.1	6.6
2005 March[p]	6.6	8.4	9.7	9.3	9.0	6.9	8.4	6.7	6.8
June[p]	9.2	8.2	10.4	7.6	10.9	7.4	8.8	6.5	7.5
Sept[p]	7.1	7.4	8.6	7.2	11.0	6.1	8.9	7.1	5.7
Dec[p]	8.4	8.9	9.0	6.5	8.8	5.3	7.9	7.0	7.1
2006 March[p]	8.0	7.9	7.1	8.6	9.6	7.1	8.3	7.3	6.5
June[p]	8.7	7.9	8.5	9.1	10.1	6.9	7.8	6.5	6.7

Note: Figures represent the numbers of deaths occurring in each year with the exception of provisional figures for 2005 and 2006 which relate to registrations.
1 Total deaths rates for 2006 have been calculated using the 2004-based population projections for 2006.
2 Perinatal mortality figures for 2003 and 2004 were revised in HSQ31 to include stillbirths data notified to ONS too late to be included in the original statistics.
p provisional.

Table 6.3 — Deaths: selected causes (International Classification)[1] and sex

England and Wales — Number (thousands) and rate for all deaths and age-standardised rates per million population for selected causes

Year and quarter	All deaths Number (thousands)	All deaths Crude rate per 100,000 population	All causes (age-standardised rates per million population[2]) A00–R99 V01–Y89	Oesophagus (C15)	Stomach (C16)	Colon (C18)	Rectosigmoid junction, rectum, and anus (C19–C21)	Trachea, bronchus and lung (C33–C34)	Melanoma of skin (C43)	Other malignant neoplasms of skin (C44)	Breast (C50)	Cervix uteri (C53)	Ovary (C56)
Males													
1971	288.4	1,207	13,466	76	317	187	144	1,066	10	12	4	:	:
1981	289.0	1,196	12,189	90	251	181	135	1,028	17	9	3	:	:
1991	277.6	1,125	10,291	117	185	194	117	842	23	10	3	:	:
1998	264.7	1,064	8,981	129	132	169	95	643	26	8	3	:	:
1999	264.3	1,044	8,862	127	127	161	90	611	27	7	2	:	:
2000	255.5	1,005	8,437	128	118	158	89	592	28	7	2	:	:
2001	252.4	987	8,188	129	111	155	89	570	26	7	3	:	:
2002	253.1	985	8,074	131	109	150	90	559	27	8	3	:	:
2003	253.9	982	7,985	134	101	145	90	538	28	8	2	:	:
2004	244.1	939	7,535	129	95	142	91	520	30	9	2	:	:
2005	243.3	929	7,337	132	92	137	92	513	28	8	2	:	:
2004 March	66.2	1,024	8,194	130	95	145	86	518	27	10	3	:	:
June	58.8	909	7,311	122	98	142	90	511	30	8	2	:	:
Sept	56.8	869	6,989	128	93	142	98	513	30	8	2	:	:
Dec	62.4	955	7,651	136	93	141	91	539	31	11	1	:	:
2005 March	67.8	1,050	8,251	134	92	139	91	528	29	7	3	:	:
June	59.1	906	7,158	135	95	131	94	489	27	7	2	:	:
Sept	55.1	834	6,624	130	95	134	89	499	27	8	3	:	:
Dec	61.3	929	7,333	130	87	145	94	538	28	8	2	:	:
2006[3] March^p	66.4	1,022	7,908	131	81	133	98	519	32	7	2	:	:
June^p	59.3	902	6,987	132	82	127	86	501	30	7	2	:	:
Females													
1971	278.9	1,104	8,189	40	149	176	79	183	14	6	379	83	126
1981	288.9	1,134	7,425	42	111	157	74	252	16	5	405	69	121
1991	292.5	1,122	6,410	50	74	146	61	300	18	4	401	54	118
1993	299.2	1,142	6,427	52	66	138	53	296	22	3	378	47	115
1994	285.6	1,088	6,115	51	67	136	52	296	22	4	371	42	114
1995	295.2	1,121	6,206	52	62	131	49	294	20	4	361	42	116
1996	291.5	1,105	6,068	52	55	126	49	293	20	3	344	41	121
1997	290.4	1,098	6,001	51	57	122	48	285	20	3	337	37	115
1998	290.3	1,108	5,945	49	54	117	47	291	21	3	328	35	116
1999	291.8	1,097	5,929	52	51	115	46	289	20	3	319	33	111
2000	280.1	1,049	5,655	51	48	107	45	285	21	3	311	33	109
2001	277.9	1,038	5,543	48	46	103	45	283	20	3	308	31	112
2002	280.4	1,044	5,526	51	44	104	44	284	19	3	302	29	112
2003	284.4	1,055	5,578	50	42	98	46	285	20	3	293	27	108
2004	268.4	992	5,259	48	42	96	47	284	19	3	285	27	102
2005	269.4	990	5,188	48	39	96	46	290	21	3	284	26	102
2004 March	74.4	1,105	5,795	51	38	97	46	292	21	3	287	28	105
June	63.4	942	5,022	46	41	94	47	265	18	4	284	25	97
Sept	61.8	908	4,863	50	43	95	45	281	19	3	276	27	102
Dec	68.9	1,013	5,359	46	44	100	49	299	20	2	293	28	101
2005 March	77.9	1,162	5,974	50	41	92	47	290	20	4	292	26	101
June	64.7	953	5,033	45	36	96	47	288	22	4	281	27	105
Sept	59.6	868	4,629	50	40	102	43	283	20	3	281	26	99
Dec	67.2	979	5,133	47	39	95	45	300	20	3	281	24	104
2006[3] March^p	74.4	1,104	5,662	48	40	90	45	308	16	4	296	26	104
June^p	64.3	943	4,899	46	34	89	46	293	18	4	265	22	101

Note: Figures represent the number of deaths registered in each year up to 1992 and the number of deaths occurring in each year from 1993 to 2005. Provisional figures for 2006 relate to registrations.
The rates by cause of death in this table are based on final underlying cause. For further details see the Explanatory Notes in the 'Report: Death registrations in England and Wales, 2004: causes' in HSQ26.
1 The Ninth Revision of the International Classification of Diseases, 1975, came into operation in England and Wales on 1 January 1979. The Tenth Revision of the International Classification of Diseases, 1992, came into operation in England and Wales on 1 January 2001. The cause descriptions and codes relate to ICD-10. For changes to this table see 'In Brief', Health Statistics Quarterly 14.
2 Directly age-standardised to the European Standard Population. See Notes to Tables.
3 Death rates for 2006 are based on the 2004-based population projections for 2006.
p provisional

Table 6.3 continued	Deaths: selected causes (International Classification)[1] and sex

England and Wales

Age-standardised rates[3] per million population for selected causes

Malignant neoplasms													
Prostate	Bladder	Leukaemia	Diabetes mellitus	Ischaemic heart disease	Cerebro vascular diseases	Pneumonia	Bronchitis, emphysema and other chronic obstructive pulmonary disease	Asthma	Gastric and duodenal ulcer	Diseases of the liver	Land transport accidents	Intentional self-harm and events of undetermined intent with inquest verdict 'Open'	Year and quarter
(C61)	(C67)	(C91–C95)	(E10–E14)	(I20–I25)	(I60–I69)	(J12–J18)	(J40–J44)	(J45–J46)	(K25–K27)	(K70–K76)	(V01–V89)	(X60–X84, Y10–Y34)	
													Males
198	124	74	82	3,801	1,541	920	944	21	107	41	209	124	1971
214	121	74	82	3,664	1,141	1,053	683	28	90	58	119	151	1981
304	121	77	131	2,984	940	391	606	31	73	76	125	160	1991
277	99	67	94	2,215	706	720	463	18	60	115	86	152	1998
272	93	67	94	2,095	673	770	474	18	64	119	86	151	1999
260	92	67	88	1,959	622	735	416	17	59	119	86	141	2000
274	93	70	94	1,872	690	388	403	16	55	139	86	134	2001
271	90	68	91	1,782	690	387	396	15	56	144	83	131	2002
272	87	71	91	1,700	661	407	411	14	53	157	84	129	2003
266	84	67	82	1,562	594	359	363	15	50	151	77	125	2004
255	80	67	79	1,466	553	351	367	12	46	156	75	118	2005
279	86	67	91	1,708	692	465	463	15	54	149	69	137	2004 March
258	82	63	80	1,538	571	332	338	13	49	144	90	133	June
260	88	70	74	1,418	519	278	293	17	44	145	79	127	Sept
267	81	66	85	1,584	594	361	360	14	52	166	71	103	Dec
264	85	67	93	1,673	644	498	489	14	55	167	75	132	2005 March
250	80	65	75	1,442	534	326	356	13	45	149	77	122	June
248	76	65	67	289	483	246	270	9	42	144	82	115	Sept
259	78	70	81	463	552	339	356	12	43	163	66	104	Dec
256	79	73	85	1,538	610	434	439	11	52	158	83	128	2006[3] March[p]
249	80	63	75	1,344	505	317	350	10	47	163	88	118	June[p]
													Females
:	32	47	89	1,668	1,352	624	193	25	44	31	82	84	1971
:	35	47	66	1,601	1,012	740	155	30	57	43	41	81	1981
:	34	44	95	1,407	812	325	211	30	46	49	45	51	1991
:	34	43	74	1,347	724	585	224	27	46	49	35	48	1993
:	35	42	69	1,237	689	512	204	24	44	50	34	44	1994
:	33	41	73	1,194	690	568	229	24	42	55	30	47	1995
:	32	41	67	1,140	680	548	222	21	43	57	30	45	1996
:	31	43	66	1,074	651	574	227	23	42	61	29	45	1997
:	32	41	65	1,055	645	546	226	22	41	64	28	43	1998
:	30	45	65	986	629	591	241	22	39	67	28	45	1999
:	31	39	62	907	577	546	216	20	41	68	24	45	2000
:	29	41	62	878	620	307	220	19	39	77	23	40	2001
:	30	43	65	844	617	316	224	20	37	79	24	41	2002
:	30	39	66	811	606	337	244	20	36	81	24	41	2003
:	28	40	60	738	550	297	214	18	35	83	21	41	2004
:	28	39	57	686	519	298	224	17	32	81	22	38	2005
:	27	43	69	806	626	399	283	23	37	84	25	46	2004 March
:	30	39	54	720	530	254	184	16	33	80	21	42	June
:	28	39	55	674	496	227	167	14	32	80	19	42	Sept
:	28	39	63	750	550	307	221	18	37	86	20	36	Dec
:	30	43	65	806	605	453	320	24	36	88	26	40	2005 March
:	29	40	54	674	496	261	207	17	32	74	20	43	June
:	27	35	50	600	462	199	157	12	28	75	21	38	Sept
:	25	40	58	665	514	281	213	16	31	85	21	33	Dec
:	29	42	60	734	553	373	282	19	37	87	24	40	2006[3] March[p]
:	27	34	55	638	477	260	213	16	27	85	26	36	June[p]

See notes opposite.

Report:

Infant and perinatal mortality by social and biological factors, 2005

This report presents statistics on stillbirths and infant deaths registered in England and Wales that occurred in 2005. Only infant deaths that have been linked to their corresponding birth records are included as linkage enables analysis of infant and perinatal deaths by risk factors collected at birth registration. These include birthweight, mother's age at birth of child, mother's country of birth, marital status, parity and father's socio-economic status based on his occupation.

In 2005, of the 3,245 infant deaths that occurred in England and Wales 3,188 (98 per cent) were linked to their birth records. Of the 57 records that were not linked, 24 were born outside England and Wales (and therefore not registered in England and Wales) and 33 were not linked because no record of the birth could be found. The linkage rate for 2005 is comparable with that for previous years since linkage began in 1975.

In 2005, of all the linked infant deaths 1,676 (53 per cent) were early neonates (babies dying under 7 days), 2,193 (69 per cent) were neonatal deaths (babies dying under 28 days) and 995 (31 per cent) were postneonatal deaths (babies dying aged 28 days and over but under one year).

Key findings

- The infant mortality rates for very low birthweight babies (under 1,500 grams) and low birthweight babies (under 2,500 grams) were 197.3 and 42.2 deaths per 1,000 live births respectively compared with a rate of 1.8 among normal birthweight babies (2,500 grams and over). Fifty per cent of infant deaths occurred among very low birthweight babies.

- There were 891 stillbirths weighing less than 1,500 grams delivered at 24–27 weeks gestation. This represented 96 per cent of all stillbirths delivered at 24–27 weeks and 57 per cent of all very low birthweight stillbirths.

- The infant mortality rate was highest among mothers aged under 20 (7.1 deaths per 1,000 live births) followed by those aged 20–24 (5.6 per 1,000 live births). The infant mortality rate was lowest among mothers in the 30–34 age group (4.2 per 1,000 live births).

- Mothers aged 40 and over had the highest stillbirth and perinatal mortality rates at 7.4 and 10.1 per 1,000 births respectively.

- Babies of mothers born in the Caribbean and Pakistan had particularly high infant mortality rates (10.7 and 8.6 deaths per 1,000 live births respectively) compared with the overall infant mortality rate of 4.9 per 1,000 live births. Stillbirth and perinatal mortality rates were also particularly high in these two groups.

- The infant mortality rate was highest for sole registered births (7.0 deaths per 1,000 live births) and for babies born outside marriage jointly registered by both parents giving different addresses (6.9 deaths per 1,000 live births). Babies born inside marriage to women with three or more previous children also had a high rate (6.2 per 1,000 live births). The perinatal mortality rates of these three groups were much higher (between 9.3 and 9.9 per 1,000 births) than the overall perinatal mortality rate of 7.9 per 1,000 births.

- For births inside marriage combined with births outside marriage jointly registered by both parents, babies of fathers in 'routine occupations' had an infant mortality rate of 6.0 deaths per 1,000 live births compared with babies of fathers in the 'large employers and higher managerial occupations' who had an infant mortality rate of 2.8 per 1,000 live births.

- Seventy-three per cent of all infant deaths were related to events occurring in pregnancy (i.e. congenital anomalies, antepartum infections and immaturity related conditions) as were 87 per cent of all neonatal deaths. For postneonatal deaths, 29 per cent were related to congenital anomalies, 16 per cent were SIDS, 13 per cent were from infections and 12 per cent were from immaturity related conditions.

Explanatory notes

Database changes

The figures presented in this report relate to live births, stillbirths and infant deaths that occurred in 2005 and were on our database at 14 August 2006. These figures are provisional.

National Statistics Socio-Economic Classification (NS-SEC)

In 2001, the National Statistics Socio-Economic Classification (NS-SEC) replaced the Registrar General's Social Class Classification. Although the eight-class version of NS-SEC is used here, the categories can be aggregated to produce five- and three-class versions of NS-SEC.

Mother's country of birth

These groupings differ slightly from those used up to 1997.
In addition, the countries included in 'Other European Union' changed in 2004 to reflect the EU enlargement that took place on 1 May 2004.

United Kingdom

England, Wales, Scotland, Northern Ireland

Elsewhere in United Kingdom

Channel Islands, Isle of Man, UK (part not stated)

Outside United Kingdom

Irish Republic

Irish Republic, Ireland (part not stated)

Other European Union

Austria, Belgium, Cyprus, Czech Republic, Denmark, Estonia, Faroe Islands, Finland, France, Germany, Greece, Greenland, Hungary, Italy, Latvia, Lithuania, Luxembourg, Malta, Netherlands, Poland, Portugal, Slovakia, Slovenia, Spain, Sweden

Rest of Europe

All other European countries including Turkey, Russia and former Soviet republics

Commonwealth

Australia, Canada and New Zealand

New Commonwealth

Asia

Bangladesh, India, Pakistan

East Africa

Kenya, Malawi, Tanzania, Uganda, Zambia

Southern Africa

Botswana, Lesotho, Namibia, South Africa, Swaziland

Rest of Africa

Cameroon, The Gambia, Ghana, Mauritius, Mozambique, Nigeria, Seychelles, Sierra Leone, Zimbabwe

Far East

Brunei, Malaysia, Singapore

Caribbean

Anguilla, Antigua, Bahamas, Barbados, Belize, Bermuda, British Virgin Islands, Cayman Islands, Dominica, Grenada, Guyana, Jamaica, Montserrat, St Christopher and Nevis, St Lucia, St Vincent, Trinidad and Tobago, Turks and Caicos Islands

Rest of the New Commonwealth

Cook Islands, Falkland Islands, Fiji, Gibraltar, Kiribati, Maldives, Nauru, New Hebrides, Papua New Guinea, St Helena, Solomon Islands, Sri Lanka, Tonga, Tuvalu, Vanuatu, Western Samoa, British Indian Ocean Territory

Rest of the World and not stated

Table 1	Live births, stillbirths and infant deaths by birthweight, 2005

England and Wales

Numbers and rates

	Numbers						Rates[1]				
	Births		Deaths								
Birthweight (grams)	Live births	Still-births	Early neonatal	Neonatal	Post-neonatal	Infants	Stillbirth	Perinatal	Neonatal	Postneonatal	Infant
All	645,881	3,484	1,676	2,193	995	3,188	5.4	7.9	3.4	1.5	4.9
Under 1,500	8,049	1,565	1,076	1,338	250	1,588	162.8	274.7	166.2	31.1	197.3
1,500–1,999	9,956	374	88	126	83	209	36.2	44.7	12.7	8.3	21.0
2,000–2,499	30,778	384	98	146	115	261	12.3	15.5	4.7	3.7	8.5
2,500–2,999	109,484	418	116	182	175	357	3.8	4.9	1.7	1.6	3.3
3,000–3,499	230,067	389	108	168	236	404	1.7	2.2	0.7	1.0	1.8
3,500 and over	255,362	299	119	157	133	290	1.2	1.6	0.6	0.5	1.1
Not stated	2,185	55	71	76	3	79	24.6	56.3	34.8	1.4	36.2

1 Stillbirths and perinatal deaths per 1,000 live births and stillbirths.
   Neonatal, postneonatal and infant deaths per 1,000 live births.

Table 2	Stillbirths: Gestation by birthweight, 2005

England and Wales

Numbers

Birthweight (grams)	All	Gestation (weeks)					
		24–27	28–31	32–35	36–39	40 and over	Not stated
All	3,484	930	579	624	830	464	57
Under 1,000	1,127	814	227	53	21	4	8
1,000–1,499	438	77	219	112	22	1	7
1,500–1,999	374	8	104	195	60	4	3
2,000–2,499	384	3	14	177	160	27	3
2,500–2,999	418	2	8	61	260	80	7
3,000–3,499	389	4	1	12	188	184	0
3,500 and over	299	11	5	7	109	162	5
Not stated	55	11	1	7	10	2	24

Table 3	Live births, stillbirths and infant deaths by mother's age, 2005

England and Wales

Numbers and rates

	Numbers						Rates[1]				
	Births		Deaths								
Mother's age	Live births	Still-births	Early neonatal	Neonatal	Post-neonatal	Infants	Stillbirth	Perinatal	Neonatal	Postneonatal	Infant
All	645,881	3,484	1,676	2,193	995	3,188	5.4	7.9	3.4	1.5	4.9
Under 20	44,828	285	154	205	113	318	6.3	9.7	4.6	2.5	7.1
20–24	122,166	638	337	444	243	687	5.2	7.9	3.6	2.0	5.6
25–29	164,365	873	411	559	233	792	5.3	7.8	3.4	1.4	4.8
30–34	188,135	910	454	573	212	785	4.8	7.2	3.0	1.1	4.2
35–39	104,131	611	260	330	163	493	5.8	8.3	3.2	1.6	4.7
40 and over	22,256	167	60	82	31	113	7.4	10.1	3.7	1.4	5.1

1 Stillbirths and perinatal deaths per 1,000 live births and stillbirths.
   Neonatal, postneonatal and infant deaths per 1,000 live births.

Table 4 — Live births, stillbirths and infant deaths by mother's country of birth, 2005

England and Wales Numbers and rates

| Country of birth | Numbers | | | | | | Rates[1] | | | | |
| | Births | | Deaths | | | | | | | | |
	Live births	Still-births	Early neonatal	Neonatal	Post-neonatal	Infants	Stillbirth	Perinatal	Neonatal	Postneonatal	Infant
All	645,881	3,484	1,676	2,193	995	3,188	5.4	7.9	3.4	1.5	4.9
United Kingdom	511,648	2,606	1,283	1,692	760	2,452	5.1	7.6	3.3	1.5	4.8
England and Wales	501,732	2,554	1,256	1,656	739	2,395	5.1	7.6	3.3	1.5	4.8
Scotland	7,321	34	21	28	16	44	4.6	7.5	3.8	2.2	6.0
Northern Ireland	2,290	14	5	7	5	12	6.1	8.2	3.1	2.2	5.2
Elsewhere	305	4	1	1	0	1	12.9	16.2	3.3	-	3.3
Outside the United Kingdom	134,233	878	393	501	235	736	6.5	9.4	3.7	1.8	5.5
Irish Republic	3,461	23	9	14	9	23	6.6	9.2	4.0	2.6	6.6
Other European Union	20,421	100	57	68	25	93	4.9	7.7	3.3	1.2	4.6
Rest of Europe	6,947	31	14	16	9	25	4.4	6.4	2.3	1.3	3.6
Commonwealth											
Australia, Canada and New Zealand	4,221	10	10	12	3	15	2.4	4.7	2.8	0.7	3.6
New Commonwealth	65,135	509	222	282	133	415	7.8	11.1	4.3	2.0	6.4
Asia											
Bangladesh	8,220	59	16	20	16	36	7.1	9.1	2.4	1.9	4.4
India	10,074	69	22	26	20	46	6.8	9.0	2.6	2.0	4.6
Pakistan	16,480	175	66	91	51	142	10.5	14.5	5.5	3.1	8.6
East Africa	4,046	23	18	23	4	27	5.7	10.1	5.7	1.0	6.7
Southern Africa	4,125	16	14	15	5	20	3.9	7.2	3.6	1.2	4.8
Rest of Africa	13,761	100	51	61	26	87	7.2	10.9	4.4	1.9	6.3
Far East	1,343	4	4	4	1	5	3.0	5.9	3.0	0.7	3.7
Caribbean	3,723	38	25	35	5	40	10.1	16.8	9.4	1.3	10.7
Rest of the New Commonwealth	3,363	25	6	7	5	12	7.4	9.1	2.1	1.5	3.6
Rest of World and not stated	34,048	205	81	109	56	165	6.0	8.3	3.2	1.6	4.8

1 Stillbirths and perinatal deaths per 1,000 live births and stillbirths.
   Neonatal, postneonatal and infant deaths per 1,000 live births.

Table 5 — Live births, stillbirths and infant deaths by marital status, parity (within marriage) and type of registration, 2005

England and Wales Numbers and rates

| Marital status / Parity/type of registration | Numbers | | | | | | Rates[1] | | | | |
| | Births | | Deaths | | | | | | | | |
	Live births	Still-births	Early neonatal	Neonatal	Post-neonatal	Infants	Stillbirth	Perinatal	Neonatal	Postneonatal	Infant
All	645,881	3,484	1,676	2,193	995	3,188	5.4	7.9	3.4	1.5	4.9
Inside marriage											
All	369,370	1,862	869	1,120	472	1,592	5.0	7.4	3.0	1.3	4.3
0	155,036	828	443	570	175	745	5.3	8.2	3.7	1.1	4.8
1	131,769	578	229	291	142	433	4.4	6.1	2.2	1.1	3.3
2	52,691	260	108	142	86	228	4.9	6.9	2.7	1.6	4.3
3 and over	29,874	196	89	117	69	186	6.5	9.5	3.9	2.3	6.2
Outside marriage											
All	276,511	1,622	807	1,073	523	1,596	5.8	8.7	3.9	1.9	5.8
Joint registration/ same address	175,572	967	481	637	262	899	5.5	8.2	3.6	1.5	5.1
Joint registration/ different address	55,774	357	199	264	119	383	6.4	9.9	4.7	2.1	6.9
Sole registration	45,165	298	127	172	142	314	6.6	9.3	3.8	3.1	7.0

1 Stillbirths and perinatal deaths per 1,000 live births and stillbirths.
   Neonatal, postneonatal and infant deaths per 1,000 live births.

Table 6	Live births[1], stillbirths and infant deaths by NS-SEC (based on father's occupation at death registration), 2005[2]

England and Wales

Numbers and rates

	Numbers						Rates[3]				
	Births		Deaths								
NS-SEC	Live births	Still-births	Early neonatal	Neonatal	Post-neonatal	Infants	Stillbirth	Perinatal	Neonatal	Post-neonatal	Infant
All[4]	600,716	3,186	1,549	2,021	853	2,874	5.3	7.8	3.4	1.4	4.8
Inside marriage											
All[5]	369,370	1,862	869	1,120	472	1,592	5.0	7.4	3.0	1.3	4.3
1.1 Large employers and higher managerial	3,602	113	56	71	27	98	3.1	4.7	2.0	0.7	2.7
1.2 Higher professional	4,943	228	99	132	54	186	4.6	6.6	2.7	1.1	3.8
2 Lower managerial and professional	8,631	373	186	221	71	292	4.3	6.4	2.6	0.8	3.4
3 Intermediate	2,303	133	67	81	33	114	5.7	8.6	3.5	1.4	5.0
4 Small employers and own-account workers	4,817	207	95	127	60	187	4.3	6.2	2.6	1.2	3.9
5 Lower supervisory and technical	4,052	177	74	94	43	137	4.3	6.2	2.3	1.1	3.4
6 Semi-routine	3,499	223	106	148	67	215	6.3	9.3	4.2	1.9	6.1
7 Routine	3,411	236	110	141	57	198	6.9	10.1	4.1	1.7	5.8
Other[6]	1,824	172	67	93	48	141	9.3	13.0	5.1	2.6	7.7
Outside marriage joint registration											
All[5]	231,346	1,324	680	901	381	1,282	5.7	8.6	3.9	1.6	5.5
1.1 Large employers and higher managerial	835	35	13	19	7	26	4.2	5.7	2.3	0.8	3.1
1.2 Higher professional	1,070	51	25	32	7	39	4.7	7.1	3.0	0.7	3.6
2 Lower managerial and professional	3,538	156	86	108	30	138	4.4	6.8	3.1	0.8	3.9
3 Intermediate	1,154	59	30	41	21	62	5.1	7.7	3.6	1.8	5.4
4 Small employers and own-account workers	3,403	139	67	97	48	145	4.1	6.0	2.9	1.4	4.3
5 Lower supervisory and technical	3,805	186	97	126	39	165	4.9	7.4	3.3	1.0	4.3
6 Semi-routine	3,129	210	125	156	58	214	6.7	10.6	5.0	1.9	6.8
7 Routine	4,482	332	152	197	80	277	7.4	10.7	4.4	1.8	6.2
Other[6]	1,788	155	69	105	72	177	8.6	12.4	5.9	4.0	9.9

1   Figures for live births in NS-SEC groups are a 10 per cent sample coded for father's occupation.
2   Information on father's occupation is not collected for births outside marriage if the father does not attend the registration of the baby's birth.
3   Stillbirths and perinatal deaths per 1,000 live births and stillbirths.
    Neonatal, postneonatal and infant deaths per 1,000 live births.
4   Inside marriage and outside marriage/joint registration only, including cases where father's occupation was not stated.
5   Includes cases where father's occupation was not stated.
6   Students; occupations inadequately described; occupations not classifiable for other reasons; never worked and long-term unemployed.

Table 7	Live births, stillbirths and infant deaths by ONS cause groups, 2005

England and Wales

Numbers and rates

	Numbers						Rates[1]				
	Births		Deaths								
Cause group	Live births	Still-births	Early neonatal	Neonatal	Post-neonatal	Infants	Stillbirth	Perinatal	Neonatal	Postneonatal	Infant
All causes	645,881	3,484	1,676	2,193	995	3,188	5.4	7.9	3.4	1.5	4.9
Congenital anomalies		493	398	552	288	840	0.8	1.4	0.9	0.4	1.3
Antepartum infections		32	25	49	7	56	0.0	0.1	0.1	0.0	0.1
Immaturity related conditions		-	1,051	1,302	124	1,426	-	1.6	2.0	0.2	2.2
Asphyxia, anoxia or trauma (intrapartum)		101	157	184	26	210	0.2	0.4	0.3	0.0	0.3
External conditions		7	3	10	44	54	0.0	0.0	0.0	0.1	0.1
Infections		-	18	29	133	162	-	0.0	0.0	0.2	0.3
Other specific conditions		208	6	7	26	33	0.3	0.3	0.0	0.0	0.1
Asphyxia, anoxia or trauma (antepartum)		930	-	-	-	-	1.4	1.4	-	-	-
Remaining antepartum deaths		1,630	-	-	-	-	2.5	2.5	-	-	-
Sudden infant deaths		-	6	28	155	183	-	0.0	0.0	0.2	0.3
Other conditions		83	12	32	192	224	0.1	0.1	0.0	0.3	0.3

1   Stillbirths and perinatal deaths per 1,000 live births and stillbirths.
    Neonatal, postneonatal and infant deaths per 1,000 live births.

Report:

Health expectancies for local authorities in England and Wales, 2001

Introduction

The Office for National Statistics publishes annual estimates of healthy life expectancy (HLE) and disability-free life expectancy (DFLE) at the national level for the UK and its four constituent countries. The most recent estimates relate to 2002 and are available on the National Statistics website.[1] HLE and DFLE are health indicators that combine mortality and morbidity data and thus measure both the quantity and quality of life. The methods and data sources used to calculate health expectancies are detailed in an earlier article.[2]

In calculating health expectancies at the national level, health rates ('good/fairly good health', 'without long standing illness') are derived by aggregating three years of combined General Household Survey (GHS) and Continuous Household Survey (CHS) data relating to Great Britain and Northern Ireland respectively. While survey data provide reliable estimates at the national level, their sample sizes are inadequate to provide robust sub-national estimates. A previous study found that even after combining GHS data over seven years, only person level (males and females combined) estimates could be calculated for the then 100 health authorities in England.[3]

In contrast, census data can be used to calculate sex-specific estimates of health expectancy for local areas with a high degree of precision. For example, the 1991 Census data on rates of limiting long term illness were used to calculate DFLE at local authority (LA) level for males and females.[4] The health questions in the 2001 Census included a question on general health (for the first time) and limiting long-term illness, although the latter was worded slightly differently from the question asked in the 1991 Census. The main drawbacks of using census data are that estimates can only be updated every ten years and are not directly comparable with the survey-based series due to differences in question wording, mode and context between these two sources.

This report presents health expectancies for local authorities and Government Office Regions (GORs) in England and Wales based on 2001 Census data. It includes health expectancies, at birth and at age 65, for males and for females, along with their confidence intervals. The geographical patterns of health inequalities as measured by health expectancies are described.

Data and methods

Health expectancies were calculated using the Sullivan method.[5] The underlying principle of the Sullivan method is to partition life expectancy into two components: (i) years lived free from ill-health, and (ii) years lived in ill-health.

Health expectancies were calculated in two steps. First, life expectancies were calculated using mortality rates derived by pooling together death registration data for the three-year period 2000-2002 (centred on 2001) and the National Statistics mid-year population estimates over the same period. Two local authorities, City of London and the Isles of Scilly, were excluded from the analysis due to small numbers of deaths and populations in these areas. The standard errors of life expectancies were calculated using the method developed by Chiang. More details about the calculation of life expectancies and data for varying geographies can be found on the National Statistics website.[6]

In the second step, the expected years of life were partitioned into healthy/unhealthy years of life. Health rates (good/fairly good health, without long-term illness) were calculated using the 2001 Census data. The 2001 Census questions on general health and long-term illness were asked of all residents including those living in communal establishments (Box one). However, the published 2001 Census tables on general health and long-term illness only relate to people living in private households.

Therefore, tables were specially commissioned from the 2001 Census to include counts of people resident in private households and communal establishments by health status categories.

The age-and sex-specific health rates were calculated by using the 2001 Census usually resident population counts as the denominators. The age groups used were under 1, 1–4, 5–9,........., 80–84, 85 and over.

Box one

Census 2001 questions on General Health and Long-term Illness

General Health

Over the last 12 months would you say your health has on the whole been: Good, Fairly good or Not good?

Long-term Illness

Do you have any long-term illness, health problem or disability which limits your daily activities or the work you can do? Yes/No. Include problems which are due to old age.

Health expectancies were calculated for local authorities, Government Office Regions (GORs) and at country level for England, Wales and England and Wales.

The method for calculation of sub-national health expectancies is identical to the method used for calculating the national health expectancy series. The difference between the two is that the former uses census data and the latter survey data.

Health expectancies at national level

In 2001, for England and Wales, DFLE at birth for males was 61.5 years, 14.5 years lower than life expectancy (75.9 years); for females it was 64.0 years, 16.6 years lower than life expectancy (80.6) (Table 1).

Although DFLE for males was lower than for females, the gender gap in DFLE (2.5 years) was almost half the gender gap in life expectancy (4.7 years). In terms of the proportion of expected life, therefore, males live a slightly higher proportion of their lives free of disability than females (80.9 per cent versus 79.4 per cent).

At age 65, DFLE for men was 8.0 years, 8.1 years lower than life expectancy at age 65 (16.1 years); for women it was 9.0 years, 10.2 years lower than life expectancy for women (19.2 years). Although DFLE at 65 for men was lower than for women, the gender gap in DFLE at 65 (1.0 years) was much lower than that at birth (2.5 years).

HLE at birth and at age 65 were generally higher than the corresponding DFLEs. In England and Wales, HLE at birth for males was 68.9 years, 7.4 years higher than DFLE at birth (61.5); for females HLE was 72.1 years, 8.2 years higher than DFLE at birth (64.0). At age 65, HLE remained higher than DFLE: a difference of 4.4 years for men (12.4 versus 8.0) and 5.4 years for women (14.4 versus 9.0).

Both HLE and DFLE for Wales were considerably lower than for England. The largest differentials between the countries were in DFLE at birth: 4.0 years lower for males and 3.7 years lower for females in Wales than in England (Table 1).

Health expectancies for Government Office Regions (GORs) and Wales

Disability-free life expectancy at birth

The distribution of DFLE by regions follows a pattern broadly similar to that observed for life expectancy: namely, a clear north-south divide, with the highest expectation of life without disability in the South East, East of England, and South West and the lowest in the North East, Wales and the North West (Figure 1). Between-region differences in DFLE were almost three times higher than equivalent differences in life expectancy. For men, DFLE ranged from 64.7 years in South East to 57.1 years in North East: a difference of 7.6 years compared with the gap in life expectancy of 2.7 years (South East: 77.2 years, North East: 74.5 years). Similarly, for women the difference in DFLE at birth was 6.5 years (South East: 67.0, North East: 60.5) while for life expectancy it was 2.4 years (South West: 81.7 and North East: 79.3).

| Table 1 | Life expectancy, healthy life expectancy and disability-free life expectancy by sex and country, 2001 |

England, Wales and England and Wales

		Life expectancy (years)	Healthy life expectancy (years)		Disability-free life expectancy (years)	
			Years in 'good' health	Years in 'not good' health	Years without disability	Years with disability
At birth						
Males	England	76.0	69.0	6.9	61.7	14.3
	Wales	75.3	66.2	9.1	57.7	17.6
	England and Wales	75.9	68.9	7.1	61.5	14.5
Females	England	80.6	72.3	8.3	64.2	16.5
	Wales	80.0	69.4	10.6	60.5	19.5
	England and Wales	80.6	72.1	8.5	64.0	16.6
At age 65						
Males	England	16.1	12.5	3.6	8.1	8.1
	Wales	15.7	11.3	4.4	6.5	9.2
	England and Wales	16.1	12.4	3.7	8.0	8.1
Females	England	19.2	14.5	4.7	9.1	10.2
	Wales	18.7	13.0	5.7	7.6	11.2
	England and Wales	19.2	14.4	4.8	9.0	10.2

Source: Office for National Statistics

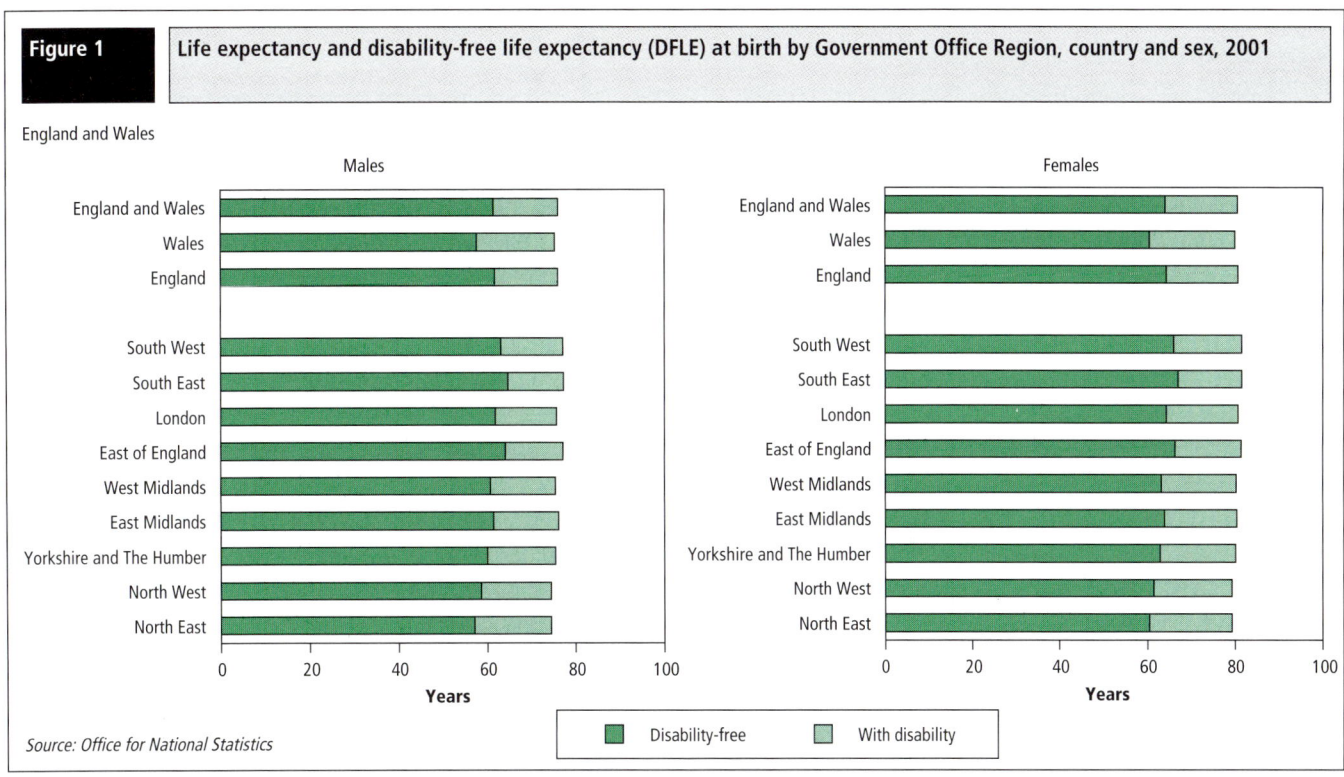

Figure 1 Life expectancy and disability-free life expectancy (DFLE) at birth by Government Office Region, country and sex, 2001

England and Wales

Source: Office for National Statistics

Not only did people in regions with the highest DFLE have higher life expectancy, they also lived fewer years of life with disability (life expectancy minus disability-free life expectancy) compared with regions with the lowest DFLE. On average males in the South East lived 77.2 years, of which 12.5 years were with disability (16.2 per cent of life expectancy) compared with 74.5 years in the North East, of which 17.4 years were with disability (23.4 per cent of life expectancy). For females the equivalent figures were 81.5 years, of which 14.6 years (17.9 per cent) were with disability in the South East compared with 79.3 years, of which 18.8 years (23.7 per cent) were with disability, in the North East.

Disability-free life expectancy at age 65

The geographical pattern for the distribution of DFLE at age 65 was similar to that for DFLE at birth, reflecting a clear north-south divide. For men, DFLE ranged from 6.2 years in the North East to 9.3 years in the South East, a gap of 3.0 years; and for women it ranged from 7.4 years in the North East to 10.3 years in the South East, a gap of 2.9 years. In terms of years lived with disability at age 65 (life expectancy minus DFLE at age 65), the overall regional distribution patterns were similar to those for years with disability at birth: years lived with disability were highest in Wales (9.2 years for men and 11.2 years for women) and lowest in the South East (7.5 years and 9.5 years, respectively).

Healthy life expectancy at birth and at age 65

The regional distribution patterns for HLE at birth and years lived in 'not good health' were similar to those for DFLEs. HLE was the highest in the South East (71.7 years for men and 74.8 years for women) and the lowest in the North East (65.5 years and 69.3 years, respectively). Correspondingly, years in 'not good health' were the highest in Wales for both men and women (9.1 years and 10.6 years respectively) and the lowest in the South East (men: 5.5 years, women: 6.7 years).

Again, regional distribution patterns for HLE at age 65 for men and women were very similar to those for DFLE at age 65. HLE at 65 was the highest in the South East (13.7 years for men, 15.8 years for women) and lowest in the North East (10.8 years for men, 12.8 years for women).

Health expectancies for local authorities

DFLE at birth

Analysis at national and regional levels masks much larger variations in DFLE found at LA level. For LAs in England and Wales, the gap in DFLE at birth for males was 18.3 years between the LA with the highest DFLE (Hart: 68.8 years) and that with the lowest DFLE (Easington: 50.5 years). In comparison, the largest difference in DFLE at GOR level was 7.6 years between South East and North East. Similarly, for women, the gap in DFLE at birth was 16.4 years between the LAs of Elmbridge (70.5 years) and Merthyr Tydfil (54.1 years) as opposed to 6.5 years between the South East and the North East regions.

Even within regions, there were marked differences in the range of DFLE between the constituent LAs with the highest and lowest estimates. Interestingly, there was less variation between LAs located in regions with a higher than average DFLE than in regions with a relatively low DFLE (Table 2). The largest within-GOR differentials in DFLEs were for LAs in the North East: a gap of 12.4 years in DFLE at birth for males (Tyndale: 62.9 years versus Easington:50.5 years) and 11.6 years for females (Alnwick: 66.3 years versus Easington 54.7 years). In contrast, the smallest differentials in DFLE were for LAs in the South West: 7.9 years for both men and women between Plymouth and Cotswold.

The detailed geographical patterns of DFLEs at LA level for males and females are shown in Map 1 and Map 2. The ranges on these maps were constructed by arranging LAs in order of descending DFLE which were then categorised into five groups (quintiles) with an approximately equal number of LAs in each group. The LAs with values not significantly different from the England and Wales national average are marked with the symbol '*'.

The broad patterns of distribution of DFLE values for males and females were similar. The LAs with the lowest DFLEs were mostly found to lie in central England and in the coastal areas of England and Wales. By contrast LAs with the highest DFLEs were located in the East of England, South East and South West. Notably, not even a single local

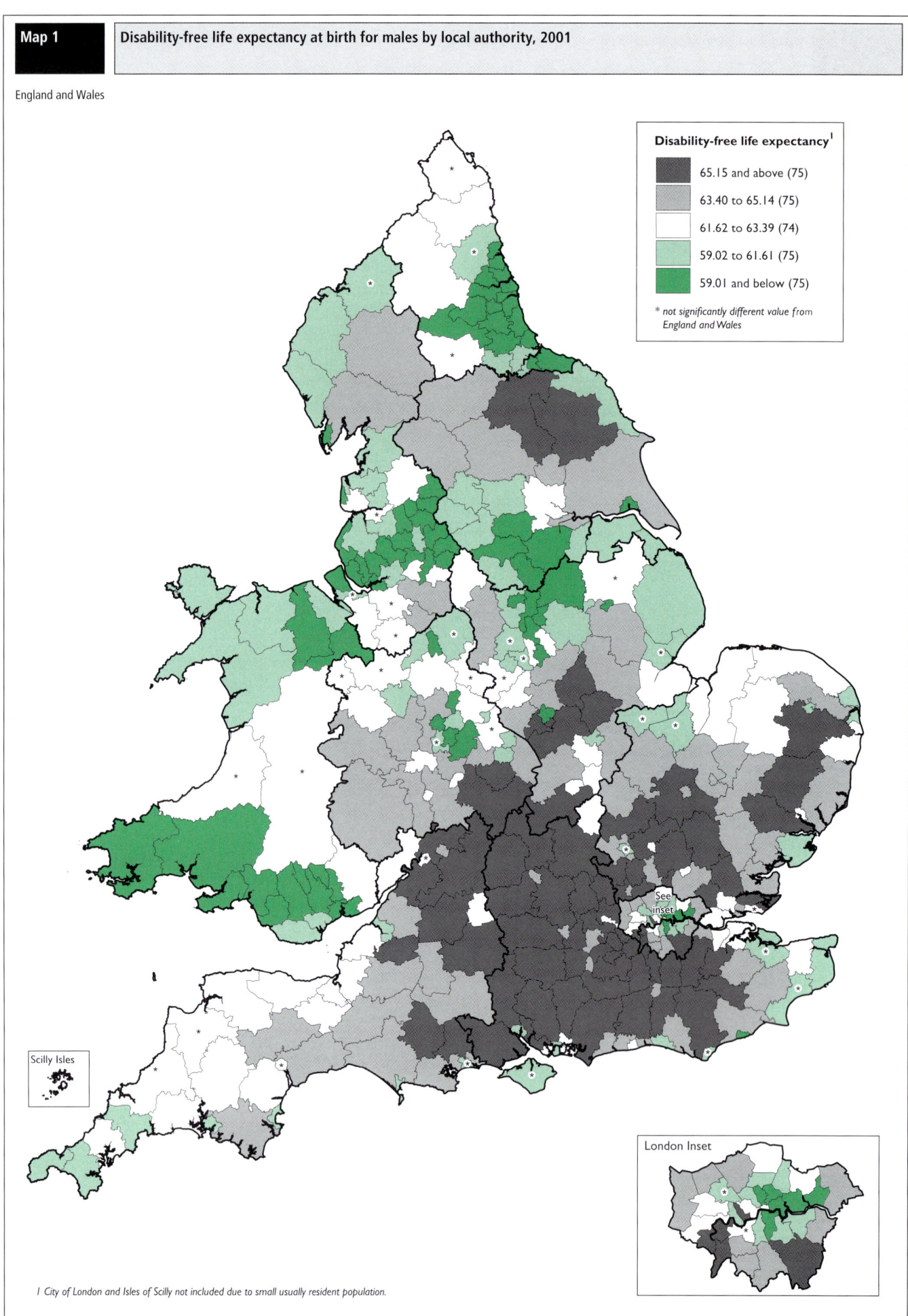

Map 1

Disability-free life expectancy at birth for males by local authority, 2001

England and Wales

Disability-free life expectancy[1]

■ 65.15 and above (75)

■ 63.40 to 65.14 (75)

□ 61.62 to 63.39 (74)

■ 59.02 to 61.61 (75)

■ 59.01 and below (75)

* not significantly different value from England and Wales

Scilly Isles

See inset

London Inset

1 City of London and Isles of Scilly not included due to small usually resident population.

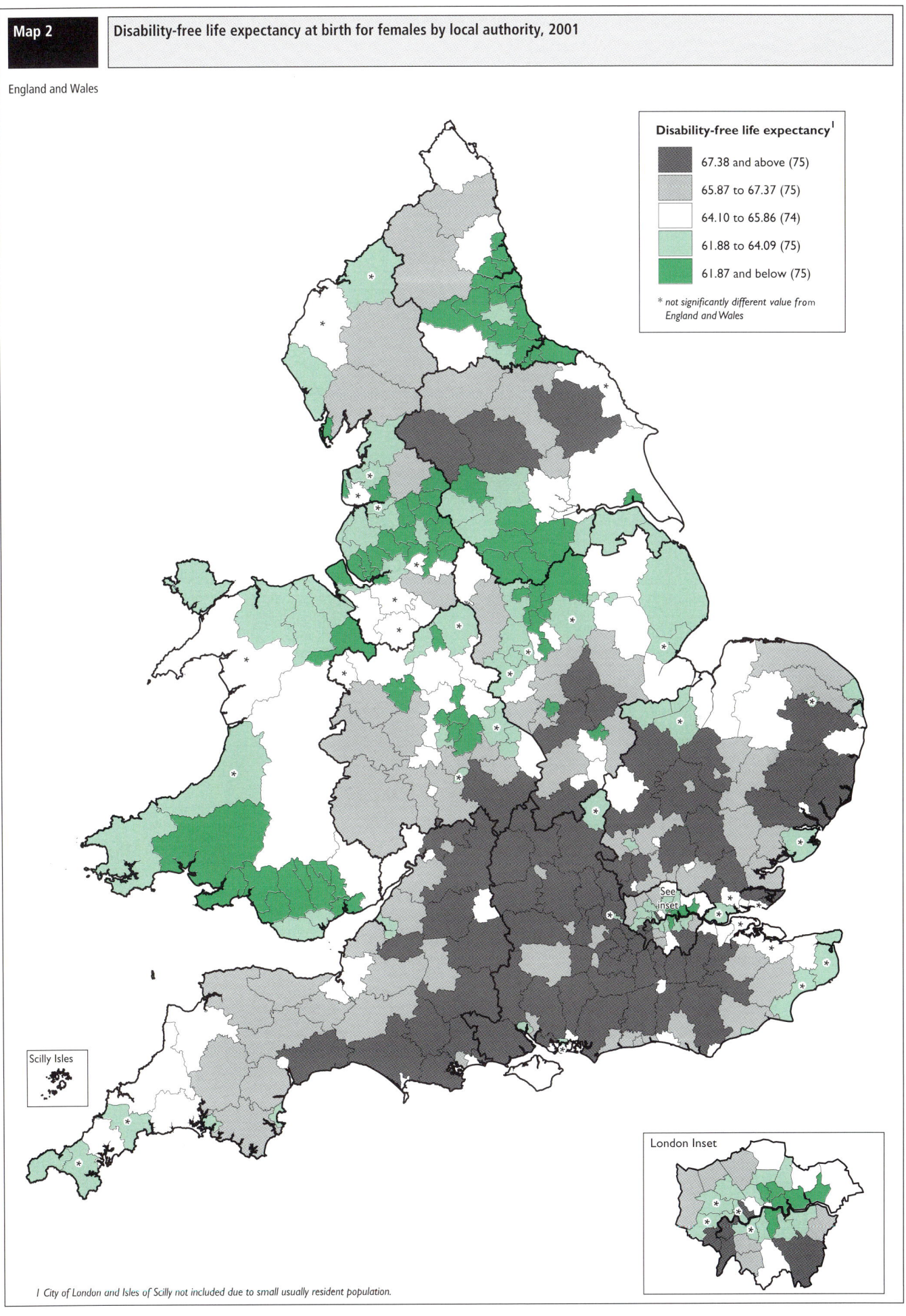

Map 2

Disability-free life expectancy at birth for females by local authority, 2001

England and Wales

Disability-free life expectancy[1]

- 67.38 and above (75)
- 65.87 to 67.37 (75)
- 64.10 to 65.86 (74)
- 61.88 to 64.09 (75)
- 61.87 and below (75)

* not significantly different value from England and Wales

Scilly Isles

See inset

London Inset

1 City of London and Isles of Scilly not included due to small usually resident population.

Table 2	Disability-free life expectancy at birth: ranges for local authorities within Government Office Regions and Wales, 2001

England, Wales and England and Wales

	Males					Females				
	Lowest DFLE		Highest DFLE		Range (years)	Lowest DFLE		Highest DFLE		Range (years)
Government Office Region	Local authority	DFLE (years)	Local authority	DFLE (years)		Local authority	DFLE (years)	Local authority	DFLE (years)	
North East	Easington	50.5	Tynedale	62.9	12.4	Easington	54.7	Alnwick	66.3	11.6
North West	Liverpool	53.6	Macclesfield	65.0	11.4	Knowsley	56.7	Macclesfield	67.0	10.2
Yorkshire and The Humber	Barnsley	54.9	Hambleton	65.4	10.5	Barnsley	58.7	Ryedale	68.3	9.6
East Midlands	Bolsover	55.4	Rutland	67.2	11.8	Bolsover	58.9	Rutland	68.4	9.5
West Midlands	Stoke-on-Trent	55.8	Stratford-on-Avon	65.6	9.8	Stoke-on-Trent	58.4	Stratford-on-Avon	68.2	9.8
East of England	Great Yarmouth	59.9	Uttlesford	67.7	7.7	Great Yarmouth	62.8	South Cambridgeshire	68.8	6.0
London	Tower Hamlets	55.7	Richmond upon Thames	66.6	10.9	Hackney	58.4	Richmond upon Thames	68.9	10.5
South East	Hastings	58.3	Hart	68.8	10.6	Hastings	62.2	Elmbridge	70.5	8.4
South West	Plymouth	59.2	Cotswold	67.1	7.9	Plymouth	62.2	Cotswold	69.1	6.9
Wales	Merthyr Tydfil	51.2	Monmouthshire	62.2	11.1	Merthyr Tydfil	54.1	Monmouthshire	65.2	11.1
England and Wales	Easington	50.5	Hart	68.8	18.3	Merthyr Tydfil	54.1	Elmbridge	70.5	16.4

Source: Office for National Statistics

authority in North East, North West and Wales was in the quintile with the highest DFLE; conversely only one LA in the South East (Hastings) and none from the East of England and South West lay in the bottom quintile. The ten LAs with the highest and lowest DFLE estimates for males and females are listed in Table 3.

In general, years lived with disability were lower in LAs with higher life expectancy. As a result, in LAs with higher life expectancy people live fewer years with disability, both in absolute and relative terms. This pattern holds for males and females and results for males are presented for illustration (see Figure 2). For example, men in Manchester (LA with the lowest life expectancy at birth of 71.0 years) live 17.2 years with disability (or 24.2 per cent of life expectancy) compared with men in Rutland (LA with the highest life expectancy of 79.5 years) who live 12.2 years with disability (or 15.4 per cent of life expectancy).

Table 3	Local authorities with the highest and lowest disability-free life expectancy (DFLE) at birth, 2001

England and Wales

	Males				Females			
Local Authority	Government Office Region	Life expectancy at birth (years)	Disability-free life expectancy at birth (years)	Local Authority	Government Office Region	Life expectancy at birth (years)	Disability-free life expectancy at birth (years)
Ten highest				**Ten highest**			
Hart	South East	79.5	68.8	Elmbridge	South East	83.0	70.5
Wokingham	South East	78.7	68.1	Chiltern	South East	82.6	69.8
Elmbridge	South East	78.5	68.0	Hart	South East	83.0	69.7
South Bucks	South East	78.1	67.8	Guildford	South East	83.9	69.7
Uttlesford	East of England	78.9	67.7	Wokingham	South East	82.7	69.6
Horsham	South East	78.6	67.5	Epsom and Ewell	South East	83.6	69.5
Waverley	South East	78.5	67.3	Mole Valley	South East	82.6	69.4
Guildford	South East	78.6	67.3	South Bucks	South East	81.6	69.3
Mid Sussex	South East	78.0	67.3	Horsham	South East	82.6	69.2
Rutland	East Midlands	79.5	67.2	Cotswold	South West	82.5	69.1
Ten lowest				**Ten lowest**			
Barnsley	Yorkshire and The Humber	74.4	54.9	Hackney	London	80.1	58.4
Knowsley	North West	72.9	53.9	Manchester	North West	77.3	57.2
Caerphilly	Wales	74.1	53.8	Liverpool	North West	77.6	57.1
Manchester	North West	71.0	53.8	Knowsley	North West	78.2	56.7
Liverpool	North West	72.5	53.6	Caerphilly	Wales	79.2	56.7
Neath Port Talbot	Wales	74.0	53.5	Rhondda, Cynon, Taff	Wales	79.1	56.4
Rhondda, Cynon, Taff	Wales	74.0	53.4	Blaenau Gwent	Wales	78.8	56.0
Blaenau Gwent	Wales	73.3	53.2	Neath Port Talbot	Wales	79.4	55.7
Merthyr Tydfil	Wales	73.3	51.2	Easington	North East	78.8	54.7
Easington	North East	74.0	50.5	Merthyr Tydfil	Wales	78.1	54.1

Source: Office for National Statistics

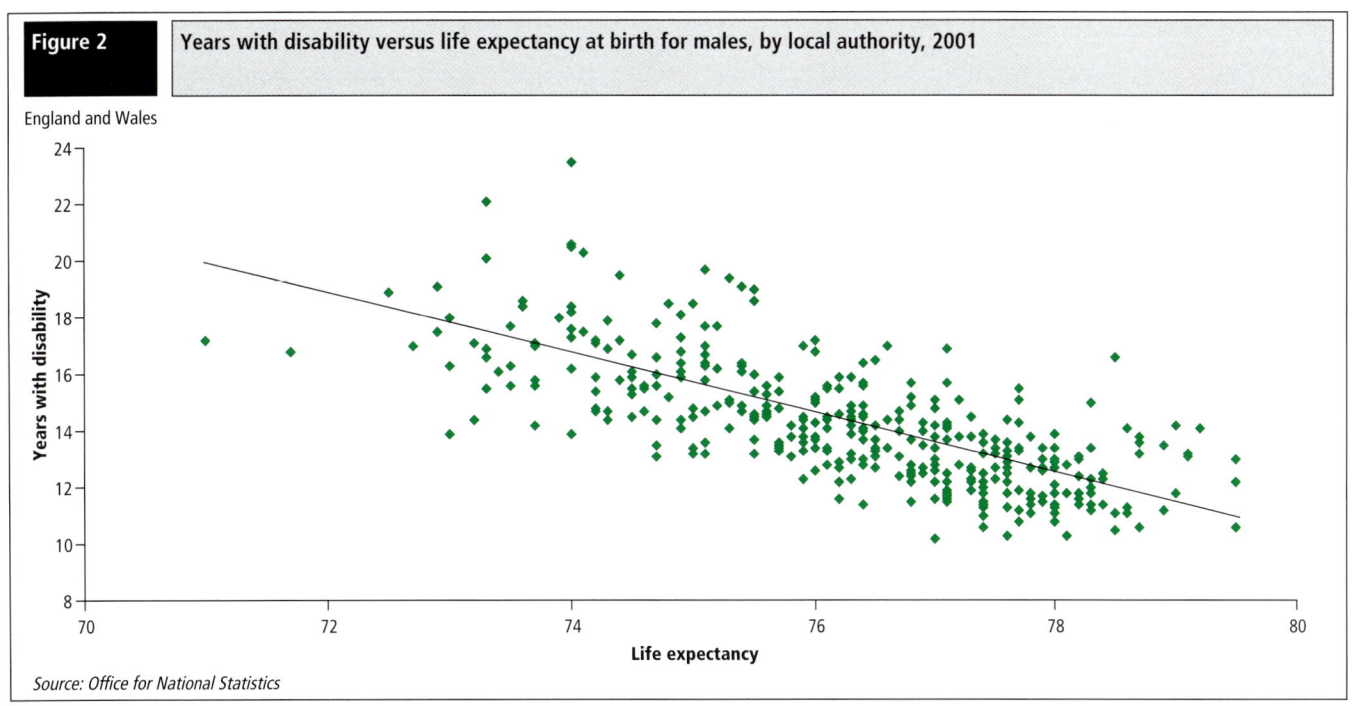

Figure 2 Years with disability versus life expectancy at birth for males, by local authority, 2001

England and Wales

Source: Office for National Statistics

DFLE at age 65

The geographical pattern for the variation of DFLE at age 65 for LAs was broadly similar to that for DFLE at birth. For both males and females, DFLEs at 65 for LAs with the highest values (for men: Hart, 10.5 years; for women: Epsom and Ewell, 11.6 years) were about two times higher than for LAs with lowest values (for men: Easington, 4.2 years; for women: Merthyr Tydfil, 5.3 years).

For both sexes, most of the local authorities with highest DFLE at 65 were situated in southern England, while most of the lowest ten LAs for DFLE at 65 were situated in Wales or in the north of England (Table 4).

As reported earlier for DFLE at birth, LAs with high life expectancy at age 65 generally have fewer years of life lived with disability. For men, years lived with disability decrease from 10.5 years for Easington to 6.7

Table 4 Local authorities with the highest and lowest disability-free life expectancy (DFLE) at age 65, 2001

England and Wales

Local Authority	Males			Females			
	Government Office Region	Life expectancy at age 65 (years)	Disability-free life expectancy at age 65 (years)	Local Authority	Government Office Region	Life expectancy at age 65 (years)	Disability-free life expectancy at age 65 (years)
Ten highest				**Ten highest**			
Hart	South East	17.7	10.5	Epsom and Ewell	South East	21.5	11.6
Rutland	East Midlands	18.2	10.5	Elmbridge	South East	20.3	11.5
Waverley	South East	17.5	10.5	Guildford	South East	21.4	11.5
Elmbridge	South East	17.5	10.5	Chiltern	South East	20.5	11.5
East Dorset	South West	18.6	10.5	Mole Valley	South East	20.4	11.4
South Bucks	South East	17.3	10.4	New Forest	South East	21.2	11.4
Kensington and Chelsea	London	18.9	10.4	Waverley	South East	20.3	11.3
Winchester	South East	17.9	10.4	East Dorset	South West	21.1	11.3
Guildford	South East	17.7	10.3	Kensington and Chelsea	London	22.0	11.3
New Forest	South East	18.0	10.3	Chichester	South East	19.8	11.2
Ten lowest				**Ten lowest**			
Barnsley	Yorkshire and The Humber	14.8	5.4	Bridgend	Wales	18.0	6.5
Knowsley	North West	14.3	5.4	Sedgefield	North East	18.1	6.5
Bolsover	East Midlands	15.2	5.3	Sunderland	North East	17.5	6.5
Sunderland	North East	14.3	5.1	Knowsley	North West	17.6	6.3
Neath Port Talbot	Wales	15.0	4.9	Blaenau Gwent	Wales	17.7	5.9
Blaenau Gwent	Wales	14.5	4.8	Caerphilly	Wales	17.9	5.9
Caerphilly	Wales	14.8	4.7	Neath Port Talbot	Wales	18.3	5.8
Rhondda, Cynon, Taff	Wales	14.8	4.6	Rhondda, Cynon, Taff	Wales	18.0	5.8
Merthyr Tydfil	Wales	14.3	4.3	Easington	North East	18.3	5.8
Easington	North East	14.7	4.2	Merthyr Tydfil	Wales	17.1	5.3

Source: Office for National Statistics

years for Mole Valley while life expectancy increases from 14.7 years for Easington to 16.8 years for Mole Valley. Correspondingly, for women years lived with disability decrease from 12.5 years for Easington to 8.5 years for Reigate and Banstead as life expectancy increases from 18.3 years for Easington to 19.3 years for Reigate and Banstead.

HLE at birth

Healthy life expectancies at birth for local authorities follow a geographical pattern broadly similar to that for DFLE at birth but the magnitude of differentials is smaller. For males, HLE at birth ranged from 75.1 years in Hart (South East) to 60.2 years in Merthyr Tydfil (Wales), with a gap of 14.9 years between the two LAs. This compares with a difference in DFLE at birth of 18.3 years between Hart (68.8 years) and Easington (50.5 years).

For women, HLE at birth ranged from 77.7 years in Epsom and Ewell to 63.5 years in Merthyr Tydfil: a gap of 14.2 years. The equivalent difference between the LAs with the highest and the lowest DFLE at birth was 16.4 years between Elmbridge (70.5 years) and Merthyr Tydfil (54.1 years).

Although LAs differ in ranking, the geographical patterns were very similar for HLE and DFLE. For example, an examination of LAs with the ten highest HLE values shows that seven of the ten LAs with highest HLE were also amongst the ten LAs with the highest DFLE values. Similarly, there was considerable overlap in LAs at the bottom end of the scale for both HLE and DFLE (Table 5, Table 3).

The relative differentials between LAs in years lived in 'not good health' were larger than in years lived with disability. For both males and females, there was a three-fold differential in years lived in 'not good health' between the LAs with the highest and lowest estimates, compared to around a two-fold differential in years lived with disability (Table 5, Table 3).

As found for years lived with disability, years lived in 'not good' health were smaller for LAs with higher than average life expectancy at birth. But the association between years lived in 'not good' health and life expectancy was slightly higher (correlation of -.82 for males and -.78 for females) than between years lived with disability and life expectancy (correlation of -.72 for both males and females).

HLE at age 65

As found for DFLE at age 65, sex and area differentials in HLE at birth continue well into older age although the magnitudes of the differentials were smaller (Table 6).

Measured in terms of years lived in 'not good health' (life expectancy minus healthy life expectancy), the relative differentials between LAs were lower at age 65 than at birth. For example, both for males and females, there were two-fold differentials in years lived in 'not good health' between the LAs with the highest and the lowest HLE at 65. This compares with three-fold differentials between the extremes of distribution of HLE at birth (Table 5, Table 6).

Table 5	Local authorities with the highest and lowest healthy life expectancy (HLE) at birth, 2001

England and Wales

	Males				Females			
Local Authority	Government Office Region	Life expectancy at birth (years)	Healthy life expectancy at birth (years)		Local Authority	Government Office Region	Life expectancy at birth (years)	Healthy life expectancy at birth (years)
Ten highest					**Ten highest**			
Hart	South East	79.5	75.1		Epsom and Ewell	South East	83.6	77.7
Wokingham	South East	78.7	74.6		Guildford	South East	83.9	77.6
Rutland	East Midlands	79.5	74.4		Elmbridge	South East	83.0	77.4
South Cambridgeshire	East of England	79.0	74.3		Hart	South East	83.0	77.3
Uttlesford	East of England	78.9	74.2		Chiltern	South East	82.6	77.2
East Dorset	South West	79.5	74.2		Wokingham	South East	82.7	77.2
Horsham	South East	78.6	74.1		South Cambridgeshire	East of England	83.0	77.1
Waverley	South East	78.5	73.9		Horsham	South East	82.6	77.1
Elmbridge	South East	78.5	73.9		Mole Valley	South East	82.6	77.0
Guildford	South East	78.6	73.8		Winchester	South East	82.5	76.9
Ten lowest					**Ten lowest**			
Caerphilly	Wales	74.1	62.8		Tower Hamlets	London	78.9	66.7
Blackpool	North West	71.7	62.7		Caerphilly	Wales	79.2	66.2
Tower Hamlets	London	72.7	62.5		Knowsley	North West	78.2	66.2
Knowsley	North West	72.9	62.5		Liverpool	North West	77.6	66.0
Rhondda, Cynon, Taff	Wales	74.0	62.4		Neath Port Talbot	Wales	79.4	66.0
Liverpool	North West	72.5	62.1		Rhondda, Cynon, Taff	Wales	79.1	65.9
Blaenau Gwent	Wales	73.3	61.9		Manchester	North West	77.3	65.4
Easington	North East	74.0	61.2		Blaenau Gwent	Wales	78.8	65.2
Manchester	North West	71.0	61.1		Easington	North East	78.8	64.9
Merthyr Tydfil	Wales	73.3	60.2		Merthyr Tydfil	Wales	78.1	63.5

Source: Office for National Statistics

Table 6	Local authorities with the highest and lowest healthy life expectancy (HLE) at age 65, 2001

England and Wales

	Males				Females			
Local Authority	Government Office Region	Life expectancy at age 65 (years)	Healthy life expectancy at age 65 (years)	Local Authority	Government Office Region	Life expectancy at age 65 (years)	Healthy life expectancy at age 65 (years)
Ten highest				**Ten highest**			
East Dorset	South West	18.6	15.5	Epsom and Ewell	South East	21.5	17.6
Rutland	East Midlands	18.2	15.3	Guildford	South East	21.4	17.4
Winchester	South East	17.9	15.0	New Forest	South East	21.2	17.3
New Forest	South East	18.0	15.0	North Dorset	South West	21.2	17.2
Christchurch	South West	18.2	14.9	Kensington and Chelsea	London	22.0	17.2
North Dorset	South West	17.8	14.9	Waverley	South East	20.3	17.1
Waverley	South East	17.5	14.9	East Dorset	South West	21.1	17.0
Hart	South East	17.7	14.9	Wealden	South East	20.9	17.0
South Cambridgeshire	East of England	17.9	14.9	Hart	South East	20.9	17.0
Guildford	South East	17.7	14.8	Chiltern	South East	20.5	16.9
Ten lowest				**Ten lowest**			
Knowsley	North West	14.3	9.8	Barnsley	Yorkshire and The Humber	17.9	11.8
Sunderland	North East	14.3	9.8	Liverpool	North West	17.1	11.7
Neath Port Talbot	Wales	15.0	9.8	Wigan	North West	17.4	11.7
Liverpool	North West	14.1	9.7	Knowsley	North West	17.6	11.7
Manchester	North West	14.0	9.7	Easington	North East	18.3	11.4
Easington	North East	14.7	9.4	Neath Port Talbot	Wales	18.3	11.4
Caerphilly	Wales	14.8	9.3	Caerphilly	Wales	17.9	11.2
Blaenau Gwent	Wales	14.5	9.3	Rhondda, Cynon, Taff	Wales	18.0	11.1
Rhondda, Cynon, Taff	Wales	14.8	9.2	Blaenau Gwent	Wales	17.7	11.1
Merthyr Tydfil	Wales	14.3	8.7	Merthyr Tydfil	Wales	17.1	10.2

Source: Office for National Statistics

Table 7	Comparison between survey- and census-based health expectancy estimates for 2001

England and Wales

		Life expectancy (years)	Healthy life expectancy (years)			Disability-free life expectancy (years)		
			Survey based[1]	2001 Census based	Difference	Survey based[1]	2001 Census based	Difference
At birth								
Males	England	76.0	67.1	69.0	-2.0	60.7	61.7	-1.0
	Wales	75.4	65.5	66.2	-0.7	57.7	57.7	-0.0
Females								
	England	80.6	70.1	72.3	-2.2	63.0	64.2	-1.2
	Wales	80.1	69.4	69.4	-0.0	61.1	60.5	0.6
At age 65								
Males	England	16.1	12.0	12.5	-0.5	8.9	8.1	0.9
	Wales	15.7	11.1	11.3	-0.2	7.3	6.5	0.8
Females								
	England	19.2	14.2	14.5	-0.3	10.4	9.1	1.4
	Wales	18.7	12.8	13.0	-0.2	8.5	7.6	0.9

1. Based on combined GHS data for 2000–2002.
Source: Office for National Statistics

Comparison with national data sources

A comparison between the Census 2001 based estimates and the GHS based estimates for 2001 shows that there were significant differences between the estimates derived from the two data sources. For England and for Wales, the GHS based estimates of HLE and DFLE were generally lower than the 2001 Census based estimates, except for DFLE at 65 for which the converse was true (Table 7).

The differences between health expectancy estimates from the two sources result from differences in the health rates calculated from the two sources. These differences arise partly due to the differences in the

question asked in the two sources – for example the limiting longstanding illness question was substantially different in the 2001 Census from the GHS question.[7] However, even when the question asked was identical – as with the general health question – there were important differences in terms of population coverage, mode of collection and context between the two sources. These are known to affect responses and may account for the differences observed.

This raises the issue 'which health expectancies to use?' at the national level. The Census-based health expectancies for England and for Wales were primarily calculated to provide a national reference value to examine the scale of sub-national variations. For the purpose of monitoring health expectancies at the national level, it is recommended to use health expectancy estimates based on surveys rather than the ones based on the Census. This is because the survey estimates of health status are based on face-to-face interviews (with no proxy reporting) asking for a subjective assessment of health status, and responses are more reliable than census returns based on postal self-completion. Furthermore, survey based estimates have the advantage of being regularly updated to allow monitoring of health trends.

Website report and results

Detailed health expectancies data including those presented in this report can be found on the National Statistics website at:

Http://www.statistics.gov.uk/StatBase/Product.asp?vlnk=12964

The website includes disability-free life expectancy and healthy life expectancy for males and females, at birth and at age 65, for local authorities and Government Office Regions in England and Wales. It also includes 95 per cent confidence intervals for the health expectancies.

Further information

If you require additional information on the data presented here please contact:

Morbidity and Cancer Team
Room D2/03
Office for National Statistics
1 Drummond Gate
London SW1V 2QQ
Tel: 020 7533 5244

Email: hle@ons.gov.uk

References

1. Health expectancies at birth and at age 65 in the United Kingdom and its constituent countries, 2001–2002. Available at www.statistics.gov.uk/StatBase/ssdataset.asp?vlnk=12964
2. Breakwell C and Bajekal M (2006) Health expectancies in the UK and its constituent countries, 2001. *Health Statistics Quarterly* **29**, 18–25.
3. Bissett B (2002) Healthy life expectancy in England at subnational level. *Health Statistics Quarterly* **14**, 21–29.
4. Bone M R, Bebbington A C, Jagger C, Morgan K and Nicolaas G (1995) *Health expectancy and its uses,* HMSO: London.
5. Jagger C (1999) *Health Expectancy Calculation by the Sullivan Method: A Practical Guide*. NUPRI Research Paper Series no 68.
6. Life expectancy at birth by health and local authorities in the United Kingdom, 1991–1993 to 2002-2004. Available at www.statistics.gov.uk/statbase/Product.asp?vlnk=8841
7. Bajekal M, Harries T, Breman R and Woodfield T (2004) *Review of disability estimates and definitions: a study carried out on behalf of the Department for Work and Pensions*. HMSO. Also available at www.dwp.gov.uk/asd/asd5/ih2004.asp#a

Report:

Life expectancy at birth by local authorities in England and Wales, 2003–2005

Introduction

This report presents the latest figures on male and female period life expectancy at birth for Government Office Regions and local authorities in England and Wales for 2003–2005. For comparison purposes results are also included for 1993–1995. The figures are three-year averages, produced by aggregating deaths and population estimates for both three-year periods, so as to provide large enough numbers to ensure that the presented figures are sufficiently robust. Two local authorities, City of London and Isles of Scilly, are excluded from the results because of small numbers of deaths and populations in these areas.

Interpretation of period life expectancy at birth

Life expectancy at birth for an area in a given time period is an estimate of the average number of years a new-born baby would survive if he or she experienced the particular area's age-specific mortality rates for that time period throughout his or her life. The figure reflects mortality among those living in the area in each time period, rather than mortality among those born in each area. It is not therefore the number of years a baby born in the area in each time period could actually expect to live, both because the death rates of the area are likely to change in the future and because many of those born in the area will live elsewhere for at least some part of their lives.

Life expectancy at birth is also not a guide to the remaining expectation of life at any given age. For example, if female life expectancy was 80 years for a particular area, life expectancy of women aged 75 years in that area would exceed 5 years. This reflects the fact that survival from a particular age depends only on the mortality rates beyond that age, whereas survival from birth is based on mortality rates at every age.

All the life expectancies quoted in this report are period life expectancies.

Summary of results

Life expectancies for Government Office Regions in 2003–2005 continued to show a familiar geographical pattern with the lowest results in the North East, North West and Wales, and the highest life expectancies in the South West, South East and East of England. For males there was a difference of 2.7 years between the regions with the lowest life expectancy (the North East and North West – both 75.4 years), and the South East and South West, where life expectancy was highest (78.1 years).The North East and South West were the regions with the lowest and highest female life expectancy (79.8 and 82.2 years respectively), although the difference between them was rather less than for males at 2.4 years.

In 2003–2005 Manchester was the local authority with the lowest male life expectancy at birth at 72.5 years. This was 9.7 years less than Kensington and Chelsea where male life expectancy was highest (82.2 years).

Kensington and Chelsea also had the highest female life expectancy at birth in 2003–2005 at 86.2 years. This was 8.1 years more than Liverpool, the local authority with the lowest female life expectancy (78.1 years).

The local authorities with the highest and lowest male and female life expectancy at birth in England and Wales in 2003–2005 are presented in Boxes 1 and 2 respectively. For comparison purposes the life expectancy and relative rank order of these areas in 1993–1995 is included. Boxes 3 and 4 present the local authorities with the highest and lowest male and female life expectancy at birth in England and Wales in 1993–1995, along with their results for 2003–2005.

Box one

Local authorities with the highest and lowest life expectancy at birth in England and Wales 2003–2005, and comparisons with 1993–1995.

Males

Highest life expectancy		2003–2005	1993–1995	1993–1995
Rank 2003–2005	Local Authority	Years	Years	Rank
1	Kensington and Chelsea	82.2	72.9	311
2	East Dorset	80.9	77.9	1
3	Hart	80.2	77.2	6
4	Uttlesford	80.0	76.5	28
5	Wokingham	80.0	77.4	3
6	South Norfolk	80.0	76.8	18
7	Chiltern	80.0	77.4	2
8	Horsham	79.9	76.8	15
9	Brentwood	79.8	75.5	111
10	Crawley	79.8	75.1	148
Lowest life expectancy				
374	Manchester	72.5	69.7	374
373	Blackpool	73.2	71.0	371
372	Liverpool	73.4	71.2	368
371	Nottingham	73.5	72.3	347
370	Stoke-on-Trent	73.7	72.1	352
369	Salford	73.8	71.1	369
368	Knowsley	73.9	71.6	360
367	Middlesbrough	74.1	71.5	362
366	Hartlepool	74.1	72.1	350
365	Blaenau Gwent	74.2	72.2	348

Box two

Local authorities with the highest and lowest life expectancy at birth in England and Wales 2003–2005, and comparisons with 1993–1995.

Females

Highest life expectancy		2003–2005	1993–1995	1993–1995
Rank 2003–2005	Local Authority	Years	Years	Rank
1	Kensington and Chelsea	86.2	80.4	99
2	Epsom and Ewell	84.5	81.7	9
3	East Dorset	84.1	83.4	1
4	South Cambridgeshire	83.9	80.8	55
5	Rutland	83.8	80.8	56
6	Purbeck	83.7	80.5	90
7	Guildford	83.6	81.9	6
8	New Forest	83.6	81.2	23
9	North Dorset	83.5	81.0	35
10	Horsham	83.4	81.0	39
Lowest life expectancy				
374	Liverpool	78.1	77.3	367
373	Halton	78.3	77.3	366
372	Hartlepool	78.3	77.6	358
371	Manchester	78.3	76.6	374
370	Blackburn with Darwen	78.4	77.6	357
369	Salford	78.4	76.8	372
368	Easington	78.4	76.9	371
367	Knowsley	78.4	76.7	373
366	Blaenau Gwent	78.4	78.4	320
365	Merthyr Tydfil	78.6	77.8	350

Box three

Local authorities with the highest and lowest life expectancy at birth in England and Wales 1993–1995, and comparisons with 2003–2005.

Males

Highest life expectancy		1993–1995	2003–2005	2003–2005
Rank 1993–1995	Local Authority	Years	Years	Rank
1	East Dorset	77.9	80.9	2
2	Chiltern	77.4	80.0	7
3	Wokingham	77.4	80.0	5
4	West Somerset	77.3	79.1	43
5	East Devon	77.3	79.6	14
6	Hart	77.2	80.2	3
7	West Oxfordshire	77.1	79.4	26
8	Christchurch	77.0	79.7	12
9	Vale of White Horse	77.0	79.2	39
10	Elmbridge	77.0	79.7	13
Lowest life expectancy				
374	Manchester	69.7	72.5	374
373	Tower Hamlets	70.6	74.9	340
372	Merthyr Tydfil	70.6	74.3	360
371	Blackpool	71.0	73.2	373
370	Hammersmith and Fulham	71.1	76.8	226
369	Salford	71.1	73.8	369
368	Liverpool	71.2	73.4	372
367	Lambeth	71.2	74.9	344
366	Preston	71.2	74.4	357
365	Islington	71.4	74.6	352

Box four

Local authorities with the highest and lowest life expectancy at birth in England and Wales 1993–1995, and comparisons with 2003–2005.

Females

Highest life expectancy		1993–1995	2003–2005	2003–2005
Rank 1993–1995	Local Authority	Years	Years	Rank
1	East Dorset	83.4	84.1	3
2	Christchurch	82.6	83.4	12
3	East Devon	82.4	83.1	19
4	Chiltern	82.0	83.0	22
5	Cotswold	82.0	82.9	27
6	Guildford	81.9	83.6	7
7	Waverley	81.8	82.7	52
8	Wealden	81.7	82.9	33
9	Epsom and Ewell	81.7	84.5	2
10	Cambridge	81.7	82.0	123
Lowest life expectancy				
374	Manchester	76.6	78.3	371
373	Knowsley	76.7	78.4	367
372	Salford	76.8	78.4	369
371	Easington	76.9	78.4	368
370	Burnley	77.0	78.6	364
369	Rochdale	77.2	78.8	360
368	Wear Valley	77.3	79.0	356
367	Liverpool	77.3	78.1	374
366	Halton	77.3	78.3	373
365	Newham	77.4	78.8	361

Table 1 includes results for all local authorities in England and Wales for both 1993–1995 and 2003–2005, and their relative rank order at each time point. Results are presented alphabetically within each Government Office Region. The difference in life expectancy between 1993–1995 and 2003–2005 is also included.

Website report and results for Scotland and Northern Ireland

The results presented in this report can also be found on the National Statistics website at:

www.statistics.gov.uk/statbase/Product.asp?vlnk=8841

The website report includes trend data for local authorities and Government Office Regions in the form of three-year rolling averages from 1991 to 1993 onwards. Results are also available for Strategic Health Authorities in England from 1991 to 1993 onwards. All life expectancy results in the website report are presented with 95 per cent confidence intervals.

The website report also includes results for local and health authorities in Scotland and Northern Ireland from 1991 to 1993 onwards. These figures were calculated by ONS except for those for Scotland for 2002–2004 and 2003–2005. These were calculated by the General Register Office for Scotland (GROS) using the same methodology used by ONS to produce results for earlier years. The Scottish life expectancies for 2003–2005 have also been published in a separate report available on the GROS website:
www.gro-scotland.gov.uk/statistics/library/life-expectancy/le2003-05/index.html

Comparison with national results

In previous years the Government Actuary's Department (GAD) published national interim life tables for the UK and constituent countries. In January 2006 responsibility for this work passed to ONS. For 2003-2005 ONS has calculated results using the same methods used by GAD. These are published on the National Statistics website at:

www.statistics.gov.uk/StatBase/Product.asp?vlnk=14459

To provide comparisons for local authority and regional figures ONS has also calculated national life expectancy results, which are included in Table 1. These were produced using the same methods as the sub-national results, with abridged life tables in which deaths and populations are aggregated into age groups. Because the national interim life tables are calculated using complete life tables (based on single years of age) the two sets of national figures may differ very slightly (normally by less than 0.1 years for England and Wales).

Figures for England will also differ slightly from the national interim life table results because of a difference in the handling of deaths of non-residents. For this report the deaths of non-residents have been included in the mortality figures for England and Wales but are excluded from the data for England and Wales separately. For the national interim tables however the deaths of non-residents in England and Wales have been included in the mortality data for England (but not Wales).

In addition, annual mortality data used in the calculation of life expectancy figures for this report have been based on all deaths registered in a year. The mortality data for England and Wales used in the national interim life tables from 1993 onwards are based on all deaths which occurred in a year. Differences in the annual numbers of occurrences and registrations may also lead to small variations in national life expectancy figures.

Methods of calculation

Abridged life tables were constructed using standard methods.[1,2] Separate tables were constructed for males and females. The tables were created using annual mid-year population estimates and deaths registered in each year. All figures presented here are for life expectancy at birth. A detailed description of the standard methods and notation associated with the calculation of life expectancy can be found on the Government Actuary's Department website:

Methods: www.gad.gov.uk/Life_Tables/methodology.htm
Notation: www.gad.gov.uk/Life_Tables/notation.htm

The calculation of confidence intervals (available on the National Statistics website) used the method developed by Chiang.[3] A report which details research undertaken by ONS to compare methodologies to allow the calculation of confidence intervals for life expectancy at birth has been published as No 33 in the National Statistics Methodology Series. This report, 'Life expectancy at birth: methodological options for small populations' also presents research carried out to establish if there is a minimum population size below which the calculation of life expectancy may not be considered feasible. It can be found on the National Statistics website at:

www.statistics.gov.uk/methods_quality/publications.asp

Using the recommendations included in this report ONS has now published experimental life expectancy at birth figures for wards in England and Wales based on deaths from 1999 to 2003:

www.statistics.gov.uk/statbase/Product.asp?vlnk=14466

An example of a life table constructed using the same method used to calculate life expectancy at birth and confidence intervals in this report can be found at.

www.statistics.gov.uk/statbase/Product.asp?vlnk=8841

Populations and Deaths

Results are based on population estimates for 2003 published in September 2004, estimates for 2004 published in August 2005, and estimates for 2005 released in August 2006. The estimates for 2004 include a correction to the female population of Harrow released 20 December 2005.

Deaths in England and Wales for 2003–2005 were allocated to current local authority boundaries.

References

1. Newell C (1994) *Methods and Models in Demography*, John Wiley & Sons: Chichester.

2. Shyrock H S and Siegel J S (1976) *The Methods and Materials of Demography* (abridged edition), Academic Press: New York.

3. Chiang C L (1968) The life table and its construction in, *Introduction to stochastic processes in Biostatistics*, John Wiley & Sons: New York, Chapter 9, 189–214.

Further information

If you require additional information on the data presented here please contact:

Email: healthgeog@ons.gov.uk

| Table 1 | Life expectancy at birth[1] (years) and relative position (rank order[2]) of local authorities in England and Wales, 2003–2005 and 1993–1995 |

	Males					Females				
	2003–2005		1993–1995			2003–2005		1993–1995		
	Life expectancy at birth	Rank order[2]	Life expectancy at birth	Rank order[2]	Difference in life expectancy between 2003–2005 and 1993–1995 (years)	Life expectancy at birth	Rank order[2]	Life expectancy at birth	Rank order[2]	Difference in life expectancy between 2003–2005 and 1993–1995 (years)
England and Wales	**76.82**		**74.06**		**2.76**	**81.07**		**79.37**		**1.70**
England	**76.92**		**74.18**		**2.74**	**81.14**		**79.44**		**1.70**
Wales	**76.15**		**73.42**		**2.73**	**80.56**		**78.99**		**1.57**
Government Office Regions and local authorities										
North East	75.39		72.71		2.68	79.83		77.95		1.88
Alnwick	76.8	227	74.6	191	2.2	82.5	75	78.8	282	3.7
Berwick-upon-Tweed	78.5	93	74.5	202	4.0	83.0	26	79.5	216	3.5
Blyth Valley	74.9	341	72.8	322	2.1	80.1	310	77.5	361	2.6
Castle Morpeth	78.2	115	74.0	241	4.2	80.9	241	78.5	307	2.4
Chester-le-Street	76.0	285	73.3	287	2.7	79.8	331	78.7	295	1.1
Darlington	75.2	326	73.2	296	2.0	80.0	314	78.1	339	1.9
Derwentside	75.2	325	71.9	358	3.3	79.8	327	77.5	362	2.3
Durham	76.7	234	74.1	234	2.6	80.2	306	79.3	236	0.9
Easington	74.2	364	72.5	337	1.7	78.4	368	76.9	371	1.5
Gateshead	75.0	337	71.9	356	3.1	79.5	337	77.6	356	1.9
Hartlepool	74.1	366	72.1	350	2.0	78.3	372	77.6	358	0.7
Middlesbrough	74.1	367	71.5	362	2.6	78.7	363	77.7	353	1.0
Newcastle upon Tyne	74.9	343	72.4	340	2.5	80.2	307	77.8	349	2.4
North Tyneside	75.6	306	73.2	295	2.4	80.4	286	78.4	315	2.0
Redcar and Cleveland	75.2	328	72.3	344	2.9	80.3	291	78.1	331	2.2
Sedgefield	75.8	295	72.9	313	2.9	79.0	355	78.0	344	1.0
South Tyneside	74.8	349	72.7	328	2.1	79.9	325	78.3	324	1.6
Stockton-on-Tees	75.7	303	73.0	308	2.7	80.0	316	78.1	336	1.9
Sunderland	75.3	320	72.3	346	3.0	79.4	343	77.4	363	2.0
Teesdale	77.1	207	73.3	288	3.8	81.3	203	79.2	245	2.1
Tynedale	77.6	164	74.6	195	3.0	81.4	186	78.6	300	2.8
Wansbeck	75.9	291	72.9	314	3.0	79.6	334	78.1	332	1.5
Wear Valley	75.2	321	72.6	331	2.6	79.0	356	77.3	368	1.7
North West	75.40		72.78		2.62	79.90		78.32		1.6
Allerdale	76.3	262	72.5	336	3.8	80.6	276	78.9	279	1.7
Barrow-in-Furness	74.8	346	73.0	309	1.8	80.4	290	78.8	289	1.6
Blackburn with Darwen	74.3	362	72.2	349	2.1	78.4	370	77.6	357	0.8
Blackpool	73.2	373	71.0	371	2.2	78.8	362	78.0	341	0.8
Bolton	74.6	350	72.8	319	1.8	79.0	357	78.0	340	1.0
Burnley	74.5	354	72.1	351	2.4	78.6	364	77.0	370	1.6
Bury	75.8	294	73.4	283	2.4	80.3	296	78.6	298	1.7
Carlisle	75.8	292	73.2	299	2.6	80.8	248	79.3	241	1.5
Chester	77.6	167	74.7	183	2.9	81.6	165	79.8	185	1.8
Chorley	76.3	257	74.0	245	2.3	80.5	279	78.8	287	1.7
Congleton	78.2	111	74.8	180	3.4	81.7	160	79.8	176	1.9
Copeland	76.1	281	72.8	324	3.3	80.4	281	78.5	314	1.9
Crewe and Nantwich	76.4	256	74.2	226	2.2	80.4	285	79.1	256	1.3
Eden	78.1	121	74.8	177	3.3	82.3	90	78.9	280	3.4
Ellesmere Port & Neston	76.8	221	73.6	269	3.2	81.1	225	79.5	215	1.6
Fylde	77.9	140	74.8	170	3.1	81.1	226	80.2	127	0.9
Halton	74.5	356	72.7	325	1.8	78.3	373	77.3	366	1.0
Hyndburn	75.2	330	72.6	332	2.6	79.4	341	78.2	329	1.2
Knowsley	73.9	368	71.6	360	2.3	78.4	367	76.7	373	1.7
Lancaster	75.9	288	73.5	272	2.4	81.0	234	79.1	253	1.9
Liverpool	73.4	372	71.2	368	2.2	78.1	374	77.3	367	0.8
Macclesfield	78.3	103	75.1	143	3.2	82.2	102	80.0	150	2.2
Manchester	72.5	374	69.7	374	2.8	78.3	371	76.6	374	1.7
Oldham	74.2	363	72.0	355	2.2	79.2	352	77.6	355	1.6
Pendle	75.3	316	73.4	278	1.9	79.8	332	79.8	183	-0.0
Preston	74.4	357	71.2	366	3.2	78.9	358	77.5	360	1.4
Ribble Valley	77.4	176	73.9	248	3.5	82.1	104	79.2	244	2.9
Rochdale	74.4	359	72.3	342	2.1	78.8	360	77.2	369	1.6
Rossendale	74.9	342	72.3	343	2.6	79.3	348	77.4	364	1.9
Salford	73.8	369	71.1	369	2.7	78.4	369	76.8	372	1.6
Sefton	75.9	287	73.3	284	2.6	80.4	288	78.8	284	1.6
South Lakeland	78.6	77	75.8	76	2.8	82.7	43	80.6	78	2.1
South Ribble	77.7	157	74.5	205	3.2	81.5	185	79.0	269	2.5
St. Helens	75.2	324	72.4	341	2.8	79.5	340	78.0	342	1.5

| Table 1 continued | **Life expectancy at birth[1] (years) and relative position (rank order[2]) of local authorities in England and Wales, 2003–2005 and 1993–1995** | | | | | | | | | |

	Males					Females				
	2003–2005		1993–1995			2003–2005		1993–1995		
	Life expectancy at birth	Rank order[2]	Life expectancy at birth	Rank order[2]	Difference in life expectancy between 2003–2005 and 1993–1995 (years)	Life expectancy at birth	Rank order[2]	Life expectancy at birth	Rank order[2]	Difference in life expectancy between 2003–2005 and 1993–1995 (years)
Stockport	76.8	222	74.5	199	2.3	81.3	204	79.4	235	1.9
Tameside	74.6	353	72.0	353	2.6	79.5	338	77.7	354	1.8
Trafford	77.3	194	74.1	229	3.2	81.1	229	79.4	231	1.7
Vale Royal	76.8	220	74.1	237	2.7	81.0	232	79.4	224	1.6
Warrington	76.1	280	72.9	316	3.2	80.7	267	78.5	310	2.2
West Lancashire	76.2	272	73.9	251	2.3	80.1	308	78.6	301	1.5
Wigan	75.1	336	72.8	323	2.3	79.4	344	77.9	345	1.5
Wirral	75.5	308	73.2	298	2.3	80.2	301	78.9	277	1.3
Wyre	76.0	286	73.4	282	2.6	81.1	218	79.5	212	1.6
Yorkshire and The Humber	76.17		73.64		2.53	80.59		78.97		1.6
Barnsley	75.0	339	72.5	335	2.5	79.4	346	78.0	343	1.4
Bradford	75.4	314	72.9	317	2.5	79.6	336	78.3	322	1.3
Calderdale	75.7	301	73.1	304	2.6	80.8	247	78.2	327	2.6
Craven	79.1	47	74.3	215	4.8	82.7	47	80.7	59	2.0
Doncaster	75.4	315	73.4	281	2.0	80.1	311	78.7	293	1.4
East Riding of Yorkshire	77.6	162	74.8	179	2.8	81.1	222	79.8	174	1.3
Hambleton	78.5	86	76.0	62	2.5	82.8	37	80.8	58	2.0
Harrogate	78.6	74	75.2	132	3.4	82.1	105	79.8	179	2.3
Kingston upon Hull, City of	74.3	361	72.8	320	1.5	78.9	359	78.1	335	0.8
Kirklees	75.9	289	73.6	268	2.3	80.1	312	78.6	303	1.5
Leeds	76.2	271	74.0	242	2.2	81.2	211	79.5	213	1.7
North East Lincolnshire	75.3	318	73.3	292	2.0	80.8	259	79.2	248	1.6
North Lincolnshire	76.2	273	73.0	307	3.2	81.1	231	78.9	275	2.2
Richmondshire	78.5	92	75.0	160	3.5	81.6	172	79.6	202	2.0
Rotherham	75.3	317	73.1	303	2.2	79.8	328	78.4	319	1.4
Ryedale	77.8	148	76.4	36	1.4	81.8	146	81.1	34	0.7
Scarborough	75.9	290	74.2	224	1.7	81.1	230	79.9	167	1.2
Selby	77.6	163	74.8	172	2.8	82.1	112	79.2	247	2.9
Sheffield	76.6	242	73.4	279	3.2	80.6	272	79.2	252	1.4
Wakefield	75.8	296	73.0	306	2.8	79.9	323	78.1	338	1.8
York	77.2	196	74.7	184	2.5	82.7	50	80.2	132	2.5
East Midlands	76.89		74.34		2.55	80.94		79.29		1.6
Amber Valley	77.2	202	74.6	189	2.6	80.9	239	79.1	260	1.8
Ashfield	75.2	327	74.3	222	0.9	80.0	317	79.0	268	1.0
Bassetlaw	76.6	240	74.1	238	2.5	79.9	319	79.3	240	0.6
Blaby	79.2	37	76.4	35	2.8	82.9	32	80.3	119	2.6
Bolsover	75.2	329	73.3	291	1.9	79.3	349	78.5	311	0.8
Boston	75.7	304	75.3	125	0.4	80.9	244	79.9	164	1.0
Broxtowe	78.1	118	74.5	196	3.6	81.9	132	80.2	122	1.7
Charnwood	77.3	190	75.6	96	1.7	81.4	189	80.2	128	1.2
Chesterfield	75.8	293	73.2	294	2.6	80.4	289	78.1	337	2.3
Corby	74.5	355	72.4	339	2.1	79.8	330	77.7	352	2.1
Daventry	77.8	141	76.3	41	1.5	81.8	151	79.8	178	2.0
Derby	76.6	245	73.6	264	3.0	81.4	195	79.2	251	2.2
Derbyshire Dales	78.2	110	75.6	92	2.6	82.1	113	80.0	156	2.1
East Lindsey	77.1	205	74.5	200	2.6	81.2	209	79.0	267	2.2
East Northamptonshire	77.3	189	75.0	152	2.3	81.1	228	79.8	177	1.3
Erewash	77.1	204	74.4	206	2.7	81.2	213	78.8	283	2.4
Gedling	78.1	116	74.7	187	3.4	81.7	162	79.8	180	1.9
Harborough	78.9	59	75.6	102	3.3	82.1	118	80.0	157	2.1
High Peak	77.8	145	73.9	252	3.9	80.4	282	78.8	286	1.6
Hinckley and Bosworth	78.6	78	75.4	117	3.2	81.3	206	80.6	72	0.7
Kettering	76.9	216	74.8	168	2.1	80.6	275	79.3	238	1.3
Leicester	74.6	351	73.0	305	1.6	79.2	353	78.6	299	0.6
Lincoln	76.3	258	73.3	290	3.0	79.4	342	78.5	308	0.9
Mansfield	75.5	310	73.8	260	1.7	79.9	324	79.0	273	0.9
Melton	78.6	76	76.2	50	2.4	82.0	120	80.6	73	1.4
Newark and Sherwood	77.2	198	74.1	236	3.1	81.4	192	78.6	302	2.8
North East Derbyshire	77.3	186	74.5	203	2.8	80.2	300	79.5	209	0.7
North Kesteven	77.9	137	75.4	116	2.5	81.5	181	79.6	207	1.9
North West Leicestershire	77.0	212	74.6	188	2.4	80.7	268	79.5	221	1.2
Northampton	76.7	233	74.1	235	2.6	80.8	251	79.1	263	1.7
Nottingham	73.5	371	72.3	347	1.2	79.3	351	78.4	317	0.9
Oadby and Wigston	78.0	126	75.9	67	2.1	81.5	182	80.3	112	1.2
Rushcliffe	79.3	32	75.4	120	3.9	82.2	103	79.7	188	2.5
Rutland	79.5	17	76.5	24	3.0	83.8	5	80.8	56	3.0

Table 1 continued	Life expectancy at birth[1] (years) and relative position (rank order[2]) of local authorities in England and Wales, 2003–2005 and 1993–1995

	Males					Females				
	2003–2005		1993–1995			2003–2005		1993–1995		
	Life expectancy at birth	Rank order[2]	Life expectancy at birth	Rank order[2]	Difference in life expectancy between 2003–2005 and 1993–1995 (years)	Life expectancy at birth	Rank order[2]	Life expectancy at birth	Rank order[2]	Difference in life expectancy between 2003–2005 and 1993–1995 (years)
South Derbyshire	77.3	184	74.3	217	3.0	80.9	243	78.6	305	2.3
South Holland	77.3	192	74.3	213	3.0	81.4	187	79.2	246	2.2
South Kesteven	77.9	138	74.4	208	3.5	82.6	66	80.5	94	2.1
South Northamptonshire	79.0	51	76.0	63	3.0	82.4	85	80.4	104	2.0
Wellingborough	76.7	230	75.0	158	1.7	82.0	121	80.1	137	1.9
West Lindsey	76.7	235	74.5	198	2.2	80.8	256	78.7	292	2.1
West Midlands	76.20		73.66		2.54	80.77		79.09		1.68
Birmingham	74.8	348	72.4	338	2.4	80.1	309	78.6	306	1.5
Bridgnorth	77.6	165	75.1	149	2.5	81.8	154	79.0	272	2.8
Bromsgrove	77.8	149	75.7	87	2.1	81.3	199	79.7	187	1.6
Cannock Chase	75.5	311	73.0	310	2.5	80.2	304	79.0	266	1.2
Coventry	75.4	313	72.9	315	2.5	80.6	273	78.6	297	2.0
Dudley	76.2	274	74.2	227	2.0	80.8	260	79.4	233	1.4
East Staffordshire	76.2	268	73.3	289	2.9	80.6	274	79.6	206	1.0
Herefordshire, County of	77.6	161	75.5	110	2.1	82.4	84	80.7	67	1.7
Lichfield	76.8	225	74.3	220	2.5	80.3	298	79.1	264	1.2
Malvern Hills	77.7	159	75.6	99	2.1	81.5	175	79.9	170	1.6
Newcastle-under-Lyme	76.1	279	73.7	261	2.4	81.1	224	79.1	255	2.0
North Shropshire	77.5	172	74.3	218	3.2	81.3	205	80.9	47	0.4
North Warwickshire	76.5	249	74.2	223	2.3	80.5	277	79.2	250	1.3
Nuneaton and Bedworth	76.1	275	73.5	276	2.6	80.0	315	78.5	313	1.5
Oswestry	77.9	136	73.7	262	4.2	81.9	140	80.5	85	1.4
Redditch	76.6	244	74.2	225	2.4	80.5	278	79.5	218	1.0
Rugby	76.7	231	74.1	239	2.6	80.3	292	79.0	270	1.3
Sandwell	74.4	358	72.0	354	2.4	79.4	347	78.2	330	1.2
Shrewsbury and Atcham	77.3	191	75.4	122	1.9	81.9	137	80.1	136	1.8
Solihull	78.5	89	75.9	75	2.6	82.6	55	80.6	77	2.0
South Shropshire	77.8	147	76.4	31	1.4	82.4	80	81.3	19	1.1
South Staffordshire	77.2	199	75.2	141	2.0	81.1	220	80.5	82	0.6
Stafford	77.4	178	74.8	169	2.6	82.0	127	79.3	237	2.7
Staffordshire Moorlands	76.9	214	73.8	257	3.1	81.0	233	78.1	334	2.9
Stoke-on-Trent	73.7	370	72.1	352	1.6	79.1	354	77.8	351	1.3
Stratford-on-Avon	78.5	85	75.7	85	2.8	81.9	130	81.3	20	0.6
Tamworth	77.7	158	73.4	277	4.3	80.3	294	78.5	312	1.8
Telford and Wrekin	76.6	243	73.6	270	3.0	80.8	255	79.1	265	1.7
Walsall	75.7	299	72.9	312	2.8	80.7	265	78.2	328	2.5
Warwick	78.0	131	75.2	138	2.8	82.9	28	80.1	138	2.8
Wolverhampton	75.1	334	72.7	326	2.4	80.0	318	78.9	276	1.1
Worcester	77.2	197	74.7	181	2.5	81.2	214	80.2	135	1.0
Wychavon	78.6	72	75.3	126	3.3	82.5	70	79.5	210	3.0
Wyre Forest	76.8	224	74.3	219	2.5	81.3	201	79.4	225	1.9
East of England	77.98		75.46		2.52	81.84		80.25		1.60
Babergh	78.9	53	76.3	38	2.6	82.6	59	81.6	13	1.0
Basildon	77.5	169	74.8	173	2.7	80.9	246	80.3	115	0.6
Bedford	77.7	152	75.0	153	2.7	81.2	210	79.9	173	1.3
Braintree	77.6	160	75.8	79	1.8	81.8	150	80.3	109	1.5
Breckland	78.3	108	75.6	104	2.7	81.9	138	80.0	154	1.9
Brentwood	79.8	9	75.5	111	4.3	82.5	69	80.0	159	2.5
Broadland	78.6	81	75.9	70	2.7	82.3	93	80.4	101	1.9
Broxbourne	78.3	107	76.1	51	2.2	82.1	117	80.8	51	1.3
Cambridge	78.1	124	76.9	13	1.2	82.0	123	81.7	10	0.3
Castle Point	78.6	75	75.8	82	2.8	81.4	191	80.4	100	1.0
Chelmsford	79.1	48	76.8	14	2.3	83.0	24	81.2	29	1.8
Colchester	78.0	129	75.5	106	2.5	82.3	94	80.5	89	1.8
Dacorum	79.0	49	76.1	53	2.9	81.6	166	80.5	96	1.1
East Cambridgeshire	78.3	102	76.6	22	1.7	83.0	23	80.5	88	2.5
East Hertfordshire	79.3	30	76.1	54	3.2	82.3	92	80.1	149	2.2
Epping Forest	77.9	139	75.6	100	2.3	81.4	188	79.6	204	1.8
Fenland	76.4	255	74.3	214	2.1	80.7	263	79.5	220	1.2
Forest Heath	78.2	112	75.6	91	2.6	81.6	168	80.1	145	1.5
Great Yarmouth	76.2	269	73.8	259	2.4	81.5	180	79.6	195	1.9
Harlow	76.6	239	75.0	164	1.6	82.7	53	79.7	189	3.0
Hertsmere	77.5	173	75.8	77	1.7	81.7	156	79.4	234	2.3
Huntingdonshire	78.5	82	75.0	156	3.5	81.8	152	80.0	160	1.8
Ipswich	77.1	203	74.5	197	2.6	81.6	170	79.9	168	1.7
King's Lynn and West Norfolk	77.9	133	75.1	144	2.8	81.8	148	79.9	165	1.9

| Table 1 continued | Life expectancy at birth[1] (years) and relative position (rank order[2]) of local authorities in England and Wales, 2003–2005 and 1993–1995 |

	Males					Females				
	2003–2005		1993–1995			2003–2005		1993–1995		
	Life expectancy at birth	Rank order[2]	Life expectancy at birth	Rank order[2]	Difference in life expectancy between 2003–2005 and 1993–1995 (years)	Life expectancy at birth	Rank order[2]	Life expectancy at birth	Rank order[2]	Difference in life expectancy between 2003–2005 and 1993–1995 (years)
Luton	75.7	300	73.7	263	2.0	79.9	326	79.5	217	0.4
Maldon	77.4	182	74.7	182	2.7	81.5	178	78.8	285	2.7
Mid Bedfordshire	78.4	96	75.3	123	3.1	81.9	136	80.4	105	1.5
Mid Suffolk	79.4	23	76.3	43	3.1	82.6	58	80.7	62	1.9
North Hertfordshire	78.0	128	75.7	90	2.3	82.0	126	80.0	163	2.0
North Norfolk	78.5	91	76.7	20	1.8	82.9	31	80.4	98	2.5
Norwich	76.8	228	74.0	240	2.8	82.4	77	81.2	26	1.2
Peterborough	76.1	277	73.9	246	2.2	80.2	303	79.6	199	0.6
Rochford	78.9	56	75.4	118	3.5	83.1	20	80.1	147	3.0
South Bedfordshire	76.6	241	75.1	145	1.5	81.4	196	79.7	194	1.7
South Cambridgeshire	79.3	27	76.8	16	2.5	83.9	4	80.8	55	3.1
South Norfolk	80.0	6	76.8	18	3.2	82.9	34	81.3	18	1.6
Southend-on-Sea	76.7	232	74.8	175	1.9	80.8	258	79.4	232	1.4
St Albans	78.8	60	75.9	72	2.9	82.4	82	80.3	114	2.1
St Edmundsbury	78.1	117	75.5	115	2.6	81.9	129	80.5	83	1.4
Stevenage	77.0	213	75.0	155	2.0	81.2	215	80.5	87	0.7
Suffolk Coastal	79.2	38	76.5	29	2.7	82.4	81	81.3	21	1.1
Tendring	76.6	238	75.2	139	1.4	81.6	169	80.1	144	1.5
Three Rivers	79.4	25	76.3	44	3.1	82.3	88	81.7	11	0.6
Thurrock	76.9	217	73.9	254	3.0	81.1	221	79.5	211	1.6
Uttlesford	80.0	4	76.5	28	3.5	81.9	135	80.8	52	1.1
Watford	77.0	210	75.2	135	1.8	80.7	266	79.8	175	0.9
Waveney	77.8	142	75.3	128	2.5	81.6	164	80.2	130	1.4
Welwyn Hatfield	78.3	105	75.7	89	2.6	82.7	51	81.2	28	1.5
London	**76.94**		**73.68**		**3.26**	**81.39**		**79.47**		**1.91**
Barking and Dagenham	75.3	319	73.2	297	2.1	79.4	345	78.7	294	0.7
Barnet	78.6	80	76.0	58	2.6	82.9	30	80.5	92	2.4
Bexley	78.3	109	75.6	95	2.7	81.9	131	80.5	93	1.4
Brent	77.4	177	73.9	247	3.5	82.8	36	79.6	198	3.2
Bromley	78.6	68	75.5	105	3.1	82.6	54	81.0	42	1.6
Camden	75.7	298	71.4	364	4.3	81.6	171	79.2	249	2.4
Croydon	77.5	174	74.9	165	2.6	81.0	235	79.6	197	1.4
Ealing	76.9	215	73.9	249	3.0	81.6	173	79.4	228	2.2
Enfield	77.1	206	75.3	124	1.8	81.3	207	80.5	91	0.8
Greenwich	74.8	347	73.1	302	1.7	80.3	297	78.8	288	1.5
Hackney	75.1	332	71.4	363	3.7	81.5	184	77.9	347	3.6
Hammersmith and Fulham	76.8	226	71.1	370	5.7	82.4	83	78.9	281	3.5
Haringey	75.2	323	72.6	330	2.6	80.9	240	78.3	321	2.6
Harrow	78.7	65	75.7	86	3.0	82.6	63	81.3	22	1.3
Havering	77.8	150	74.8	171	3.0	81.4	193	79.9	171	1.5
Hillingdon	77.3	185	75.3	127	2.0	81.6	163	80.1	140	1.5
Hounslow	76.2	270	74.0	243	2.2	80.2	305	80.0	162	0.2
Islington	74.6	352	71.4	365	3.2	79.6	335	77.8	348	1.8
Kensington and Chelsea	82.2	1	72.9	311	9.3	86.2	1	80.4	99	5.8
Kingston upon Thames	78.5	87	76.0	60	2.5	82.1	110	80.3	118	1.8
Lambeth	74.9	344	71.2	367	3.7	79.8	329	78.2	326	1.6
Lewisham	75.1	335	72.3	345	2.8	79.6	333	78.5	309	1.1
Merton	78.0	125	75.2	140	2.8	82.5	74	80.3	107	2.2
Newham	74.9	345	71.6	359	3.3	78.8	361	77.4	365	1.4
Redbridge	77.5	168	75.5	112	2.0	81.6	174	80.1	141	1.5
Richmond upon Thames	79.3	28	74.8	167	4.5	82.7	41	81.0	37	1.7
Southwark	75.5	309	71.5	361	4.0	80.9	242	78.3	323	2.6
Sutton	77.9	135	75.0	163	2.9	81.7	159	80.2	131	1.5
Tower Hamlets	74.9	340	70.6	373	4.3	79.9	322	77.5	359	2.4
Waltham Forest	75.4	312	73.5	273	1.9	80.3	293	79.3	242	1.0
Wandsworth	76.3	266	72.6	333	3.7	80.8	253	78.6	296	2.2
Westminster	78.9	54	72.5	334	6.4	83.1	21	80.0	161	3.1
South East	**78.13**		**75.44**		**2.70**	**82.01**		**80.38**		**1.6**
Adur	77.4	180	75.5	109	1.9	81.4	194	80.7	61	0.7
Arun	77.7	153	75.0	161	2.7	82.3	97	80.6	76	1.7
Ashford	79.0	50	75.0	151	4.0	81.7	157	80.0	151	1.7
Aylesbury Vale	77.9	132	75.3	130	2.6	81.6	167	79.6	203	2.0
Basingstoke and Deane	78.4	94	75.1	150	3.3	82.1	115	80.7	68	1.4
Bracknell Forest	78.2	114	75.0	157	3.2	82.1	107	80.2	129	1.9
Brighton and Hove	76.1	278	73.5	275	2.6	81.3	202	79.7	193	1.6
Canterbury	77.3	193	75.6	98	1.7	81.4	190	80.0	153	1.4

Table 1 continued	Life expectancy at birth[1] (years) and relative position (rank order[2]) of local authorities in England and Wales, 2003–2005 and 1993–1995

	Males					Females				
	2003–2005		1993–1995			2003–2005		1993–1995		
	Life expectancy at birth	Rank order[2]	Life expectancy at birth	Rank order[2]	Difference in life expectancy between 2003–2005 and 1993–1995 (years)	Life expectancy at birth	Rank order[2]	Life expectancy at birth	Rank order[2]	Difference in life expectancy between 2003–2005 and 1993–1995 (years)
Cherwell	78.1	123	75.8	80	2.3	82.4	78	80.6	80	1.8
Chichester	78.8	63	75.9	66	2.9	82.7	46	81.0	38	1.7
Chiltern	80.0	7	77.4	2	2.6	83.0	22	82.0	4	1.0
Crawley	79.8	10	75.1	148	4.7	81.5	179	80.7	63	0.8
Dartford	77.2	200	73.8	258	3.4	80.4	287	79.1	257	1.3
Dover	76.5	246	74.1	231	2.4	81.5	176	80.1	146	1.4
East Hampshire	79.1	45	75.2	131	3.9	81.9	141	79.6	200	2.3
Eastbourne	76.8	223	75.0	154	1.8	81.7	161	80.6	81	1.1
Eastleigh	78.8	64	76.1	55	2.7	81.9	142	80.7	66	1.2
Elmbridge	79.7	13	77.0	10	2.7	83.3	13	81.1	31	2.2
Epsom and Ewell	79.2	34	75.4	119	3.8	84.5	2	81.7	9	2.8
Fareham	79.5	19	75.9	69	3.6	83.3	15	81.0	44	2.3
Gosport	76.7	236	74.6	192	2.1	80.9	237	79.1	262	1.8
Gravesham	77.5	170	74.8	176	2.7	81.4	197	79.7	190	1.7
Guildford	79.4	22	76.3	37	3.1	83.6	7	81.9	6	1.7
Hart	80.2	3	77.2	6	3.0	83.3	14	81.1	30	2.2
Hastings	75.7	302	73.4	280	2.3	79.9	321	79.4	223	0.5
Havant	78.2	113	75.1	146	3.1	82.0	124	79.6	205	2.4
Horsham	79.9	8	76.8	15	3.1	83.4	10	81.0	39	2.4
Isle of Wight	78.1	120	74.5	204	3.6	82.6	57	80.5	84	2.1
Lewes	78.4	95	75.8	78	2.6	83.2	17	81.1	33	2.1
Maidstone	77.4	181	75.7	88	1.7	82.0	125	80.1	148	1.9
Medway	76.4	254	73.6	265	2.8	80.4	284	79.0	271	1.4
Mid Sussex	78.6	69	75.9	73	2.7	81.8	145	80.9	48	0.9
Milton Keynes	76.5	247	74.7	186	1.8	80.2	302	79.1	261	1.1
Mole Valley	79.5	18	76.5	26	3.0	83.0	25	80.7	70	2.3
New Forest	79.5	20	76.3	42	3.2	83.6	8	81.2	23	2.4
Oxford	77.7	154	75.2	136	2.5	81.8	147	79.9	172	1.9
Portsmouth	76.1	276	73.9	255	2.2	80.9	245	79.8	182	1.1
Reading	76.4	253	74.3	216	2.1	81.2	208	80.0	152	1.2
Reigate and Banstead	78.3	104	75.6	103	2.7	81.5	183	80.1	142	1.4
Rother	77.8	151	76.2	49	1.6	82.1	116	81.0	41	1.1
Runnymede	78.7	67	76.3	39	2.4	82.3	96	80.3	121	2.0
Rushmoor	78.0	130	74.4	212	3.6	81.5	177	78.9	278	2.6
Sevenoaks	79.4	21	76.2	47	3.2	83.4	11	80.7	69	2.7
Shepway	76.5	251	74.4	209	2.1	81.1	219	79.4	229	1.7
Slough	77.3	187	73.2	300	4.1	80.7	271	79.1	258	1.6
South Bucks	79.5	16	75.9	74	3.6	82.1	119	80.0	158	2.1
South Oxfordshire	79.1	46	76.1	52	3.0	82.5	68	81.5	16	1.0
Southampton	76.5	250	73.5	274	3.0	81.2	212	79.9	166	1.3
Spelthorne	78.8	62	76.9	12	1.9	81.7	158	80.7	64	1.0
Surrey Heath	79.1	44	76.5	27	2.6	82.1	108	80.7	60	1.4
Swale	76.6	237	74.4	211	2.2	80.7	269	79.5	219	1.2
Tandridge	79.3	31	76.4	32	2.9	82.8	40	80.6	74	2.2
Test Valley	78.5	88	76.6	23	1.9	82.3	89	80.7	65	1.6
Thanet	75.0	338	73.9	250	1.1	80.0	313	79.1	259	0.9
Tonbridge and Malling	78.7	66	75.5	107	3.2	82.4	86	80.3	108	2.1
Tunbridge Wells	78.5	90	76.0	59	2.5	81.9	134	80.5	86	1.4
Vale of White Horse	79.2	39	77.0	9	2.2	82.7	42	81.6	14	1.1
Waverley	78.9	55	76.7	21	2.2	82.7	52	81.8	7	0.9
Wealden	79.3	29	76.4	34	2.9	82.9	33	81.7	8	1.2
West Berkshire	78.4	99	75.9	68	2.5	82.4	79	80.3	116	2.1
West Oxfordshire	79.4	26	77.1	7	2.3	82.1	109	80.9	50	1.2
Winchester	79.7	11	76.0	56	3.7	82.7	45	81.1	32	1.6
Windsor and Maidenhead	78.4	100	75.5	114	2.9	82.6	64	79.6	196	3.0
Woking	79.2	36	76.2	46	3.0	82.6	62	80.2	125	2.4
Wokingham	80.0	5	77.4	3	2.6	83.2	16	81.0	40	2.2
Worthing	76.7	229	75.0	159	1.7	80.8	252	80.3	117	0.5
Wycombe	78.6	71	76.3	45	2.3	82.6	61	80.6	75	2.0
South West	**78.10**		**75.45**		**2.66**	**82.21**		**80.60**		**1.61**
Bath and North East Somerset	78.9	58	75.2	134	3.7	82.8	39	81.0	43	1.8
Bournemouth	77.3	195	75.0	162	2.3	81.9	133	80.4	102	1.5
Bristol, City of	76.3	261	74.0	244	2.3	80.8	257	79.9	169	0.9
Caradon	78.0	127	75.6	97	2.4	82.1	111	80.3	111	1.8
Carrick	78.4	98	75.4	121	3.0	82.3	87	80.9	46	1.4
Cheltenham	78.6	73	75.6	93	3.0	82.3	98	80.4	103	1.9
Christchurch	79.7	12	77.0	8	2.7	83.4	12	82.6	2	0.8
Cotswold	79.2	35	76.7	19	2.5	82.9	27	82.0	5	0.9

| Table 1 continued | Life expectancy at birth[1] (years) and relative position (rank order[2]) of local authorities in England and Wales, 2003–2005 and 1993–1995 |

	Males					Females				
	2003–2005		1993–1995			2003–2005		1993–1995		
	Life expectancy at birth	Rank order[2]	Life expectancy at birth	Rank order[2]	Difference in life expectancy between 2003–2005 and 1993–1995 (years)	Life expectancy at birth	Rank order[2]	Life expectancy at birth	Rank order[2]	Difference in life expectancy between 2003–2005 and 1993–1995 (years)
East Devon	79.6	14	77.3	5	2.3	83.1	19	82.4	3	0.7
East Dorset	80.9	2	77.9	1	3.0	84.1	3	83.4	1	0.7
Exeter	77.1	208	74.8	178	2.3	82.6	65	80.2	126	2.4
Forest of Dean	76.9	218	74.6	194	2.3	82.3	99	79.8	186	2.5
Gloucester	76.3	260	74.3	221	2.0	80.8	254	79.3	243	1.5
Kennet	78.4	101	75.6	94	2.8	82.3	91	81.0	36	1.3
Kerrier	77.3	188	74.7	185	2.6	81.8	144	79.8	184	2.0
Mendip	77.5	171	75.7	84	1.8	81.9	128	80.8	57	1.1
Mid Devon	78.1	119	76.5	30	1.6	82.8	38	81.2	24	1.6
North Cornwall	77.6	166	75.1	142	2.5	82.0	122	80.5	95	1.5
North Devon	77.4	175	75.5	113	1.9	81.9	139	80.2	123	1.7
North Dorset	79.4	24	77.0	11	2.4	83.5	9	81.0	35	2.5
North Somerset	78.3	106	75.8	83	2.5	82.2	100	80.8	53	1.4
North Wiltshire	78.5	83	76.0	57	2.5	82.1	106	80.1	143	2.0
Penwith	77.2	201	74.8	174	2.4	81.1	217	79.7	192	1.4
Plymouth	76.0	283	73.3	286	2.7	80.9	238	79.4	226	1.5
Poole	78.1	122	75.9	71	2.2	82.5	72	80.9	45	1.6
Purbeck	79.2	41	76.0	64	3.2	83.7	6	80.5	90	3.2
Restormel	77.8	144	74.1	232	3.7	81.8	149	79.6	208	2.2
Salisbury	78.8	61	75.6	101	3.2	82.5	73	80.3	120	2.2
Sedgemoor	77.8	146	75.5	108	2.3	82.1	114	80.3	113	1.8
South Gloucestershire	79.2	42	76.5	25	2.7	82.7	44	81.4	17	1.3
South Hams	79.0	52	76.8	17	2.2	83.1	18	81.6	12	1.5
South Somerset	79.2	40	76.0	61	3.2	82.4	76	81.2	25	1.2
Stroud	78.6	79	75.8	81	2.8	82.3	95	80.3	110	2.0
Swindon	77.4	183	74.6	193	2.8	80.7	262	79.4	230	1.3
Taunton Deane	77.7	155	75.1	147	2.6	82.6	60	80.6	79	2.0
Teignbridge	79.3	33	76.3	40	3.0	82.9	35	80.9	49	2.0
Tewkesbury	78.5	84	76.4	33	2.1	82.5	71	80.4	106	2.1
Torbay	76.5	252	75.2	137	1.3	81.7	155	80.7	71	1.0
Torridge	77.8	143	74.6	190	3.2	81.9	143	80.2	133	1.7
West Devon	78.9	57	75.9	65	3.0	82.9	29	80.0	155	2.9
West Dorset	78.6	70	76.2	48	2.4	82.6	56	81.5	15	1.1
West Somerset	79.1	43	77.3	4	1.8	82.6	67	81.2	27	1.4
West Wiltshire	79.5	15	75.3	129	4.2	82.7	48	80.2	124	2.5
Weymouth and Portland	77.4	179	74.1	233	3.3	81.8	153	80.4	97	1.4
Wales	76.15		73.4		76.15	80.56		78.99		1.57
Blaenau Gwent	74.2	365	72.2	348	2.0	78.4	366	78.4	320	0.0
Bridgend	75.5	307	73.3	285	2.2	79.9	320	78.6	304	1.3
Caerphilly	75.2	322	72.9	318	2.3	79.3	350	78.1	333	1.2
Cardiff	76.3	263	73.6	266	2.7	80.7	264	79.3	239	1.4
Carmarthenshire	75.6	305	73.1	301	2.5	80.7	270	79.1	254	1.6
Ceredigion	77.7	156	74.9	166	2.8	82.2	101	80.2	134	2.0
Conwy	76.2	267	74.4	207	1.8	81.1	227	80.1	139	1.0
Denbighshire	76.5	248	74.1	230	2.4	80.3	295	79.7	191	0.6
Flintshire	76.3	259	73.9	253	2.4	80.7	261	78.7	291	2.0
Gwynedd	76.9	219	74.4	210	2.5	81.0	236	79.6	201	1.4
Isle of Anglesey	77.1	209	73.6	271	3.5	81.3	200	79.4	222	1.9
Merthyr Tydfil	74.3	360	70.6	372	3.7	78.6	365	77.8	350	0.8
Monmouthshire	78.4	97	75.2	133	3.2	82.7	49	80.8	54	1.9
Neath Port Talbot	75.2	331	72.6	329	2.6	80.4	283	78.4	318	2.0
Newport	76.0	284	73.2	293	2.8	80.4	280	78.4	316	2.0
Pembrokeshire	76.0	282	74.1	228	1.9	81.2	216	79.5	214	1.7
Powys	77.9	134	74.5	201	3.4	81.4	198	79.8	181	1.6
Rhondda, Cynon, Taff	75.1	333	71.9	357	3.2	79.5	339	77.9	346	1.6
Swansea	75.7	297	73.6	267	2.1	80.8	250	79.0	274	1.8
The Vale of Glamorgan	77.0	211	73.8	256	3.2	80.8	249	79.4	227	1.4
Torfaen	76.3	265	72.7	327	3.6	81.1	223	78.2	325	2.9
Wrexham	76.3	264	72.8	321	3.5	80.3	299	78.7	290	1.6

1 95 per cent confidence intervals for these results are available on the National Statistics website at: http://www.statistics.gov.uk/statbase/Product.asp?vlnk=8841
2 Life expectancy figures are presented to one decimal place. The rankings in this table reflect differences in the unrounded numbers.
1= Highest, 374 = Lowest

Report:

Estimated daily mortality during July 2006 in England and Wales

Summary

During July 2006, temperatures in England and Wales triggered the Government to initiate its Heatwave Plan and issue advice to the public on how to keep healthy during hot weather, and guidance to health care professionals on minimising heat-related health risks. This report presents provisional daily mortality during July by age and region, and estimates excess deaths at the hottest times. The high temperatures during July 2006 did not affect mortality in England and Wales to the extent seen in August 2003 – the first hot period of July 2006 showed no increase in mortality nationally and there was a 4 per cent increase over baseline mortality in the second hot period (680 excess deaths). This compares to a 16 per cent increase during the August 2003 heat wave.

Introduction

England and Wales generally experiences higher levels of mortality in the winter than in the summer. However, previous analysis[1–5] has shown that during 'heat waves,' when temperatures remain abnormally high over more than one or two days, mortality increases proportionally, though remaining at levels lower than those experienced in winter. The most severe heat wave of recent times occurred in August 2003, when temperature records were broken in England and Wales. Brogdale, Kent recorded the UK's highest ever temperature of 38.5°C on 10th August 2003. Between 4th to 13th August in England, an estimated 2,139 excess deaths occurred compared to the average for the same period over the previous five years.[1] The percentage increase in mortality, at 16 per cent in England, was greater than during the heat waves of 1976 and 1995. During the 2003 heat wave, the increase in mortality was greatest in London, although Central and Southern England were also affected, and people aged 75 and over were most affected.

This heat wave prompted the development of the *Heat wave Plan for England* which was published by the Department of Health in 2004,[6] and was updated in 2005[7] and May 2006.[8] One of the core elements of the plan was a 'Heat-Health watch' system, which would operate from 1st June to 15th September, based on Met Office forecasts, and which would trigger levels of response from DH and other bodies. The 'Heat-Health watch' system comprises 4 levels of response and is based on threshold day and night-time temperatures defined by the Met Office. These vary by region but the average threshold temperature is 30°C during the day and 15°C overnight. The levels of response are:

- **Level 1** – a state of awareness and the minimum state of vigilance which covers the entire period
- **Level 2** – a state of alert (the Met Office has forecast threshold temperatures for at least three days ahead)
- **Level 3** – the heat wave state, which is triggered as soon as the Met Office confirms that threshold temperatures have been reached in any one region or more
- **Level 4** – a state of emergency, which is triggered when a heat wave is so severe and/or prolonged that its effects extend outside health and social care, e.g. power or water shortages

During July 2006, there were 12 days when the 'Heat-Health watch' for any region reached Level 2 or higher, and seven days when Level 3 was attained. Of these, one day, 19th July 2006, had all regions of England, and Wales, reach Level 3. A Level 4 state of emergency was not reached in 2006 in any region. For the four-day period between 1st July and 4th July, and for the seven-day period between 17th July and 23rd July, a Level 2 state or above was reached across consistent days.

The Office for National Statistics (ONS) and predecessors have published weekly estimates of deaths registered in England and Wales since the 1850s.[9, 10] An increase in the estimated number of deaths registered in the weeks ending 21st and 28th July 2006 compared to the average for the previous five years was reported by ONS on 1st and 8th August 2006. This report examines the July period in more detail and, rather than examining weekly deaths by date of registration, presents provisional daily mortality data during July by age and region based on the date deaths occurred, and estimates excess deaths at the hottest times.

Methods

Mortality data are collected from death registration. Every Friday, ONS receives data on the deaths that have been registered that week (from Saturday to Friday) from the Register Offices of England and Wales. These data are processed by ONS and stored on a live database. By law, a death should be registered 'before the expiration of five days from the date of death,' but, in the case of suspected violent deaths, where a coroner needs to hold an inquest before reaching a verdict, this is almost impossible as in most cases the death can only be registered after the inquest. However, unpublished analysis of delays in registration of deaths in 2001, showed that 93 per cent of all deaths for that year were registered within seven days of the death occurring.

The daily mortality data from ONS for July 2006 used in this analysis were estimated to account for late registrations of deaths, using factors based on the number of deaths occurring between weeks 26 and 31 of 2004 that had been registered and received by ONS by the end of week 34 of 2004, compared to the final number of actual deaths occurring each day in July 2004. This estimation was needed because approximately 5 per cent of deaths occurring during these weeks remained unregistered by this date and at the time of our analysis ONS only had data on deaths registered in 2006 by the end of week 34. Thus, to use actual numbers of deaths on the ONS database for 2006 would underestimate the true number of deaths occurring in July. Data were estimated by age and region of England, and Wales.

The Met Office supplied daily mean, maximum day, and minimum night-time temperatures for Central England for July from 2001 to 2006. The hottest periods were defined using the same method which was used for previous research[2] examining the 2003 heat wave – starting when maximum daily Central England Temperatures (CET) first exceeded average values by 8°C and ending when temperatures returned to average

levels. This gave two hot periods within July 2006 – 1st to 7th and 16th to 28th, referred to in this article as the 'first hot period' and the 'second hot period'. A baseline daily temperature was calculated as the average CET of 2001 to 2005. Figure 1 shows daily maximum temperatures and night-time minimum temperatures for July 2006 compared to the average maximum and minimum threshold temperatures used in the 'Heat-health watch' system.

Excess mortality was calculated as observed daily deaths in 2006 minus baseline (average of 2001 to 2005) mortality. As regions vary in size, an excess death index for the two hot periods was produced so that comparisons between areas could be made. This was calculated as the number of excess deaths divided by the baseline daily deaths, expressed as a percentage. Confidence intervals for the index were calculated for the excess values using Poisson methods, as in previous analysis.[2]

ONS publishes mortality data for all deaths occurring in England and Wales. Mortality data by area are produced using the area of usual residence of the deceased. If the deceased does not live in England or Wales these deaths are coded with an area of residence of 'elsewhere,' or non-resident, and are not included in analyses by area. For consistency with other data published by ONS, data on non-residents have been included in this analysis when data for England and Wales as a whole are presented. Therefore, national data for 'England and Wales' refer to all deaths occurring in England and Wales, of residents of England and Wales and of non-residents.

Results

Figure 2 shows daily mortality and mean daily temperature in July for 2006 and the baseline average years (2001–2005). During the first hot period, between 1st and 7th July, there was a peak in deaths on the 3rd July and then a fall in daily mortality to below the average baseline level. This was followed by over a week of mortality substantially lower than the 2001/05 average which corresponded with a period of lower temperatures. Daily mortality began to increase from the start of the second hot period, and peaked on 19th July. On this day the 'Heat-health Watch' system reached Level 3 status for all regions of England, and Wales. Daily mortality fell after this day but was still higher than the baseline average for most days until 28th July.

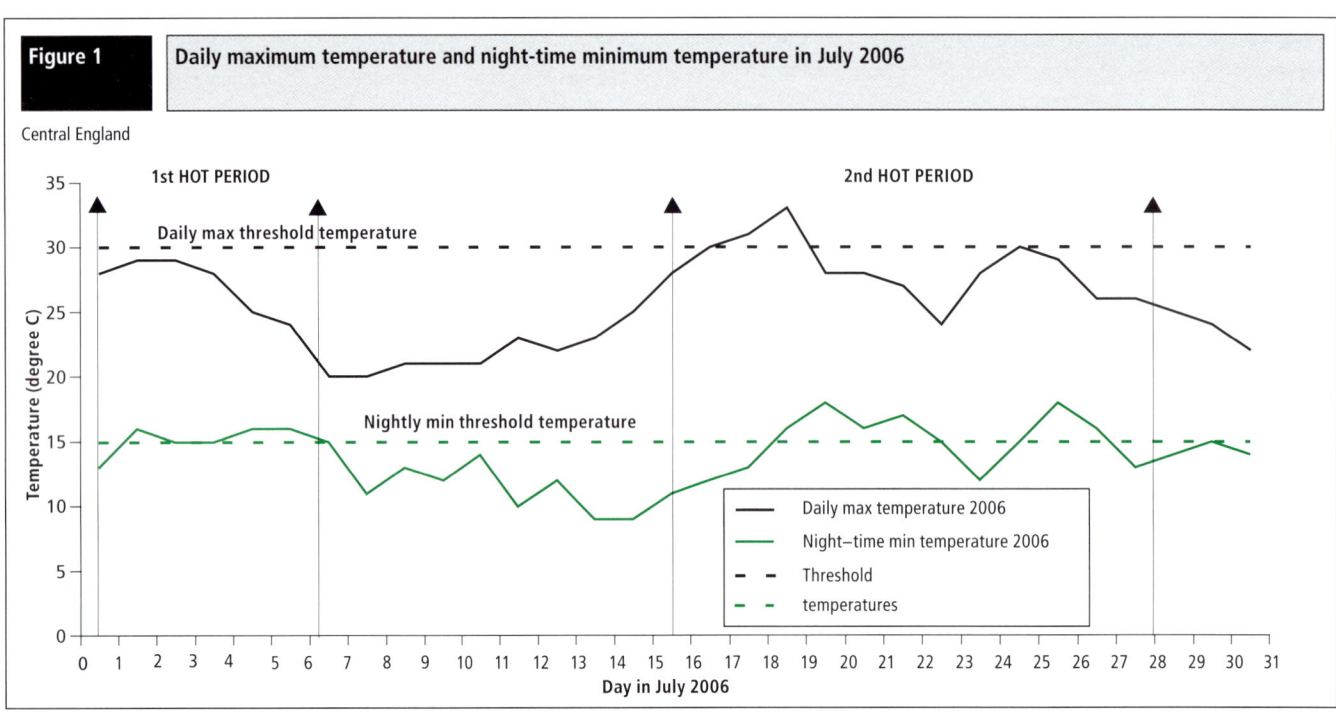

Figure 1 — Daily maximum temperature and night-time minimum temperature in July 2006

Central England

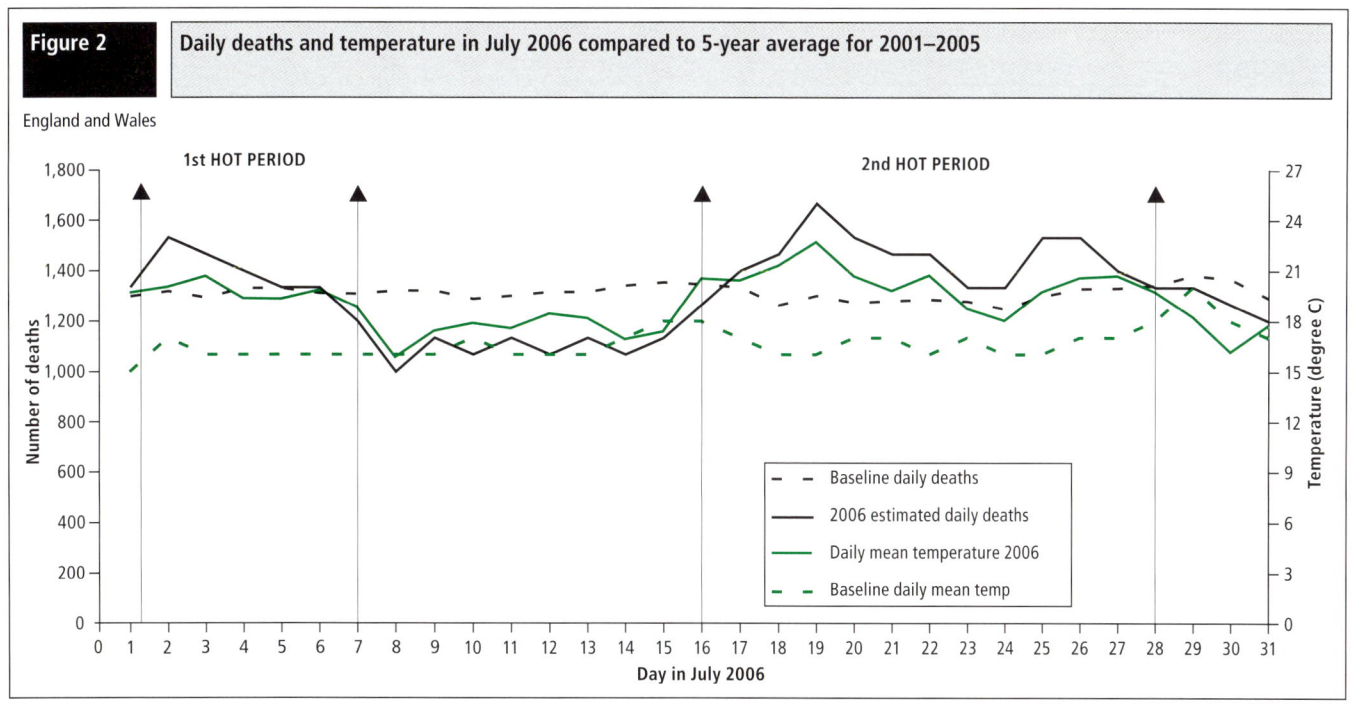

Figure 2 — Daily deaths and temperature in July 2006 compared to 5-year average for 2001–2005

England and Wales

During the first hot period between 1st and 7th July 2006, there were less deaths than for the baseline average for the previous 5 years, that is there was no excess mortality during this time, but during the second hot period between 16th and 28th July 2006 there were 680 excess deaths (4.0 per cent increase on baseline average deaths).

Figures 3a and 3b show excess deaths by Government Office Region of England, and Wales, for the two hot periods. The charts show the number of excess deaths and the excess deaths index (including 95% confidence intervals) for each area. During 1st to 7th July, although there were no excess deaths overall, there was variability by region (Figure 3a).

Five regions had a raised mortality during this period – North West, East Midlands, Eastern, London, and Wales, although the 95% confidence intervals for all regions included 0. Wales had the highest excess deaths index at 6.5 per cent (CI: -2.1;15.1). During 16th to 28th July 2006, all

regions except the South West showed increased mortality (Figure 3b), although only 5 of these regions showed 95% lower confidence interval that did not include a negative value. The West Midlands had the highest excess deaths index with a 10.0 per cent (CI: 5.0;15.0) increase on baseline average mortality.

Table 1 shows the number and proportion of excess deaths by region in England, and Wales and age group for 1st to 7th July 2006 (including 95% confidence intervals). In England and Wales as a whole, lower than baseline mortality was seen for the younger age groups, but there was an increase of 2.2 per cent (CI: -0.4;4.7) on baseline figures for people aged 75 and over, though this figure was not statistically significant. No region or age group had excess mortality that was statistically significant in this time period.

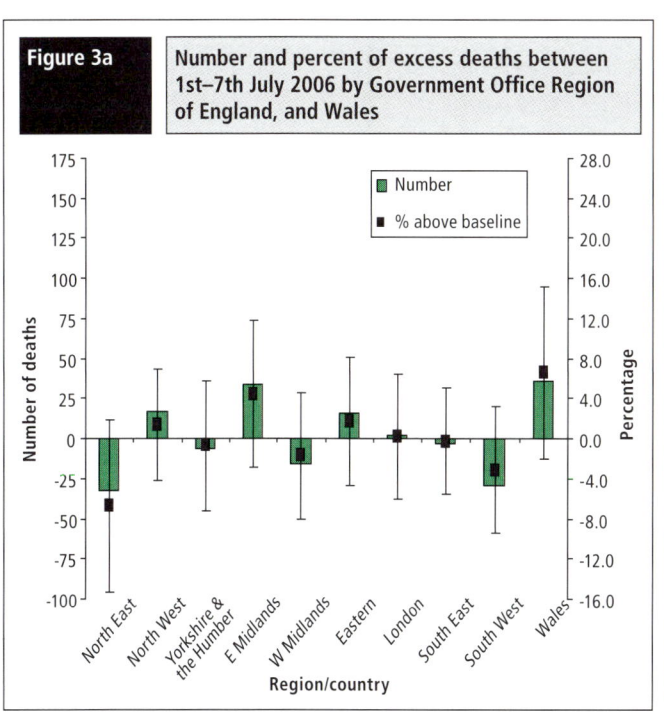

Figure 3a — Number and percent of excess deaths between 1st–7th July 2006 by Government Office Region of England, and Wales

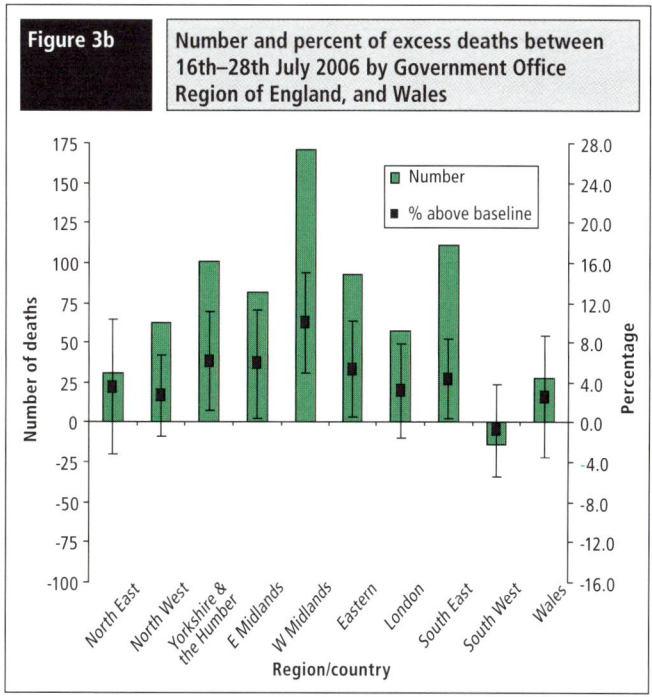

Figure 3b — Number and percent of excess deaths between 16th–28th July 2006 by Government Office Region of England, and Wales

Table 1 — Number[1] and proportion of excess deaths by Government Office Region of England, and Wales, and age group, 1st–7th July 2006

Region	0–64 Number	% above baseline (95% confidence limit)	LCL	UCL	65–74 Number	% above baseline (95% confidence limit)	LCL	UCL	75 and over Number	% above baseline (95% confidence limit)	LCL	UCL	All ages Number	% above baseline (95% confidence limit)	LCL	UCL
North East	-10	-10.7	(-30.2 :	8.8)	-10	-5.3	(-24.8 :	14.1)	-20	-5.9	(-17.0 :	5.2)	-30	-6.7	(-15.3 :	1.9)
North West	-10	-2.3	(-14.5 :	9.9)	-20	-8.6	(-20.6 :	3.5)	40	5.7	(-1.6 :	12.9)	20	1.4	(-4.2 :	6.9)
Yorkshire and the Humber	-10	-8.0	(-22.7 :	6.6)	-10	-6.5	(-21.2 :	8.1)	20	3.1	(-5.2 :	11.3)	-10	-0.7	(-7.2 :	5.8)
East Midlands	20	13.7	(-4.5 :	31.9)	10	6.8	(-10.9 :	24.5)	10	1.3	(-7.6 :	10.3)	30	4.5	(-2.9 :	11.8)
West Midlands	-10	-7.0	(-20.9 :	7.0)	-20	-12.6	(-26.4 :	1.2)	20	3.2	(-5.0 :	11.4)	-20	-1.7	(-8.0 :	4.6)
Eastern	-10	-5.4	(-20.5 :	9.6)	0	-1.0	(-16.4 :	14.5)	30	4.2	(-3.7 :	12.1)	20	1.7	(-4.7 :	8.1)
London	-20	-10.7	(-22.9 :	1.5)	-10	-3.7	(-18.3 :	10.9)	30	5.7	(-2.7 :	14.1)	0	0.2	(-6.0 :	6.5)
South East	10	6.4	(-7.3 :	20.0)	-30	-11.8	(-23.9 :	0.2)	10	1.1	(-5.4 :	7.6)	0	-0.2	(-5.5 :	5.0)
South West	0	-0.1	(-16.3 :	16.2)	-10	-3.4	(-18.7 :	11.9)	-20	-3.7	(-11.3 :	3.8)	-30	-3.1	(-9.4 :	3.2)
Wales	20	21.7	(-0.6 :	43.9)	10	8.6	(-11.2 :	28.4)	10	1.9	(-8.7 :	12.4)	40	6.5	(-2.1 :	15.1)
England	-40	-2.7	(-7.6 :	2.2)	-90	-5.9	(-10.8 :	-1.1)	120	2.1	(-0.6 :	4.8)	-20	-0.2	(-2.3 :	1.9)
England and Wales[2]	-40	-2.3	(-7.0 :	2.4)	-90	-5.6	(-10.3 :	-0.9)	130	2.2	(-0.4 :	4.7)	0	-0.1	(-2.1 :	2.0)

1. Rounded to the nearest 10.
2. Includes deaths of non-residents.

Table 2 shows these figures for 16th to 28th July 2006. In England and Wales, unlike the first hot period, the youngest age group (aged under 65) had a positive excess death index – with mortality 2.9 per cent (CI: -0.7; 6.5) higher than baseline – although excess deaths were higher in those aged 75 and over – 6.5 per cent increase (CI: 4.6; 8.4). All regions had raised mortality in those aged 75 and over although this was not statistically significant in all regions. Two regions had their highest excess death indexes in the youngest age group – North West and London – and two regions had their highest excess death indexes in those aged 65 to 74 – Yorkshire and the Humber, and Wales, although these were not statistically significant. The highest excess deaths index was seen in those aged 75 and over in the East Midlands (14.2 per cent increase on baseline deaths – CI: 7.2; 21.3). For those aged 65–74 years, the highest excess deaths index was in Yorkshire and the Humber (12.0 per cent – CI: 0.0; 24.0), and for the youngest age group the highest index was in West Midlands (11.1 per cent – CI: -0.4; 22.6).

Discussion

During July 2006, there were 12 days when the 'Heat-Health watch' system for any region reached Level 2 or higher, and 7 days when Level 3 was reached. Of these, one day, 19th July 2006, had all regions of England, and Wales, reach Level 3. These high temperatures during July 2006 did not affect mortality in England and Wales to the extent that the heat wave of August 2003 did – the first hot period of July 2006 showed no increase in mortality nationally and there was a 4 per cent increase over baseline mortality in the second hot period (680 excess deaths). This compares to a 16 per cent increase in mortality in England and Wales during the August 2003 heat wave.[1] Examining the reasons for this is beyond the scope of this report. The two periods examined showed day and night-time temperatures where health might be at risk. Analysis across the whole of July shows overall lower than average mortality. Lower than average day and night-time temperatures during the middle of July (8th to 15th July) coincided with very low mortality for these days.

Table 2 — Number[1] and proportion of excess deaths by Government Office Region of England, and Wales, and age group, 16th–28th July 2006

Region	0–64 Number	% above baseline (95% confidence limit)	LCL	UCL	65–74 Number	% above baseline (95% confidence limit)	LCL	UCL	75 and over Number	% above baseline (95% confidence limit)	LCL	UCL	All ages Number	% above baseline (95% confidence limit)	LCL	UCL
North East	0	-0.2	(-15.4 :	15.1)	10	4.3	(-10.6 :	19.1)	20	4.4	(-4.2 :	13.0)	30	3.5	(-3.2 :	10.2)
North West	40	8.1	(-1.6 :	17.8)	-30	-5.6	(-14.4 :	3.2)	50	3.7	(-1.6 :	9.0)	60	2.7	(-1.4 :	6.8)
Yorkshire and the Humber	10	4.1	(-7.6 :	15.9)	40	12.0	(-0.0 :	24.0)	50	5.1	(-1.1 :	11.3)	100	6.2	(1.2 :	11.1)
East Midlands	10	3.8	(-9.2 :	16.7)	-50	-19.5	(-30.3 :	-8.8)	120	14.2	(7.2 :	21.3)	80	5.9	(0.5 :	11.3)
West Midlands	40	11.1	(-0.4 :	22.6)	0	-1.1	(-12.2 :	10.0)	140	12.8	(6.5 :	19.2)	170	10.0	(5.0 :	15.0)
Eastern	-20	-5.6	(-17.0 :	5.9)	10	2.0	(-9.6 :	13.7)	100	8.7	(2.8 :	14.7)	90	5.3	(0.5 :	10.2)
London	40	10.0	(-0.5 :	20.6)	-60	-17.0	(-26.9 :	-7.1)	70	6.8	(0.7 :	13.0)	60	3.2	(-1.5 :	7.9)
South East	10	2.9	(-6.8 :	12.6)	-20	-4.8	(-14.1 :	4.6)	120	6.9	(2.0 :	11.9)	110	4.4	(0.4 :	8.3)
South West	-10	-5.5	(-17.4 :	6.4)	0	-0.8	(-12.3 :	10.6)	0	0.2	(-5.5 :	5.9)	-10	-0.8	(-5.5 :	3.9)
Wales	-10	-4.2	(-17.8 :	9.5)	20	9.4	(-5.1 :	23.9)	20	2.5	(-5.1 :	10.2)	30	2.6	(-3.5 :	8.6)
England	110	4.0	(0.3 :	7.8)	-110	-3.9	(-7.5 :	-0.3)	690	6.8	(4.8 :	8.8)	690	4.4	(2.8 :	6.0)
England and Wales[2]	90	2.9	(-0.7 :	6.5)	-120	-3.8	(-7.3 :	-0.3)	710	6.5	(4.6 :	8.4)	680	4.0	(2.5 :	5.5)

1. Rounded to the nearest 10.
2. Includes deaths of non-residents.

Increases in mortality varied by age group and region. The percentage increase in mortality was greatest at older ages, as in 2003. The regional pattern was not as consistent as in 2003, which may reflect different patterns of hot temperatures throughout England and Wales during July 2006, whereas the hot temperatures in 2003 were very concentrated in the south and east of England.

This report has made available rapidly a summary of estimated mortality during July 2006. Further more detailed work on the patterns shown could be carried out once final figures are available in October 2007.

Key findings

- There was a 4 per cent increase over baseline mortality between 16th and 28th July 2006 (680 excess deaths) in England and Wales.
- This increase was not as great as that seen in August 2003 (16 per cent excess).
- Increased mortality in the two hot periods of July 2006 did not affect all regions and age groups equally.
- People aged 75 and over were more affected than other age groups.
- There was no consistent regional pattern of increased mortality, whereas in 2003 excess mortality was concentrated in the south and east of England.

Acknowledgements:

Clare Bryden and Tish Laing-Morton of the Met Office.

References

1. Johnson H, Kovats R S, McGregor G, Stedman J, Gibbs M and Walton H (2005) The impact of the 2003 heat wave on daily mortality in England and Wales and the use of rapid weekly mortality estimates. *Eurosurveillance* **10**, 168–171.
2. Johnson H, Kovats R S, McGregor G, Stedman J, Gibbs M, Walton H, Cook L and Black E (2005) The impact of the 2003 heat wave on mortality and hospital admissions in England. *Health Statistics Quarterly* **25**, 6–11.
3. Rooney C, McMichael A J, Kovats R S and Coleman M (1998) Excess mortality in England and Wales, and in Greater London, during the 1995 heat wave. *Journal of Epidemiology and Community Health* **52**, 482–486.
4. McMichael A J and Kovats R S (1998) *Assessment of the impact of mortality in England and Wales of the heat wave and associated air pollution episode of 1976.* Report to Department of Health. London: Department of Epidemiology and Population Health, London School of Hygiene and Tropical Medicine.
5. Hajat S, Kovats R S, Atkinson R W and Haines A (2002) Impact of hot temperatures on deaths in London: a time series approach. *Journal of Epidemiology and Community Health* **56**, 367–372.
6. Department of Health (2004) NHS Heat wave plan for England. Protecting health and reducing harm from extreme heat and heat waves.
7. Department of Health (2005) NHS Heat wave plan for England. Protecting health and reducing harm from extreme heat and heat waves, updated 2005. Available at www.dh.gov.uk/ assetRoot/04/11/57/33/04115733.pdf
8. Department of Health (2006) NHS Heat wave plan for England. Protecting health and reducing harm from extreme heat and heat waves, updated 2006. Available at www.dh.gov.uk/ assetRoot/04/13/52/97/04135297.pdf
9. Kelly S and Lawes H (1999) Weekly deaths in England and Wales. *Health Statistics Quarterly* **01**, 40–43.
10. Office for National Statistics. *Weekly Deaths registered in England and Wales: weekly release of provisional figures.* Available at www. statistics.gov.uk/StatBase/ssdataset.asp?vlnk=6157

Report:

Excess winter mortality in England and Wales, 2005/06 (provisional) and 2004/05 (final)

Introduction

Provisional estimated figures on excess winter mortality (EWM) for the winter period 2005/06, and final figures for the winter period 2004/05 for deaths occurring in England and Wales were published on the National Statistics website on 27th October 2006. This report analyses EWM for these periods in more detail. Historical trends in EWM are presented for persons in England and Wales from 1950/51 to 2005/06, and by sex, age, and Government Office Region of England, and Wales for the five-year period 2001/02 to 2005/06, and by cause of death from 2002/03 to 2004/05.

Background

England and Wales experiences higher levels of mortality in the winter than in the summer. A measure of this increase is provided on an annual basis, in the form of the EWM figure and index. The elderly are more vulnerable than others during the winter and these figures are used to monitor health targets at a national and local level. Policies aimed at tackling EWM, such as winter fuel payments,[1] and influenza vaccinations[2] particularly focus on the elderly. Although EWM is associated with low temperatures, conditions directly relating to cold, such as hypothermia, are not the main cause of excess winter mortality. A previous article[3] on EWM showed that circulatory and respiratory diseases exhibited marked seasonal fluctuations with deaths from respiratory illnesses having the largest percentage seasonal increase.

Excess Winter Mortality (EWM) is calculated by comparing the number of deaths occurring in winter with the number occurring in a non-winter period. Previous analysis compared methods of calculating EWM using different winter and non-winter periods.[3] The method for calculating EWM used in this report can be found in Box One.

Box one

Method for calculating EWM

The current ONS standard method defines the winter period as December to March, and compares the number of deaths which occurred in this winter period with the average number of deaths occurring in the preceding August to November and the following April to July:

$$EWM = winter\ deaths - average\ non\text{-}winter\ deaths$$

This produces a number of excess winter deaths which is rounded to the nearest 10 for final data and to the nearest 100 for provisional data.

The EWM index is calculated so that comparisons can be made between sexes, age groups and regions, and is calculated as the number of excess winter deaths divided by the average non-winter deaths, expressed as a percentage:

$$EWM\ Index = (EWM\ /\ average\ non\text{-}winter\ deaths) * 100$$

The EWM index is presented with 95 per cent confidence intervals in this report.

Mortality data are collected from death registration. Most deaths (over 95 per cent) are registered within 1 month of the date of occurrence, although violent or unexpected deaths, which need further investigation from a coroner, can take much longer. So that timely EWM figures can be produced, ONS produces a special extract of mortality data in September for deaths which were registered by this month but which occurred up to the end of July. These figures are then adjusted using the number of deaths from the previous years extract, compared with the final number. This produces a provisional estimated number of deaths for January to July in the current year so that EWM can be calculated for the previous winter. As these figures are provisional they are rounded to the nearest 100 and are not produced for areas smaller than Government Office Region of England or by cause of death. Appendix A and Appendix B at the end of this report contains mortality data by age, sex, area of usual residence – Government Office Region of England , and Wales, and month of occurrence from January to December 2005.

Results

Total EWM in England and Wales

Figure 1 shows EWM in England and Wales from the winter of 1950/51 to 2005/06. There has been a log-linear decrease over time, showing a general downward trend in EWM over a period of years rather than in any particular time period.

In the winter of 2005/06 there were an estimated 25,700 more deaths in England and Wales compared to levels in the non-winter period. This was a decrease on the number seen in the previous winter but was not as low as the number seen in the winter of 1988/89 (Figure 1), which had

the lowest EWM in the past 55 years. There were almost 6,000 fewer winter deaths in 2005/06 compared to 2004/05, a decrease of 19 per cent.

The number of extra deaths occurring in winter varies depending on temperature and the level of disease (particularly influenza) in the population, as well as other factors. Figure 2 shows that the decrease in EWM in 2005/06 did not correspond to an increase in the average temperature across the winter period. When monthly mortality data for 2005/06 were compared to the five-year average between 2000/01 and 2004/05 (Figure 3), March was the only month which reported a higher number of deaths than the five-year average. This corresponded to a wintry snap with very low temperatures for the time of year, although lower than average temperatures were also seen across the other winter months (December to February).

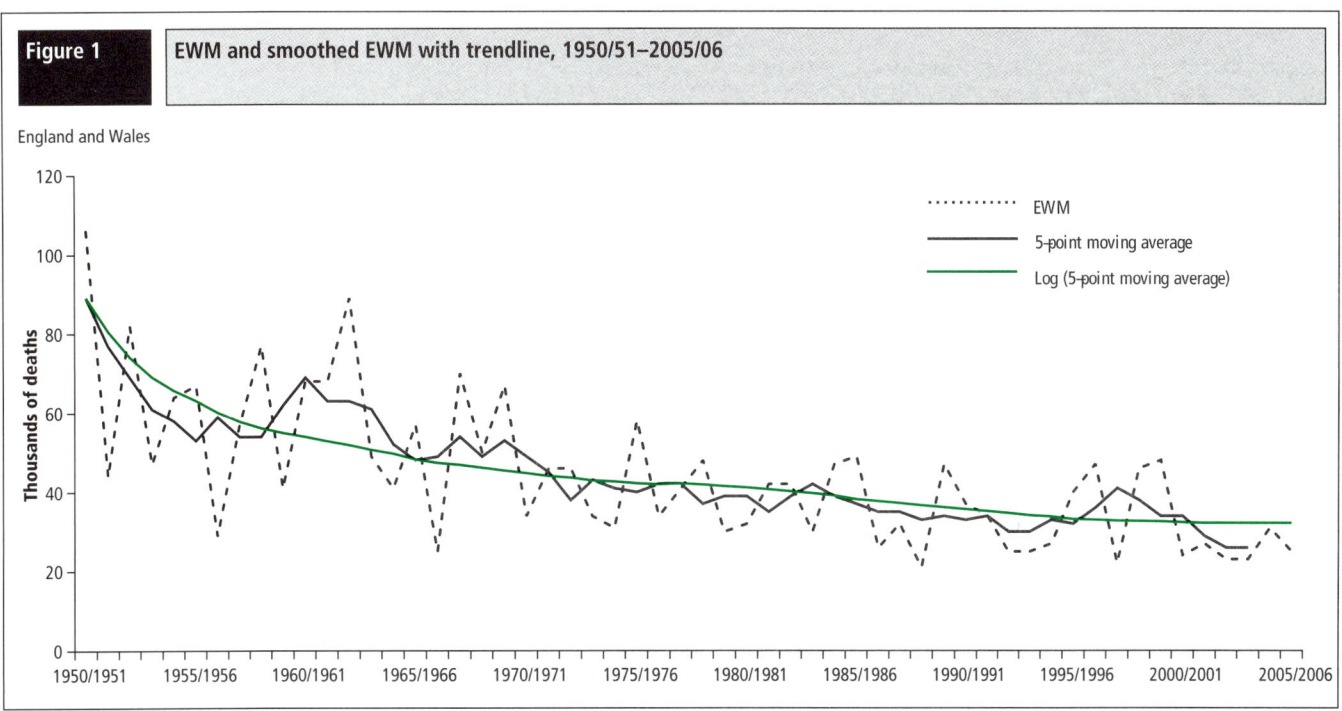

Figure 1   EWM and smoothed EWM with trendline, 1950/51–2005/06

England and Wales

EWM
5-point moving average
Log (5-point moving average)

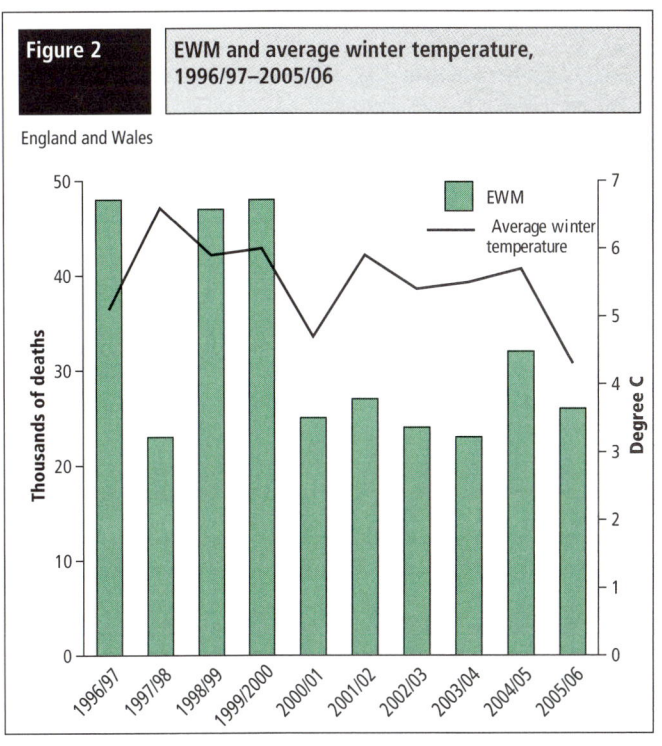

Figure 2   EWM and average winter temperature, 1996/97–2005/06

England and Wales

EWM
Average winter temperature

When daily deaths were examined between 1st August 2005 and 31st July 2006 compared to the five-year average for 2000/01 to 2004/05 (Figure 4) it could be seen that for the winter months December to February, there were fewer deaths than average for those months. Only in March did the number of deaths exceed the average number for the previous five years. This is probably related to the wintry conditions and below average temperatures experienced in this month.[4]

EWM by sex and age

The elderly (aged 75 and over) experience the greatest increase in deaths each winter. There is a greater proportion of the female population that are elderly than men (9 per cent of females were aged 75 and over and 6 per cent of males, in 2005), which may wholly or partially account for the higher number of excess winter deaths seen in women. Figure 5 shows the numbers of excess winter deaths by sex and age in England and Wales for 2003/04 to 2005/06.

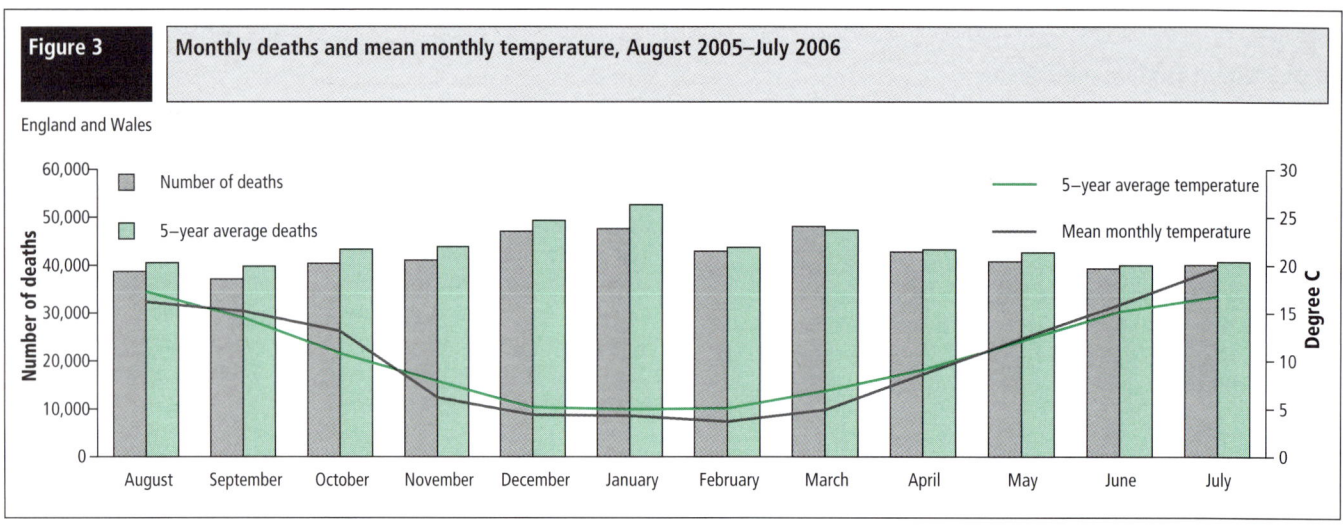

Figure 3 Monthly deaths and mean monthly temperature, August 2005–July 2006

England and Wales

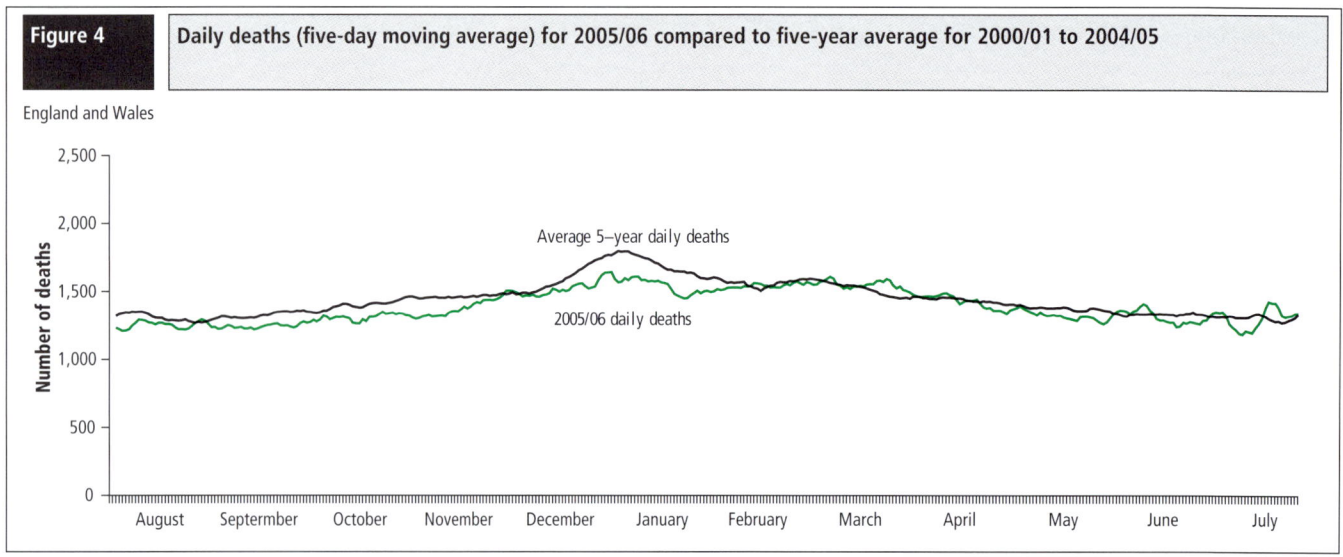

Figure 4 Daily deaths (five-day moving average) for 2005/06 compared to five-year average for 2000/01 to 2004/05

England and Wales

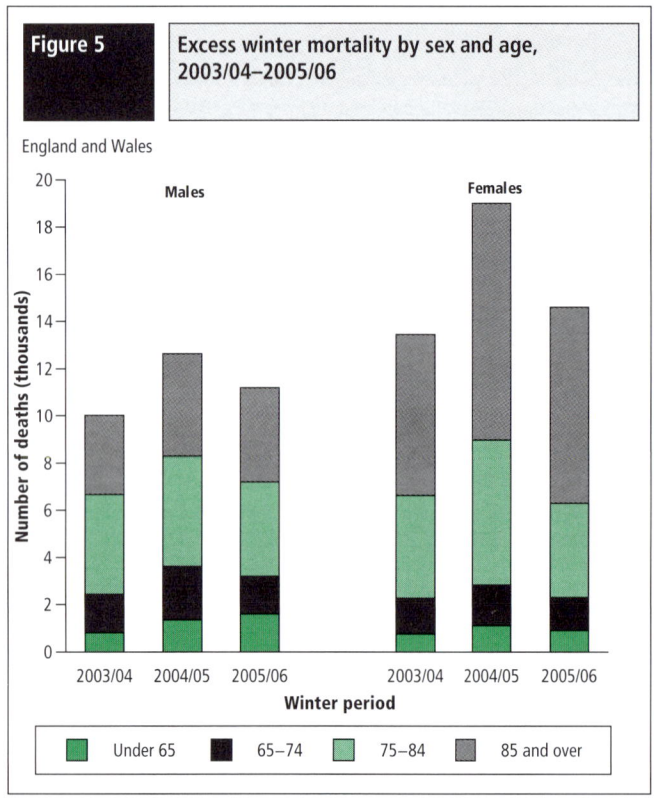

Figure 5 Excess winter mortality by sex and age, 2003/04–2005/06

England and Wales

In 2005/06, there were 11,100 and 14,600 excess winter deaths in males and females respectively. The majority of these deaths occurred at ages 75 and over in both sexes, although proportions varied by sex. Among those aged under 75, there were more excess winter deaths in males than females with a male: female ratio of 1.39. In those aged 75 and over, there were more excess winter deaths in women than men, with a male: female ratio of 0.65.

Overall, there were a smaller number of excess winter deaths for both males and females in 2005/06 compared to the previous winter (2004/05), but this was not as low as EWM in 2003/04. In 2005/06, EWM for males decreased by 12 per cent and for females by almost a quarter (23 per cent) compared to the winter of 2004/05. In males, the number of deaths in those aged under 65 increased by 19 per cent but due to the smaller proportion of deaths which occur at these ages this did not affect the overall decrease in EWM for males. In females, the majority (88 per cent) of the decrease was seen in elderly women aged 75 and over.

EWM for Government Office Region of England, and Wales

Table 1 presents EWM and the EWM index by age and Government Office Region of England, and Wales. There are substantial year-on-year changes in the rank order of regions for EWM – for example London had the highest EWM index in the winter of 2002/03 and the lowest EWM index for the following winter of 2003/04. Previous research[5] examining EWM amongst the elderly, found little evidence for any consistent variation by geographical region within the UK.

| Table 1 | | Excess winter mortality by age group and usual residence of deceased – Government Office Region of England, and Wales, 2001/2002–2004/2005 and 2005/2006 (provisonal) | | | | | | | | | |

		2001/2002		2002/2003		2003/2004		2004/2005		2005/2006	
		EWM[1]	EWM Index	EWM[1]	EWM Index	EWM[1]	EWM Index	EWD[1]	EWD Index	EWD[2]	EWD Index
England, Wales and elsewhere	0–64	1,670	5.7	1,780	6.1	1,570	5.4	2,460	8.7	2,500	9.4
	65–74	3,350	10.8	3,050	10.1	3,140	10.6	4,000	14.1	3,000	10.8
	75–84	9,310	16.8	7,960	13.9	8,590	15.0	10,810	19.7	8,000	15.1
	85+	12,890	24.9	11,180	21.3	10,160	19.4	14,380	28.3	12,200	23.2
	All ages	27,230	16.2	23,970	14.2	23,450	13.9	31,640	19.5	25,700	16.1
North East	0–64	150	9.5	150	9.1	60	3.7	50	3.3	200	10.9
	65–74	200	10.3	290	15.8	200	10.7	210	11.5	200	9.1
	75–84	480	15.7	500	15.6	570	17.7	480	15.2	400	12.2
	85+	690	30.3	330	13.8	370	15.8	730	31.7	500	19.4
	All ages	1,530	17.1	1,260	14.0	1,190	13.2	1,460	16.6	1,100	13.4
North West	0–64	280	6.3	220	5.0	320	7.4	520	12.1	400	9.2
	65–74	530	11.2	410	8.8	500	11.3	750	17.7	300	7.8
	75–84	1,640	21.4	1,180	14.9	1,390	17.5	1,520	19.9	1,100	15.5
	85+	1,590	23.7	1,370	20.6	1,340	20.3	1,650	25.8	1,300	19.3
	All ages	4,040	17.2	3,180	13.5	3,560	15.2	4,440	19.7	3,100	14.1
Yorkshire and the Humber	0–64	200	7.1	130	4.6	290	10.2	260	9.1	300	11.1
	65–74	400	12.7	220	7.0	370	12.4	410	14.2	200	8.6
	75–84	930	16.9	870	15.2	940	16.4	1,270	23.6	600	10.5
	85+	1,300	27.0	1,010	20.6	1,110	22.3	1,320	27.5	1,000	19.8
	All ages	2,840	17.3	2,230	13.4	2,710	16.4	3,250	20.5	2,100	13.2
East Midlands	0–64	180	7.8	110	4.6	160	6.9	140	5.8	200	9.5
	65–74	360	14.3	200	7.9	240	9.7	340	14.4	200	10.8
	75–84	680	14.8	720	15.2	750	15.9	860	18.9	700	15.7
	85+	1,080	27.1	1,020	24.8	850	20.4	1,130	28.0	900	20.5
	All ages	2,300	17.2	2,050	14.9	1,990	14.6	2,460	18.6	2,000	15.4
West Midlands	0–64	310	10.4	250	8.2	290	9.4	290	9.7	100	3.7
	65–74	340	10.1	340	10.8	270	8.5	430	14.2	500	17.0
	75–84	930	15.9	840	14.0	860	14.4	1,240	21.7	1,000	17.5
	85+	1,100	22.5	1,170	23.4	1,140	23.0	1,630	33.0	1,200	23.1
	All ages	2,670	15.7	2,610	15.1	2,560	14.9	3,590	21.5	2,800	16.7
East	0–64	90	3.4	250	9.5	50	2.0	210	8.2	300	12.1
	65–74	360	12.3	290	10.1	390	14.0	420	15.6	200	13.0
	75–84	970	16.9	740	12.7	840	14.3	1,120	19.7	800	14.5
	85+	1,360	24.3	1,210	21.3	990	17.1	1,540	27.9	1,300	23.4
	All ages	2,790	16.4	2,480	14.7	2,280	13.3	3,290	20.0	2,600	17.1
London	0–64	170	4.5	200	5.3	40	1.2	370	10.5	300	9.9
	65–74	380	11.4	450	13.9	270	8.3	340	11.5	200	8.5
	75–84	880	15.5	810	14.0	720	12.6	1,150	21.5	800	15.1
	85+	1,310	24.5	1,350	25.2	1,010	18.6	1,580	31.3	1,300	25.4
	All ages	2,750	15.1	2,810	15.5	2,040	11.3	3,440	20.4	2,600	16.1
South East	0–64	100	2.6	300	7.6	210	5.3	310	8.2	400	9.8
	65–74	320	7.6	430	10.6	370	9.3	430	11.2	600	15.4
	75–84	1,320	16.3	1,070	12.9	1,140	13.5	1,500	18.4	1,500	18.9
	85+	2,390	27.3	1,870	20.8	1,580	17.9	2,350	27.4	2,400	26.7
	All ages	4,140	16.5	3,670	14.5	3,310	13.1	4,590	18.8	4,700	19.9
South West	0–64	190	7.5	120	4.7	90	3.4	170	7.0	200	8.3
	65–74	220	7.9	250	9.0	230	8.6	380	15.0	200	6.9
	75–84	950	16.8	770	13.0	890	15.2	1,010	17.8	800	14.4
	85+	1,370	22.0	1,210	19.3	1,080	17.1	1,650	27.0	1,700	27.7
	All ages	2,740	15.9	2,360	13.4	2,290	13.1	3,220	19.2	2,800	17.3
Wales	0–64	20	1.2	60	3.2	70	3.6	140	8.0	200	12.7
	65–74	240	11.9	200	10.3	310	16.4	300	16.2	200	10.9
	75–84	530	14.5	490	13.3	480	13.2	670	18.9	400	13.1
	85+	690	22.7	650	20.4	700	22.4	810	26.3	700	21.6
	All ages	1,480	14.2	1,400	13.1	1,550	14.9	1,930	18.8	1,500	15.3
England	0–64	1,690	6.2	1,730	6.4	1,510	5.6	2,320	8.8	2,300	9.2
	65–74	3,110	10.7	2,860	10.2	2,850	10.3	3,700	14.1	2,800	10.9
	75–84	8,790	16.9	7,490	14.0	8,110	15.2	10,150	19.8	7,600	15.3
	85+	12,200	25.1	10,540	21.4	9,460	19.2	13,570	28.5	11,500	23.3
	All ages	25,790	16.4	22,620	14.3	21,930	13.9	29,740	19.6	24,200	16.2
England and Wales	0–64	1,710	5.9	1,790	6.1	1,570	5.4	2,460	8.8	2,500	9.5
	65–74	3,350	10.8	3,070	10.2	3,160	10.7	4,000	14.2	3,000	10.9
	75–84	9,320	16.8	7,980	14.0	8,590	15.0	10,820	19.7	8,000	15.1
	85+	12,890	24.9	11,190	21.3	10,160	19.4	14,390	28.3	12,200	23.2
	All ages	27,270	16.3	24,020	14.2	23,480	14.0	31,670	19.6	25,700	16.1

1 Rounded to the nearest 10.
2 Provisional, rounded to the nearest 100.

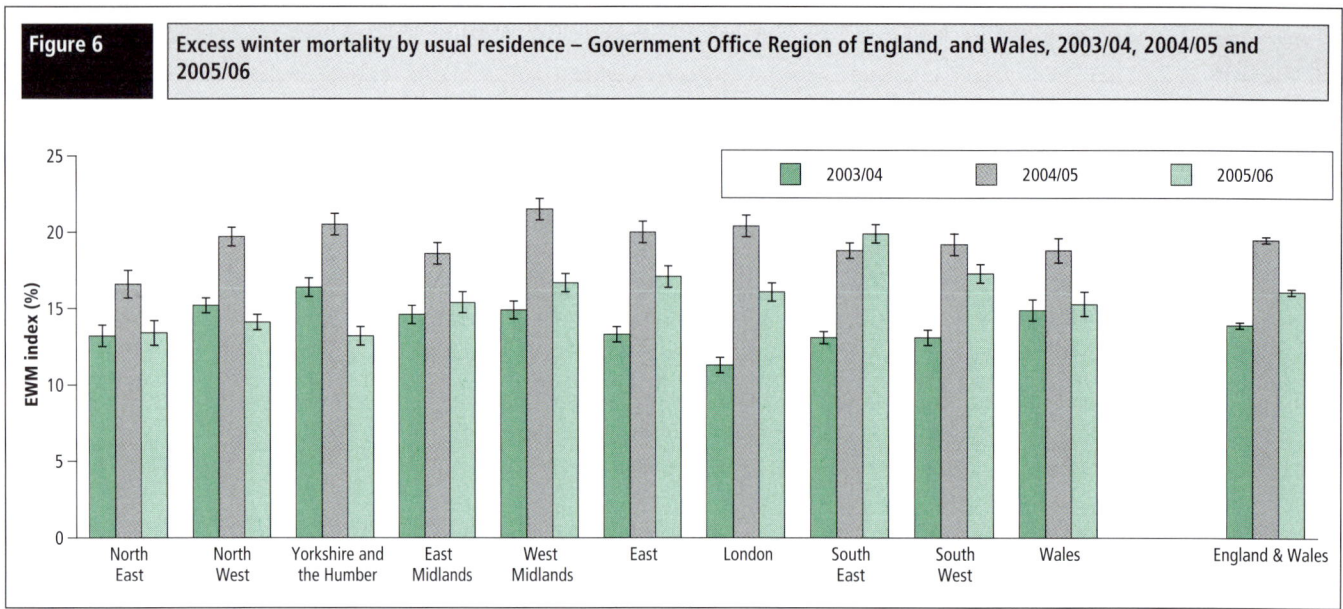

Figure 6 Excess winter mortality by usual residence – Government Office Region of England, and Wales, 2003/04, 2004/05 and 2005/06

Figure 6 shows the EWM index by Government Office Region of England, and Wales, for the winters of 2003/04 to 2005/06. The EWM index was significantly lower in 2005/06 than the previous winter for all regions, except the South East. This region had the highest EWM index for 2005/06 winter and the index increased by 1 percentage point. The region with the lowest EWM index in 2005/06 was Yorkshire and the Humber.

EWM by underlying cause of death

Figure 7 shows EWM and EWM index for circulatory diseases, respiratory diseases, external causes of injury and poisoning, and neoplasms (or cancers) for the winters of 2002/03 to 2004/05. Although neoplasms account for a quarter of all deaths annually, previous research[3] found that there was no clear seasonal pattern for these deaths which accounts for the low EWM and EWM index for these causes seen in Figure 7. Injury and poisoning deaths, however, include accidental falls which can be affected by wintry conditions – for example, icy pavements, and the EWM index was 11 per cent for this cause in 2005/06.

There were roughly the same number of excess winter deaths with an underlying cause of circulatory disease and respiratory disease for the winters of 2003/04 and 2004/05, and a greater number of excess winter circulatory disease deaths in 2002/03 (Figure 7). However, when the EWM index is examined we can see that the index is much lower for circulatory diseases than for respiratory diseases for all of the winter periods. This means that a greater number of circulatory disease deaths occurred during the non-winter periods compared to respiratory disease deaths, for all of the winter periods 2002/03 to 2004/05.

For all of these causes, both numbers of excess winter deaths and the EWM index increased between 2003/04 and 2004/05. Respiratory disease deaths had the highest EWM index for all of the winters analysed. In the winter of 2004/05, the EWM index was 60 per cent. This was an increase of 18 percentage points from the previous winter.

Table 2 shows the number of excess winter deaths and the EWM index by sex and age group for circulatory and respiratory diseases, injury

Figure 7 Excess winter mortality by underlying cause of death, persons, 2002/03–2004/05

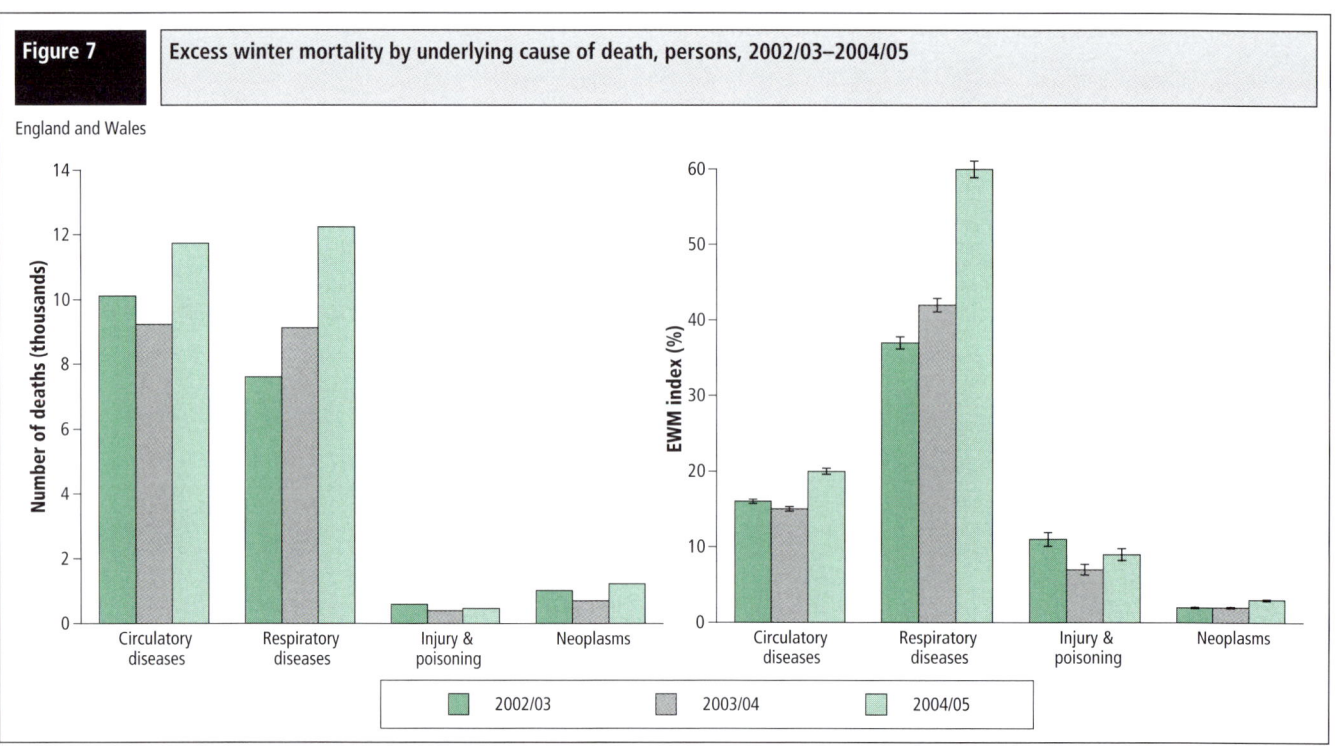

| Table 2 | Excess winter mortality by sex, age group and underlying cause of death, England and Wales, 2002/2003–2004/2005 |

		2002/2003		2003/2004		2004/2005	
		EWM[1]	EWM Index	EWM[1]	EWM Index	EWM[1]	EWM Index
Males							
Circulatory diseases	0–64	510	9.9	520	10.5	440	9.1
(ICD-10 I00–I99)	65–74	940	13.7	780	11.8	1,070	17.8
	75–84	1,930	16.2	1,800	15.4	2,030	18.6
	85 and over	1,440	20.8	1,310	19.4	1,580	23.8
	All ages	4,830	15.6	4,410	14.7	5,110	18.0
Respiratory diseases	0–64	250	26.0	320	32.3	440	46.5
(ICD-10 J00–J99)	65–74	410	23.3	680	38.6	690	42.0
	75–84	990	25.3	1,450	35.8	1,780	47.0
	85 and over	1,290	42.8	1,290	40.3	1,690	54.7
	All ages	2,930	30.5	3,740	37.4	4,600	48.6
Injury & poisoning	0–64	110	4.7	−80	−3.4	−10	−0.6
(ICD-10 V01–Y89)	65–74	30	9.8	50	20.1	30	9.2
	75–84	80	22.1	80	19.9	30	6.0
	85 and over	50	18.5	40	12.5	50	14.9
	All ages	270	8.3	90	2.7	90	2.7
Neoplasms	0–64	30	0.6	−150	−2.7	0	0.0
(ICD-10 C00–D48)	65–74	90	1.3	−40	−0.5	230	3.4
	75–84	90	1.1	310	3.7	100	1.1
	85 and over	150	4.8	150	4.7	190	5.8
	All ages	370	1.5	270	1.1	510	2.1
Females							
Circulatory diseases	0–64	160	7.6	110	5.7	240	12.7
(ICD-10 I00–I99)	65–74	470	11.8	390	10.0	480	13.9
	75–84	1,630	13.1	1,820	15.3	2,410	22.2
	85 and over	3,030	19.2	2,510	16.3	3,510	24.4
	All ages	5,290	15.4	4,830	14.6	6,630	21.7
Respiratory diseases	0–64	190	28.5	270	38.2	430	71.5
(ICD-10 J00–J89)	65–74	450	33.7	660	49.9	780	63.4
	75–84	1,430	39.8	1,690	43.2	2,330	64.1
	85 and over	2,610	47.0	2,760	47.3	4,100	76.2
	All ages	4,680	41.9	5,390	45.7	7,640	70.4
Injury & poisoning	0–64	−20	−2.7	50	7.6	10	1.0
(ICD-10 V01–Y89)	65–74	20	9.3	10	8.5	30	19.8
	75–84	110	26.2	90	20.1	130	29.1
	85 and over	220	31.9	150	21.7	220	28.8
	All ages	330	15.8	310	15.3	390	18.4
Neoplasms	0–64	90	1.6	80	1.5	120	2.3
(ICD-10 C00–D48)	65–74	200	3.8	220	4.3	140	2.7
	75–84	240	3.3	30	0.5	250	3.5
	85 and over	130	2.9	100	2.3	200	4.7
	All ages	650	2.9	430	1.9	720	3.3

1 Rounded to the nearest 10.

& poisoning deaths, and neoplasms in England and Wales between the winters of 2002/03 and 2004/05. For circulatory diseases, elderly adults aged 85 and over had the highest EWM index in both males and females, with the EWM index increasing with age in both sexes across all of the winter periods. For respiratory diseases, elderly adults aged 85 and over also had the highest EWM index for males and females for the winter periods 2002/03 and 2004/05. However, for the winter of 2003/04, although this was still the case in elderly men aged 85 and over, women aged 65-74 had the highest EWM index for these diseases. For deaths from injury & poisoning, EWM varied across the age groups for males and steadily increased with age for females up to 2004/05 when the EWM index was slightly higher in women aged 75–84 than for those aged 85 and over. Deaths from neoplasms varied across age groups for both sexes, but increased with age for females in 2004/05.

References

1. Department for Work and Pensions (2006) *Your guide to Winter Fuel Payments 2006/2007.* Available at www.thepensionservice.gov. uk/pdf/winterfuel/wfpl1jul06.pdf Accessed 8 August 2006.
2. Department of Health (2006) *Flu Watch.* Available at www. dh.gov.uk/AboutUs/MinistersAndDepartmentLeaders/ ChiefMedicalOfficer/Features/FeaturesArticle/fs/en?CONTENT_ ID=4103271&chk=2ijGJ5 Accessed 8 August 2006.
3. Johnson H and Griffiths C (2003) Estimating excess winter mortality in England and Wales. *Health Statistics Quarterly* **20**, 19–24.
4. www.metoffice.com/climate/uk/2006/index.html
5. Wilkinson P, Pattenden S, Armstrong B, Fletcher A, Kovats R S, Mangtani P and McMichael A J (2004) Vulnerability to winter mortality in elderly people in Britain: population based study. *British Medical Journal*, **18**; 329: 647–652.

Appendix A | **Number of deaths by month, age group and area of usual residence – Government Office Region of England, and Wales, males, 2005**

		January	February	March	April	May	June	July	August	Septmeber	October	November	December	Total
England, Wales [1] and elsewhere	0–64	4,954	4,313	4,751	4,426	4,537	4,166	4,359	4,122	4,148	4,314	4,167	4,604	52,861
	65–74	4,932	4,294	4,715	4,232	4,192	3,968	4,001	3,991	3,859	4,093	4,157	4,583	51,017
	75–84	8,595	7,461	7,935	7,171	7,050	6,440	6,435	6,454	6,013	6,692	6,845	7,709	84,800
	85+	5,728	4,808	5,286	4,492	4,359	4,102	3,986	3,938	3,815	4,342	4,481	5,399	54,736
	All ages	24,209	20,876	22,687	20,321	20,138	18,676	18,781	18,505	17,835	19,441	19,650	22,295	243,414
North East	0–64	268	212	236	246	270	231	218	216	215	227	251	263	2,853
	65–74	293	299	257	262	267	250	243	238	211	273	258	257	3,108
	75–84	450	368	397	378	395	393	377	365	355	377	360	401	4,616
	85+	260	157	223	199	188	176	149	172	175	204	196	223	2,322
	All ages	1,271	1,036	1,113	1,085	1,120	1,050	987	991	956	1,081	1,065	1,144	12,899
North West	0–64	792	664	787	683	713	628	659	610	618	644	662	717	8,177
	65–74	811	631	690	627	602	570	619	605	596	594	611	699	7,655
	75–84	1,221	1,060	1,032	979	982	847	876	833	820	896	988	1,036	11,570
	85+	709	533	570	536	538	478	470	471	447	506	570	635	6,463
	All ages	3,533	2,888	3,079	2,825	2,835	2,523	2,624	2,519	2,481	2,640	2,831	3,087	33,865
Yorkshire and the Humber	0–64	489	462	476	455	431	425	463	418	436	396	444	440	5,335
	65–74	542	421	436	447	404	412	419	356	412	387	413	421	5,070
	75–84	952	726	775	660	674	629	629	653	610	677	676	730	8,391
	85+	558	440	428	409	419	348	367	336	353	425	401	527	5,011
	All ages	2,541	2,049	2,115	1,971	1,928	1,814	1,878	1,763	1,811	1,885	1,934	2,118	23,807
East Midlands	0–64	412	331	356	385	363	353	333	360	324	352	325	388	4,282
	65–74	403	347	422	362	329	341	311	318	327	346	360	413	4,279
	75–84	750	602	654	605	599	601	496	561	477	554	573	669	7,141
	85+	460	392	389	381	337	325	347	346	288	364	384	451	4,464
	All ages	2,025	1,672	1,821	1,733	1,628	1,620	1,487	1,585	1,416	1,616	1,642	1,921	20,166
West Midlands	0–64	551	480	475	497	503	453	492	469	438	521	455	476	5,810
	65–74	536	478	526	467	470	418	442	453	391	441	443	570	5,635
	75–84	914	778	815	769	765	686	666	676	641	687	698	854	8,949
	85+	565	480	553	448	428	407	368	374	369	425	464	510	5,391
	All ages	2,566	2,216	2,369	2,181	2,166	1,964	1,968	1,972	1,839	2,074	2,060	2,410	25,785
East	0–64	434	373	400	388	416	389	376	348	398	415	360	428	4,725
	65–74	494	394	490	407	424	367	346	396	360	393	384	418	4,873
	75–84	936	763	851	726	759	691	661	652	643	738	710	824	8,954
	85+	653	557	597	486	510	449	439	485	465	497	502	646	6,286
	All ages	2,517	2,087	2,338	2,007	2,109	1,896	1,822	1,881	1,866	2,043	1,956	2,316	24,838
London	0–64	614	540	637	530	567	509	567	509	524	553	533	575	6,658
	65–74	487	453	487	416	450	423	397	455	389	405	460	474	5,296
	75–84	820	787	803	759	664	612	669	641	581	655	641	756	8,388
	85+	608	486	554	445	471	426	393	390	362	431	420	506	5,492
	All ages	2,529	2,266	2,481	2,150	2,152	1,970	2,026	1,995	1,856	2,044	2,054	2,311	25,834
South East	0–64	663	561	617	576	569	563	583	553	570	583	529	623	6,990
	65–74	579	580	647	570	559	539	549	522	528	582	547	615	6,817
	75–84	1,188	1,090	1,217	1,013	1,019	917	971	946	828	991	1,022	1,161	12,363
	85+	938	817	984	742	682	739	668	651	635	722	735	901	9,214
	All ages	3,368	3,048	3,465	2,901	2,829	2,758	2,771	2,672	2,561	2,878	2,833	3,300	35,384
South West	0–64	399	381	430	395	393	332	372	370	358	374	331	376	4,511
	65–74	424	411	435	399	380	343	384	392	382	404	402	407	4,763
	75–84	841	784	872	789	769	658	673	705	645	678	716	793	8,923
	85+	632	632	667	572	538	501	526	474	493	516	552	678	6,781
	All ages	2,296	2,208	2,404	2,155	2,080	1,834	1,955	1,941	1,878	1,972	2,001	2,254	24,978
Wales	0–64	296	277	309	240	267	256	262	243	235	215	242	289	3,131
	65–74	347	265	315	264	292	285	272	239	252	262	268	306	3,367
	75–84	514	493	515	480	416	391	409	412	402	428	452	474	5,386
	85+	343	310	320	271	243	249	256	236	222	249	255	320	3,274
	All ages	1,500	1,345	1,459	1,255	1,218	1,181	1,199	1,130	1,111	1,154	1,217	1,389	15,158
England	0–64	4,622	4,004	4,414	4,155	4,225	3,883	4,063	3,853	3,881	4,065	3,890	4,286	49,341
	65–74	4,569	4,014	4,390	3,957	3,885	3,663	3,710	3,735	3,596	3,825	3,878	4,274	47,496
	75–84	8,072	6,958	7,416	6,678	6,626	6,034	6,018	6,032	5,600	6,253	6,384	7,224	79,295
	85+	5,383	4,494	4,965	4,218	4,111	3,849	3,727	3,699	3,587	4,090	4,224	5,077	51,424
	All ages	22,646	19,470	21,185	19,008	18,847	17,429	17,518	17,319	16,664	18,233	18,376	20,861	227,556
England and Wales	0–64	4,918	4,281	4,723	4,395	4,492	4,139	4,325	4,096	4,116	4,280	4,132	4,575	52,472
	65–74	4,916	4,279	4,705	4,221	4,177	3,948	3,982	3,974	3,848	4,087	4,146	4,580	50,863
	75–84	8,586	7,451	7,931	7,158	7,042	6,425	6,427	6,444	6,002	6,681	6,836	7,698	84,681
	85+	5,726	4,804	5,285	4,489	4,354	4,098	3,983	3,935	3,809	4,339	4,479	5,397	54,698
	All ages	24,146	20,815	22,644	20,263	20,065	18,610	18,717	18,449	17,775	19,387	19,593	22,250	242,714

1. Includes non-residents of England and Wales.

Appendix B	**Number of deaths by month, age group and area of usual residence – Government Office Region of England, and Wales, females, 2005**

		January	February	March	April	May	June	July	August	Septmeber	October	November	December	Total
England, Wales[1] and elsewhere	0–64	3,191	2,722	3,033	2,787	2,896	2,670	2,729	2,822	2,628	2,728	2,716	2,935	33,857
	65–74	3,523	3,065	3,394	2,927	3,068	2,785	2,769	2,773	2,617	2,905	2,843	3,307	35,976
	75–84	9,073	7,659	8,529	7,170	7,207	6,517	6,366	6,478	6,192	6,628	6,807	7,793	86,419
	85+	12,178	10,194	11,376	9,389	8,965	8,289	8,250	8,138	7,839	8,716	9,047	10,775	113,156
	All ages	27,965	23,640	26,332	22,273	22,136	20,261	20,114	20,211	19,276	20,977	21,413	24,810	269,408
North East	0–64	166	130	169	147	145	126	144	152	132	126	142	161	1,740
	65–74	237	197	207	200	203	156	189	168	183	188	180	205	2,313
	75–84	534	439	487	421	438	356	360	382	344	380	390	462	4,993
	85+	629	464	524	445	466	388	387	402	374	432	447	475	5,433
	All ages	1,566	1,230	1,387	1,213	1,252	1,026	1,080	1,104	1,033	1,126	1,159	1,303	14,479
North West	0–64	480	408	477	422	440	428	418	426	391	419	406	454	5,169
	65–74	563	455	531	423	456	415	383	449	392	417	466	496	5,446
	75–84	1,304	1,124	1,159	1,007	1,028	965	955	926	888	953	883	1,172	12,364
	85+	1,600	1,281	1,366	1,151	1,135	1,072	1,074	1,060	979	1,111	1,151	1,346	14,326
	All ages	3,947	3,268	3,533	3,003	3,059	2,880	2,830	2,861	2,650	2,900	2,906	3,468	37,305
Yorkshire and the Humber	0–64	376	271	277	287	278	254	266	297	252	281	269	300	3,408
	65–74	374	319	323	307	305	273	278	295	293	302	269	361	3,699
	75–84	991	692	809	687	737	663	610	657	613	651	732	751	8,593
	85+	1,265	924	932	916	865	832	779	725	780	827	906	1,060	10,811
	All ages	3,006	2,206	2,341	2,197	2,185	2,022	1,933	1,974	1,938	2,061	2,176	2,472	26,511
East Midlands	0–64	278	239	226	230	264	221	218	206	205	246	213	251	2,797
	65–74	281	252	267	240	249	230	247	232	216	253	228	270	2,965
	75–84	768	601	673	627	541	524	490	572	502	566	592	625	7,081
	85+	1,079	806	793	774	705	619	658	692	624	728	724	857	9,059
	All ages	2,406	1,898	1,959	1,871	1,759	1,594	1,613	1,702	1,547	1,793	1,757	2,003	21,902
West Midlands	0–64	356	289	324	269	305	270	321	330	272	269	280	316	3,601
	65–74	350	346	323	311	322	287	263	268	252	315	288	353	3,678
	75–84	971	810	894	676	747	661	674	667	664	678	704	782	8,928
	85+	1,208	1,037	1,128	896	865	784	796	816	765	833	884	1,032	11,044
	All ages	2,885	2,482	2,669	2,152	2,239	2,002	2,054	2,081	1,953	2,095	2,156	2,483	27,251
East	0–64	292	280	307	273	276	266	248	270	269	276	272	266	3,295
	65–74	327	251	323	275	282	289	274	276	233	258	252	300	3,340
	75–84	890	834	831	725	731	636	667	652	622	685	723	794	8,790
	85+	1,258	1,105	1,264	995	994	890	881	891	864	960	978	1,173	12,253
	All ages	2,767	2,470	2,725	2,268	2,283	2,081	2,070	2,089	1,988	2,179	2,225	2,533	27,678
London	0–64	370	335	372	353	339	311	339	312	328	309	308	346	4,022
	65–74	353	316	364	311	309	290	288	265	247	290	324	343	3,700
	75–84	876	724	830	699	706	631	599	621	616	648	653	760	8,363
	85+	1,184	1,044	1,192	907	870	780	816	802	774	879	796	1,050	11,094
	All ages	2,783	2,419	2,758	2,270	2,224	2,012	2,042	2,000	1,965	2,126	2,081	2,499	27,179
South East	0–64	417	338	430	374	389	392	354	398	386	377	384	406	4,645
	65–74	470	428	490	384	447	400	394	389	375	396	375	451	4,999
	75–84	1,319	1,147	1,319	1,082	1,085	967	924	963	909	962	972	1,151	12,800
	85+	1,970	1,669	2,019	1,576	1,487	1,453	1,397	1,384	1,293	1,411	1,577	1,838	19,074
	All ages	4,176	3,582	4,258	3,416	3,408	3,212	3,069	3,134	2,963	3,146	3,308	3,846	41,518
South West	0–64	234	256	247	232	246	226	240	259	227	243	254	243	2,907
	65–74	322	270	337	283	280	255	273	242	246	279	274	288	3,349
	75–84	843	785	898	743	730	668	640	630	611	656	728	794	8,726
	85+	1,330	1,237	1,394	1,165	1,044	933	969	870	902	1,007	1,047	1,298	13,196
	All ages	2,729	2,548	2,876	2,423	2,300	2,082	2,122	2,001	1,986	2,185	2,303	2,623	28,178
Wales	0–64	205	159	179	187	188	166	159	161	153	168	174	176	2,075
	65–74	238	222	225	190	201	182	171	185	173	198	177	234	2,396
	75–84	565	498	624	496	454	435	434	394	417	439	425	490	5,671
	85+	650	626	760	560	530	533	493	491	479	524	532	644	6,822
	All ages	1,658	1,505	1,788	1,433	1,373	1,316	1,257	1,231	1,222	1,329	1,308	1,544	16,964
England	0–64	2,969	2,546	2,829	2,587	2,682	2,494	2,548	2,650	2,462	2,546	2,528	2,743	31,584
	65–74	3,277	2,834	3,165	2,734	2,853	2,595	2,589	2,584	2,437	2,698	2,656	3,067	33,489
	75–84	8,496	7,156	7,900	6,667	6,743	6,071	5,919	6,070	5,769	6,179	6,377	7,291	80,638
	85+	11,523	9,567	10,612	8,825	8,431	7,751	7,757	7,642	7,355	8,188	8,510	10,129	106,290
	All ages	26,265	22,103	24,506	20,813	20,709	18,911	18,813	18,946	18,023	19,611	20,071	23,230	252,001
England and Wales	0–64	3,174	2,705	3,008	2,774	2,870	2,660	2,707	2,811	2,615	2,714	2,702	2,919	33,659
	65–74	3,515	3,056	3,390	2,924	3,054	2,777	2,760	2,769	2,610	2,896	2,833	3,301	35,885
	75–84	9,061	7,654	8,524	7,163	7,197	6,506	6,353	6,464	6,186	6,618	6,802	7,781	86,309
	85+	12,173	10,193	11,372	9,385	8,961	8,284	8,250	8,133	7,834	8,712	9,042	10,773	113,112
	All ages	27,923	23,608	26,294	22,246	22,082	20,227	20,070	20,177	19,245	20,940	21,379	24,774	268,965

1. Includes non-residents of England and Wales.

Annual Update:

Mortality statistics 2004: general

Introduction

This update summarises some of the findings from the annual reference volume *Mortality statistics: general 2004* (series DH1 no. 37),[1] which was published in October 2006. It presents data and analysis on various measures of mortality and details recorded at death registration in England and Wales, including:

- Mortality rates by single year of age
- Years of life lost
- Monthly variation in mortality
- Place of occurrence of death
- Country of birth of the deceased
- Type of death certification
- Geographical variation in mortality

The annual reference volume contains more detailed information on these, and other, themes. It contains long-term time series for crude death rates, standardised mortality ratios (SMRs) and age-specific mortality rates, some going back to 1841. Infant mortality rates are also given from the 19th century onwards, as well as stillbirth and perinatal mortality rates from 1931. The volume also presents mortality data by country of residence within the UK, and by region of residence within England. More detailed information for areas such as local and health authorities can be found in *Key Population and Vital Statistics.*[2]

Mortality rates in 2004

In 2004, there were 244,130 male deaths and 268,411 female deaths in England and Wales. Figure 1 shows age-specific mortality rates for single years of age for both males and females in 2004. This shows a typical age-specific pattern of mortality. Beyond the age of 1, mortality rates fall rapidly and are at their lowest among children under 10 years – at age 5 for males and age 9 for females. Usually the rate of increase/decrease is similar for males and females except for two instances: female mortality rates between the ages of 6 and 9 show a decrease not seen in males; and male mortality rates show the more rapid increase from 16 to 18 years. However in all single years of age, male mortality rates are higher than those for females.

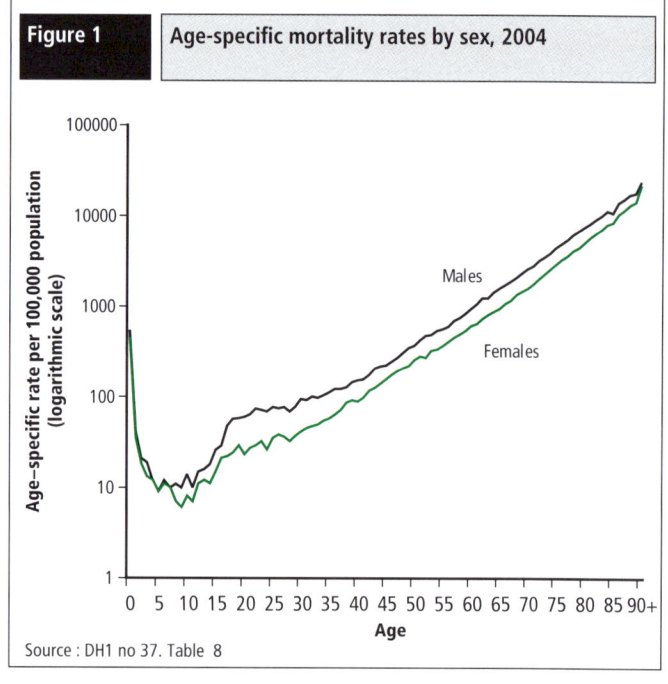

Figure 1   Age-specific mortality rates by sex, 2004

Source : DH1 no 37. Table 8

Years of life lost

Analyses of the effects of premature death can be expressed by the number of years of life lost. In calculating this, it is assumed that everyone may live to some arbitrarily chosen age (65, 75 or 85 in the DH1 volume) and that death at a younger age means that some future years of life have been lost. Using age 65 for both males and females, it is also possible to estimate years of working life lost due to premature death. Comparisons can be made between selected causes with the aim of illustrating their relative effects.

A total of 767,000 years of working life (ages 15–64) were lost for males in 2004, compared with 476,000 for females. Of the selected causes in Table 25 of the annual reference volume, the cancers that are presented in total account for a large proportion of these: 115,000 years for men and 136,000 for women. However, when cancers are considered on a site-specific basis, the causes of death that contributed most to the total for men were ischaemic heart disease (87,000 years lost), suicide including open verdicts (70,000 years) and land transport accidents (56,000 years). For women, breast cancer caused the highest number of years of working life lost (45,000), diseases of the liver (22,000 years) followed by lung cancer and suicide including open verdicts (both 21,000 years). Land transport accidents caused the loss of 13,000 years of working life for women; this is less than a quarter of the number lost for men due to such accidents.

Monthly variation

Annualised monthly ratios show seasonal variation in mortality over the year. They allow for the variation in the number of days between months, and include all deaths where the date of occurrence was known. Figure 2 shows how these ratios change through the year for males and females. The pattern for males and females is very similar although the female ratios were higher than males in the winter months but lower for the remaining months. The ratios for each sex in 2004 were highest in both January and December, while the lowest were in July for males and August for females. From the peak in January, the ratios decreased through the spring and summer months, and then increased again from July through to December. This pattern shows the higher mortality that is experienced in the winter than in other months.[3] The seasonal pattern is found for most causes of death, particularly respiratory and circulatory diseases. Deaths from cancer, however, show little variation over the year.

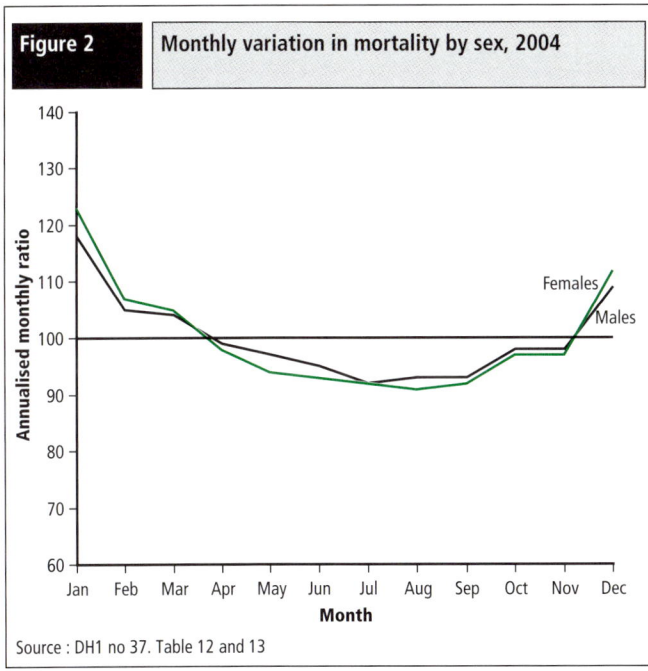

| Figure 2 | Monthly variation in mortality by sex, 2004 |

Source : DH1 no 37. Table 12 and 13

Place of occurrence

More than half of all deaths in England and Wales occur in NHS hospitals or in other NHS communal establishments for the care of the sick: 60 per cent of male and 57 per cent of female deaths occurred in such places in 2004 (Table 1). Over a fifth (22 per cent) of male deaths occurred in the deceased's own home, while 15 per cent of female deaths occurred here. Conversely, a greater proportion of female deaths than male deaths occurred in other communal establishments such as residential homes for the elderly: 10 per cent of female deaths compared

| Table 1 | Place of occurrence of death by sex, 2004 |

Place of occurrence[1]		Males		Females	
		Number	Percentage	Number	Percentage
Total deaths		244,130	100.0	268,411	100.0
Psychiatric hospitals	NHS	615	0.3	683	0.3
	Non-NHS	619	0.3	998	0.4
Hospices		12,000	4.9	11,551	4.3
Other hospitals & communal establishments for care of the sick	NHS	146,387	60.0	151,785	56.5
	Non-NHS	16,119	6.6	33,314	12.4
Other communal establishments		8,896	3.6	25,572	9.5
At home		52,670	21.6	41,237	15.4
In other private houses & other places		6,824	2.8	3,271	1.2

1 The definition for groups of establishments can be found in DH1 no. 37 section 2.4
Source: DH1 no.37, Table 19.

with 4 per cent of male deaths. This most likely reflects women's longer life expectancy: at the same ages, more women will have been widowed than men and so are more likely to be living in residential or nursing care homes for the elderly at the time of death.

Just over 4 per cent of all deaths occurred in hospices. However, this figure is an underestimate because hospice or palliative care wards that are situated within NHS hospitals may not be identified separately by the person registering the death. This means that ONS is unable to include these deaths with those in freestanding hospices.

Country of birth of deceased

Of those who died in 2004, 7.9 per cent had been born outside the UK, compared with 4.8 per cent in 1981 and 5.9 per cent in 1991. Half (50 per cent) of those born outside the UK were born in another European country. The increasing trend partly reflects migration patterns earlier in the 20th century. For example, 0.2 per cent of deaths in 1981 were people born in the Caribbean, rising to 0.4 per cent in 1991 and 0.6 per cent in 2004.

Type of death certification

More than three-quarters (78 per cent) of deaths in 2004 were certified by a doctor. Twenty-two per cent of the deaths certified by a coroner (5 per cent of all deaths) were subject to an inquest, while the remaining 78 per cent were subject to a post-mortem only (Table 2).

The proportion of deaths certified by a coroner varied considerably by cause of death. Most injury and poisoning deaths (84 per cent) were certified by a coroner and nearly all of these (96 per cent) were subject to an inquest (with or without post mortem). Deaths due to ischaemic heart disease had a relatively high proportion certified by a coroner (47 per cent), which reflects the fact that deaths from this cause can be sudden and unexpected. Deaths from long-term illnesses such as cancer, however, have a far lower proportion (6 per cent in 2004) certified by a coroner.

Table 2	Method of death certification by selected underlying cause, 2004

Cause		Total deaths	Certified by coroner Inquest held		Post-mortem without inquest		Certified by medical pratitioner (with or without post-mortem)		Uncertified	
			Number	Percentage	Number	Percentage	Number	Percentage	Number	Percentage
All causes		512,541	24,498	4.8	87,898	17.1	399,275	77.9	870	0.2
Neoplasms	C00–D48	138,062	2,754	2.0	5,044	3.7	130,013	94.2	251	0.2
Diseases of the circulatory system	I00–99	190,603	2,375	1.2	61,161	32.1	126,795	66.5	272	0.1
Ischaemic heart diseases	I20–I25	92,528	1,254	1.4	42,188	45.6	48,964	52.9	122	0.1
Cerebrovascular diseases	I60–I69	52,899	225	0.4	3,217	6.1	49,358	93.3	99	0.2
Diseases of the respiratory system	J00–J99	69,213	1,442	2.1	9,297	13.4	58,370	84.3	104	0.2
Diseases of the digestive system	K00–K93	24,912	851	3.4	7,240	29.1	16,803	67.4	18	0.1
Injury and poisoning	V01–Y89	16,497	13,282	80.5	535	3.2	2,671	16.2	9	0.1

Source: DH1 no.37, Table 22

Geographical variation

The annual reference volume presents standardised mortality ratios (SMRs) for the constituent countries of the UK. The SMRs are based on the standard of UK = 100 for each cause and sex. Scotland had the highest all causes SMR for both males and females in 2004, while England had the lowest. Looking at selected cause groups, Scotland had the highest SMRs for the majority of groups. However Northern Ireland had the highest SMRs for diseases of the nervous, respiratory and genito-urinary systems whilst England had highest SMRs for diseases of the musculoskeletal system. In 2004, amongst the government office regions, the North East had the highest SMRs for both males and females while the South West had the lowest. Further geographical analyses of mortality can be found in *Key Population and Vital Statistics*[2] and *Health Statistics Quarterly*.[4]

Background note

Revised population estimates for mid-2004 were published on 20 December 2005. These population estimates were the most up-to-date at the time of publication and have been used for calculating mortality rates in this update. These estimates incorporate the findings of the local authority population studies, the results of which were published in July 2004. Further information on population estimates, and their methodology, can be found on the National Statistics website www.statistics.gov.uk/popest.

References

1. Office for National Statistics (2006) *Mortality statistics: general 2004* (series DH1 no. 37). Available on the National Statistics website www.statistics.gov.uk/statbase/Product.asp?vlnk=620

2. Office for National Statistics (2006) *Key Population and Vital Statistics* 2004 (series VS no. 31, PP1 no. 27), Palgrave MacMillan: Basingstoke. Also available on the National Statistics website www.statistics.gov.uk/statbase/Product.asp?vlnk=539

3. Johnson H and Griffiths C (2003) Estimating excess winter mortality in England and Wales. *Health Statistics Quarterly* **20**, 19–24.

4. Office for National Statistics (2006) Report: Death registrations in England and Wales, 2005: area of residence. *Health Statistics Quarterly* **31**, 87–97.

Other population and health articles, publications and data

Population Trends 126

Planned articles:
- Population review of 2004 and 2005: England and Wales
- 2007 Census Test

Report:
- Mid-2005 population estimates

Annual Update:
- Births in 2005 in England and Wales

Health Statistics Quarterly 33

Planned articles:
- Trends and geographical variations in alcohol-related deaths in the UK, 1991–2004
- Pilot linkage of NHS Numbers for Babies data with birth registrations

Reports:
- Conceptions in England and Wales, 2005
- Deaths related to drug poisoning: England and Wales, 1993–2005
- Deaths involving MRSA: England and Wales, 2001–2005
- Deaths involving *Clostridium difficile*: England and Wales, 2001–2005
- Health expectancies in the UK, 2003

Annual Updates:
- Congenital anomaly statistics: notifications, 2005, England and Wales
- 2005 mortality statistics: cause (England and Wales)

Forthcoming Annual Reference Volumes

Title	Planned publication
Birth statistics 2005, FM1 no.34*	December 2006
Cancer statistics: registrations 2004, MB1 no.35*	December 2006
Congenital anomaly statistics 2005, MB3 no.20*	December 2006
Mortality statistics: cause 2005, DH2 no.32*	December 2006

* Available through the National Statistics website only; www.statistics.gov.uk